Inside Countries

Although comparative politics is conventionally seen as the study of politics across countries, the field has a longstanding and increasingly prominent tradition in national contexts, focusing on subnational units, institutions, actors, and processes. This book offers the first comprehensive assessment of the substantive, theoretical, and methodological contributions of subnational research to comparative politics. With empirical chapters from across the contemporary Global South, including India, Mexico, and China, as well as Russia, the contributors show how subnational research provides useful insights about major substantive themes in political science, from regimes and representation, to states and security, to social and economic development. In addition to methodological chapters with specific guidance about best practices for doing subnational research, this volume also proposes a set of strategies for subnational research, assesses their strengths and weaknesses, and offers illustrative empirical applications.

AGUSTINA GIRAUDY is Assistant Professor at American University. Her research focuses on subnational democracy and subnational institutions in developing countries. She is the author of *Democrats and Autocrats* (2015).

EDUARDO MONCADA is Assistant Professor of Political Science at Barnard College, Columbia University. His research focuses on crime, violence, and the political economy of development. He is the author of *Cities, Business and the Politics of Urban Violence in Latin America* (2016).

RICHARD SNYDER is Professor of Political Science at Brown University. He is the author of *Politics after Neoliberalism: Reregulation in Mexico* (2001) and *Passion, Craft and Method in Comparative Politics* (2007) with Gerardo L. Munck.

Inside Countries

Subnational Research in Comparative Politics

Edited by

AGUSTINA GIRAUDY
American University, Washington DC

EDUARDO MONCADA
Barnard College, Columbia University, New York

RICHARD SNYDER
Brown University, Rhode Island

CAMBRIDGE
UNIVERSITY PRESS

CAMBRIDGE
UNIVERSITY PRESS

University Printing House, Cambridge CB2 8BS, United Kingdom

One Liberty Plaza, 20th Floor, New York, NY 10006, USA

477 Williamstown Road, Port Melbourne, VIC 3207, Australia

314–321, 3rd Floor, Plot 3, Splendor Forum, Jasola District Centre,
New Delhi – 110025, India

79 Anson Road, #06–04/06, Singapore 079906

Cambridge University Press is part of the University of Cambridge.

It furthers the University's mission by disseminating knowledge in the pursuit of
education, learning, and research at the highest international levels of excellence.

www.cambridge.org
Information on this title: www.cambridge.org/9781108496582
DOI: 10.1017/9781108678384

First published 2019

Printed and bound in Great Britain by Clays Ltd, Elcograf S.p.A.

A catalogue record for this publication is available from the British Library.

Library of Congress Cataloging-in-Publication Data
Names: Giraudy, Agustina, editor. | Moncada, Eduardo, 1977– editor. | Snyder, Richard
(Richard Owen), 1967– editor.
Title: Inside countries : subnational research in comparative politics / edited by Agustina
Giraudy, Eduardo Moncada, Richard Snyder.
Description: Cambridge, United Kingdom ; New York, NY : Cambridge University Press,
2019. | Includes bibliographical references.
Identifiers: LCCN 2018051437 | ISBN 9781108496582 (hardback) | ISBN 9781108721707
(paperback)
Subjects: LCSH: Subnational governments – Case studies. | Comparative politics. | BISAC:
POLITICAL SCIENCE / General.
Classification: LCC JS251 .I67 2019 | DDC 320.3–dc23
LC record available at https://lccn.loc.gov/2018051437

ISBN 978-1-108-49658-2 Hardback
ISBN 978-1-108-72170-7 Paperback

Contents

Figures, Tables, and Maps

FIGURES

TABLES

MAPS

Contributors

Ana Arjona, Associate Professor of Political Science, Northwestern University

Caroline Beer, Associate Professor of Political Science, University of Vermont

Gavril Bilev, Associate Professor of Political Science, Merrimack College

Agustina Giraudy, Assistant Professor, School of International Service, American University

Imke Harbers, Associate Professor of Political Science, University of Amsterdam

Matthew C. Ingram, Associate Professor of Political Science, SUNY-Albany

Sunila S. Kale, Associate Professor of International Studies, University of Washington, Seattle

Sandra Ley, Assistant Professor of Political Studies, Centro de Investigación y Docencia Económicas (CIDE)

Nimah Mazaheri, Associate Professor of Political Science, Tufts University

Eduardo Moncada, Assistant Professor of Political Science, Barnard College, Columbia University

Meg Rithmire, Associate Professor of Business Administration, Harvard Business School

Prerna Singh, Associate Professor of Political Science, Brown University

Richard Snyder, Professor of Political Science, Brown University

Hillel Soifer, Associate Professor of Political Science, Temple University

Guillermo Trejo, Associate Professor of Political Science, University of Notre Dame

Preface and Acknowledgments

This collective volume stems from a series of invitations. The first invitation came in 2010 from Bryon Moraski and Michael Bernhard, both at the University of Florida, in their capacities as Editors of *Comparative Democratization*, the newsletter of the Comparative Democratization Section of the American Political Science Association (APSA). They invited Richard Snyder, who had previously published on the subnational comparative method, to participate in a symposium on subnational research on democratization proposed by Agustina Giraudy. Giraudy had recently completed her PhD at the University of North Carolina, Chapel Hill, and her dissertation on the persistence of subnational undemocratic regimes in Argentina and Mexico had won the Comparative Democratization Section's Juan J. Linz Prize for the Best Dissertation in the Comparative Study of Democracy. Snyder, in turn, invited Eduardo Moncada, then an advanced doctoral student at Brown University and completing a subnational dissertation on violent cities in Colombia, to collaborate with him in writing the piece for *Comparative Democratization*. As a result of our participation in this symposium, and aware of exciting subnational research by young scholars working on other important substantive topics across the globe in addition to democratization, we decided to invite some of the best of these scholars to collaborate with us. The goal was to produce a collective volume that not only highlighted the theoretical and methodological contributions of subnational research but also offered compelling exemplars of how it can be used to tackle a broad range of humanly important problems. The volume, in turn, would help publicize and consolidate the increasingly prominent role of subnational research as a powerful option for doing comparative politics.

Taking advantage of Snyder's access to staff and organizational resources as director of the Center for Latin American and Caribbean Studies (CLACS) at Brown University, we organized an initial conference in May 2013 on "Subnational Research in Comparative Politics" at Brown's Watson Institute for International and Public Affairs. At the conference, most of the contributors to the volume presented initial drafts of the chapters that appear here. A second conference, at which the contributors presented revised versions of their papers, was held at the Weatherhead Center for International Affairs at Harvard University in March 2014, under the auspices of the Harvard Academy for International and Area Studies, where Giraudy, by then an assistant professor at American University's School of International Service, had recently held a two-year post-doctoral fellowship. The chapters collected here are carefully and, in most cases, substantially revised versions of papers presented at the Brown and Harvard conferences.

For their indispensable administrative support of the two conferences, we thank Katherine Goldman, Susan Hirsch, and Emma Strother of CLACS at Brown University and Laurence Winnie of the Harvard Academy. We also wish to acknowledge the helpful comments and input that we and the other contributors to this book received from colleagues who participated in one or both of the conferences by serving as discussants or presenting their own work. This includes Jorge Alves, Matthew Amengual, Enrique Desmond Arias, Michael Bernhard, Ravi Bhavnani, Jordan Branch, Elizabeth Carlson, Matthew Cleary, Michael Coppedge, Jorge I. Domínguez, Thad Dunning, Angélica Durán-Martínez, Todd Eisenstadt, Tulia Falleti, Candelaria Garay, John Gerring, Edward Gibson, Steven Levitsky, Richard M. Locke, Kristen Looney, Edmund Malesky, Zachariah Mampilly, Akshay Mangla, James McGuire, Kelly McMann, Jeremy Menchik, Alfred Montero, Bryon Moraski, Lorena Moscovich, Suhas Palshikar, Thomas Pepinsky, Rachel Riedl, Rodrigo Rodrígues, Lily Tsai, Ashutosh Varshney, Yogendra Yadav, Erik Wibbels, and Daniel Ziblatt. We also thank our editor at Cambridge University Press, Robert Dreesen, for his enthusiastic and patient support of this project; our copy editor, Wade Guyitt; production manager, Gayathri Tamilselvan; and two anonymous reviewers for the Press.

Snyder wishes to acknowledge three senior friends and colleagues who provided crucial support and encouragement for his subnational research over the past twenty-five years: David Collier, Gerardo L. Munck, and the late Juan J. Linz. David, who served as Snyder's doctoral adviser at the University of California, Berkeley, saw from the start the value of the subnational comparative study of economic policy reforms across Mexican states that he was carrying out for his dissertation in the mid-1990s, optimistically predicting that the research would "put the study of state politics in Mexico 'on the map.'" Munck, who was Snyder's senior colleague at the University of Illinois at Urbana-Champaign in the late 1990s, invited him to present a paper on methodological issues in subnational comparative research at a conference he organized at Illinois in 1999 on political regimes in Latin America. Subsequently, Gerry provided detailed comments that greatly improved the paper, helping prepare it for publication in a special issue of the journal *Studies in Comparative International Development* (SCID) that he coedited with Collier. The late Juan J. Linz, himself a subnational researcher and the author of a classic paper on subnational variation in Spain, was a kind and generous supporter of Snyder's work, both subnational and cross-national. Juan's wisdom and insightfulness and the powerful example he set of scholarship as a noble vocation are fondly remembered and greatly missed.

Beyond the professional realm, Giraudy wishes to acknowledge the love, company, and support of her two daughters, Chiara and Sofia. Moncada acknowledges the love, support, and patience of his son, Elisio, his daughter, Nacine, his wife, Angie, and his parents, Damary and Manuel. Snyder acknowledges the love and support of his mother, Margaret, his late father, Roger, his sister, Karen, and his teenage daughter, Ellen.

INTRODUCTION

I

Subnational Research in Comparative Politics

Substantive, Theoretical, and Methodological Contributions

Agustina Giraudy
Eduardo Moncada
Richard Snyder

Comparative politics is conventionally seen as the study of politics across countries. Still, the field has a prominent and long-standing tradition of studying politics not across countries but *inside* them, especially by zooming down to subnational units. Indeed, political science was arguably born subnational: One of the discipline's oldest canonical texts, *The Politics*, written by Aristotle in the fourth century BC, offered a typology of political systems based on a comparative study of 158 city constitutions in ancient Greece. A focus on subnational politics also plays an important role in subsequent classic works of social science. In *Democracy in America*, Alexis de Tocqueville drew inferences about the negative consequences of slavery for industrialization by studying "slavery's borderlands," that is, the Kentucky and Ohio banks of the Ohio River, which he argued varied "only in a single respect: Kentucky has admitted slavery, but the state of Ohio has prohibited the existence of slaves within its borders."[1] A century later, V. O. Key (1949) used a subnational approach to explore political competition across the US South and discovered surprising variation across states in levels of political conservatism at a time when political attitudes were assumed to be uniform in the so-called Solid South. Seymour Martin Lipset (1950) compared the political leanings of farmers in the Canadian and American "wheat belts" during the 1930s to explain variation in the emergence of agrarian socialism. And Robert A. Dahl (1961) studied the city

An earlier version of this chapter was presented at the Annual Meeting of the American Political Science Association (APSA), August 28–31, 2014, in Washington, DC. For helpful comments and suggestions on this chapter, we thank Jordan Branch, Liesbet Hooghe, Rodrigo Mardones, Gary Marks, Sebastián Mazzuca, Camilla Reuterswaerd, Margaret Weir, and participants in seminars at the Catholic University of Chile, Princeton University, Johns Hopkins University, and the University of Wisconsin-Madison.

[1] Tocqueville continues, "Thus the traveler who floats down the current of the Ohio to the spot where that river falls into the Mississippi may be said to sail between liberty and servitude; and a transient inspection of surrounding objects will convince him which of the two is more favorable to humanity" (1831, Chapter XVIII).

of New Haven, Connecticut, to answer the question "who governs?" and, in turn, advance his pluralist theory of democracy.[2]

Subnational research (SNR) also figures notably in more recent agenda-setting works of comparative politics. In *Making Democracy Work*, Robert Putnam (1994) explained sharp variation in subnational government performance between the Northern and Southern regions of Italy by highlighting how associational life, or "social capital," determined service delivery and governance.[3] Theda Skocpol (1992) developed a novel historical-institutional explanation for the birth of modern social policy in the United States by looking at subnational variation in the strength and strategies of locally based women's and veterans' organizations. Work on European integration also focuses on subnational factors. For example, Liesbet Hooghe and Gary Marks (2001, 2016; see also Hooghe, Marks, & Schakel, 2010) showed that European integration was driven not only by national governments but also by a host of subnational political actors who operated directly in the supranational arena, often having a stronger impact on the integration process than national governments. In *Why Nations Fail*, Daron Acemoglu and James Robinson (2012) opened their book by offering a vivid subnational vignette about two adjacent border cities – Nogales, Arizona, and Nogales, Mexico. Despite their shared political, social, and cultural histories, these two neighboring cities are located in distinct national political and economic institutional contexts that, according to the authors, explain the stark differences between them in security, equity, provision of public goods, and the quality of democracy.[4]

Moreover, the past two decades have witnessed a strong surge of interest in SNR, as evident in the sharp increase in the number of studies with a subnational focus published by top-ranked political science presses and journals. For example, the share of books with a subnational focus published by the comparative politics series of Cambridge University Press, Cornell University Press, and University of Michigan Press increased from 24 percent in 1989–2001 to 34 percent in 2002–2016.[5] Whereas 20 percent of the empirical

---

[2] Juan J. Linz's (1986) work comparing the politics of the Basque regions in Spain and France offers another classic example of the subnational tradition. See also Linz and De Miguel (1966) on the "eight Spains." Charles Tilly's *The Vendee* (1964) and the work of Stein Rokkan offer further examples (Rokkan & Urwin, 1983; Rokkan et al., 1987).

[3] Other prominent works by political scientists that apply a subnational perspective to the Italian case include Tarrow (1977), Locke (1995), and Ziblatt (2006).

[4] The subnational tradition of research is also reflected in the organization of the political science profession: In the field of American politics, for example, there is an organized section of the American Political Science Association (APSA) dedicated exclusively to state and local politics. Likewise, the Latin American Studies Association (LASA) has a section on Subnational Politics and Society.

[5] The data presented in this paragraph on the prevalence of subnational research in political science books and journals is drawn from Sellers (in press, Table 1). See also Pepinsky (2018), which shows that single-country studies have made a remarkable resurgence across the top US general interest and comparative politics journals, with a large share consisting of subnational, especially quantitative, studies.

articles published in 1989–2001 by the discipline's leading journal, *American Political Science Review*, focused on subnational units of analysis, this amount increased to 28 percent in 2004–2016. Although the share of subnational articles published by the three top comparative politics journals (i.e., *Comparative Politics, Comparative Political Studies,* and *World Politics*) was smaller, this amount also increased notably, rising from 12 percent in 1989–2001 to 16 percent in 2004–2016. Today, SNR stands as a prominent and widely used approach to comparative politics.

Moreover, as indicated by the agenda-setting subnational works listed in the previous paragraphs, without SNR we would know far less about major substantive issues at the heart of political science. Indeed, as summarized in Table 1.1, this book is guided by the premise that SNR makes important substantive as well as theoretical and methodological contributions to the study of politics. With regard to substance, SNR makes it easier to see important phenomena obscured by a national-level focus. A good example of phenomena "under the radar" of national research can be found in what Guillermo O'Donnell (1993) evocatively labeled *brown areas,* that is, regions inside countries where the presence of state institutions, and hence the possibility of effective citizenship, were severely attenuated. Other humanly important outcomes that are difficult to detect with a national-level lens include subnational authoritarian regimes that curtail political and civil rights in certain areas of otherwise democratic countries, special economic zones and industrial clusters that can have a significant impact on national economic

TABLE 1.1 *Contributions of Subnational Research to Substance, Theory, and Methods in Comparative Politics*

Substance	Theory	Methods
Helps researchers see humanly important variation inside countries. Brings into focus subnational actors, institutions, and units of analysis that are often neglected. Prompts new research questions, especially when subnational observations cannot be explained by national-level theories.	Mitigates the problem of "theory stretching," that is, the inappropriate application to subnational levels of theories developed to explain national-level phenomena. Spurs new theory-building to explain subnational outcomes. Makes it easier to build multilevel theories that explain outcomes caused by variables at different scales.	Expands the menu of units of analysis, thereby making possible new strategies of comparative research. Opens opportunities to employ conventional and vanguard tools of social science research, including case studies, small-N, large-N, mixed, and experimental methods, in new and powerful ways.

performance, and local inequalities across small distances that translate into large differences in life expectancy, access to social services, vulnerability to crime, and other fundamental aspects of well-being. By opening a window on important variation inside countries, SNR prompts us to pose new research questions, inviting us to explain why phenomena of both scholarly and public interest are distributed unevenly across territory. A subnational perspective also shifts the focus to a host of actors (such as mayors, governors, provincial legislators, local civic organizations and indigenous communities), institutions (including provincial legislatures, local courts, and subnational government agencies), and units of analysis that are too often neglected by comparative politics because of the dominant national-level perspective.

SNR spurs theoretical innovation by offering new data and political units with which to build, test, and refine theories. The contributions collected in this volume show that well-established theories of executive–legislative relations, citizenship, property rights, public goods provision, and criminal violence, among others, fail to explain outcomes at the subnational level. Because these theories were mostly developed to explain national-level phenomena, their limited explanatory power at subnational levels highlights what we call the problem of *theory stretching*, that is, the inappropriate application of a theory from one level of analysis to another level.[6] SNR not only mitigates theory stretching by reining in overextended theories, it also underscores the importance of defining scope conditions for theories by specifying not just their international and historical scope but also the *scales* at which they operate. Moreover, as illustrated by the chapters in this volume, the inability of many existing theories to explain subnational outcomes prompts the building of new theories that offer stronger explanations for important phenomena inside countries.

SNR contributes to methodological innovation by providing fresh opportunities for deploying vanguard tools of social inquiry, including mixed methods that combine quantitative and qualitative analysis, promising new techniques for spatial analysis,[7] and experiments. With regard to experimental research, for example, national-level policy and institutional changes are often implemented unevenly within countries, and the exogenous and spatially uneven nature of these changes in relation to subnational units, in turn, may justify viewing them as "treatments," with unaffected subnational units serving as a control group. Likewise, shifts in administrative, jurisdictional, and other boundaries can occur in an "as-if random" manner with respect to outcomes of interest and can thus offer potential sources of

---

[6] Theory stretching is distinct from *theoretical stretching*, which Collier (1995) defines as the construction of concepts that are so ontologically distinct from their root concepts that they may be more fruitfully analyzed as subtypes of neighboring concepts in the semantic field. The term "theory stretching," as used in this chapter, is an extension of Sartori's (1970) notion of "conceptual stretching."

[7] On the affinity between SNR and new tools for spatial analysis, including Geographic Information Systems (GIS), see Harbers and Ingram (Chapter 2 of this volume).

	Political and Administrative Units		Other Territorial Units
National	Countries, National electoral districts, National supreme court jurisdictions.		National economies.
Subnational	*Jurisdictional Units:* Precincts, Wards, Boroughs, Townships, Cities, Counties, Municipalities, Cantons, States, Provinces, Regions, Territories, Special economic zones, Indigenous reservations, Tribal homelands; Legislative, Court, Police, School, and Military Districts.		*Formal Units:* Census tracts, Diocese, Districts of private voluntary organizations (e.g., trade unions, professional and civic associations), Public utility districts, Industrial parks, Legal parcels of property.
	Non-Jurisdictional Units: Squatter settlements, Shanty towns, Areas controlled or governed by non-state actors (e.g., paramilitary groups, gangs, criminal organizations, and insurgencies).		*Informal Units:* Regional economies, Extralegal parcels of property, Ecological zones.

FIGURE 1.1 Varieties of Territorial Units

natural experiments.[8] Precisely for these reasons, SNR and experimental methods are frequently used in tandem.

Before elaborating on these substantive, theoretical, and methodological contributions, we first offer clarification about what SNR is and is not. We define SNR as a strategy of social science inquiry that focuses on actors, organizations, institutions, structures, and processes located in territorial units inside countries, that is, below the national and international levels. Phenomena located within countries yet lacking a prominent territorial dimension, such as individuals, families, and interest groups, sit outside the scope of our definition of SNR. As seen in Figure 1.1, a subnational focus offers researchers a rich menu of political, administrative, and socioeconomic units of analysis, one that is far broader and more diverse than the set of units available in national-level research.[9] Moreover, territorial units in SNR can be formal/jurisdictional or informal/non-jurisdictional. Formal territorial units have clearly demarcated, legally defined boundaries. Examples of formal units include provinces, states, municipalities, counties, departments, wards, voting precincts, school districts, police districts, judicial circuits, military regions, census tracts and blocks, and special-purpose districts that manage the provision of public goods like water,

---

[8] The division of ethnic groups by a national boundary was employed implicitly as a natural experiment by Linz (1986) and Miles (1994) and explicitly by Posner (2004) and by Acemoglu and Robinson in the vignette mentioned in the second paragraph of this chapter. On natural experiments in social science research, see Dunning (2012) and Diamond and Robinson (2010).

[9] The expanded set of units made available by SNR creates both opportunities and challenges, especially concerning the selection of appropriate units of analysis. The methodological chapters in this volume by Harbers and Ingram (Chapter 2) and by Soifer (Chapter 3) discuss these issues.

electricity, natural gas, waste collection, and transportation. Informal territorial units, by contrast, are not legally constituted and typically lack crisp boundaries, although actors equipped with local knowledge may be able to identify them.[10] Informal subnational units include squatter settlements, shantytowns, areas controlled by gangs, rebels, criminal organizations, and other non-state groups, economic regions (e.g., "Silicon Valley" and the "Third Italy"[11]), and extralegal parcels of property. It bears emphasis that SNR does not necessarily focus on units that are spatially contiguous or even proximate to each other. Indeed, scholars routinely study subnational units located in different countries.[12] Also, as discussed in Sections 1.2 and 1.3 of this chapter, SNR often has a multilevel scope that spans different subnational scales and can also include variables that operate at the national and even transnational level.

Second, we do not view SNR as a research method per se, although it is compatible with and can enhance the power of conventional social science methods, including case study, small-N, large-N, and experimental methods. It also bears emphasis that SNR cuts across the conventional schools and paradigms in comparative politics.[13] As illustrated by the contributions in this book, scholars working in the historical institutional, rational choice, and interpretivist traditions fruitfully employ a focus on subnational politics.

Finally, this book does not aim to displace national and cross-national studies: We do not claim that all comparative research should be subnational. The choice of levels and units of analysis should depend on the nature of the research question. For example, it is hard to imagine a compelling study of foreign policy that does not focus on the national level. Still, as highlighted by the contributors to this book, a *multilevel* perspective that focuses on interactions between national and subnational factors can offer a stronger understanding of national policymaking. Moreover, in our increasingly globalized and interconnected world, the capacity of the national level to stand as an autonomous filter between the supra- and subnational levels may be attenuated, as suggested by recent research on how cities bypass the national level and connect directly with international markets (Davis, 2005; Robinson, 2002; Sassen, 2001).

---

[10] See, for example, the Peruvian economist Hernando De Soto's (2003) discussion of how informal property boundaries are signaled by barking dogs in settings where formal property rights are absent.

[11] The Third Italy refers to the industrial districts clustered within northeastern and central Italy that emerged in the late twentieth century.

[12] Recent studies that compare subnational units across different countries include Apaydin (2012, 2018); Arnold (2010); Durán-Martínez (2018); Gibson (2013); Holland (2016); Pasotti (2010); and Posner (2004). Sellers (in press) finds a striking recent increase in the number of studies that compare subnational units across countries.

[13] Lichbach and Zuckerman (2009).

The rest of this introductory chapter provides an overview of the substantive, theoretical, and methodological contributions of SNR in comparative politics. Section 1 shows how SNR has advanced knowledge about substantive themes at the center of the field. Section 2 explores how SNR can strengthen theory building, especially by mitigating the problem of "theory stretching" and making it possible to craft multilevel theories. Section 3 turns to issues of method and research design, proposing a new set of strategies for SNR and showing how a subnational focus can be fruitfully combined with widely used methodologies.

1.1 THE SUBNATIONAL TURN IN COMPARATIVE POLITICS: SUBSTANTIVE ACHIEVEMENTS

Whereas foundational works of SNR in comparative politics focused mainly on developed countries in Europe and North America, the empirical scope of SNR has widened over the last 25 years to include developing countries, or the "Global South."[14] To assess the contributions to knowledge resulting from the "subnational turn" in comparative politics, we focus on three broad themes, because they are central to the field and are also addressed by the substantive chapters in this book: political regimes and representation; state institutions and the provision of security and welfare; and economic inequality and development.

Subnational Regimes and Representation

The Third Wave of democratization that swept the globe over the past 45 years (Huntington, 1991) did not spread evenly inside countries. As scholars of newly democratic countries including Mexico, Russia, the Philippines, Argentina, and Brazil found, authoritarian regimes often persisted at the subnational level. The observation that democratization at the national level did not necessarily produce democratization at the subnational level spurred a first generation of research on the origins, maintenance, and consequences of subnational authoritarian regimes (Cornelius et al., 1999; Fox, 1994; Gibson, 2005; Hagopian, 1996; Heller, 2000; McMann, 2006; O'Donnell, 1993; Sidel, 1999; Snyder, 1999a; Solt, 2003; Stoner-Weiss, 2002).[15] A surprising finding emerged from this research: Subnational authoritarian regimes often were not isolated "backwaters" disconnected from the newly democratic national

---

[14] Moncada and Snyder (2012).

[15] Some scholars argue that the term "authoritarian" inappropriately characterizes subnational units where rulers wield power in a less-than-democratic fashion (Behrend, 2011; Gervasoni, 2010a; Giraudy, 2010, 2015). Behrend and Whitehead (2016) object not only to the usage of "authoritarian" but also to the term "regime" to describe subnational units that deviate from national-level democracy, preferring to describe such cases as instances of "illiberal practices."

political arena but were instead important sources of votes and other forms of political support for popularly elected national politicians. The previously dominant focus on national democratic regimes thus turned out to be doubly blind: Not only did a national-level perspective obscure the persistence of authoritarian regimes at the subnational level, a phenomenon that Edward Gibson (2005) labeled "regime juxtaposition," but it also made it harder to see that the maintenance of democracy at the national level could, ironically, depend on support produced through undemocratic means by subnational authoritarian regimes.[16]

A second generation aimed to systematically measure levels of democracy (or non-democracy) across subnational units within democratic countries,[17] while seeking also to explain the persistence of subnational authoritarian regimes. Studies in this second generation focused on the exclusionary practices of political elites, such as distorting local electoral rules and procedures,[18] stacking electoral commissions with allies,[19] politicizing local judiciaries,[20] and targeting extralegal violence against opponents.[21] Others looked instead to economic factors to explain the emergence and durability of subnational authoritarianism, including local political economies,[22] inter-governmental fiscal transfers,[23] and how subnational units were inserted into global markets.[24] Still other studies proposed multilevel theoretical frameworks that centered on strategic interactions between local and national political actors to explain both the endurance and breakdown of subnational authoritarian regimes.[25] Alongside these studies of subnational authoritarianism, researchers also assessed the origins and consequences of subnational democracies in the context of nondemocratic "hybrid" national regimes, including their potential to serve as beachheads for advancing national democratization.[26]

In sum, the line of research on subnational political regimes offered new insights into territorial variation in representation, highlighting how interactions across levels of government help explain the origins and survival of such regimes. Moreover – as discussed later in this chapter in the section on "theory stretching," as well as in Gavril Bilev's Chapter 4 on subnational

---

[16] See Gibson (2005, 2013) and Giraudy (2015).

[17] See Benton (2012); Borges (2007); Gerring et al. (2015); Gervasoni (2010a, 2010b); Giraudy (2010, 2013, 2015); Lankina and Getachew (2006, 2012); McMann (2006); Montero (2007, 2010); Petrov (2005); Rebolledo (2011); Reisinger and Moraski (2010); Remington (2009, 2010a, 2010b); and Saikkonen (2016), among others.

[18] Behrend and Whitehead (2016); Benton (2012); Calvo and Micozzi (2005); Green (2010). See also Snyder and Samuels (2001, 2004).

[19] Rebolledo (2011).   [20] Brinks (2007); Castagnola (2012); Chavez (2004); Leiras et al. (2015).

[21] Gibson (2005).   [22] McMann (2006); Behrend (2011); Hale (2003).

[23] Gervasoni (2010b); Díaz-Rioseco (2016).   [24] Libman and Obydenkova (2014).

[25] Gibson (2005, 2015); Giraudy (2013, 2015); Reuter and Robertson (2012).

[26] Lankina and Getachew (2006). On hybrid national regimes, see Karl (1995), Schedler (2006), and Levitsky and Way (2010).

executive-legislative relations in Russia and Caroline Beer's Chapter 5 on women's rights across Mexico's states – the inability of theories of national political regimes to provide satisfactory explanations at the subnational level prompted efforts to build new theories that can account for the sharp variation in regimes and representation observed inside countries.

The Uneven Reach of the State: Citizenship, Security, and Public Goods

Another key area where SNR helped advance knowledge involved the territorially uneven reach and capacity of state institutions inside countries. A subnational perspective made it easier to see the uneven presence of state institutions and, in turn, to explore the consequences for important substantive outcomes, including effective citizenship and the provision of security and other public goods that have increasingly come under the authority of subnational institutions, actors, and interests because of the administrative and political decentralization that occurred across the world in the late twentieth century.

SNR revealed within-country variation in the accessibility and capacity of state institutions, which, in turn, resulted in sharply divergent opportunities for citizens to exercise their rights, even among citizens who lived in close proximity to each other.[27] To explain this variation in what O'Donnell (1993) called the "intensity of citizenship," researchers focused on a variety of subnational political factors that affected the state's territorial reach, including local partisan competition,[28] whether local judicial officials were affiliated with the governing national political party,[29] the political beliefs of local authorities,[30] informal institutions and norms,[31] and efforts by local politicians to escape central government oversight.[32]

SNR also contributed to a stronger understanding of security, especially in the face of the many "internal wars" that proliferated across the globe in the post–Cold War era. As discussed by Ana Arjona in her Chapter 7 on civilian support for rebel groups, a burgeoning literature on the micro-dynamics of civil war aimed to explain subnational variation in wartime violence,[33] patterns of recruitment,[34] forced displacement,[35] and post-war conflicts.[36] Recent research on civil wars found that rebel groups built different types of institutions at the local level for the provision of goods and services to civilians – in some

---

[27] Luna and Medel (2017). On subnational state capacity, see Luna and Soifer (2017).

[28] Chavez (2004); Leiras et al. (2015); Pribble (2015).

[29] Castagnola (2012); Niedzwiecki (2016). [30] Ingram (2015).

[31] Brinks (2007); Smulovitz (2015). [32] Trochev (2004).

[33] Balcells (2010, 2011); Kalyvas (2006); Kalyvas and Kocher (2009); Schutte and Weidmann (2011); Urdal (2008); Wood (2003).

[34] Fearon, Humphreys, and Weinstein (2009); Humphreys and Weinstein (2008); Straus (2015); Weinstein (2006).

[35] Lubkemann (2005); Steele (2017). [36] Autesserre (2010); Bateson (2013); Grandi (2013).

instances, ironically, in coordination with the very state they ostensibly aimed to topple and replace.[37]

Likewise, as elaborated in Chapter 6 by Guillermo Trejo and Sandra Ley on the lethal consequences of national anti-narcotics policies for local politicians in Mexico, SNR played a central role in recent research on the politics of criminal violence.[38] To explain variation in both levels and forms of violence, recent subnational studies showed that criminal violence could be exacerbated by insufficient intergovernmental coordination,[39] different political parties holding power at the subnational and national levels,[40] "iron-fist" law enforcement strategies targeting the leadership of criminal organizations,[41] and local socioeconomic crises.[42] Other studies focused on law enforcement, showing how differences in the local political contexts where policing objectives and practices were defined caused subnational variation in crime[43] and, more broadly, in local state–society relations.[44] A subnational perspective also revealed significant local variation in how citizens, social groups, and state agencies responded to criminal violence and, in turn, constructed different kinds of local institutions for enforcing order.[45]

The study of ethnic conflict also relied increasingly on SNR. By focusing on variation in levels of ethnic violence across neighborhoods, cities, regions and other subnational units, scholars produced new explanations. This can be seen especially in work on Hindu–Muslim violence in India, which generated a set of influential, if partly competing, explanations for ethnic conflict. For example, Ashutosh Varshney (2002) looked at pairs of Indian cities matched across demographic and socioeconomic factors yet with sharply contrasting levels of ethnic violence, finding that associational ties bridging ethnic groups differentiated peaceful from violent cities. Steven Wilkinson (2006) found instead that the electoral incentives of state-level politicians were a better predictor of ethnic violence, because these incentives determined whether state protection was extended to ethnic minorities facing violent threats. By contrast, Anjali Bohlken and Ernest Sergenti (2010) found that subnational economic conditions, specifically the annual growth rate of per capita GDP in each Indian state, was a far better predictor of ethnic violence than political, social or cultural factors.

---

[37] Arjona (2016); Arjona et al. (2015); Mampilly (2011); Staniland (2012).

[38] See also Harbers and Ingram's Chapter 2 in this volume, as well as Barnes (2017); Hilgers and Macdonald (2017); Osorio (2013).

[39] Snyder and Durán-Martínez (2009a, 2009b); Ríos (2013); Shirk and Wallman (2015)

[40] Trejo and Ley (Chapter 6 of this volume).   [41] Calderón et al. (2015); Phillips (2015).

[42] Cotte Poveda (2012); Ingram (2014).   [43] Arias and Ungar (2009).

[44] Eaton (2008); Hinton (2006); Moncada (2009, 2016a).

[45] Arias (2009, 2013, 2017); Auyero (2007); Auyero and Sobering (2017); Durán-Martínez (2015); LeBas (2013); Leeds (1996); Moncada (2013b, 2016a, 2016b, 2017); Weinstein (2013); Wolff (2015).

As seen in the chapters on subnational social development in India by Prerna Singh (Chapter 8) and by Sunila S. Kale and Nimah Mazaheri (Chapter 9), SNR on the uneven reach and capacity of state institutions inside countries has also contributed to a stronger understanding of the provision of public goods, such as social welfare, both by state and non-state actors. Subnational studies revealed how the ability of state agencies to deliver public goods depended on a host of local contextual factors, including the stock of social capital,[46] the administrative capacity and fiscal solvency of subnational governments, grassroots mobilization by political parties, partisan alignments across levels of government, and the linkage of regional economies to global markets.[47] Building on pioneering work by Elinor Ostrom (1996) and Peter Evans (1996), subnational researchers identified ecologies of governance formed by local governments and authorities working in tandem with citizens, interest associations, and civil society organizations.[48] An especially fruitful line of research focused on participatory local governance in Africa,[49] Asia,[50] and Latin America.[51]

SNR on the provision of public goods highlighted key explanatory factors overlooked or de-emphasized as a result of the national-level focus in prior research. For example, subnational researchers found that clientelist networks played an important role in provision of social welfare, especially in cities and neighborhoods.[52] And, as illustrated by recent work on non-state social welfare, a subnational approach brought into focus the crucial role played by non-state actors and institutions, such as local political factions and social groups, in providing public goods and services in areas where state institutions were weak or simply nonexistent.[53]

---

[46] Here scholars have built on Putnam's (1994) seminal work in this area, including Tsai (2007).

[47] Early and influential studies in this vein include Kohli (1987), Tendler (1997), and Tendler and Freedheim (1994). More recent analyses include Alves (2015); Chibber and Nooruddin (2004); Díaz-Cayeros et al. (2014); Boulding and Brown (2014); Faguet (2009); Hecock (2006); Hiskey (2003); Kale (2014); Mcguire (2017); Niedzwiecki (2016); Saez and Sinha (2009); and Ziblatt (2008).

[48] See, for example, Post et al. (2017).

[49] Heller (2008); Crook (2003). For cross-national subnational studies of the influence that participatory governance has on public goods provisions, see Blair (2000) and Heller (2009).

[50] Corbridge (2005); Heller (2000); Krishna (2002).

[51] Abers (2000); Abers and Keck (2013); Alberti (2016, in press); Avritzer (2009); Baiocchi (2005); Boulding and Wampler (2010); Falleti and Riofrancos (2018); Goldfrank (2011); Heller et al. (2007); Montambeault (2015); Touchton and Wampler (2014); Wampler (2007).

[52] For a subnational study of clientelism in two Italian cities, see Chubb (1982). More recent subnational studies of clientelism in Latin America include Calvo and Murillo (2004); Hunter and Sugiyama (2014); Szwarcberg (2013, 2015); Stokes et al. (2013); Sugiyama and Hunter (2013); and Weitz-Shapiro (2014), among others. Recent subnational studies of clientelism in Africa include Koter (2013); Resnick (2012, 2013); and Wantchekon (2003). For a subnational analysis of the politics of clientelism in the Middle East, see Corstange (2016). And for a cross-national subnational analysis of the breakdown of urban clientelist machines across Bogotá (Colombia), Naples (Italy), and Chicago (USA), see Pasotti (2010).

[53] Cammett and Issar (2010); MacLean (2010); Cammett (2014); and the contributions collected in Cammett and MacLean (2014); Amengual (2016).

From National to Subnational Development

Like regimes and states, patterns of economic development can also vary widely inside countries. By zooming in on vibrant regional economies driven by clusters of firms specializing in similar products, such as the industrial districts of the "Third Italy" and cutlery producers in the German state of North Rhine-Westphalia, pioneering studies by Richard M. Locke (1995) and Gary Herrigel (1996) challenged the "national models" approach that had previously dominated the field of comparative political economy. Subsequent SNR on the political economy of development focused on the Global South, exploring how distinct regional economies emerged as a result of divergent patterns of industrialization[54] and, as illustrated by Meg Rithmire's Chapter 10 on the politics of regulating land markets across China's cities, the postindustrial transformation of urban economies.[55]

A related line of research looked at the subnational consequences of national policies that aimed to promote economic and human development. These studies converged in finding that the implementation of national policies depended on local political conditions. For example, studies of market-oriented, or "neoliberal," policy reforms in countries as different as Brazil, China, Mexico, Russia, and Argentina found that these initiatives often ended up producing new institutions for regulating markets at the subnational level instead of territorially uniform "free markets."[56] These new subnational institutions, in turn, had contrasting consequences for capital–labor and state–labor relations.[57] Researchers have also taken what we describe in Section 2 as a "bottom up" approach, exploring how subnational political and economic factors themselves drove national development outcomes, ranging from economic recoveries to the sustainability of economic policy reforms.[58]

The recent reconceptualization of development to include participatory and deliberative components, a move largely inspired by the work of Amartya Sen

---

[54] Montero (2010); Naseemullah (2016); Sinha (2005).

[55] Logan and Swanstrom (2009); Sellers (2002). The analysis of urban political economies is part of a broader movement in the field of urban studies that seeks to add a comparative focus, both within and across countries, to the single-case studies that have traditionally characterized research in this area (Denters & Mossberger, 2006; Kantor & Savitch, 2005; Pierre, 2005; Robinson, 2011; Sellers, 2005).

[56] Amengual (2010); Coslovsky and Locke (2013); Jayasuriya (2008); Snyder (1999b, 2001b); Herrera (2014, 2017); Contarino (1995); Rithmire (2014); Stoner-Weiss (2006); Wengle (2015).

[57] Contarino (1995); Locke (1992); Hurst (2004, 2009).

[58] See, for example, Katznelson (2013) and Mickey (2015) on how the support of authoritarian and racist subnational elites in the US South proved essential for implementing the progressive New Deal social policies. On the role of subnational elites in shaping the sustainability of economic reforms in Argentina in the 1990s, see Gibson and Calvo (2000). See Pogrebinschi and Samuels (2014) on how local experiences with participatory governance had a transformative effect on national policymaking in Brazil.

(1999), also spurred new subnational research. It is at local scales where public policies that impact the day-to-day lives of citizens are often formulated and implemented. Moreover, the possibilities for deliberation and other forms of consultation designed to increase citizen engagement in policy making are likely to be greater at smaller scales, as reflected in the city and municipal-level focus of recent research on participatory budgeting and participatory security.[59]

The burgeoning literature on the political and economic consequences of natural-resource wealth also focused increasingly on subnational units. Mineral and other natural resources are rarely, if ever, distributed evenly within countries, and researchers effectively exploited this subnational variation in the distribution of natural resources to test, refine, and even challenge the well-known national "resource curse" hypothesis that mineral wealth leads to authoritarianism and economic underdevelopment.[60] While most of these subnational studies offered new evidence that supported the resource curse hypothesis, they also showed that some of the causal mechanisms proposed in the national-level literature to explain the association between resource wealth and underdevelopment either did not travel to the subnational level or required modifications when applied there. For example, in a study of the US states, Ellis Goldberg et al. (2008) concluded that the "Dutch disease" mechanism, whereby natural resource booms caused an appreciation of the exchange rate which, in turn, resulted in poor economic performance, could not explain why resource-rich states in the United States performed worse economically, because all the US states shared the same currency and real prices varied little among them. Similarly, in a study of the political consequences of an offshore oil boom in Brazil's municipalities, Joana Monteiro and Claudio Ferraz (n.d.) showed that, as predicted by the national-level resource curse literature, oil windfalls also stifled political competitiveness at the municipal level by providing incumbents with increased resources to spend on patronage, especially in the form of expanded public employment. However, they also found that the mechanism of resource-driven patronage as a source of incumbency advantage worked differently at the subnational level, because of federal regulations in Brazil that constrained the use of oil rents to hire public employees on a permanent basis. As a result of an increase in the enforcement of these federal constraints, the large incumbency advantage at the municipal level associated with the oil windfall boom proved fleeting, disappearing after two elections.

Other studies went further, using a subnational perspective to challenge the notion of a resource curse altogether. For example, in his analysis of oil wealth

---

[59] On participatory budgeting, see: Abers (2000); Abers and Keck (2013); Avritzer (2009); Baiocchi (2005); Boulding and Wampler (2010); Goldfrank (2011); Heller et al. (2007); Montambeault (2015); Touchton and Wampler (2014); Wampler (2007). On participatory security, see: Arias and Ungar (2009); Baker (2002); Bénit-Gbaffou (2008); González (2016); Moncada (2009).

[60] Beblawi and Luciani (1987); Mahdavy (1970). See also Sachs and Warner (1995); Smith (2004); and Ross (2012).

in the Argentine provinces, Diego Díaz-Rioseco (2016) showed that, in some instances, oil actually led to more, not less, political contestation at the subnational level. To explain the contrasting consequences of oil on levels of political competitiveness at the provincial level, Díaz-Rioseco focused on "rent sharing regimes," that is, the fiscal institutions for sharing resource revenues among levels of government. When these institutions distributed rents to municipal governments, rather than concentrating them under the control of provincial governments, the result was an increase in political competitiveness at the provincial level.[61] SNR has thus provided a stronger and more nuanced understanding of the contrasting political and economic consequences of natural resource wealth.

In sum, the proliferation of SNR in comparative politics over the past 25 years yielded new and often surprising insights about regimes, states, and development, thereby advancing knowledge about important substantive issues at the heart of political science.

I.2 SUBNATIONAL RESEARCH AND THEORETICAL PROGRESS

A subnational perspective spurs theoretical progress by giving researchers new ways both to refine existing theories and build new ones. We focus on three specific contributions of SNR to theory building. First, SNR mitigates what we call theory stretching, that is, the inappropriate application of a theory from one level of analysis to another. Second, SNR drives the development of new theories with an explicitly subnational scope. Third, SNR fosters multilevel theories that highlight causal relationships across levels of analysis to explain subnational and also national outcomes of interest.

The Problem of Theory Stretching

Theories in comparative politics traditionally have focused on the national level, relying on national-level variables to explain national outcomes. This national-level focus is evident across well-known theories of political regimes,[62] elections,[63] institutional change,[64] and public policy.[65] As seen most notably in the chapters in this volume by Kale and Mazaheri (Chapter 9), by Singh (Chapter 8), and by Bilev

---

[61] Additional recent subnational studies of the political and economic consequences of resource wealth include Mahdavi (2015); Saikkonen (2016); González (2018); and González and Lodola (n.d.). See also Gervasoni (2010b), who finds that federal transfers, like natural resource rents, have a negative effect on political contestation at the subnational level. Gervasoni argues that such monies are similar to resource rents because they also consist of funds that incumbents can spend without taxing.

[62] Collier and Collier (1991); Dahl (1971); Huntington (1968, 1993); Lijphart (1992); Linz and Stepan (1996); Lipset (1959); Moore (1966); Przeworksi (2000).

[63] Duverger (1978); Downs (1957).   [64] Knight (1992); North (1990).

[65] Shonfield (1965); Bates (1981); Pierson (1994).

(Chapter 4), SNR highlights surprising outcomes that cannot be explained by national-level theories. This, in turn, prompts these authors to propose new theories attuned to subnational contexts and thus able to explain subnational outcomes. Moreover, the evidence they provide that national-level theories can be ill equipped to explain subnational outcomes serves to underscore the risk of "theory stretching," that is, drawing on theories designed to explain phenomena at one level of analysis to account for outcomes at other levels. Whether or not theories can travel across levels of analysis is an important matter that has received insufficient attention in comparative politics: When a theoretical framework is proposed, the level of analysis, in contrast to international and historical scope, is more often assumed than specified.[66]

In Chapter 9, on policies intended to improve the welfare of indigenous people in India, Kale and Mazaheri consider two hypotheses drawn from national-level theories of public goods provision: (i) socio-cultural homogeneity increases citizens' support for public goods; and (ii) political units anchored in a clearly defined group identity offer more robust welfare benefits. Kale and Mazaheri's comparative analysis across Indian states shows that states with strong subnational identities surprisingly failed to implement robust welfare agendas unless they also had vibrant civil society organizations (CSOs). By focusing on subnational units, the authors are thus able to identify a key factor, undertheorized in prior national-level studies, that influences the provision of public goods: the strength of local CSOs. Kale and Mazaheri find that CSOs serve as a critical intervening variable that determines the relationship between group identities and welfare provision at the subnational level. Drawing on these findings, the authors propose a new theory of provision of public goods, one that provides a stronger explanation of the variation in the implementation of welfare-enhancing policies observed across Indian states.

Singh's Chapter 8 also highlights the inability of national-level theories to explain important subnational outcomes. Through a comparative historical analysis of social development in two Indian states, Kerala and Uttar Pradesh, Singh challenges well-known theories that predict a strong and positive relationship between economic and social development. She shows instead that robust cultural solidarities in subnational units, a phenomenon she calls "subnationalism," can help surmount barriers to development predicted by national-level theories and, in turn, yield surprisingly positive educational and health outcomes even in places with low levels of economic development. Moreover, because powerful collective solidarities may be more likely to arise and persist at scales smaller than countries, Singh's Chapter 8 highlights more generally the importance of a subnational perspective for understanding how sociocultural forces shape political outcomes.

---

[66] As discussed in Soifer's Chapter 3 in this volume, some theories operate equally well at more than one level of analysis and are therefore less susceptible to inappropriate stretching.

In his Chapter 4 on executive-legislative relations in Russia, Bilev finds that the institutional incentives faced by subnational elected officials differ starkly from those faced by national officeholders. In Russia, as in many countries, whereas the national legislative assembly is a full-time, professional body, subnational assemblies are not. Consequently, subnational legislators are often compelled to combine their work as elected representatives with extra-legislative private work. In Russia's provinces (*Oblast*), this phenomenon of part-time legislators, who depend on income from other sources, makes subnational deputies especially vulnerable to pressure from monied interests, undercuts their professionalism, and weakens their ability to challenge governors and hold them accountable. Bilev further documents a range of tools available only at the subnational level which governors use to neutralize the capacity of the provincial assembly to check their power – for example, by supporting mayors as candidates for the assembly. Mayors in Russia typically depend on the governor's discretionary allocation of revenue transfers, which renders them a reliable base of support for governors. Sponsoring mayors as candidates for the assembly thus serves as a way for governors to try to stack it with loyal deputies. A focus on subnational political actors and the distinct institutional environments in which they operate thus provides a foundation for a stronger theory of executive–legislative relations, one that explains variation in the power and influence of legislative assemblies and executives both across subnational units and also at different levels of the political system.

Together, these and other chapters show that successful theory building in comparative politics requires specifying the level(s) of analysis at which the theory operates. Prior work on scope conditions focuses on risks that arise when theories are stretched beyond their historical and international scope.[67] SNR, by contrast, highlights the importance of including the level of analysis, and therefore the scales and types of territorial units to which a theory applies, as a further – and indispensable – component of scope conditions for theories.[68]

Multilevel Theory Building

By making it possible to study causal relationships among variables at different scales and levels of analysis inside countries, SNR fosters the building of

---

[67] Geddes (2003); Mahoney and Goertz (2004). For an example of a substantive debate framed explicitly in terms of the historical and international scope of theories, see Bunce (1995); Schmitter and Karl (1994); and Karl and Schmitter (1995) concerning the applicability to the Soviet Union and Eastern Europe of theories of regime change developed to explain transitions from authoritarianism in Southern Europe and South America. See also Gans-Morse (2004).

[68] Relatedly, Soifer (Chapter 3 in this volume) divides theories into three categories: "those that are *unit-independent* and can apply to any unit of analysis we might imagine, those that are *unit-specific* to certain units of analysis, those that are *unit-limiting* in that they can be evaluated with certain units of analysis but not others." Soifer notes that "unit-independent" theories are rare in political science.

multilevel theories that combine national and subnational factors to offer stronger explanations for outcomes of interest (Rokkan, 1970; Tarrow, 1978; Rokkan & Urwin, 1982, 1983). Multilevel theories have a long pedigree in the field of international relations (Evans et al., 1993; Gourevitch, 1978; Singer, 1961), and, because of the recent proliferation of SNR, they are now increasingly common in comparative politics (Hooghe & Marks, 2001, 2016). Two kinds of multilevel theory are routinely employed in SNR: (i) *bottom-up theories*, where subnational variables explain national-level outcomes; and (ii) *top-down theories*, where, conversely, national-level variables explain subnational outcomes.[69]

Bottom-Up Theories

Bottom-up theories identify how national, and even international,[70] phenomena are shaped by subnational factors. From this standpoint, national politics cannot be properly understood without paying attention to subnational institutions, actors, and events. Indeed, scholars attuned to bottom-up causation often aim to destabilize theories that fail to incorporate subnational forces, showing how this neglect results, at best, in incomplete explanations and, at worst, in fundamental misunderstandings of national-level outcomes.

Research on national social policy in the United States provides a good example of bottom-up analysis. Studies of the New Deal social programs proposed by Franklin D. Roosevelt's administration during the 1930s show that their successful implementation depended on the political support of racist southern Democrats, whose elected representatives were the dominant force in the US Congress, counting among their ranks several Speakers of the House and many chairpersons of key committees. As historian Harvard Sitkoff (1981, p. 51) succinctly observed, "Congress held the power of the purse, and the South held power in Congress." In turn, President Roosevelt remained ambivalent about black civil rights, largely because raising this issue would have jeopardized his social policies by angering southern congressional leaders. The successful implementation of the New Deal thus hinged on the maintenance of Jim Crow in the "Solid South," an unsavory fact obscured by a strictly national vantage point (Katznelson, 2013; Mickey, 2015).

Research on the implementation of market-oriented, "neoliberal" reforms further illustrates how bottom-up theories can help provide a stronger understanding of national politics.[71] In their study of economic reforms

---

[69] As discussed in Section 3, top-down and bottom-up perspectives can be combined into theories characterized by *reciprocal causality*, where factors at one level shape and, in turn, are shaped by factors at other levels.

[70] See, for example, Bates (1997), which shows how the policy preferences and political power of the coffee-producing states in Brazil and regions in Colombia had an important impact both on global prices for coffee and the evolution of an international regulatory framework under the auspices of the International Coffee Organization (ICO).

[71] Gibson and Calvo (2000). See also Gibson (2004).

implemented by the national government in Argentina in the 1990s, Edward Gibson and Ernesto Calvo (2000) showed how a focus on subnational coalitions helps explain the puzzling political sustainability of the new policies, despite their unpopularity among the vital urban working-class constituency of the governing Peronist Party. Whereas prior research on the politics of neoliberal economic reforms focused mainly on the national level, the authors shifted the focus to the provincial level, arguing that the overrepresentation of rural provinces by Argentina's malapportioned electoral system made it possible for the Peronist Party to pursue a regionally segmented strategy of building new alliances with rural elites and voters who had not traditionally supported the Peronists.[72] The government of President Carlos Menem (1990–1999) was thus able to target public spending to "low maintenance," mostly rural constituencies in overrepresented districts, thereby cushioning these groups from the costs inflicted by the economic reforms. By contrast, "high maintenance" constituencies in underrepresented districts located in urban areas saw large cuts in public spending and bore the brunt of the hardships resulting from the new policies. The resulting patchwork coalition, which reflected the territorially uneven distribution of the costs of the neoliberal reforms, ensured the national electoral viability of the Peronist Party and, hence, the political sustainability of new policies.[73]

Bottom-up perspectives have also spurred theoretical progress in the comparative study of industrialization. For example, Herrigel (1996) challenged the widely accepted idea, introduced by Alexander Gerschenkron (1962), that Germany was a paradigmatic example of centralized industrialization dominated by large firms and big, national-level banks. Instead, Herrigel showed that key regions of Germany actually experienced a different kind of industrialization rooted in small firms and regional banks. By situating the process of industrialization in a regionally differentiated framework, Herrigel "recodes" German industrialization as a bimodal phenomenon. What emerges is a reconfigured national composite formed by two distinct modes of industrialization: centralized, "organized capitalism" in some regions and a "decentralized industrial order" in others. In light of these findings, it would be a mistake to conclude based on the German case that an entire country could follow the path of centralized, organized capitalism. Rather, Herrigel's study suggests that organized capitalism is suited only for specific regions and kinds of firms, not entire countries. Moreover, to the degree that Germany's centralized industrialization was not an independent,

---

[72] On electoral malapportionment and the over- and underrepresentation of subnational political units in Latin America and beyond, see Samuels and Snyder (2001) and also Snyder and Samuels (2001).

[73] See Luna (2014) and Alves and Hunter (2017) for further studies that focus on the territorially segmented strategies of political parties. For a bottom-up theory that links local experiences with participatory governance to national policy decisions, see Pogrebinschi and Samuels (2014).

separately determined process but was in fact causally related to the decentralized industrial order, a failure to analyze the latter phenomenon could lead to a serious misunderstanding of the former (Snyder, 2001a).[74] In this instance, a bottom-up focus thus destabilized a long-standing national theory of industrialization.[75]

Top-Down Theories: Homogenous versus Heterogeneous Effects

Whereas bottom-up theories focus on national effects of subnational causes, top-down theories focus on the opposite, that is, subnational effects of national-level causes. Moreover, in contrast to bottom-up theories, which justify, at least implicitly, their focus on subnational factors as a way to provide stronger explanations for national outcomes, top-down theories stake a different claim: Subnational outcomes are worth explaining and understanding in their own right, and, therefore, a subnational focus is legitimate whether or not it sheds light on national-level phenomena. We identify two kinds of top-down multilevel theories depending on whether national-level factors are understood to have homogenous or, alternatively, heterogeneous effects at subnational levels. The first treats major national events and phenomena, such as decentralization, democratization, and economic liberalization, as having similar consequences across subnational units. For instance, Alfred Montero and David Samuels (2004) argue that national policies of decentralization, which swept across Latin America in the late 1980s and 1990s, shifting political, fiscal, and administrative power to subnational governments, gave local elected officials more resources and independence, which, in turn, had the convergent effect of strengthening subnational incumbents. And Carla Alberti (in press) shows how national-level political strategies, especially populist mobilization by ruling parties, hinder the implementation of indigenous autonomy at the local level in Bolivia and Ecuador.

A second approach to top-down theory begins with the opposite premise, namely that national causes have heterogeneous effects with divergent consequences across subnational units. From this standpoint, subnational actors and institutions are seen not as passive recipients of national policies and initiatives but as active agents with the potential to engage, challenge, and even modify, top-down forces. Depending on subnational actors and institutions, therefore, a variety of different outcomes can result across subnational units.[76] Theoretical frameworks that emphasize heterogeneous top-down effects are

---

[74] See also Anderson (1992) for a subnational study of the political economy of Germany.

[75] On the emergence of distinct subnational modes of industrialization in Brazil and Spain, see Montero (2002). On this phenomenon in India, see Sinha (2005).

[76] See, for example, Eaton's (2004) study of waves of decentralization and recentralization in Latin America; Vergara's (2015) study of center–periphery relations in Bolivia and Peru; González's (2017) study of intergovernmental relations in Argentina and Brazil.

increasingly common in SNR.[77] The chapters in this book by Trejo and Ley (Chapter 6) and by Rithmire (Chapter 10) show how top-down multi-level theories can advance knowledge about policy implementation, violence and state capacity, and economic reforms.

Trejo and Ley propose a top-down theory to explain subnational variation in the nature and consequences of the coercive strategies of criminal organizations in Mexico. They explore why a group that had previously not been targeted by drug-trafficking organizations (DTOs) – municipal officials and political candidates – suddenly became victims of hundreds of lethal criminal attacks starting in 2007. To explain this rapid shift, the authors focus on two key national-level variables: a major change in federal policy toward confronting DTOs militarily; and the federal government's decision to provide protection from criminal attacks to local officials who were co-partisans and political allies yet deny it to those affiliated with opposition parties, especially in states where the governor belonged to the leftist party that had opposed the president and his conservative party since the 2006 election. The authors use quantitative and qualitative evidence to test these propositions. Based on statistical analyses of criminal attacks across more than 2,000 municipalities, they show that violence against local authorities was more common in municipalities experiencing the most intense levels of inter-cartel violence, where DTOs were engaged in bitter conflicts over drug trafficking routes and in need of fresh resources to finance turf wars.[78] They also show that local authorities affiliated with the opposition parties in states ruled by leftist governors were far more likely to become targets of criminal attacks than local authorities in states ruled by the president's co-partisans. Trejo and Ley thus show how a combination of national and local factors, including intergovernmental partisan conflict, explains the emergence of subnational regions where DTOs and their criminal associates enjoyed a monopoly on violence, security, and taxation: DTOs sought to tap new sources of revenue by targeting local officials, and national officials, in turn, tolerated, and even tacitly supported, the resulting violence in regions where their co-partisans were not in power. More broadly, Trejo and Ley's attention to how partisan preferences can shape the behavior of federal officials responsible for providing security challenges the assumption in much of the vast social science literature on state institutions that national authorities

---

[77] See, for example, Snyder (2001b); Boone (2003, 2014); Ziblatt (2006); Giraudy (2010, 2015); Moncada (2013a, 2013b); and Alves (2015). The logic of this approach to theory building corresponds to the "most similar systems" research design proposed by Przeworski and Teune (1970), which is also known as John Stuart Mill's "method of difference."

[78] According to Trejo and Ley, DTOs discovered two lucrative markets that set municipal authorities at the center of their operations: extortion and kidnapping for ransom. Acting as racketeers, criminals could levy a "tax" on municipal authorities and also get illegal access to the local property-tax registry, using this privileged information to extort local businesses and carry out lucrative kidnappings for ransom.

will always seek a monopoly of violence. Instead, national elites may prefer selectively abdicating local control of violence to criminals over sharing it with their partisan foes.[79]

Rhitmire's Chapter 10 on China shows that, even in a highly centralized authoritarian regime, the implementation of national economic reforms can produce sharply contrasting institutions for regulating markets at the local level. Focusing on land markets and property rights across three cities in the "rust belt" region of northeastern China, Rithmire proposes a theoretical framework that combines national and subnational variables to explain the distinct local economic orders that resulted from economic reforms launched by the national government in the 1980s and 1990s. Her framework focuses on how these new national policies interacted with two critical subnational variables: intra-governmental cohesion, which includes the degree of bureaucratic coherence at the municipal level, and state–firm relations, which refers to the amount and kind of control that local governments exert over economic actors. The resulting economic orders, in turn, led to different property rights systems across cities, with local governments emerging in some instances as the monopoly owners of urban land in order to capitalize monetarily on its value, whereas local governments in other instances distributed land as a political resource, selectively enforcing claims to property and allowing illegal land use by politically important constituencies. Rithmire's study challenges dominant explanations of the emergence of property rights institutions, which operate at the national level and emphasize broad changes in economic structure or national regimes.[80] Consequently, these explanations fail to account for the diverse political uses of property rights that Rithmire shows can occur across subnational units. A focus on property rights institutions at the local level highlights how they can emerge as a product of political bargaining about matters far removed from either questions of economic development or the intentions of the architects of national economic reforms. By taking a subnational perspective, Rithmire thus finds that "sometimes property rights are not about property rights at all."[81]

Together, these chapters show how SNR can help build new multilevel theories that challenge established national-level theories and offer stronger explanations for a variety of humanly important outcomes.

---

[79] See Díaz Cayeros et al. (2015) for an analysis of subnational variation in relations between drug trafficking organizations and communities across Mexico.

[80] See, for example, Acemoglu and Johnson (2005); North and Weingast (1989); North (1990); North and Thomas (1973).

[81] Albertus (2015) uses a subnational approach to show that – contrary to the conventional wisdom – land redistribution is greater under autocratic national regimes than under democracies. See also Saffon (n.d.).

I.3   SUBNATIONAL RESEARCH AND METHODOLOGICAL
       INNOVATION: NEW STRATEGIES AND OPPORTUNITIES

In addition to contributing to theoretical progress, SNR also fosters methodological innovation. Nearly 20 years ago, Richard Snyder (2001a) argued that subnational research offered important methodological advantages for research design, measurement, and theory building in comparative politics. Focusing on "small-N" comparative research, he argued that a subnational perspective helped mitigate the problem of "many variables, small-N" (Lijphart, 1971) both by increasing the number of observations and by making it easier to design controlled comparisons.[82] Snyder identified two strategies of subnational research – within-nation comparisons, which focus on subnational cases inside a single country; and between-nation comparisons, which focus on subnational cases across countries – discussing exemplary works that deployed each strategy. Over the past two decades, as SNR has proliferated in comparative politics, advances in theory and methods now make it possible to propose an expanded set of strategies of SNR.[83] Moreover, these advances invite us to consider how a subnational perspective can be combined effectively not only with conventional small-N comparisons but with new and increasingly popular methodologies such as "mixed methods," sophisticated tools for spatial analysis, and experiments.

New Strategies of Subnational Research

A focus on subnational units opens many new options for designing comparative research. As seen earlier in Figure 1.1, scholars can choose to study outcomes in a broad set of different kinds of subnational territorial units. Moreover, they can seek explanations by looking at variables at the same subnational scale as outcomes of interest – for example, a study that focuses on state-level elections to explain state-level policies. Alternatively, as discussed in the previous section, scholars can craft multilevel research designs, seeking to explain subnational outcomes by focusing on variables at lower or higher scales, including at the national and even international levels. For example, explanations for state-level policies might be found at lower scales, perhaps in the political power and strategies of city mayors or municipal interest groups, or at higher scales, say in the partisan composition of the national government or in the performance of the international economy. Finally, as

---

[82] With regard to measurement, Snyder (2001a) argued that subnational research improved the capacity of researchers to code cases accurately and thus make valid causal inferences. With regard to theory building, he argued that subnational research played an indispensable role in developing explanations of spatially uneven phenomena.

[83] Recent contributions that address important methodological and inferential challenges involved in subnational research include Tsai and Ziblatt (n.d.); Pepinsky (2017); and Sellers (in press).

illustrated by the examples of "bottom-up" theorizing already discussed, scholars can choose to focus not on subnational outcomes but on national ones, seeking explanations in variables that operate at subnational scales.

To organize this new set of research design options, Table 1.2 identifies distinct strategies of SNR defined by two dimensions: (i) the number of levels of analysis; and (ii) the type of causal relationship among variables. With regard to levels of analysis, strategies are defined by whether they are unilevel, focusing on variables at a single scale, or, alternatively, multilevel, focusing on variables at two or more scales. The type of causal relationship among variables, in turn, takes one of three forms: no relationship, unidirectional, or reciprocal.[84]

Together, these two dimensions result in seven strategies of SNR. A freestanding units strategy (Quadrant I) treats subnational units as self-contained entities in which variables located at higher scales (for example,

TABLE 1.2 *Strategies of Subnational Research*

| | | Number of Levels of Analysis | |
		Unilevel	*Multilevel*
Type of Causal Relationship	*None*	I. **Freestanding Units** *Subnational units at a single scale are independent entities.*	II. **Freestanding Levels** *Levels are independent entities.*
	Unidirectional	III. **Horizontal** *Causes at a single subnational scale have effects only at that scale.*	IV. **Top-down** *Causes at higher scales have effects at lower scales.* V. **Bottom-up** *Causes at lower scales have effects at higher scales.*
	Reciprocal	VI. **Reciprocal Horizontal** *Causes at a single subnational scale affect and are affected by other causes at that same scale.*	VII. **Reciprocal Vertical** *Causes at one scale affect and are affected by causes at higher and lower scales.*

[84] These different strategies are not unique to subnational research. Scholars of international relations implement multilevel research designs to assess, for instance, how international organizations affect national policy making or domestic politics. Likewise, comparativists who carry out cross-national research on a wide variety of subjects adopt strategies resembling the unilevel ones in Table 1.2.

national government policy) or even in other subnational units at any scale have no causal effect.[85] A freestanding levels strategy (Quadrant II), by contrast, sets subnational phenomena in a multilevel framework. Still, only variables at the same scale as the outcome of interest are understood to have a causal effect, although variables at higher or lower scales may provide contextual information.[86] A horizontal strategy (Quadrant III) seeks causal effects at a single scale. In studies that deploy a horizontal strategy, processes of diffusion and contagion across units located at the same scale often play a key role in explaining subnational outcomes.[87] When levels of analysis are seen not as freestanding but as causally connected, multilevel strategies can be used to explore the causal effects of variables on outcomes at lower and higher scales. The top-down strategy (Quadrant IV) focuses on causal effects of variables at higher scales on outcomes at lower scales.[88] Conversely, the bottom-up strategy (Quadrant V) explores the causal impact of variables at lower scales on outcomes at higher scales. Studies that employ a bottom-up strategy often highlight how actors, interests, and institutions have causal consequences far beyond the formal or informal borders of the subnational units in which they are located.[89] Finally, reciprocal causality can be studied among variables at the same scale, with a reciprocal horizontal strategy (Quadrant VI), or among variables at different scales with a reciprocal vertical strategy (Quadrant VII). The former approach often focuses on reciprocal causation across neighboring subnational units, for example through diffusion.[90]

None of these seven strategies is inherently superior. Each has strengths and weaknesses, and researchers should be aware of the trade-offs involved when choosing one strategy over another. To illustrate these trade-offs, we compare

---

[85] Recent works that employ a freestanding units strategy include Alves (2015), Ingram (2014, 2015), and Pribble (2015), among others. When multiple units are compared, this kind of research could be called *cross-subnational analysis*, in line with the conventional label *cross-national analysis*. See Slater and Ziblatt (2013, p. 1306) for a discussion of how a cross-subnational approach can provide stronger external validity than a subnational approach limited to a single country.

[86] Research on civil wars, for example, commonly employs a freestanding levels strategy, treating national-level conflicts as a contextual backdrop for subnational groups, whose actions are understood to be driven by preexisting local cleavages that are often far removed from the "master cleavage" that defines the national conflict (Kalyvas, 2003, 2006).

[87] For a study that deploys a horizontal strategy to explain patterns of homicides at the municipal level in Brazil, see Ingram and da Costa (2016). See Sugiyama (2008) for a study that uses a horizontal strategy to explain the subnational diffusion of social policies in Brazil.

[88] Examples of top-down strategies include studies of subnational authoritarian regimes (Gibson, 2013; Gervasoni, 2010a, 2010b; Giraudy, 2015) and subnational patterns of drug-related violence (Phillips 2015).

[89] Examples of bottom-up strategies include Gibson and Calvo (2000), Herrigel (1996), and Pogrebinschi and Samuels (2014). See also Schiller's (1999) analysis of how subnational political geography affects national trade policy in the United States.

[90] See, for example, Sugiyama's (2012) study of the implementation of conditional cash transfers (CCTs) in Brazil during the 1990s and 2000s.

two strategies located in opposite quadrants in Table 1.2: the freestanding units (Quadrant I) and reciprocal vertical (Quadrant VII) strategies. Because the freestanding units strategy treats subnational units as self-contained entities in which outcomes are driven fully by variables inside each unit, it offers advantages for making causal inferences. Most notably, this strategy attenuates the threats that spatial dependence among units of analysis can pose to causal inference, especially when studying outcomes in spatially proximate units. Still, as Harbers and Ingram caution in Chapter 2, subnational units are often highly permeable to external forces, which produces a strong potential both for structural dependence among observations and unobserved spatial correlation among units. Researchers employing a freestanding units strategy will thus need to give a convincing justification, ideally supported by evidence showing the absence of spatial dependence, that the units are indeed self-contained.

The reciprocal vertical strategy of SNR, by contrast, highlights not the independence but the interdependence of units and variables at different scales. From this perspective, variables operate both as causes and effects. Moreover, reciprocal causation is understood to occur among variables at different scales. For example, a subnational policy innovation, perhaps resulting from factors internal to a specific subnational unit, can reshape national policy if the national government decides to emulate it. In turn, with the national government's endorsement and support, the policy innovation, possibly in a modified form, may propagate across subnational units, including back to the source unit where it originated.[91] As this example suggests, effectively deploying the reciprocal vertical strategy requires careful attention to cross-level causal sequences. This strategy offers the advantage of fostering multilevel process tracing and holistic explanations that highlight causal relationships across variables at different scales, relationships that may be hidden when using other strategies of subnational analysis. Still, the broad compass of the reciprocal vertical strategy is a source of both strength and weakness, because the complex interdependence among variables at different scales can make it hard to manage threats to causal inference posed by endogeneity.[92] Moreover, the reciprocal vertical strategy does not have a strong affinity with parsimonious research designs or theories.

The various strategies of subnational research can be productively combined, as illustrated by Beer's Chapter 5 on women's rights in Mexico, which draws on multiple strategies to explain contrasting outcomes across Mexico's states in legislation concerning both abortion and violence against women (VAW). With legislation prohibiting VAW, a pattern of policy convergence emerged in the 2000s, as similarly robust laws spread quickly across all Mexican states. With

---

[91] For an example of this kind of multilevel policy diffusion, see Sugiyama (2012).

[92] The logic of causation in the reciprocal vertical strategy resembles the principle of interconnectedness central to systems theory. See, for example, Jervis (1998).

abortion rights, however, the result was not policy convergence but divergence, with some states passing conservative restrictions on abortion whereas others moved to liberalize access. To explain these contrasting outcomes across the two policy areas, Beer combines several strategies of subnational research. First, she argues that understanding the subnational heterogeneity in abortion policy requires a dual focus that encompasses both the internal characteristics of Mexico's states, as highlighted by the freestanding units strategy, and cross-state influences, as emphasized by the horizontal strategy. States governed by the leftist *Partido de la Revolución Democrática* (PRD) and where secular values dominated were likely to try to liberalize abortion whereas states governed by the right-wing *Partido Acción Nacional* (PAN) and with predominantly conservative Catholic populations were likely to restrict abortion. In addition to such factors internal to states, horizontal influences *across* states also help explain the divergence in abortion policies. For example, Mexico City's move to liberalize abortion in 2007 raised fears among conservatives across the country that legal abortion would soon spread to other jurisdictions. These fears, in turn, galvanized a preemptive backlash of restrictive legislation across many states. Beer thus concludes that, without the threat posed by liberalization of abortion in Mexico City, constitutional amendments restricting abortion would probably not have passed so quickly across so many states.

The subnational policy convergence in VAW legislation, on the other hand, cannot be explained by a unilevel focus on variables internal to states or on horizontal influences across them. Instead, a multilevel, reciprocal vertical strategy, attuned both to top-down and bottom-up interactions, is required to explain why similar VAW legislation resulted across all Mexican states. Beer shows that the subnational proliferation of VAW laws started in the 1990s with appeals by local activists and human rights advocates who mobilized to protest the murders and disappearances of a large number of young women in Ciudad Juárez, in the northern state of Chihuahua. When the government of Chihuahua failed to investigate seriously and prosecute the crimes, these activists appealed both to the national government and international organizations, specifically the Inter-American Court of Human Rights (IACHR). This "bottom-up" pressure from local activists resulted in new national legislation addressing violence against women in 2007 and a ruling by the IACHR in 2009 ordering the Mexican government to investigate the murders in Ciudad Juárez, improve its response to violence against women, and create a database to help find missing people and keep track of violence against women. The resulting "top-down" pressures on state governments from both the national government and the IACHR, in turn, drove a rapid replication of new VAW laws across all the Mexican states. Beer's chapter thus highlights the advantages of drawing on several strategies of SNR to build a multilevel theoretical framework that combines international, national, and subnational factors to provide a stronger explanation for humanly important outcomes.

In sum, by offering this new set of strategies for subnational research, we aim to make it easier for scholars to: (i) specify the kind of strategy they are employing, which, in turn, could aid the accumulation of knowledge by fostering focused and constructive dialogues both among subnational researchers deploying the same strategy and among researchers deploying different ones; (ii) evaluate the strengths and weaknesses of their research strategies; and (iii) assess the trade-offs involved in choosing one strategy over another.

Combining Subnational and Cross-National Strategies

The strategies of SNR can also be combined fruitfully with cross-national research (Sellers, in press; Riedel, 2017).[93] One advantage of this approach is that subnational units in different countries may match each other more closely across variables of interest than would the two countries as a whole. Closer matching, in turn, can mitigate the risk that causal inferences will be biased by confounding variables. For example, Juan J. Linz and Amando de Miguel (1966, p. 269) argue that a comparison between "advanced and backward" regions of Italy and Spain, with similar cultural and socioeconomic profiles, is an effective way to assess how different political institutions in the two countries affect participation in voluntary organizations. Similarly, O'Donnell (1973, p. 21) proposes a "cross-modern areas" comparison that juxtaposes the most developed regions of Brazil and Argentina.

Adjacent subnational units located on opposite sides of a national border can offer especially strong opportunities for matching. In his seminal article on the comparative method, Arend Lijphart (1971, pp. 689–690) thus proposes that in order to study the effects of presidential and parliamentary systems, rather than comparing the United States and Great Britain, it may be more fruitful to compare North Dakota and Manitoba, because this comparison would minimize variation in potentially confounding factors like levels of economic development and education.[94] Along similar lines, in his study of agrarian radicalism in the North American wheat belt, Lipset (1950, p. 215) compares North Dakota and Saskatchewan, which he describes as near replicas in economic, demographic, and ecological terms. The close matching of the cases across these variables increases confidence in Lipset's argument that cross-national differences in federal social policy explain the divergent fortunes of agrarian radicalism: In the wheat belt of the United States, the New Deal weakened rural socialist movements, whereas in Canada the absence of robust federal social policies during the Great Depression favored such

---

[93] Sellers (in press) uses the label "transnational subnational" to refer to strategies that combine subnational and cross-national perspectives.

[94] Lijphart acknowledges Naroll (1966) as the source of this recommendation.

movements.[95] More recently, scholars have carried out subnational cross-national studies of adjacent units to explore how different kinds of colonialism influenced contemporary African politics. William Miles (1994) and Kathryn Firmin-Sellers (2001), for example, look at villages and regions located across an international border separating a former French from a former British colony (see also Laitin, 1986).

In addition to improving causal inference through closer matching, subnational cross-national research can further strengthen causal inference through natural experiments. To understand why cultural differences become politically salient, Daniel N. Posner (2004) takes advantage of a natural experiment produced by the division of the Chewa and Tumbuka ethnic groups by the border between Zambia and Malawi. Despite identical objective cultural differences, such as language and appearance, between Chewas and Tumbukas on both sides of the border, intergroup relations differ sharply in each country, with Chewas and Tumbukas treating each other as political allies in Zambia and as rivals in Malawi. Posner argues that the division of the Chewa and Tumbuka ethnic groups by the Zambia–Malawi border "provides a laboratory-like setting" for studying the salience of an identical cultural cleavage in different settings. Posner (2004, p. 530) further notes that "like many African borders, the one that separates Zambia and Malawi was drawn purely for administrative purposes, with no attention to the distribution of groups on the ground." According to Posner, the resulting "as-if random" sorting of Chewa and Tumbuka people into Zambia and Malawi helps control for confounding factors, thereby increasing confidence that observed differences in intergroup relations result from his preferred explanation, that is, the different sizes of each group relative to each country's national political arena. Acemoglu and Robinson (2012) make a similar claim that the international border separating two cities, Nogales, Arizona, and Nogales, Mexico, offers a natural experiment that rules out local sociocultural, political, or ecological factors as credible explanations for their sharply divergent trajectories of development, security, and equity.

Still, spatial proximity offers a double-edged sword for causal inference. On the one hand, focusing on contiguous subnational units separated by a border can help strengthen causal inference through closer matching and natural experiments. On the other, the very proximity of the units can hinder causal inference by producing spatial dependence, spillovers, and other forms of "interference" among units. At first glance, subnational units divided by an international border may seem less prone to spatial dependence than units located in the same country, because, *ceteris paribus*, international borders should be less porous than administrative and other boundaries inside countries. Yet international borders may actually be highly permeable, either

---

[95] Similarly, to study ethnic conflict, Linz (1986, pp. 372–398) focuses on the adjacent Spanish and French Basque regions.

by design, as among the European Union countries, or by default, because of weak state capacity, as in many developing countries. Porous international borders, in turn, weaken claims, such as Posner's (2004), that borders serve as plausible sources of natural experiments because they assign subjects in an as-if random way to mutually insulated "treatment" and "control" groups.[96]

One way to reduce spatial dependence, spillovers, and the associated threats they pose to causal inference is to select noncontiguous subnational units located in different countries.[97] For instance, Eleonora Pasotti (2010) studies the breakdown of urban clientelist machines by focusing on three cities located in distant and quite different countries: Bogota, Chicago, and Naples. Despite the contrasting national-level socioeconomic and political contexts in which these cities are located, Pasotti finds that the shift from clientelism to programmatic politics resulted from surprisingly similar patterns of local party building, urban fiscal autonomy, and municipal electoral institutions.[98] Another good example of subnational cross-national research focusing on spatially distant units can be seen in Angélica Durán-Martínez's (2018) study of drug violence in five cities across two countries, Colombia (Cali, Medellin) and Mexico (Culiacán, Ciudad Juárez, and Tijuana). This set of cases makes it possible to combine the methods of "most similar" and "most different" comparisons in creative ways.[99] By pairing cities in the same countries that experienced contrasting patterns of violence, as in Cali and Medellin in Colombia, or Ciudad Juárez and Tijuana in Mexico, Durán-Martínez gains inferential leverage from a most similar comparison. By contrast, pairing cities in different countries that experienced similar patterns of violence, such as Cali in Colombia and Culiacán in Mexico, provides a most different comparison. Durán-Martínez supplements these comparisons with a longitudinal analysis of periods of violence within each city, which offers an even stronger most similar systems design.

Although these examples of subnational cross-national research focus on cities, other kinds of subnational units can also be used. For example, Gibson's (2013) study of subnational authoritarianism compares states and provinces across three countries, Argentina, Mexico, and the United States. And Agustina Giraudy (2015) builds and tests a novel theoretical framework to explain the

---

[96] As Dunning (2012) notes in his assessment of Posner's research design, "subsequent migration and other factors could have mitigated the as-if randomness on one side of the border or the other." As Posner (2004, p. 531) himself notes, "Indeed, both pairs of villages are so close to each other that several respondents reported regularly visiting friends and relatives across the border in the other village."

[97] This approach essentially deploys the freestanding strategy of subnational research cross-nationally.

[98] Yue Zhang's (2013) study of policies for urban historic preservation in Beijing, Chicago, and Paris offers a similar example of subnational cross-national research focusing on spatially distant units. Zhang finds that sharp differences in these policies are driven by cross-national variation in the coherence of decision-making processes between levels of government.

[99] On "most similar" and "most different" systems designs, see Przeworski and Teune (1970).

maintenance of what she calls "subnational undemocratic regimes" (SURs) by combining within-country comparisons among states in Argentina and Mexico with cross-national comparisons.[100] Creative and carefully constructed combinations of subnational and cross-national strategies such as these can help researchers increase confidence in their causal inferences.

Methodological Challenges and Opportunities in Subnational Research

Whereas Snyder (2001a) focused on the advantages of combining the methodology of "small-N" comparisons with a focus on subnational units, the increasing popularity of "mixed methods," new tools for analyzing spatial dependence, and experiments invites us to consider how these methodologies can be employed fruitfully in SNR. As seen in Table 1.3, which shows the set of methodological options in social science research, SNR offers a "crosscutting" strategy of inquiry that can be deployed in conjunction with a wide variety of methods, from qualitative case studies to small-N comparisons to large-N quantitative studies to field and natural experiments.

Mixed Methods
A clear affinity can be seen between SNR and the increasingly common use in comparative politics of "mixed methods," that is, research designs that combine two or more methodologies to help bolster confidence in causal inferences.

TABLE I.3 *Methodological Options in the Social Sciences: Subnational Research as a Crosscutting Strategy of Inquiry*

Observational Research		Experimental Research
SMALL-N/QUALITATIVE	LARGE-N/QUANTITATIVE	
Case Studies	Survey Research	Laboratory Experiments
Comparative Method (systematic analysis of a small number of cases)	Quantitative Cross-National Research (QCN)	**Field Experiments**
Subnational Comparative Method (systematic analysis of a small number of subnational cases)	**Quantitative Subnational Research (QSN)**	**Natural and Quasi-Experiments**

Note: Methodologies highlighted in boldface are routinely employed in SNR.

[100] Different kinds of subnational units can be combined in a single study. See, for example, Heller's (2001) study of the politics of democratic decentralization, which compares the Brazilian city of Porto Alegre, the Indian state of Kerala, and the country of South Africa.

Subnational researchers routinely combine in-depth qualitative case studies with quantitative analysis, often by implementing a "nested" research design that integrates small-N comparative case studies with large-N analysis of quantitative data drawn from the full universe of subnational political and administrative units in one or more countries.[101] By situating subnational case studies within a larger "out-of-sample" population of subnational cases, nested designs can help scholars assess the external validity of their results. Nested subnational studies have shed light on a wide range of topics, including the provision of public goods (Tsai, 2007), the politics of regulation and privatization (Herrera, 2014; Post, 2014), ethnic politics and development (Lieberman, 2009), the "resource curse" (González, in press; González & Lodola, n.d.), clientelism (Weitz-Shapiro, 2014), and ethnic violence (Varshney, 2002). Still, as Harbers and Ingram caution in Chapter 2, the strong potential for spatial dependence among subnational units located in the same country poses challenges for such nested mixed-methods designs. Specifically, studies relying on estimation techniques, such as OLS, that treat subnational observations and units as independently distributed run a significant risk of getting incorrect estimates. Fortunately, as Harbers and Ingram also point out, new tools of spatial analysis offer effective ways to manage spatial dependence.

Spatial Dependence: Threat or Opportunity?

Spatial dependence among units and observations is conventionally viewed as a serious threat to causal inference, which is understood to require independent observations. To be sure, spatial dependence also occurs among national units, as cross-national research on diffusion (Brinks & Coppedge, 2006), international demonstration effects, and dependent development (Cardoso & Faletto, 1979; Evans, 1979) has long recognized. Still, *ceteris paribus*, spatial dependence will likely be stronger among subnational units located in the same country, because the boundaries between such units are probably more permeable than those between countries. Spatial dependence is thus seen as an especially vexing problem for SNR.[102]

Recent advances in both qualitative and quantitative methods, however, give reason to view spatial dependence not as an insurmountable threat to causal inference but as a manageable challenge and even as a welcome

---

[101] On nested research designs, see Lieberman (2005). See also Coppedge (2012, pp. 219–220; chapter 3) for a discussion of nested analysis and the potential to build "nested theories" in the study of democratization. See Pepinsky (2018) on the upsurge of quantitative single-country studies in comparative politics over the past 15 years; many of these studies are subnational.

[102] This is also referred to as "Galton's problem," a reference to the objection raised by Francis Galton at the meeting of the Royal Anthropological Institute in 1889 to a paper by Edward B. Tylor introducing the cross-cultural survey method. Galton pointed out that, because traits often spread by diffusion, borrowing or migration, observations of such traits across culture were not necessarily independent instances (Naroll, 1961, p. 15).

opportunity for building stronger theories. Recent research on qualitative methods emphasizes the value of case-based "causal process observations" (CPOs) both for testing and building theories (Collier et al., 2010, p. 2). And CPOs, in turn, are prone to spatial dependence by virtue of their location in the same case. The very contextual knowledge required to carry out effective CPOs can, in turn, make it easier to comprehend and disentangle spatial autocorrelation among the linked observations that form a causal process.[103]

Moreover, as Ingram and Harbers show in Chapter 2, new spatial analytic estimation techniques offer powerful ways to model spatial dependence among subnational units. They thus emphasize the importance of testing empirically for spatial dependence in order to determine the appropriate statistical estimation technique that should be employed to assess causal relationships.[104] If subnational units are *not* spatially dependent, then OLS statistical models may very well be appropriate. By contrast, when dealing with spatially dependent units, estimation techniques capable of accounting for this dependence should be employed.

By making it easier to handle spatial dependence, these new qualitative and quantitative tools lower the methodological barriers to doing SNR. Moreover, instead of seeing spatial dependence as an unwelcome, if manageable, threat to causal inference, scholars increasingly view it as an exciting opportunity for theory building. Indeed, "horizontal" and especially "reciprocal horizontal" strategies of SNR, as discussed, are premised on spatial dependence, and scholars have effectively used these strategies to propose new theories of policy diffusion (Sugiyama, 2008) and violence (Ingram & da Costa, 2016).

Experiments

The growing use of both field and natural experiments in comparative politics also opens new possibilities for SNR. Carrying out true experimentation, where the treatment, or intervention, is manipulated by the researcher, is rarely possible for national-level institutions or policies. Experiments in the social sciences thus typically focus on smaller subnational units, such as villages and municipalities, where manipulation of treatment variables by the researcher is feasible, making it possible to boost the internal validity of causal inference. Recent research in comparative politics uses field experiments to identify the causes of subnational variation in a wide range of outcomes, including political

---

[103] Moreover, a subnational perspective, by potentially allowing researchers to get "closer" to their cases, offers advantages with regard to acquiring valid contextual information in the first place.

[104] The same can be said for choices about the appropriate strategy of subnational research: An empirical test showing little or no spatial dependence among units would set a freestanding unit strategy on firm ground. Likewise, a test showing high levels of spatial dependence would call for horizontal or reciprocal horizontal strategies.

participation,[105] public goods provision,[106] dispute resolution and violence,[107] empowerment of women,[108] and ethnic voting.[109]

Although they may not be suitable for true, "randomized controlled" experiments, national-level policy and institutional changes can serve as sources of natural experiments if a plausible case can be made that these changes are exogenous to subnational units and affect them in an "as-if random" manner.[110] Opportunities for combining natural experiments with a focus on subnational units may be especially strong when national-level changes are implemented in a spatially uneven manner, leaving some subnational units unaffected, or with temporal lags that result in some units being affected earlier or later than others. The uneven implementation of national-level initiatives across subnational units, in addition to providing opportunities for what we call "top-down" strategies of research, can make it easier to sort these units into "treatment" and "control" groups.

Likewise, changes in administrative, jurisdictional, and even non-jurisdictional boundaries inside countries can also occur in an "as-if random" fashion with respect to subnational outcomes of interest and may thus provide a fruitful source of natural experiments. The division of ethnic groups by arbitrary national boundaries is implicitly employed as a natural experiment by Linz (1986) in his study of Catalans in France and Spain, by Miles (1994) in his study of Hausa-speaking people in Niger and Nigeria, and explicitly by Posner (2004) in his study of Chewas and Tumbukas in Zambia and Malawi.[111] *Ceteris paribus*, boundary changes inside countries should occur more frequently than boundary changes between countries, and natural experiments with boundaries as treatments should thus be plentiful at subnational levels. Still, researchers looking to use subnational or international borders as sources of natural experiments face several methodological challenges.

First, a plausible case needs to be made that the boundaries were indeed drawn in an "as-if random" manner and thus serve as exogenous treatments.[112]

---

[105] Wantchekon (2003); Fujiwara and Wantchekon (2013); Chong et al. (2015). On field experiments in the social sciences more generally, see Gerber and Green (2012); and Druckman et al. (2011).

[106] Blair, Morse, and Tsai (2017); Fearon, Humphreys, and Weinstein (2009, 2015).

[107] Blattman, Hartman, and Blair (2014); Blair, Blattman, and Hartman (2017).

[108] Beath, Christia, and Enikolopov (2013).   [109] Dunning and Harrison (2010).

[110] Natural experiments are distinguished from both laboratory and field experiments by the source of their data, which are produced not through the manipulation of a treatment by the researcher but by "naturally" occurring phenomena. Moreover, natural experiments may only partially share the attribute of random assignment of subjects to treatment and control groups that characterizes true, or "randomized controlled," experiments. On natural experiments in the social sciences, see Dunning (2012) and Diamond and Robinson (2010).

[111] Other examples of studies that use borders as sources of natural experiments include Banerjee and Iyer (2005), Berger (2009), Laitin (1986), and Miguel (2004).

[112] As Hillel Soifer notes in Chapter 3 of this volume, with the exception of the study of electoral institutions, where regression discontinuity designs (RDDs) are common, scholars looking for

This requires providing evidence about how the boundaries were created, including perhaps the motives, goals, and capabilities of the boundary makers (Kocher & Monteiro, 2016). Relatedly, researchers should consider the possibility of self-selection by individuals both into and out of border units, as occurred with Hindus and Muslims as a result of the partitioning of the British Indian empire into India and Pakistan in 1947. When such self-selection occurs, it weakens the credibility of the claim that subjects are assigned in an as-if random manner to treatment and control groups.

The effective use of boundaries as sources of natural experiments also requires an assessment of whether *spillover* occurs between treatment and control subjects and units. Spillover arises when one unit is affected by the treatment status of another unit, for example, when increased law enforcement in one area causes crime to increase in nearby areas, and it is especially likely where treatment and control subjects live in close proximity and can interact regularly. Spillover violates the "noninterference assumption," also known as the "stable unit-treatment value assumption" (SUTVA), routinely invoked in causal inference. This violation, in turn, can result in significantly biased estimates of treatment effects. Techniques are available for detecting and estimating spillover effects, such as multilevel experiments, and also for avoiding spillovers in the first place, such as selecting noncontiguous units located far away from each other.[113] The latter technique assumes that spillover occurs only through spatial proximity and not through nongeographic mechanisms, such as Internet, telephone, television, or radio.[114]

Lastly, subnational researchers looking for natural experiments likely face the challenge of "bundling," also known as the "compound treatment problem." This problem emerges when the treatment encompasses multiple explanatory factors, thus making it difficult to pinpoint which factor actually causes the effect. As Thad Dunning (2012, p. 300) notes, the problem of bundling can be especially vexing in natural experiments that exploit jurisdictional and other kinds of borders, because units on either side of the border may differ in many more ways than just their location in relation to the border. The treatment of being located on one side of a border or the other may

---

natural experiments have tended to avoid subnational administrative jurisdictions, focusing instead on subnational units divided by boundaries drawn arbitrarily and with little contemporary meaning. Soifer offers the example of Berger's (2009) study of the contemporary effects of an obscure British colonial administrative boundary drawn in 1900 and erased permanently in 1914.

[113] Sinclair, McConnell, and Green (2012). See also http://egap.org/methods-guides/10-things-you-need-know-about-spillovers (accessed on December 14, 2016).

[114] This technique for mitigating spillover effects is sometimes described as relying on "buffer rows." This refers to agricultural studies in which experimental crop rows were physically separated by non-experimental "buffer" rows to prevent interference from local changes in soil, water usage, or insect behavior.

thus entail so many different components that it becomes difficult to identify precisely which one actually does the causal work. One technique suggested by Dunning (2012, pp. 300–302) for potentially mitigating the compound treatment problem is to make "pre-tests" and "post-tests" in both treatment and control groups. For example, in their study of the impact of raising the minimum wage on employment in fast-food restaurants, David Card and Alan B. Krueger (1994) compare restaurants on either side of the border between the US states of New Jersey, which increased the minimum wage in 1992, and Pennsylvania, which did not make an increase. By drawing on time-series data, the authors are able to make pre- and post-comparisons of employment levels on either side of the border during a small temporal window around the date that New Jersey's new minimum-wage law went into effect. This makes it possible to "unbundle" the treatment of "being in New Jersey" as opposed to "being in Pennsylvania," thereby increasing confidence that the change in the minimum-wage law, not some other aspect of the compound treatment, explains the observed shifts in employment levels. By drawing on techniques such as these, subnational researchers will be better able to take advantage of opportunities opened by experimental methods for crafting stronger research designs.

1.4 CONCLUSION

SNR offers a long-standing and increasingly prominent option that contributes to substantive, theoretical, and methodological progress in comparative politics. The chapters that follow show how a subnational perspective produces knowledge across core substantive themes that define comparative politics, from regimes and representation to states, security, and public goods to social and economic development. The chapters also illustrate how SNR drives theoretical innovation, especially multilevel theory building that combines variables and causal processes at different scales. Lastly, SNR offers novel strategies for comparative research and, as highlighted in the next two chapters, provides exciting possibilities for strengthening research design and exploiting new methodological tools for spatial analysis. In the concluding chapter, Chapter 11, we consider the challenges and directions for future research opened by the substantive, theoretical, and methodological achievements of SNR.

BIBLIOGRAPHY

Abers, Rebecca. (2000). *Inventing local democracy: Grassroots politics in Brazil.* Boulder, CO: Lynne Rienner Publishers.

Abers, Rebecca, & Keck, Margaret E. (2013). *Practical authority: Agency and institutional change in Brazilian water politics.* Oxford, England: Oxford University Press.

Acemoglu, Daron, & Johnson, Simon. (2005). Unbundling institutions. *Journal of Political Economy 113*, 949–995.

Acemoglu, Daron, & Robinson, James A. (2012). *Why nations fail: The origins of power, prosperity, and poverty.* New York, NY: Crown Publishers.

Alberti, Carla (2016). *Projecting hegemony: Parties, organizations, and indigenous forms of governance in Bolivia.* (Doctoral dissertation). Brown University, Providence, RI.

Alberti, Carla (in press). Populist multiculturalism in the Andes: Balancing political control and societal autonomy. *Comparative Politics.*

Albertus, Michael. (2015). *Autocracy and redistribution.* Cambridge, England: Cambridge University Press.

Alves, Jorge Antonio. (2015). (Un?) healthy politics: The political determinants of subnational health systems in Brazil. *Latin American Politics and Society 57*(4), 119–142.

Alves, Jorge Antonio, & Hunter, Wendy. (2017). From right to left in Brazil's northeast: Transformation. *Comparative Politics 49*(4), 437–455.

Amengual, Matthew. (2010). Complementary labor regulation: The uncoordinated combination of state and private regulators in the Dominican Republic. *World Development 38*(3), 405–414.

Amengual, Matthew. (2016). *Politicized enforcement in Argentina: Labor and environmental regulation.* Cambridge, England: Cambridge University Press.

Anderson, Jeffrey. (1992). *The territorial imperative.* New York, NY: Cambridge University Press.

Apaydin, Fulya. (2012). Partisan preferences and skill formation policies: New evidence from Turkey and Argentina. *World Development 40*(8), 1522–1533.

Apaydin, Fulya. (2018). *Technology, institutions and labor: Manufacturing automobiles in Argentina and Turkey.* Cham, Switzerland: Palgrave Macmillan.

Arias, Enrique Desmond. (2009). *Drugs and democracy in Rio de Janeiro: Trafficking, social networks, and public security.* Durham, NC: University of North Carolina Press.

Arias, Enrique Desmond. (2013). The impacts of differential armed dominance of politics in Rio de Janeiro, Brazil. *Studies in Comparative International Development 48*(3), 263–284.

Arias, Enrique Desmond. (2017). *Criminal enterprises and governance in Latin America and the Caribbean.* Cambridge, England: Cambridge University Press.

Arias, Enrique Desmond, & Ungar, Mark. (2009). Community policing and Latin America's citizen security crisis. *Comparative Politics 41*(4), 409–429.

Arjona, Ana. (2016). *Rebelocracy: Social order in the Colombian Civil War.* Cambridge, England: Cambridge University Press.

Arjona, Ana, Kasfir, Nelson, & Mampilly, Zachariah (Eds.). (2015). *Rebel governance in civil war.* Cambridge, England: Cambridge University Press.

Arnold, Caroline E. (2010.). Where the low road and the high road meet: Flexible employment in global value chains. *Journal of Contemporary Asia 40*(4), 612–637.

Autesserre, Séverine. (2010). *The trouble with the Congo: Local violence and the failure of international peacebuilding.* Cambridge, England: Cambridge University Press.

Auyero, Javier. 2007. *Routine politics and violence in Argentina: The gray zone of state power.* Cambridge, England: Cambridge University Press.

Auyero, Javier, & Sobering, Katherine. (2017). Violence, the state, and the poor: A view from the south. *Sociological Forum 32*(1), 1018–1031.

Avritzer, Leonardo. (2009). *Participatory institutions in democratic Brazil*. Baltimore, MD: Johns Hopkins University Press.

Baiocchi, Gianpaolo. (2005). *Militants and citizens: The politics of participatory democracy in Porto Alegre*. Stanford, CA: Stanford University Press.

Baker, Bruce. (2002). Living with non-state policing in South Africa: The issues and dilemmas. *The Journal of Modern African Studies 40*(1), 29–53.

Balcells, Laia. (2010). Rivalry and revenge: Violence against civilians in conventional civil wars. *International Studies Quarterly 54*(2), 291–313.

Balcells, Laia. (2011). Continuation of politics by two means: Direct and indirect violence in civil war. *Journal of Conflict Resolution 55*(3), 397–422.

Banerjee, Abhijit, & Iyer, Lakshmi. (2005). History, institutions, and economic performance: The legacy of colonial land tenure systems in India. *The American Economic Review 95*(4), 1190–1213.

Barnes, Nicholas. (2017). "Criminal politics: An integrated approach to the study of organized crime, politics, and violence. *Perspectives on Politics 15*(4), 967–987.

Bates, Robert H. (1981). *Markets and states in tropical Africa: The political basis of agricultural policies*. Berkeley, CA: University of California Press.

Bates, Robert H. (1997). *Open-economy politics: The political economy of the world coffee trade*. Princeton, NJ: Princeton University Press.

Bateson, Regina Anne. (2013). *Order and violence in postwar Guatemala*. (Doctoral dissertation). Yale University, Boston, MA.

Beath, Andrew, Christia, Fotini, & Enikolopov, Ruben (2013). "Empowering women through development aid: Evidence from a field experiment in Afghanistan. *American Political Science Review 107*(3), 540–557.

Beblawi, Hazem, & Luciani, Giacomo. (1987). *The rentier state*. London: Croom Helm.

Behrend, Jacqueline. (2011). The unevenness of democracy at the subnational level: Provincial closed games in Argentina. *Latin American Research Review 46*(1), 150–176.

Behrend, Jacqueline, & Whitehead, Laurence. (2016). *Illiberal practices: Territorial variance within large federal democracies*. Baltimore, MD: Johns Hopkins University Press.

Bénit-Gbaffou, Claire. (2008). Community policing and disputed norms for local social control in post-apartheid Johannesburg. *Journal of Southern African Studies 34*(1), 93–109.

Benton, Allyson Lucinda. (2012). Bottom-up challenges to national democracy: Mexico's (legal) subnational authoritarian enclaves. *Comparative Politics 44*(3), 253–271.

Berger, Daniel. (2009). *Taxes, institutions and local governance: Evidence from a natural experiment in colonial Nigeria*. (Unpublished manuscript).

Blair, Harry. (2000). Participation and accountability at the periphery: Democratic local governance in six countries. *World Development 28*(1), 21–39.

Blair, Robert A., Blattman, Christopher, & Hartman, Alexandra. (2017). Predicting local violence: Evidence from a panel survey in Liberia. *Journal of Peace Research 54* (2), 298–312.

Blair, Robert A., Morse, Benjamin S., & Tsai, Lily L. (2017). Public health and public trust: Survey evidence from the Ebola virus disease epidemic in Liberia. *Social Science & Medicine 172*, 89–97.

Blattman, Christopher, Hartman, Alexandra C., & Blair, Robert A. (2014). How to promote order and property rights under weak rule of law? An experiment in changing dispute resolution behavior through community education. *American Political Science Review 108*(1), 100–120.

Bohlken, Anjali Thomas, & Sergenti, Ernest John. (2015). Economic growth and ethnic violence: An empirical investigation of Hindu-Muslim riots in India. *Journal of Peace Research 47*(5), 589–600.

Boone, Catherine. (2003). *Political topographies of the African state: Territorial authority and institutional choice.* Cambridge, England: Cambridge University Press.

Boone, Catherine. (2014). *Property and political order in Africa: Land rights and the structure of politics.* Cambridge, England: Cambridge University Press.

Borges, André. (2007). Rethinking state politics: The withering of state dominant machines in Brazil. *Brazilian Political Science Review 2*(se).

Boulding, Carew, & Brown, David S. (2014). Political competition and local social spending: Evidence from Brazil. *Studies in Comparative International Development 49*(2), 197–216.

Boulding, Carew, & Brian Wampler. (2010). Voice, votes, and resources: Evaluating the effect of participatory democracy on well-being. *World Development 38*(1), 125–135.

Brinks, Daniel, & Coppedge, Michael. (2006). Diffusion is no illusion: Neighbor emulation in the third wave of democracy. *Comparative Political Studies 39*(4), 463–489.

Brinks, Daniel M. (2007). *The judicial response to police killings in Latin America: Inequality and the rule of law.* Cambridge, England: Cambridge University Press.

Bunce, Valerie. (1995). Should transitologists be grounded? *Slavic Review 54*(1), 111–127.

Calderón, Gabriela, Robles, Gustavo, Díaz-Cayeros, Alberto, & Magaloni, Beatriz. (2015). The beheading of criminal organizations and the dynamics of violence in Mexico. *Journal of Conflict Resolution 59*(8), 1455–1485.

Calvo, Ernesto, & Micozzi, Juan Pablo. (2005). The governor's backyard: A seat-vote model of electoral reform for subnational multiparty races. *Journal of Politics 67*(4), 1050–1074.

Calvo, Ernesto, & Murillo, Maria Victoria. (2004). Who delivers? Partisan clients in the Argentine electoral market. *American Journal of Political Science 48*(4), 742–757.

Cammett, Melani. (2014). *Compassionate communalism: Welfare and sectarianism in Lebanon.* Ithaca, NY: Cornell University Press.

Cammett, Melani, & MacLean, Lauren M. (Eds.). (2014). *The politics of non-state welfare.* Ithaca, NY: Cornell University Press.

Cammett, Melani, & Issar, Sukriti. (2010). Bricks and mortar clientelism: Sectarianism and the logics of welfare allocation in Lebanon. *World Politics 62*(3), 381–421.

Card, David, & Krueger, Alan B. (1994). Minimum wages and employment: A case study of the fast-food industry in New Jersey and Pennsylvania. *American Economic Review 84*(4), 772–793.

Cardoso, Fernando Henrique, & Faletto, Enzo. (1979). *Dependency and development in Latin America.* Berkeley, CA: University of California Press.

Castagnola, Andrea. (2012). I want it all, and I want it now: The political manipulation of Argentina's provincial high courts. *Journal of Politics in Latin America 4*(2), 39–62.

Chavez, Rebecca Bill. (2004). *The rule of law in nascent democracies: Judicial politics in Argentina.* Stanford, CA: Stanford University Press.

Chibber, Pradeep, & Nooruddin, Irfan. (2004). Do party systems count? The number of parties and government performance in the Indian states. *Comparative Political Studies 37*(2), 152–187.

Chong, Alberto, De La O, Ana L., Karlan, Dean, & Wantchekon, Leonard. (2015). Does corruption information inspire the fight or quash the hope? A field experiment in Mexico on voter turnout, choice, and party identification. *Journal of Politics 77*(1), 55–71.

Chubb, Judith. (1982). *Patronage, power and poverty in Southern Italy: A tale of two cities*. Cambridge, England: Cambridge University Press.

Collier, David. (1995). Trajectory of a concept: "Corporatism" in the study of Latin American politics. In Peter H. Smith (Ed.), *Latin America in Comparative Perspective* (pp. 135–162). Boulder, CO: Westview Press.

Collier, David, Brady, Henry E., & Seawright, Jason. (2010). Introduction to the second edition: A sea change in political methodology. In Henry E. Brady & David Collier (Eds.), *Rethinking social inquiry: Diverse tools, shared standards* (pp. 1–10). Lanham, MD: Rowman & Littlefield Publishers.

Collier, Ruth Berins, & Collier, David. (1991). *Shaping the political arena: Critical junctures, the labor movement, and regime dynamics in Latin America*. Princeton, NJ: Princeton University Press.

Contarino, Michael. (1995). The local political economy of industrial adjustment: Variations in trade union responses to industrial restructuring in the Italian textile-clothing sector. *Comparative Political Studies 28*(1), 62–86.

Coppedge, Michael. (2012). *Democratization and research methods*. Cambridge, England: Cambridge University Press.

Corbridge, Stuart. (2005). *Seeing the state: Governance and governmentality in India*. Cambridge, England: Cambridge University Press.

Cornelius, Wayne A., Eisenstadt, Todd A., & Hindley, Jane (Eds.). (1999). *Subnational politics and democratization in Mexico*. La Jolla, CA: Center for US-Mexican Studies, University of California, San Diego.

Corstange, Daniel. (2016). *The price of a vote in the middle east: Clientelism and communal politics in Lebanon and Yemen*. Cambridge, England: Cambridge University Press.

Coslovsky, Salo V., & Locke, Richard M. (2013). Parallel paths to enforcement private compliance, public regulation, and labor standards in the Brazilian sugar sector. *Politics & Society 41*(4), 497–526.

Cotte Poveda, Alexander. (2012). Violence and economic development in Colombian cities: A dynamic panel data analysis. *Journal of International Development 24*(7), 809–827.

Crook, Richard C. (2003). Decentralisation and poverty reduction in Africa: The politics of local–central relations. *Public Administration and Development 23*(1), 77–88.

Dahl, Robert A. (1961). *Who governs? Democracy and power in an American city*. New Haven, CT: Yale University Press.

Dahl, Robert A. (1971). *Polyarchy*. New Haven, CT: Yale University Press.

Davis, Diane E. (2005). Cities in global context: A brief intellectual history. *International Journal of Urban and Regional Research 29*(1), 92–109.

De Soto, Hernando. (2003). Listening to the barking dogs: Property law against poverty in the non-West. *FOCAAL-UTRECHT 41*, 179–186.

De Tocqueville, Alexis. (1956). *Democracy in America*. New York, NY: New American Library. (Original work published 1831).

Denters, Bas, & Mossberger, Karen. (2006). Building blocks for a methodology for comparative urban political research. *Urban Affairs Review 41*(4), 550–571.

Diamond, Jared, & Robinson, James A. (2010). *Natural experiments of history.* Cambridge, MA: Harvard University Press.

Díaz-Cayeros, Alberto, Magaloni, Beatriz, & Ruiz-Euler, Alexander. (2014). Traditional governance, citizen engagement, and local public goods: Evidence from Mexico. *World Development 53*, 80–93.

Díaz-Cayeros, Alberto, Magaloni, Beatriz, Matanock, Aila M., & Romero, Vidal. (2015). *Living in fear: The dynamics of extortion in Mexico's criminal insurgency.* Working Paper. Center for International Development, Stanford University.

Diaz-Rioseco, Diego. (2016). Blessing and curse: Oil and subnational politics in the Argentine provinces. *Comparative Political Studies 49*(14), 1930–1964.

Downs, Anthony. (1957). An economic theory of political action in a democracy. *The Journal of Political Economy 65*(2), 135–150.

Druckman, James N., Green, Donald P., Kuklinski, James H., & Lupia, Arthur (Eds.). (2011). *Cambridge handbook of experimental political science.* New York, NY: Cambridge University Press.

Dunning, Thad. (2012). *Natural experiments in the social sciences: A design-based approach.* Cambridge, England: Cambridge University Press.

Dunning, Thad, & Harrison, Lauren. (2010). Cross-cutting cleavages and ethnic voting: An experimental study of cousinage in Mali. *American Political Science Review 104* (1), 21–39.

Durán-Martínez, Angélica. (2015). To kill and tell? State power, criminal competition, and drug violence. *Journal of Conflict Resolution 59*(8), 1377–1402.

Durán-Martínez, Angélica. (2018). *Criminals, cops and politicians: Drug violence in Colombia and Mexico.* Oxford, England: Oxford University Press.

Duverger, Maurice. (1978). *Political parties.* London, England: Methuen.

Eaton, Kent. (2004). *Politics beyond the capital: The design of subnational institutions in South America.* Stanford, CA: Stanford University Press.

Eaton, Kent. (2008). Paradoxes of police reform: federalism, parties, and civil society in Argentina's public security crisis. *Latin American Research Review 43*(3), 5–32.

Evans, Peter. (1979). *Dependent development: The alliance of multinational, state and local capital in Brazil.* Princeton, NJ: Princeton University Press.

Evans, Peter. (1996). Government action, social capital and development: Reviewing the evidence on synergy. *World Development 24*(6), 1119–1132.

Evans, Peter B., Jacobson, Karan, Harold, & Putnam, Robert D. (1993). *Double-edged diplomacy: International bargaining and domestic politics.* Berkeley, CA: University of California Press.

Faguet, Jean-Paul. (2009). Governance from below in Bolivia: A theory of local government with two empirical tests. *Latin American Politics and Society 51*(4), 29–68.

Falleti, Tulia G., & Riofrancos, Thea N. (2018). Endogenous participation: Strengthening prior consultation in extractive economies. *World Politics 70*(1), 86–121.

Fearon, James D., Humphreys, Macartan, & Weinstein, Jeremy M. (2009). Can development aid contribute to social cohesion after civil war? Evidence from a field experiment in post-conflict Liberia. *The American Economic Review 99*(2), 287–291.

Fearon, James D., Humphreys, Macartan, & Weinstein, Jeremy M. (2015). How does development assistance affect collective action capacity? Results from a field experiment in post-conflict Liberia. *American Political Science Review 109*(3), 450–469.

Firmin-Sellers, Kathryn. (2001). The reconstruction of society: Understanding the indigenous response to French and British rule in Cameroon. *Comparative Politics 34*(1), 43–62.

Fox, Jonathan. (1994). The difficult transition from clientelism to citizenship: Lessons from Mexico. *World Politics 46*(2), 151–184.

Fujiwara, Thomas, & Wantchekon, Leonard 2013. "Can informed public deliberation overcome clientelism? Experimental evidence from Benin," *American Economic Journal: Applied Economics 5*(4), 241–255.

Gans-Morse, Jordan. (2004). Searching for transitologists: Contemporary theories of post-communist transitions and the myth of a dominant paradigm. *Post-Soviet Affairs 20*(4), 320–349.

Geddes, Barbara. (2003). *Paradigms and sand castles: Theory building and research design in comparative politics.* Ann Arbor: University of Michigan Press.

Gerber, Alan S., & Green, Donald. (2012). *Field experiments: Design, analysis, and interpretation.* New York, NY: W. W. Norton.

Gerring, John, Palmer, Maxwell, Teorell, Jan, & Zarecki, Dominic. (2015). Demography and democracy: A global, district-level analysis of electoral contestation. *American Political Science Review 109*(3), 574–591.

Gerschenkron, Alexander. (1962). *Economic backwardness in historical perspective: A book of essays.* Cambridge, MA: Belknap Press of Harvard University Press.

Gervasoni, Carlos. (2010a). Measuring variance in subnational regimes: Results from an expert-based operationalization of democracy in the Argentine provinces. *Journal of Politics in Latin America 2*(2), 13–52.

Gervasoni, Carlos. (2010b). A rentier theory of subnational regimes: Fiscal federalism, democracy, and authoritarianism in the Argentine provinces. *World Politics 62*(2), 302–340.

Gibson, Edward L. (2005). Boundary control: Subnational authoritarianism in democratic countries. *World Politics 58*(1), 101–132.

Gibson, Edward L. (2013). *Boundary control: Subnational authoritarianism in federal democracies.* Cambridge, England: Cambridge University Press.

Gibson, Edward L., & Calvo, Ernesto. (2000). Federalism and low-maintenance constituencies: Territorial dimensions of economic reform in Argentina. *Studies in Comparative International Development 35*(3), 32–55.

Gibson, Edward L. (Ed.). (2004). *Federalism and democracy in Latin America.* Baltimore, MD: Johns Hopkins University Press.

Giraudy, Agustina. (2010). The politics of subnational undemocratic regime reproduction in Argentina and Mexico. *Journal of Politics in Latin America 2*(2), 53–84.

Giraudy, Agustina. (2013). Varieties of subnational undemocratic regimes: Evidence from Argentina and Mexico. *Studies in Comparative International Development 48*(1), 51–80.

Giraudy, Agustina. (2015). *Democrats and autocrats: Pathways of subnational undemocratic regime continuity within democratic countries.* Oxford, England: Oxford University Press.

Goldberg, Ellis, Wibbels, Erik, & Mvukiyehe, Eric. (2008). Lessons from strange cases: Democracy, development, and the resource curse in the US states. *Comparative Political Studies 41*(4–5), 477–514.

Goldfrank, Benjamin. (2011). *Deepening local democracy in Latin America: Participation, decentralization, and the left.* University Park: Penn State University Press.

González, Yanilda. (2016). Varieties of participatory security: Assessing community participation in policing in Latin America. *Public Administration and Development 36*(2), 132–143.

González, Lucas I. (2017). *Presidents, governors and the politics of distribution in federal democracies: Primus contra pares in Argentina and Brazil.* New York, NY: Routledge.

González, Lucas I. (in press). Oil rents and patronage: The fiscal effects of oil booms in the Argentine provinces. *Comparative Politics*.

González, Lucas I., & Lodola, Germán. (n.d.). *The impact of oil windfalls on subnational development: Evidence from Argentina.* Unpublished manuscript.

González, Lucas I., & Nazareno, Marcelo. (n.d.). *The unequal distribution of inequality subnational politics and income distribution in the Argentine provinces, 2003–2011.* Unpublished manuscript.

Gourevitch, Peter. (1978). The second image reversed: The international sources of domestic politics. *International Organization 32*(4), 881–912.

Grandi, Francesca. (2013). Why do the victors kill the vanquished? Explaining political violence in post-World War II Italy. *Journal of Peace Research 50*(5), 577–593.

Green, Elliot. (2010). Patronage, district creation, and reform in Uganda. *Studies in Comparative International Development 45*(1), 83–103.

Hagopian, Frances. (1996). *Traditional politics and regime change in Brazil.* New York, NY: Cambridge University Press.

Hale, Henry E. (2003). Explaining machine politics in Russia's regions: Economy, ethnicity, and legacy. *Post-Soviet Affairs 19*(3), 228–263.

Hecock, R. Douglas. (2006). Electoral competition, globalization, and subnational education spending in Mexico, 1999–2004. *American Journal of Political Science 50*(4), 950–961.

Heller, Patrick. (2000). Degrees of democracy: Some comparative lessons from India. *World Politics 52*(4): 484–519.

Heller, Patrick. (2001). Moving the state: The politics of democratic decentralization in Kerala, South Africa, and Porto Alegre. *Politics and Society 29*(1), 131–163.

Heller, Patrick. (2008). Local democracy and development in comparative perspective. In Mirjam van Donk (Ed.), *Consolidating developmental local government: Lessons from the South African experience* (pp. 153–174). Cape Town, South Africa: UCT Press.

Heller, Patrick. (2009). Democratic deepening in India and South Africa. *Journal of Asian and African Studies 44*(1), 123–149.

Heller, Patrick, Harilal, K. N., & Chaudhuri, Shubham. (2007). Building local democracy: Evaluating the impact of decentralization in Kerala, India. *World Development 35*(4), 626–648.

Herbst, Jeffrey. (2000). *States and power in Africa: Comparative lesson in authority and control.* Princeton, NJ: Princeton University Press.

Herrera, Veronica. (2014). Does commercialization undermine the benefits of decentralization for local services provision? Evidence from Mexico's urban water and sanitation sector. *World Development 56*, 16–31.

Herrera, Veronica. (2017). *Water and politics: Clientelism and reform in urban Mexico.* Ann Arbor: University of Michigan Press.

Herrigel, Gary. (1996). *Industrial constructions: The sources of German industrial power.* Cambridge, England: Cambridge University Press.

Hilgers, Tina, & Macdonald, Laura. (2017). *Violence in Latin America and the Caribbean: Subnational structures, institutions, and clientelism.* Cambridge, England: Cambridge University Press.

Hinton, Mercedes S. (2006). *The state on the streets: Police and politics in Argentina and Brazil.* Boulder, CO: Lynne Rienner.

Hiskey, Jonathan T. (2003). Demand-based development and local electoral environments in Mexico. *Comparative Politics 36*(1), 41–59.

Holland, Alisha. (2016). Forbearance. *American Political Science Review 110*(2), 232–246.

Hooghe, Liesbet, & Marks, Gary. (2001). *Multi-level governance and European integration.* Lanham, MD: Rowman & Littlefield.

Hooghe, Liesbet, & Marks, Gary. (2016). *Community, scale, and regional governance: A postfunctionalist theory of governance.* Oxford, England: Oxford University Press.

Hooghe, Liesbet, Marks, Gary, & Schakel, Arjan H. (2010). *The rise of regional authority: A comparative study of 42 democracies.* New York, NY: Routledge.

Humphreys, Macartan, & Weinstein, Jeremy M. (2008). Who fights? The determinants of participation in civil war. *American Journal of Political Science 52*(2), 436–455.

Hunter, Wendy, & Sugiyama, Natasha Borges. (2014). Transforming subjects into citizens: Insights from Brazil's Bolsa Família. *Perspectives on Politics 12*(4), 829–845.

Huntington, Samuel P. (1968). *Political order in changing societies.* New Haven, CT: Yale University Press.

Huntington, Samuel P. (1991). *The third wave: Democratization in the late twentieth century.* Norman, OK: University of Oklahoma Press.

Hurst, William. (2004). Understanding contentious collective action by Chinese laid-off workers: The importance of regional political economy. *Studies in Comparative International Development 39*(2), 94–120.

Hurst, William. (2009). *The Chinese worker after socialism.* Cambridge, England: Cambridge University Press.

Ingram, Matthew C. (2014). *The local educational and regional economic foundations of violence: A subnational, spatial analysis of homicide rates across Mexico's municipalities.* Working Paper. Mexico Institute, Woodrow Wilson International Center for Scholars.

Ingram, Matthew C. (2015). *Crafting courts in new democracies: The politics of subnational judicial reform in Brazil and Mexico.* Cambridge, England: Cambridge University Press.

Ingram, Matthew C., & da Costa, Marcelo Marchesini. (2016). A spatial analysis of homicide across Brazil's municipalities. *Homicide Studies 21*(2), 87–110.

Jayasuriya, Kanishka. (2008). Regionalising the state: Political topography of regulatory regionalism. *Contemporary Politics 14*(1), 21–35.

Jervis, Robert. (1998). *System effects: Complexity in political and social life.* Princeton, NJ: Princeton University Press.

Kale, Sunila. (2014). *Electrifying India: Regional political economies of development.* Stanford, CA: Stanford University Press.

Kalyvas, Stathis N. (2003). The ontology of "political violence": Action and identity in civil wars. *Perspectives on Politics 1*(3), 475–494.

Kalyvas, Stathis N. (2006). *The logic of violence in civil war.* Cambridge, England: Cambridge University Press.

Kalyvas, Stathis N., & Kocher, Matthew Adam. (2009). The dynamics of violence in Vietnam: An analysis of the hamlet evaluation system (HES). *Journal of Peace Research 46*(3), 335–355.

Kantor, Paul, & Savitch, Hank V. (2005). How to study comparative urban development politics: A research note. *International Journal of Urban and Regional Research 29*(1), 135–151.

Karl, Terry Lynn. (1995). The hybrid regimes of Central America. *Journal of Democracy* 6(3), 72–86.

Karl, Terry Lynn, & Schmitter, Philippe C. (1995). From an iron curtain to a paper curtain: Grounding transitologists or students of postcommunism? *Slavic Review 54* (4), 965–978.

Katznelson, Ira. (2013). *Fear itself: The new deal and the origins of our time.* New York, NY: W. W. Norton & Company.

Key, V. O. (1949). *Southern politics in state and nation.* New York, NY: Knopf.

Knight, Jack. (1992). *Institutions and social conflict.* Cambridge, England: Cambridge University Press.

Kocher, Matthew A., & Monteiro, Nuno P. (2016). Line of demarcation: Causation design-based inference, and historical research. *Perspectives on Politics 14*(4), 952–975.

Kohli, Atul. (1987). *The state and poverty in India: The politics of reform.* New York, NY: Cambridge University Press.

Koter, Dominika. (2013). King makers: Local leaders and ethnic politics in Africa. *World Politics 65*(2), 187–232.

Krishna, Anirudh. (2002). Enhancing political participation in democracies: What is the role of social capital? *Comparative Political Studies 35*(4), 437–460.

Laitin, David D. (1986). *Hegemony and culture: Politics and change among the Yoruba.* Chicago, IL: University of Chicago Press.

Lankina, Tomila, & Getachew, Lullit. (2012). Mission or empire, word or sword? The human capital legacy in postcolonial democratic development. *American Journal of Political Science 56*(2), 465–483.

Lankina, Tomila V., & Getachew, Lullit. (2006). A geographic incremental theory of democratization: Territory, aid, and democracy in postcommunist regions. *World Politics 58*(4), 536–582.

LeBas, Adrienne. (2013). Violence and urban order in Nairobi, Kenya and Lagos, Nigeria. *Studies in Comparative International Development 48*(3), 240–262.

Leeds, Elizabeth. (1996). Cocaine and parallel polities in the Brazilian urban periphery: Constraints on local-level democratization. *Latin American Research Review 31*(3), 47–83.

Leiras, Marcelo, Tuñón, Guadalupe, & Giraudy, Agustina. (2015). Who wants an independent court? Political competition and supreme court autonomy in the Argentine provinces (1984–2008). *Journal of Politics 77*(1), 175–187.

Levitsky, Steven, & Way, Lucan A. (2010). *Competitive authoritarianism: Hybrid regimes after the Cold War.* Cambridge, England: Cambridge University Press.

Libman, Alexander, & Obydenkova, Anastassia. (2014). International trade as a limiting factor in democratization: An analysis of subnational regions in post-communist Russia. *Studies in Comparative International Development 49*(2), 168–196.

Lichbach, Mark Irving, & Zuckerman, Alan S. (2009). *Comparative politics: Rationality, culture, and structure.* Cambridge, England: Cambridge University Press.

Lieberman, Evan S. (2005). Nested analysis as a mixed-method strategy for comparative research. *American Political Science Review 99*(3), 435–452.

Lieberman, Evan S. (2009). *Boundaries of contagion: How ethnic politics have shaped government responses to AIDS.* Princeton, NJ: Princeton University Press.

Lijphart, Arend. (1971). Comparative politics and the comparative method. *American Political Science Review 65*(3), 682–693.

Lijphart, Arend. (1992). *Parliamentary versus presidential government.* Oxford, England: Oxford University Press.

Linz, Juan J. (1986). *Conflicto en Euskadi.* Madrid, Spain: Espasa Calpe.

Linz, Juan J., & De Miguel, Amando. (1966). Within-nation differences and comparisons: The eight Spains. In Richard L. Merritt & Stein Rokkan (Eds.), *Comparing nations: The use of quantitative data in cross-national research* (pp. 267–319). New Haven, CT: Yale University Press.

Linz, Juan J., & Stepan, Alfred (1996). *Problems of democratic transition and consolidation: Southern Europe, South America, and post-communist Europe.* Baltimore, MD: Johns Hopkins University Press.

Lipset, Seymour Martin. (1950). *Agrarian socialism: The cooperative commonwealth federation in Sakatchewan.* Berkeley, CA: University of California Press.

Lipset, Seymour Martin. (1959). Some social requisites of democracy: Economic development and political legitimacy. *American Political Science Review 53*(1), 69–105.

Locke, Richard M. (1992). The demise of the national union in Italy: Lessons for comparative industrial relations theory. *Industrial & Labor Relations Review 45*(2), 229–249.

Locke, Richard M. (1995). *Remaking the Italian economy.* Ithaca, NY: Cornell University Press.

Logan, John, & Swanstrom, Todd. (2009). *Beyond the city limits: Urban policy and economic restructuring in comparative perspective.* Philadelphia, PA: Temple University Press.

Lubkemann, Stephen C. (2005). Migratory coping in wartime Mozambique: An anthropology of violence and displacement in "fragmented wars." *Journal of Peace Research 42*(4), 493–508.

Luna, Juan Pablo. (2014). *Segmented representation: Political party strategies in unequal democracies.* Oxford, England: Oxford University Press.

Luna, Juan Pablo, & Medel, Rodrigo. (2017). *Local citizenship regimes in contemporary Latin America: Inequality, state capacity, and segmented access to civil, political, and social rights.* Paper presented at the Annual Meeting of the American Political Science Association (APSA), San Francisco, CA.

Luna, Juan Pablo, & Soifer, Hillel David. (2017). Capturing subnational variation in state capacity: A survey-based approach. *American Behavioral Scientist 61*(8), 887–907.

MacLean, Lauren M. (2010). *Informal institutions and citizenship in rural Africa: Risk and reciprocity in Ghana and Cote d'Ivoire*. Cambridge, England: Cambridge University Press.

Mahdavy, Hossein. (1970). The patterns and problems of economic development in rentier states: The case of Iran. In M. A. Cook (Ed.). *Studies in economic history of the Middle East* (pp. 37–61). London, England: Oxford University Press.

Mahdavi, Paasha. (2015). Explaining the oil advantage: Effects of natural resource wealth on incumbent reelection in Iran. *World Politics 67*(2), 226–267.

Mahoney, James, & Goertz, Gary. (2004). The possibility principle: Choosing negative cases in comparative research. *American Political Science Review 98*(4), 653–669.

Mampilly, Zachariah Cherian. (2011). *Rebel rulers: Insurgent governance and civilian life during war*. Ithaca, NY: Cornell University Press.

McGuire, James W. (2017). *Politics, gender, and health: Insight from Argentina's provinces*. Paper prepared for a talk at the Institute of the Americas, University College, London.

McMann, Kelly M. (2006). *Economic autonomy and democracy: Hybrid regimes in Russia and Kyrgyzstan*. Cambridge, England: Cambridge University Press.

Mickey, Robert. (2015). *Paths out of Dixie: The democratization of authoritarian enclaves in America's Deep South, 1944–1972*. Princeton, NJ: Princeton University Press.

Miguel, Edward. (2004). Tribe or nation? Nation building and public goods in Kenya versus Tanzania. *World Politics 56*(3), 328–362.

Miles, William F. S. (1994). *Hausaland divided: Colonialism and independence in Nigeria and Niger*. Ithaca, NY: Cornell University Press.

Moncada, Eduardo. (2009). Toward democratic policing in Colombia? Institutional accountability through lateral reform. *Comparative Politics 41*(4), 431–449.

Moncada, Eduardo. (2013a). The politics of urban violence: Challenges for development in the Global South. *Studies in Comparative International Development 48*(3), 217–239.

Moncada, Eduardo. (2013b). Business and the politics of urban violence in Colombia. *Studies in Comparative International Development 48*(3), 308–330.

Moncada, Eduardo. (2016a). *Cities, business, and the politics of urban violence in Latin America*. Stanford, CA: Stanford University Press.

Moncada, Eduardo. (2016b). Urban violence, political economy, and territorial control: Insights from Medellin. *Latin American Research Review 51*(4), 225–248.

Moncada, Eduardo. (2017). Varieties of vigilantism: Conceptual discord, meaning and strategies. *Global Crime 18*(4), 403–423.

Moncada, Eduardo, & Snyder, Richard. (2012). Subnational comparative research on democracy: Taking stock and looking forward. *CD-APSA: The Newsletter of the Comparative Democratization Section of the American Political Science Association (APSA) 10*, 4–9.

Montambeault, Françoise. (2015). *The politics of local participatory democracy in Latin America: Institutions, actors, and interactions*. Stanford, CA: Stanford University Press.

Monteiro, Joana, & Ferraz, Claudio. (n.d.). *Does oil make leaders unaccountable? Evidence from Brazil's offshore oil boom*. Unpublished manuscript.

Montero, Alfred P. (2002). *Shifting states in global markets: Subnational industrial policy in contemporary Brazil and Spain*. University Park: Penn State University Press.

Montero, Alfred P. (2007, September 5–8). *Uneven democracy? Subnational authoritarianism in democratic Brazil.* Paper presented at the Latin American Studies Association Annual Meeting, Montreal, Quebec, Canada.

Montero, Alfred P., & Samuels, David. (2004). *Decentralization and democracy in Latin America.* Notre Dame, IN: University of Notre Dame Press.

Moore, Barrington, Jr. (1966). *Social origins of dictatorship and democracy: Lord and peasant in the making of the modern world.* Boston, MA: Beacon Press.

Naroll, Raoul. (1961). Two solutions to Galton's problem. *Philosophy of Science 28* (January), 15–39.

Naroll, Raoul. (1966). Scientific comparative politics and international relations. In R. Farrell (Ed.), *Approaches to Comparative and International Politics* (pp. 329–337). Evanston, IL: Northwestern University Press.

Naseemullah, Adnan. (2016). *Development after statism.* Cambridge, England: Cambridge University Press.

Niedzwiecki, Sara. (2016). Social policies, attribution of responsibility, and political alignments: A subnational analysis of Argentina and Brazil. *Comparative Political Studies 49*(4), 457–498.

North, Douglass C. (1990). *Institutions, institutional change and economic performance.* Cambridge, England: Cambridge University Press.

North, Douglass C., & Weingast, Barry R. (1989). Constitutions and commitment: The evolution of institutions governing public choice in seventeenth-century England. *The Journal of Economic History 49*(4), 803–832.

O'Donnell, Guillermo. (1993). On the state, democratization and some conceptual problems: A Latin American view with glances at some postcommunist countries. *World Development 21,* 1355–1369.

O'Donnell, Guillermo. (1973). *Modernization and bureaucratic-authoritarianism: Studies in South American politics.* Berkeley, CA: Institute of International Studies, University of California.

Osorio, Javier. (2013). *Hobbes on drugs: Understanding drug violence in Mexico.* (Doctoral dissertation). University of Notre Dame, Notre Dame, IN.

Ostrom, Elinor. (1996). Crossing the great divide: Coproduction, synergy, and development. *World Development 24*(6), 1073–1087.

Pasotti, Eleonora. (2010). *Political branding in cities: The decline of machine politics in Bogotá, Naples, and Chicago.* Cambridge, England: Cambridge University Press.

Pepinsky, Thomas B. (2017). Regions of exception. *Perspectives on Politics 15*(4), 1034–1052.

Pepinsky, Thomas B. (2018). *The return of the single country study.* Available at SSRN: https://ssrn.com/abstract=3197172.

Petrov, Nikolai. (2005). Regional models of democratic development. In Michale McFaul, Nikolai Petrov, & Andrei Ryabov (Eds.), *Between Dictatorship and Democracy: Russian post-communist political reform* (pp. 239–267). Washington, DC: Carnegie Endowment for International Peace.

Phillips, Brian J. (2015). How does leadership decapitation affect violence? The case of drug trafficking organizations in Mexico. *Journal of Politics 77*(2), 324–336.

Pierre, Jon. (2005). Comparative urban governance: Uncovering complex causalities. *Urban Affairs Review 40*(4), 446–462.

Pierson, Paul. (1994). *Dismantling the welfare state? Reagan, Thatcher, and the politics of retrenchment.* New York, NY: Cambridge University Press.

Pogrebinschi, Thami, & Samuels, David. (2014). The impact of participatory democracy: Evidence from Brazil's National Public Policy Conferences. *Comparative Politics 46*(3), 313–332.

Posner, Daniel N. (2004). The political salience of cultural difference: Why Chewas and Tumbukas are allies in Zambia and adversaries in Malawi. *American Political Science Review 98*(4), 529–545.

Post, Alison E. (2014). *Foreign and domestic investment in Argentina: The politics of privatized infrastructure.* Cambridge, England: Cambridge University Press.

Post, Alison E., Bronsoler, Vivian, & Salman, Lana. (2017). Hybrid regimes for local public goods provision: A framework for analysis. *Perspectives on Politics 15*(4), 952–966.

Pribble, Jennifer. (2015). The politics of building municipal institutional effectiveness in Chile. *Latin American Politics and Society 57*(3), 100–121.

Przeworski, Adam. (2010). *Democracy and the limits of self-government.* Cambridge, England: Cambridge University Press.

Przeworski, Adam, Alvarez, Michael E., Cheibub, Jose Antonio, & Limongi, Fernando. (2000). *Democracy and development: Political institutions and well-being in the world, 1950–1990.* Cambridge, England: Cambridge University Press.

Przeworski, Adam, & Teune, Henry. (1970). *The logic of comparative social inquiry.* New York, NY: John Wiley.

Putnam, Robert D., Leonardi, Robert, & Nanetti, Raffaella Y. (1994). *Making democracy work: Civic traditions in modern Italy.* Princeton, NJ: Princeton University Press.

Rebolledo, Juan. (2011). *Voting with the enemy: Democratic support for subnational authoritarians.* (Doctoral dissertation). Yale University, Boston, MA.

Reisinger, William M., & Moraski, Bryon J. (2010). Regional changes and changing regional relations with the centre. In Vladimir Gel'man & Cameron Ross (Eds.), *The politics of sub-national authoritarianism in Russia* (pp. 67–84). London, England: Routledge.

Remington, Thomas. (2009). *Democracy and inequality in the postcommunist transition.* Paper presented at the Annual Meeting of the Midwestern Political Science Association (MPSA), Chicago, IL.

Remington, Thomas. (2010a). *Accounting for regime differences in the Russian regions: Historical and structural influences.* Paper presented at the Annual Meeting of the Midwestern Political Science Association (MPSA), Chicago, IL.

Remington, Thomas. (2010b). *Politics in Russia.* Boston, MA: Longman.

Resnick, Danielle. (2012). Opposition parties and the urban poor in African democracies. *Comparative Political Studies 45*(11), 1351–1378.

Resnick, Danielle. (2013). *Urban poverty and party populism in African democracies.* Cambridge, England: Cambridge University Press.

Reuter, Ora John, & Robertson, Graeme B. (2012). Subnational appointments in authoritarian regimes: Evidence from Russian gubernatorial appointments. *Journal of Politics 74*(4), 1023–1037.

Riedl, Rachel Beatty. (2017). Sub-national–cross-national variation: Method and analysis in sub-saharan Africa. *American Behavioral Scientist 61*(8), 932–959.

Ríos, Viridiana. (2013). Why did Mexico become so violent? A self-reinforcing violent equilibrium caused by competition and enforcement. *Trends in organized crime 16*(2), 138–155.

Rithmire, Meg. (2014). China's 'new regionalism': Subnational analysis in Chinese political economy. *World Politics 66*(1), 165–94.

Robinson, Jennifer. (2002). Global and world cities: A view from off the map. *International Journal of Urban and Regional Research 26*(3), 531–554.

Robinson, Jennifer. (2011). Cities in a world of cities: The comparative gesture. *International Journal of Urban and Regional Research 35*(1), 1–23.

Rokkan, Stein. (1970). *Citizens, elections, parties: Approaches to the comparative study of the processes of development.* New York, NY: David McKay Company.

Rokkan, Stein, & Urwin, Derek W. (1982). *The politics of territorial identity: Studies in European regionalism.* London, England: Sage Publications.

Rokkan, Stein, & Urwin, Derek W. (1983). *Economy, territory, identity: Politics of West European peripheries.* London, England: Sage Publications.

Rokkan, Stein, Urwin, Derek W., Aerobrot, Frank H., Malaba, Pamela, & Sande, Terje. (1987). *Centre-Periphery structures in Europe: An ISSC workbook in comparative analysis.* Frankfurt, Germany: Campus Verlag.

Ross, Michael L. (2012). *The oil curse: How petroleum wealth shapes the development of nations.* Princeton, NJ: Princeton University Press.

Sachs, Jeffrey D., & Warner, Andrew M. (1995). *Natural resource abundance and economic growth.* NBER Working Paper No. w5398. Available at SSRN: https://ssrn.com/abstract=225459.

Saez, Lawrence, & Sinha, Aseema. (2010). Political cycles, political institutions and public expenditure in India, 1980–2000. *British Journal of Political Science 40*(1), 91–113.

Saffon, Maria Paula. (n.d.). *When theft becomes grievance: The violation of land rights as a cause of land reform claims in Latin America.* Unpublished manuscript.

Saikkonen, Inga A-L. (2016). Variation in subnational electoral authoritarianism: Evidence from the Russian Federation. *Democratization 23*(3), 437–458.

Samuels, David, & Snyder, Richard. (2001). The value of a vote: Malapportionment in comparative perspective. *British Journal of Political Science 31*(4), 651–671.

Samuels, David, & Snyder, Richard. (2004). Legislative Malapportionment in Latin America: Historical and comparative perspectives. In Edward L. Gibson (Ed.), *Federalism and Democracy in Latin America* (pp. 131–172). Baltimore, MD: Johns Hopkins University Press.

Sartori, Giovanni. (1970). Concept misformation in comparative politics. *American Political Science Review 64*(4), 1033–1053.

Sassen, Saskia. (2001). *The global city: New York, London, Tokyo.* Princeton, NJ: Princeton University Press.

Schedler, Andreas (Ed.). (2006). *Electoral authoritarianism: The dynamics of unfree competition.* Boulder, CO: Lynne Rienner.

Schiller, Wendy J. (1999). Trade politics in the American congress: A study of the interaction of political geography and interest group behavior. *Political Geography 18*(7), 769–789.

Schmitter, Philippe C., & Karl, Terry Lynn. (1994). The conceptual travels of transitologists and consolidologists: How far to the east should they attempt to go?" *Slavic Review 53*(1), 173–185.

Schumpeter, Joseph Alois. (1942). *Socialism, capitalism and democracy.* New York, NY: Harper and Brothers.

Schutte, Sebastian, & Weidmann, Nils B. (2011). Diffusion patterns of violence in civil wars. *Political Geography 30*(3), 143–152.

Sellers, Jefferey M. (2002). *Governing from below: Urban regions and the global economy*. Cambridge, England: Cambridge University Press.

Sellers, Jefferey M. (2005). "Re-placing the nation: An agenda for comparative urban politics. *Urban Affairs Review 40*(4), 419–445.

Sellers, Jefferey M. (in press). From within to between nations: Subnational comparison across borders. *Perspectives on Politics*.

Sen, Amartya. (1999). *Development as freedom*. New York, NY: Knopf.

Shirk, David, & Wallman, Joel. (2015). Understanding Mexico's drug violence. *Journal of Conflict Resolution 59*(8), 1348–1376.

Shonfield, Andrew. (1965). *Modern capitalism: The changing balance of public and private power*. New York, NY: Oxford University Press.

Sidel, John Thayer. (1999). *Capital, coercion, and crime: Bossism in the Philippines*. Stanford, CA: Stanford University Press.

Sinclair, Betsy, McConnell, Margaret, & Green, Donald P. (2012). Detecting spillover effects: Design and analysis of multilevel experiments. *American Journal of Political Science 56*(4), 1055–1069.

Singer, J. David. (1961). The level-of-analysis problem in international relations. *World Politics 14*(1), 77–92.

Singh, Prerna. (2017). The theoretical potential of the within-nation comparison: How subnational analyses can enrich our understandings of the national welfare state. *American Behavioral Scientist 61*(8), 861–886.

Sinha, Aseema. (2005). *The regional roots of developmental politics in India: A divided leviathan*. Bloomington: Indiana University Press.

Sitkoff, Harvard. (1981). *A new deal for blacks: The emergence of civil rights as a national issue: The depression decade*. New York, NY: Oxford University Press.

Skocpol, Theda. (1992). *Protecting soldiers and mothers: The political origins of social policy in the United States*. Cambridge, MA: Harvard University Press.

Slater, Dan, & Ziblatt, Daniel. (2013). The enduring indispensability of the controlled comparison. *Comparative Political Studies 46*(10), 1301–1327.

Smith, Benjamin. (2004). Oil wealth and regime survival in the developing world, 1960–1999. *American Journal of Political Science 48*(2), 232–246.

Smulovitz, Catalina. (2015). Legal inequality and federalism: Domestic violence laws in the Argentine provinces. *Latin American Politics and Society 57*(3), 1–26.

Snyder, Richard. (1999a). After the state withdraws: Neoliberalism and subnational authoritarian regimes in Mexico. In Wayne A. Cornelius, Todd A. Eisenstadt, & Jane Hindley (Eds.), *Subnational politics and democratization in Mexico* (pp. 295–341). La Jolla: Center for U.S.-Mexican Studies, University of California, San Diego.

Snyder, Richard. (1999b). After neoliberalism: The politics of reregulation in Mexico. *World Politics 51*(2), 173–204.

Snyder, Richard. (2001a). Scaling down: The subnational comparative method. *Studies in Comparative International Development 36*(1), 93–110.

Snyder, Richard. (2001b). *Politics after neoliberalism: Reregulation in Mexico*. Cambridge, England: Cambridge University Press.

Snyder, Richard, & Durán-Martínez, Angélica. (2009a). Does illegality breed violence? Drug trafficking and state-sponsored protection rackets. *Crime, Law and Social Change 52*(3), 253–273.

Snyder, Richard, & Durán-Martínez, Angélica. (2009b). Drugs, violence, and state-sponsored protection rackets in Mexico and Colombia. *Colombia Internacional 70*, 61–91.

Snyder, Richard, & Samuels, David. (2001). Devaluing the vote in Latin America. *Journal of Democracy 12*(1), 146–159.

Solt, Frederick. (2003). Explaining the quality of new democracies: Actors, institutions, and socioeconomic structure in Mexico's states. (Doctoral dissertation). University of North Carolina, Chapel Hill.

Staniland, Paul. (2012). States, insurgents, and wartime political orders. *Perspectives on Politics 10*(2), 243–264.

Steele, Abbey. (2017). *Democracy and displacement in Colombia's civil war.* Ithaca, NY: Cornell University Press.

Stokes, Susan C., Dunning, Thad, Nazareno, Marcelo, & Brusco, Valeria. (2013). *Brokers, voters, and clientelism: The puzzle of distributive politics.* Cambridge, England: Cambridge University Press.

Stoner-Weiss, Kathryn. (2002). *Local heroes: The political economy of Russian regional governance.* Princeton, NJ: Princeton University Press.

Stoner-Weiss, Kathryn. (2006). *Resisting the state: Reform and retrenchment in post-Soviet Russia.* Cambridge, England: Cambridge University Press.

Straus, Scott. (2015). *Making and unmaking nations: War, leadership, and genocide in modern Africa.* Ithaca, NY: Cornell University Press.

Sugiyama, Natasha Borges. (2008). Ideology and networks: The politics of social policy diffusion in Brazil. *Latin American Research Review 43*(3), 82–108.

Sugiyama, Natasha Borges. (2012). *The diffusion of good government: Social sector reforms in Brazil.* Notre Dame, IN: University of Notre Dame Press.

Sugiyama, Natasha Borges, & Hunter, Wendy. (2013). Whither clientelism? Good governance and Brazil's Bolsa Família Program. *Comparative Politics 46*(1), 43–62.

Szwarcberg, Mariela. (2013). The microfoundations of political clientelism: Lessons from the Argentine case. *Latin American Research Review 48*(2), 32–54.

Szwarcberg, Mariela. (2015). *Mobilizing poor voters: Machine politics, clientelism, and social networks in Argentina.* Cambridge, England: Cambridge University Press.

Tarrow, Sidney. (1978). *Territorial politics in industrial nations.* New York, NY: Praeger.

Tarrow, Sidney G. (1977). *Between center and periphery: Grassroots politicians in Italy and France.* New Haven, CT: Yale University Press.

Tendler, Judith. (1997). *Good government in the tropics.* Baltimore, MD: Johns Hopkins University Press.

Tendler, Judith, & Freedheim, Sara. (1994). Trust in a rent-seeking world: Health and government transformed in northeast Brazil. *World Development 22*(12), 1771–1791.

Tilly, Charles. (1964). *The Vendee.* Cambridge, MA: Harvard University Press.

Touchton, Michael, & Wampler, Brian. (2014). Improving social well-being through new democratic institutions. *Comparative Political Studies 47*(10), 1442–1469.

Trochev, Alexei. (2004). Less democracy, more courts: A puzzle of judicial review in Russia. *Law & Society Review 38*(3), 513–548.

Tsai, Lily, & Ziblatt, Daniel. (n.d.). *The rise of subnational and multilevel comparative politics.* Unpublished manuscript.

Tsai, Lily L. (2007). *Accountability without democracy: Solidary groups and public goods provision in rural China.* Cambridge, England: Cambridge University Press.

Urdal, Henrik. (2008). Population, resources, and political violence: A subnational study of India, 1956–2002. *Journal of Conflict Resolution 52*(4), 590–617.

Varshney, Ashutosh. (2002). *Ethnic conflict and civic life: Hindus and Muslims in India.* New Haven, CT: Yale University Press.

Vergara, Alberto. (2015). *La danza hostil: Poderes subnacionales y estado central en Boliva y Perú (1952–2012).* Lima, Peru: Instituto de Estudios Peruanos.

Wampler, Brian. (2007). *Participatory budgeting in Brazil: Contestation, cooperation, and accountability.* University Park: Penn State University Press.

Wantchekon, Leonard. (2003). Clientelism and voting behavior: Evidence from a field experiment in Benin. *World Politics 55*(3), 399–422.

Weinstein, Jeremy M. (2006). *Inside rebellion: The politics of insurgent violence.* Cambridge, England: Cambridge University Press.

Weinstein, Liza. (2013). Demolition and dispossession: Toward an understanding of state violence in millennial Mumbai. *Studies in Comparative International Development 48*(3), 285–307.

Weitz-Shapiro, Rebecca. (2014). *Curbing clientelism in Argentina: Politics, poverty, and social policy.* Cambridge, England: Cambridge University Press.

Wengle, Susanne A. (2015). *Post-Soviet power.* Cambridge, England: Cambridge University Press.

Wilkinson, Steven I. (2006). *Votes and violence: Electoral competition and ethnic riots in India.* Cambridge, England: Cambridge University Press.

Wolff, Michael Jerome. (2015). Building criminal authority: A comparative analysis of drug gangs in Rio de Janeiro and Recife. *Latin American Politics and Society 57*(2), 21–40.

Wood, Elisabeth Jean. (2003). *Insurgent collective action and civil war in El Salvador.* Cambridge, England: Cambridge University Press.

Zhang, Yue. (2013). *The fragmented politics of urban preservation.* Minneapolis: University of Minnesota Press.

Ziblatt, Daniel. (2006). *Structuring the state: The formation of Italy and Germany and the puzzle of federalism.* Princeton, NJ: Princeton University Press.

Ziblatt, Daniel. (2008). Why some cities provide more public goods than others: A subnational comparison of the provision of public goods in German cities in 1912. *Studies in Comparative International Development 43*(3–4), 273–289.

PART I

ISSUES OF METHOD AND RESEARCH DESIGN

2

Politics in Space

Methodological Considerations for Taking Space Seriously in Subnational Research

Imke Harbers
Matthew C. Ingram

Throughout the twentieth century, methodological nationalism has been the predominant form of thinking about political phenomena. In recent years, there has been a critical reevaluation of how readily social scientists, and especially scholars of comparative politics and international relations, accepted the nation-state as the most important level of analysis. Letting go of the simplifying assumption that the primary causes and consequences of political phenomena are located in the national arena enables scholars to more adequately map and explain the spatially uneven nature of contemporary political and economic transformations (Snyder, 2001). Indeed, over the past two decades a rich research program has emerged in which scholars draw on the subnational approach to better understand phenomena such as state formation, democratization, and development. Despite its undisputed potential, however, the subnational approach also creates specific challenges for researchers throughout the research cycle that have yet to be resolved.

This chapter explores how insights from Geographic Information Systems (GIS) and spatial analysis can help us work through some of these challenges. Furthermore, we highlight how a spatial perspective can strengthen the subnational approach by opening up new opportunities for theory development and analysis. While some of the techniques discussed below have been available since the 1980s (Doreian, 1980, 1982; Cliff & Ord, 1981; Anselin, 1988), political science has been slower than other social science disciplines to adopt a spatial perspective. Moreover, current work in comparative politics has tended to use GIS primarily for visualizing data at the level of subnational jurisdictions, without recognizing its potential for

We thank Richard Snyder, Agustina Giraudy, and Eduardo Moncada; workshop participants at Brown University in 2013 and Harvard University in 2014, especially Lily Tsai and Daniel Ziblatt; and two anonymous readers for their comments on an earlier draft. We are grateful to Alejandro Trelles and Miguel Carreras for sharing their municipal-level data on homicide rates from Mexico. All remaining errors are our own.

theory development or analysis.[1] Throughout this chapter, we include citations to key texts in spatial analysis to enable further reading and a more in-depth look at the techniques discussed.

Our central argument is that there is much to gain by thinking more explicitly about how the phenomena we study are situated in space and how space may, in turn, structure or condition outcomes and causal relationships of interest. By "space" we mean the geographic connectivity among units of observation. This connectivity can be conceptualized in multiple ways (e.g., contiguity, distance), but we emphasize its geographic or territorial nature (see Appendix on spatial weights). The spatial nature of connectivity comes into clearer focus if contrasted with the relational nature of connectivity in the field of network analysis. For instance, in a study of voting behavior, network analysts would be more interested in the associational ties and social closeness among individuals (e.g., Huckfeldt & Sprague, 1995), whereas spatial analysts would be more interested in their geographic proximity (e.g., Darmofal, 2006). Closeness, distance, and proximity can have overlapping connotations in both spatial and network research, but the key difference is that network connectivity is relational or affective whereas spatial connectivity is geographic.

"Taking space seriously" has key conceptual as well as theoretical implications. A major implication is the need for a more thorough recognition of the structural dependence that exists among units of observation. To be sure, this recognition is also important in international relations and cross-national comparative studies,[2] but the analytic shift is perhaps most important at the subnational level, where units of analysis have boundaries that are more porous than international borders. In quantitative research or mixed-methods designs with a quantitative component – which have recently become the norm in subnational comparative analyses (Moncada & Snyder, 2012) – treating these units as independently distributed is often untenable. Analyses drawing on estimation techniques that do not account for this spatial dependence then run the risk of obtaining incorrect, biased estimates and missing key factors influencing phenomena of interest. Yet most studies in comparative politics have so far left the issue of spatial dependence unaddressed.

More importantly, however, the value added of spatial analysis for subnational research lies not only in getting "right" answers to existing questions but also in bringing to the table exciting methods for (a) seeing existing questions in a new light and (b) identifying new and interesting questions that might otherwise go unnoticed. Taking space seriously thus also implies considering how spatial

---

[1] Among political science subfields, the international relations literature has been most proactive about embracing the notion of "politics in space" (e.g., Cederman & Gleditsch, 2009), and there has been a push to make GIS and related tools accessible to a larger audience (e.g., Gleditsch & Ward, 2005; Gleditsch & Weidman, 2012; Ward & Gleditsch, 2018). In comparative politics, see Franzese and Hays (2008).

[2] See, e.g., Ward and Gleditsch (2018) for spatial dependence in international relations or Hafner-Burton et al. (2009) for network dependence.

dependence structures outcomes and relationships of interest, and it invites researchers to question the assumption that units are self-contained. Moreover, in conventional, large-N analyses, the relationship between an explanatory variable and the dependent variable is generally assumed to be the same among all units, and the relationship in one unit is assumed to be unaffected by the outcome or explanatory variables in nearby units. As discussed in the introduction to this volume, the research program on subnational democracy, for instance, has looked for the causes of subnational undemocratic regimes mostly within the units themselves or in the vertical interactions between subnational units and higher levels of government. In light of the permeability of subnational borders, however, it may also be valuable to explore more systematically horizontal interactions among units and issues of spillover, diffusion, contagion, and similar phenomena among observations. Schedler (2014), for instance, raises the question of how the spread of violence in Mexico subverts democracy. Applying a spatial lens to violence, as we show in this chapter, allows analysts to more fully theorize and assess how such phenomena are also spatial processes – i.e., causal processes structured by space.

In making our plea for a "spatial turn" in subnational research, we recognize that we are guilty ourselves of the sins we are exposing, namely, of practicing the "dark art" of treating subnational units as independently distributed observations and of not considering the effect of spatial structures on outcomes and relationships of interest (e.g., Ingram, 2013, 2016; Harbers, 2014). Further, we acknowledge that a spatial perspective is not a simple, cool trick, nor does it reduce to a quick methodological fix. Instead, this chapter is intended as a contribution to a conversation about how to study subnational politics in a more disciplined and self-conscious way by examining the implications of spatial thinking across three stages of research design: (1) conceptualization; (2) theorizing; and (3) analysis. Within each of these phases there are lessons to be learned from taking space more seriously, and there are important analytic costs of not doing so.[3]

The chapter follows the structure outlined in Table 2.1. Looking ahead, a major concern in the subnational literature is the marked variation within countries in outcomes of interest, especially democracy and security. Throughout the chapter, we draw on the substantive examples of subnational democracy and the territorial dimension of violence. As the editors highlight in their introduction to the volume, these are areas of research where insights from the subnational approach have been particularly valuable. In our discussion, we highlight current practices and explain how taking space seriously can open new directions for research. The first section of the paper focuses on conceptualization where closer attention to how concepts are related to spatial and institutional

---

[3] In our discussion, we assume some basic familiarity with the vocabulary of spatial analysis. For readers unfamiliar with the logic of spatial analysis, we have included a brief appendix on spatial weights.

TABLE 2.1 *Strengthening Subnational Research: Implications of a Spatial Perspective for Conceptualization, Theory, and Analysis*

	Current Practices and Associated Challenges for Improving Subnational Research	Contributions of a Spatial Perspective to Improving Subnational Research
Conceptualization	Practice: Emphasis on adapting national-level concepts for subnational units Challenge: Make explicit how space and/or institutional categories are related to the phenomenon of interest	• Distinguish unbound from institutional phenomena • Identify appropriate level of analysis
Theory	Practice: Explaining causes and consequences of territorial variation (i.e., unevenness) but treat subnational units as independent of one another Challenge: Conceptualize nature of spatial dependence among units	• Recognize relationship between structures of spatial dependence and outcomes of interest • Elucidate whether sources of territorial variation are place-based or propagation-based, and what the underlying causal process entails
Analysis	Practice: Mixed-methods designs, where quantitative analyses draw on estimation techniques for time-series cross-sectional data Challenge: Incorporate spatial dependence and interactions into analyses	• Identify and specify connectivity among subnational units • Detect nature of spatial dependence in data: spatial error, spatial lag of DV, or mixed process, including spatial lag of IVs (i.e., correlated relationship, endogenous interaction, or exogenous interaction; Manski, 1993)

categories can help clarify the causes and consequences of territorial unevenness. Core research questions include whether this variation has local, contextual sources – what we call *place-based* processes – or whether the variation is due to factors that help or hinder the diffusion, spread, transfer, or spillover of the outcome of interest – what we call *propagation-based* processes. The section on theory argues that more deliberate attention to the role of space can generate shifts in our framework of analysis and yield valuable insights about causation in both place- and propagation-based processes. Lastly, we examine tools for exploratory and confirmatory spatial analysis, focusing on how a variety of techniques can advance quantitative analyses of spatial patterns in the data.

Across all three stages of research design, we draw on concrete examples to illustrate our points, including an extended analysis of homicide rates across Mexico's municipalities.

2.1 CONCEPTUALIZATION: INCLUDING SPACE IN CONCEPT FORMATION

The subnational turn has sparked a lively debate about concept formation. One important debate in subnational comparative analyses centers on whether and how concepts initially formulated at the national level can "travel" to subnational units. The classic issue in comparative politics concerns whether concepts can usefully be applied to different historical and cultural contexts without the risk of "stretching" (Sartori, 1970). This debate has recently been broadened to the question of whether concepts can travel across levels of analysis (e.g., Hilgers, 2011; Gibson & Suárez-Cao, 2010). Sartori (2005 [1976]) was highly skeptical about applying concepts developed for the national arena – like democracy – to subnational units. He specifically cautions against "jump unit fallacies," where "a sub-state, i.e. a member of a federal state, is made equal to a sovereign state." Discussing politics in the US South, Sartori stated that "with respect to 'democracy' ... the single states are granted only a subordinate and limited autonomy. Hence Florida or Louisiana or Mississippi ... are not states in the sense in which Mexico and Tanzania are such" (Sartori, 2005 [1976], p. 73). In light of a wealth of empirical evidence demonstrating territorial unevenness in democratization (e.g., Lankina & Getachew, 2006; Gervasoni, 2010; Giraudy, 2010; Schedler, 2014), however, the idea that we cannot meaningfully study intra-country variation in democracy is clearly unsatisfactory. Scholarship has therefore consciously discussed conditions under which concepts originally developed for the national arena can be applied to subnational units and whether acknowledging the presence of multiple levels of analysis (and power) creates the need to refine concepts, also at the national level (e.g., Harbers & Ingram, 2014).[4]

Beyond this debate, a more fundamental challenge arising from taking space seriously is choosing the appropriate subnational level of analysis. As Soifer's Chapter 3 in this volume points out, the issue of *unit selection* is particularly pressing in subnational research. Because many subnational analyses move into uncharted methodological territory, existing conceptualizations and theories may offer little guidance on whether the theory about a causal relationship of interest is *unit-independent, unit-specific*, or *unit-limiting*. In light of this, we

---

[4] Refining concepts appears to be the course of action recommended by Sartori (2005 [1976], p. 74), because in federal systems "each level is of itself incomplete and/or reflective of the other level. With respect to 'democracy', for instance, the state level has a wholly subordinate jurisdiction (a clear case of incompleteness)." Sartori's own commitment to multi-level concepts remains haphazard, however, as Gibson and Suárez-Cao (2010) point out. Even though the national level is supposedly incomplete without the subnational level, Sartori makes no attempt to incorporate this in his typology of party systems.

echo Soifer's advice that scholars make explicit which theoretical and practical considerations have entered into choosing the units for analyses. In the following paragraphs we also outline why distinguishing between *institutional* and *unbound* phenomena may be helpful at the stage of concept formation. Here a spatial perspective allows us to recognize more explicitly how a phenomenon of interest is anchored in space.

Even though GIS software appeared in the social sciences only around the 2000s, the idea of analyzing how political and social phenomena relate to space is by no means novel. A classic example familiar to most political scientists is John Snow's investigation of the 1854 cholera epidemic in London. By visualizing where in the city cholera victims lived, Snow was able to identify the Broad Street water pump as one of the culprits in the outbreak. GIS facilitates such analyses of spatial patterns by providing software that can store and process large quantities of information and connect them to space in meaningful ways. The potential contribution of GIS for the social sciences arises from the ability to connect non-spatial observations and their properties to a specific location. GIS is therefore "a methodological and conceptual approach that allows for the linking together of spatial data, or data that is based on a physical space, with non-spatial data, which can be thought of as any data that contains no direct reference to physical location" (Parker & Asencio, 2009, p. 1). The process by which non-spatial data is linked to spatial locations is called "geocoding" or "georeferencing."

The issue of how the phenomena we study are related to institutional or spatial categories has received relatively scant attention in comparative politics. Most comparativists intuitively choose to study subnational politics within the boundaries of territorially delimited jurisdictions, and the decision to focus on these units as the relevant objects of inquiry has often seemed so natural that it is almost nonconscious. Spatially uneven processes such as democratization have therefore generally been studied by focusing on provinces, or states – i.e., "the territorially-defined subunits of a political system" (Snyder, 2001, p. 94). Yet formal jurisdictions or administrative units are by no means the only lens through which we can study spatially uneven processes, and whether they are always the most appropriate lens deserves careful consideration.[5]

---

[5] We are, of course, by no means the first to point out that social, economic, and political phenomena do not necessarily align with administrative divisions, either at the national or the subnational level. Moncada and Snyder (2012) highlight that "coping with spatially complex, uneven, and unbound processes and flows" presents important challenges for comparative research. Rodrigues-Silveira (2013, p. 4) recently introduced the term "institutional unbounded-ness" to denote a "territorial mismatch between state administrative boundaries and social, political and economic processes." This is slightly different from distinguishing types of phenomena, as we propose, because the idea of a "mismatch" suggests that the relevant comparison is between institutional boundaries and broader processes, not whether the occurrence of the phenomenon is tied to the institution itself. For examples in criminology literature, see Mears and Bhati (2006).

To appreciate why this approach has been so prevalent, it is useful to consider the origins of many concepts in comparative politics. Comparativists – like Sartori – have generally studied concepts such as regimes, party systems, and parliaments in which the state and its jurisdictional boundaries play a key role. Methodological nationalism tended to assume that national borders circumscribed the most relevant social and political phenomena. This "whole nation bias" (Rokkan, 1970; also Snyder, 2001) took for granted an alignment of institutional and spatial categories. Theories of the state as well as of democracy thus tended to assume "a high degree of homogeneity in the scope, both territorial and functional, of the state and of the social order it supports" (O'Donnell, 1999, pp. 137–138). This assumption of homogeneity was always an analytic shortcut, even for advanced industrial countries. What is striking, though, is that not just phenomena clearly associated with the jurisdiction of the state were conceptualized and measured at the national level. In addition to regimes, party systems, and parliaments, phenomena such as crime rates, child mortality, and ethno-linguistic fractionalization were also conceived of as properties of countries. As Soifer highlights in his chapter, those in the latter category share the feature of being aggregates and thus raise concerns about the modifiable areal unit problem (MAUP).

Subnational research provides an opportunity to unpack more systematically how the phenomena we study are related to spatial categories. Rather than simply adapting categories to a lower level of aggregation, we suggest instead that it may be more useful to consider whether the phenomenon of interest is indeed related to institutional categories and circumscribed by jurisdictional boundaries. In geocoding non-spatial data it is important to make explicit to which spatial feature the phenomenon or attribute in question belongs. Comparativists have often intuitively linked non-spatial data to polygons representing formal, subnational administrative jurisdictions – sometimes without realizing that this move constitutes a conceptual choice, and that other options are available.

In line with the discussion of varieties of territorial units in the introduction to this volume, Map 2.1 offers an illustration of three different ways to leverage subnational research designs and increase the number of observations – as Snyder (2001) suggests – by focusing on subnational units. The first two maps in Map 2.1 reflect instances of subnational jurisdictional units – i.e., states and municipalities – and will be familiar to many comparativists. These units "have clearly demarcated, legally constituted boundaries" (see Introduction). Moreover, the boundaries are endogenous to particular institutional arenas and political processes.[6] The third map divides Mexico into equal squares according to the PRIO-GRID, a unified spatial data structure for conflict research, which

---

[6] Even though all subnational boundaries are endogenous to political processes, the extent to which subnational or national factors, as well as considerations of regional community or scale efficiency, determine jurisdictional design varies considerably across countries and over time. For an insightful discussion of this issue, see Hooghe and Marks (2016).

MAP 2.1 Different Approaches to Mapping Subnational Units in Mexico

has a resolution of 0.5 x 0.5 decimal degrees latitude/longitude or about 50 x 50 km at the equator. In contrast to the first two maps, these gridcells are "insensitive to political boundaries and developments, and they are completely exogenous to likely features of interest" (Tollefsen, Strand, & Buhaug, 2012, p. 363). Thus, whereas the units in the first two maps are politically meaningful, gridcells are intended to be arbitrary divisions of the territory.

The key issue to consider at the stage of concept formation is whether the phenomenon of interest is necessarily tied to an institutional arena. Even though political institutions are part and parcel of political science thinking, not all concepts are equally attached to the domain of institutions. Whereas some phenomena, such as cabinets or party systems, cannot be conceived apart from a political institutional setting, others, like criminal violence or disease, may not be circumscribed by institutional jurisdictions. In many other instances, the difference between institutional and unbound phenomena may not be so clear-cut, making it especially important to think about alternative levels of analysis.

Let us illustrate what this might look like with an example. One of the key insights provided by subnational research is that democratization within countries is a spatially uneven process. There is no consensus, however, about how democracy varies within countries. At least two ways are possible. In the first, variation in democracy is captured at the level of subnational jurisdictions. In the second, we might observe considerable variation even within subnational jurisdictions. Each of these two interpretations of unevenness implies distinct choices at the stage of concept formation.

According to the first logic, intra-country variation in democracy occurs because subnational jurisdictional units have democratic characteristics to varying degrees. Giraudy (2013) – following Goertz (2006) – conceptualizes subnational democracy in terms of four secondary dimensions: turnover; contestation for the executive; contestation for the legislature; and clean elections. These dimensions are all necessary and jointly sufficient to classify a regime as democratic. All dimensions contain an explicit reference to institutional categories, thus implying that democracy varies at the level of that particular institutional framework. An important implication of this conceptual choice is that only federal or politically decentralized countries display subnational variation in democracy (see also Lankina & Getachew, 2006; Gervasoni, 2010; Behrend, 2011).

An alternative view classifies democratic unevenness on the basis of variation in secondary dimensions. Goertz (2006, p. 107), for instance, identifies four secondary-level dimensions of national democracy: (1) competitiveness of participation; (2) executive recruitment; (3) constraints on the executive; and (4) political liberties. Whereas the first three dimensions are associated with institutions, the fourth dimension, political liberties, is not necessarily linked to an institutional arena. Liberties are under threat where the rule of law is weak and citizens fear for their safety and bodily integrity. Large-scale criminal, interpersonal, or state-sanctioned violence, such as exists in contemporary

Mexico, thus subverts democracy (Schedler, 2014). Yet, while levels of violence can be influenced by jurisdictional boundaries (Snyder and Durán-Martínez, 2009), violence itself is not tied to specific institutional settings (Messner et al., 1999; Baller et al., 2001; Mears & Bhati, 2006; Deane et al., 2008). Both violence and liberties can therefore vary within jurisdictional units, and, following this logic, even unitary countries and politically centralized countries can display subnational variation in democracy. This approach opens up the possibility of studying unevenness in democracy at the level of non-jurisdictional units, such as squatter settlements, shanty towns, or areas controlled or governed by non-state actors – e.g., gangs or criminal organizations.

An illustration of this approach is O'Donnell's (1999) conceptual map of the state according to what he calls blue, green, and brown areas, where each color denotes progressively greater deficits in the rule of law. State capacity and the quality of institutions often vary significantly within countries (e.g., Harbers, 2015). While residents of shanty towns may formally be entitled to the same rights and protections as residents of upper-middle-class neighborhoods, they generally cannot expect proper treatment from the justice system. This, O'Donnell argues, results in "low intensity citizenship" – often structured along territorial lines – which undermines democracy.[7] Even within jurisdictions, we are therefore likely to encounter blue, green, and brown areas – and hence, variation in one of the constituent dimensions of democracy.

The answer to the question about how democracy varies within countries thus depends, in part, on the conceptualization of democracy. Our purpose is not to take sides in the debate about which concept of democracy is preferable but to point out that making explicit the ways in which concepts relate to spatial features is not a trivial matter. How, why, and at which level variation arises is important if we are to develop a better understanding of the causes and consequences of spatially uneven processes. Moreover, how the concept is defined can be helpful in identifying the appropriate subnational unit for comparative analyses. If we are interested in examining how variation in civil liberties shapes democracy, it is probably appropriate to collect data at smaller levels of aggregation than provinces or states and perhaps at an even lower level of analysis than municipalities (e.g., localities, neighborhoods).

The distinction between institutional and unbound phenomena arises at a very early stage in the research cycle, and it is different from concerns about the modifiable areal unit problem. Soifer's Chapter 3 focuses primarily on relationships between variables and on spelling out at which level the mechanism proposed by a given theory operates. Our focus until now, by contrast, has been univariate and conceptual. Questions about how

---

[7] O'Donnell (1999) identifies Bolivia, Colombia, and Peru as countries characterized by extreme territorial heterogeneity. Yet, when the paper was first published in 1993, political decentralization in these countries was in its infancy and limited primarily to the municipal level. "Brown areas" therefore do not correspond to subnational jurisdictions.

phenomena are anchored in space thus arise even *prior* to the formulation of causal arguments.

What level of analysis is appropriate depends fundamentally on the research problem at hand. Ideally, theory relevant to answering the research question would guide selection. Yet, practical considerations like data availability may restrict choices (Baller et al., 2001, p. 569; see also Soifer, Chapter 3 in this volume). Still, from a spatial perspective, researchers should be wary of two common pitfalls when selecting levels of analysis: (1) selecting areas that are *too large*; and (2) selecting areas that are *too small*. If the research examines an individual-level phenomenon, even small areal units may overlook individual-level variation, and any attempt at causal inferences may be vulnerable to an ecological fallacy (King, 1997). Similarly, if the chosen areal unit is too large, meaningful variation in an outcome of interest at a lower level of aggregation remains unseen. Alternately, if units are too small and a researcher examines a phenomenon covering geographic areas larger than the chosen level of analysis, then splitting this area into smaller pieces will artificially produce spatial autocorrelation.

While remaining cognizant of these pitfalls, scholars might also consider the following practical criteria when choosing levels of analysis: (1) what level of analysis maximizes the number of observations; (2) what is the lowest level of analysis that still offers contiguous areas across the full national territory – i.e., complete contiguity; (3) what level of analysis maximizes comparability with existing studies; (4) what level of analysis maximizes boundary stability over time, thereby facilitating longitudinal studies[8]; and (5) what is the lowest level of analysis that still offers data availability, maximizing opportunities to "scale up" in the future. For most research questions, there will be trade-offs among these criteria, and scholars may seek to balance them in different ways. For many studies, multiple levels of analysis are plausible choices. Explicit attention to these issues, however, and a discussion of how tension between criteria for selecting levels of analysis is resolved will contribute not only to transparency but also to the accumulation of knowledge about core concepts and theories.

2.2   THEORY: RECOGNIZING SPATIAL DEPENDENCE IN CAUSAL ARGUMENTS

The key analytic insight of spatial analysis is the spatially dependent structure of data. Contrary to conventional regression analysis where individual observations are regarded as distributed independently, spatial analysis explicitly acknowledges that observations are connected in space. In this regard, spatial analysis shares important conceptual and analytic features with network, temporal, and multilevel analysis. Whereas network analysis

---

[8] See Weidmann, Kuse, and Gleditsch (2010) for an approach that accounts for changing boundaries over time.

emphasizes social ties among observations, temporal analysis examines the influence of past aspects of a unit on present aspects of the unit, and multilevel analysis examines the embeddedness of observations in vertical structures, spatial analysis allows scholars to examine horizontal cross-unit interactions between observations located in space. Spatial dependence, similar to other types of dependent structures, is seen as both substantively meaningful and a methodological challenge that requires the use of diagnostic tools to determine appropriate modeling techniques.

To be sure, in his seminal piece on subnational research, Snyder (2001) highlighted the interdependence of subnational units. Yet his article was geared more toward small-N, controlled comparisons, and the implications of dependent or independent data structures may not resonate as strongly with scholars pursuing small-N work as they might for scholars pursuing large-N statistical analyses.[9] More recently, Moncada and Snyder (2012) note that much subnational work has progressed to mixed-methods designs, integrating small-N, qualitative techniques with large-N, quantitative ones (see also the Introduction to this volume). Still, the issue of the dependent structure of subnational data and the nature of spatial dynamics has received limited attention in subnational research. Thus, despite drawing scholarly attention to the analytic leverage gained from "scaling down" and to the added leverage of multi-method research designs, subnational research in comparative politics – especially quantitative work – has largely ignored the structural dependence among observations. As we noted in the introduction to this chapter, it is precisely in the subnational context where we might expect territorial boundaries to be permeable and geographic units to be dependent – and therefore spatial analysis to be especially relevant.

Acknowledging that subnational units may be dependent raises questions about how outcomes of interest are distributed across space and why different types of spatial patterns emerge. Outcomes of interest may cluster in space in three principal ways. Figure 2.1 shows three stylized graphs (a–c, from left to right); each square within each of the three graphs represents a territorial unit. If there is no clustering, then we observe spatial randomness (a). That is, the outcome of interest exhibits no dependence on the underlying spatial structure. However, if high values of the outcome of interest tend to appear close to other high values, and low values near other low values, then the data exhibit clustering of similar values (b). By contrast, if high and low values appear near each other, then there is clustering of dissimilar values, as in c (see, e.g., Griffith, 1987, p. 37; Darmofal, 2015). These stylized patterns offer simplified versions of the different types of spatial patterns in cluster maps generated by

---

[9] Though Franzese and Hays (2008, pp. 756, 760 n. 33) warn that even qualitative studies that neglect interdependence are vulnerable to biased estimates in the form of an inflated impression of the weight of nonspatial factors.

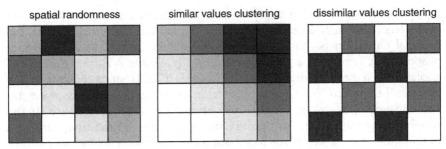

FIGURE 2.1 Varieties of Clustering Patterns

using the local indicators of spatial autocorrelation (LISA values, which we discuss in the analysis of Exploratory Spatial Analysis in Section 2.3).

Turning to more theory-oriented concerns, "[t]o interpret spatial patterns, we need spatial theories" (Logan et al., 2010, p. 15). From a spatial perspective, the causal process producing a spatial pattern of interest may come in two forms: (1) place-based, and (2) propagation-based. While theoretically distinct, empirically these two types of processes are not mutually exclusive, and may be present at the same time. Questions about place-based processes ask whether there is something about a particular area or region that creates a similar data-generating process for a set of units within that area, thereby producing a similar pattern in an outcome of interest across neighboring territorial units. In this respect, place-based relationships are instances of what Manski calls "correlated relationships" or what Franzese and Hays call "common exposure." In practice, questions about place-based processes essentially try to identify a regional omitted variable. For instance, fertile soil is conducive to agriculture, which in turn contributes to the emergence of certain social structures (e.g., reliance on non-free labor and inequality) and thus encourages particular types of political order (e.g., strong local elites). Soil characteristics may vary across regions but not as rapidly as variation in administrative boundaries, so a study of a large set of adjacent units that overlooks their soil characteristics might miss an important determinant of political patterns within the units of observation. The notion of "neighborhoods" implied by this example is common in studies of a wide range of phenomena. Conversely, different geographic or place-specific conditions might help explain divergent patterns of electoral behavior in neighboring units if, for instance, there is a structural or geologic feature of the terrain that produces a different pattern of interactions within that unit.[10] In this manner, research on place-based processes resembles work in the field of

---

[10] For an example of how soil characteristics have shaped voting patterns in the United States, see www.npr.org/blogs/krulwich/2012/10/02/162163801/obama-s-secret-weapon-in-the-south-small-dead-but-still-kickin.

international relations that explores whether there is a particular "stock" or characteristic of an area covering multiple countries and whether, in turn, this regional characteristic has far greater explanatory power than unit-specific properties or attributes (e.g., Kopstein & Reilly, 2000). A further example of a place-based process draws from Schedler's (2014) study of patterns of violence in Mexico. In his review of existing research, Schedler notes the "labor supply" of young men as an untested correlate of violence. If this supply is spread over, or proximate to, many neighboring units of observation, then a key place-based source of violence may be obscured by studies that ignore this demographic feature.

The second kind of causal process that produces spatial patterns, propagation-based, involves the spread or diffusion of a phenomenon of interest between or among territorial units. Unpacking this idea further, diffusion can occur in both (a) the outcome of interest (Manski's "endogenous interaction," i.e., endogenous spread or diffusion) and (b) a predictor of the outcome of interest (Manski's "exogenous interaction," i.e., exogenous spread or diffusion). That is, the outcome of interest propagates itself (endogenous) or, alternatively, a change in a causal factor in nearby units produces a change in the outcome of interest in the focal unit (exogenous). When analyzing a propagation-based process, emphasis is given to cross-space data-generation, e.g., spatial contours that affect the connectedness or dependence among units and therefore help or hinder the spread of either the outcome of interest itself or of a predictor of this outcome located in nearby units. Propagation-based explanations resemble arguments in the international relations field that focus on "flows" as opposed to "stocks" (e.g., Kopstein & Reilly, 2000). Returning to Schedler's review of research on violence in Mexico, he notes two major unanswered questions: (1) we do not know the boundaries or contours of the problem of violence in Mexico; and (2) while violence has generally been concentrated geographically, it has begun to spill over or diffuse to a larger number of units, yet we do not adequately understand how this happens. While spatial approaches can help answer both of these questions, they lend themselves especially well to addressing the second one, which concerns diffusion processes. Overall, a spatial perspective allows us both to conceptualize and theorize more effectively how geography affects the causal processes we are interested in.

These examples of place-based and propagation-based processes align with the way spatial dependence can be modeled mathematically. For instance, "unmeasured causes of crime [might] cluster in geographic space," resulting in a place-based process. Conversely, a "diffusion process that causes crime to spill over from one district to a neighboring district" yields an endogenous propagation-based process. "The former process is modeled by a 'spatial error' term, while the latter process is more closely approximated by a 'spatial lag' term" (Messner et al., 2011, p. 9, citing Anselin & Bera, 1998; Baller et al., 2001). More specifically, endogenous propagation is modeled by a spatial lag of the dependent variable; whereas exogenous propagation would be modeled by the spatial lag of an independent variable (LeSage & Pace, 2010).

In sum, spatially confined phenomena are associated with a place-based causal process whereas spatially interconnected phenomena are associated with a propagation-based causal process. The next section considers how the spatial error model captures the effect of spatially confined, yet unmeasured, variables and is thus especially useful for identifying relevant omitted variables and gaining leverage to generate new hypotheses and develop theory. The spatial lag model, on the other hand, captures propagation and diffusion effects. For both types of phenomena, theoretical arguments should explicate the causal process. Spatial analysis, which provides tools for assessing causal processes of diffusion and reciprocal influence across subnational units, is therefore especially useful for what the editors of the volume call a *horizontal strategy* (Table 2.2, Quadrant III) and a *reciprocal horizontal strategy* (Table 2.2, Quadrant VI) for subnational research.

2.3   ANALYSIS: IDENTIFYING SPATIAL DEPENDENCE

Because research in comparative politics has increasingly deployed mixed-methods designs, and time-series cross-sectional data have become a standard data structure, it is worth revisiting what a spatial perspective means for analytic techniques in the study of subnational politics. Specifically, how might scholars go about operationalizing the spatial structure of data and assessing the consequence of this structure, just as earlier methodological research placed a premium on operationalizing the temporal dynamics and serial autocorrelation present in such data structures (e.g., Beck & Katz, 1996; also Beck, Gleditsch, & Beardsley, 2006).

As with conceptualization, there are myriad ways to analyze "politics in space." We start with some exploratory techniques but then focus on deductive, confirmatory approaches, acknowledging that these and other tools can also be employed in a more inductive fashion. A running example explores homicide rates across Mexico's municipalities (homicides per 1,000 people), because violence has important implications for the territorial dimension of democracy (Schedler, 2014). From a place-based perspective, attributes or characteristics of a particular location may be predictors or determinants of violence in that space. From a propagation-based perspective, on the other hand, the attributes of a particular area encompassing several units may not matter, but the *connectedness* among communities may lead to high levels of violence in one community to increase violence in nearby communities (endogenous relationship), or, alternatively, the predictors of violence may exert an effect across territorial units, thereby influencing violence in neighboring units (exogenous relationship). Notably, existing research suggests that spatial patterns of violence were diminishing over time within Mexico since the 1980s and were largely absent by 2003 (Snyder & Durán-Martínez, 2009, pp. 266–267). Thus, 2010 presents a "least likely" scenario for finding spatial patterns of violence. If any spatial patterns are found, then, they are that much more remarkable and deserving of attention.

Exploratory Spatial Analysis

Exploratory techniques or exploratory spatial data analysis (ESDA) is "a critical first step for visualizing patterns in the data, identifying spatial clusters and spatial outliers, and diagnosing possible misspecification in analytic models" (Baller et al., 2001, p. 563). Although maps are not a necessary step, "[g]raphical displays provide an auxiliary method [to data tables] that may allow patterns to be discovered visually, quickly" (Ward & Gleditsch, 2018, p. 23). For instance, the decile map in Map 2.2 visualizes municipal-level data on homicide rates in Mexico for the year 2010.[11]

In the decile map, light shading identifies municipalities with low homicide rates, and the color darkens as the homicide rate increases. The darkest shades identify the municipalities with the highest homicide rates. Even a cursory

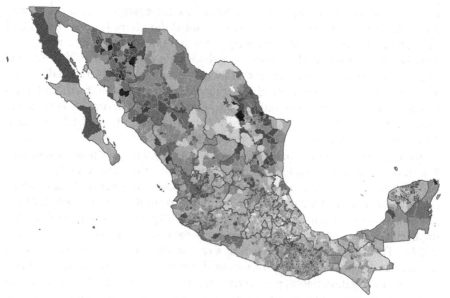

MAP 2.2 Decile Map of Homicide Rates in Mexican Municipalities (2010)

---

[11] Homicide data is from Trelles and Carreras (2012), and the municipal shapefile and georeferenced data are from INEGI (www.inegi.org.mx/geo/contenidos/geoestadistica/catalogoclaves .aspx; last accessed April 5, 2013).

glance at this map reveals concentrations of darker, violent areas in (1) the upper west coast of Mexico (across the states of Nayarit, Sinaloa, and Sonora), (2) the northeast (covering parts of three states: Coahuila, Nuevo León, Tamaulipas), (3) southern Mexico, and (4) portions of the Yucatán peninsula. Moreover, there are a few areas in northern, central, and southern Mexico that are almost clear of any color, i.e., have low homicide rates.

Helpful variants of this kind of visualization include standard deviation maps – maps that identify units that are one or more standard deviations above or below the mean. Even a quick glance at this kind of map would help identify spatial units that represent outliers or extreme values.

Two additional techniques include global and local tests of spatial autocorrelation, which can be used to assess the degree of structural dependence among units. Specifically, global and local tests of spatial autocorrelation posit a null hypothesis of no spatial dependence among observations, i.e., spatial randomness, and then test whether this null hypothesis is supported. One global test is the global Moran's I, which examines whether there are any regular patterns among geographically connected units (Moran, 1948; Cliff & Ord, 1981). If there are no regular patterns of spatial association, then the statistic is not significant. On the other hand, if there are significant spatial associations, the statistic can be positive or negative. A positive global Moran's I indicates that territorial units that are connected exhibit similar values on the outcome of interest; a negative result indicates territorial units that are connected have divergent or dissimilar values.

Table 2.2 lists global Moran's I values (and corresponding z-value) for homicide rates across Mexico's municipalities in 2010, as well as the average values for three time periods (2007–2009, 2001–2006, and 1995–2000), and the year with the highest value in the available data, 1996. All values are statistically significant at the .01 level.[12]

Looking only at 2010, the high z-value allows us to confidently reject the null hypothesis of spatial randomness in the data. This suggests that standard regression techniques would not only be inappropriate but would also overlook a key characteristic of the phenomenon of violence. Further, the highest Moran's I values appear prior to 2000, i.e., prior to the end of the PRI's 71-year rule that marked the national transition to democracy. Complementing Snyder and Durán-Martínez's (2009) suggestion that state-sponsored protection rackets that may have existed prior to 2000 were dissolved by the weakening of the PRI in the 1990s, these municipal-level data

[12] The population at risk in each Mexican municipality can vary considerably, so it is important to account for the variance instability of rates. Following Baller et al. (2001, p. 589) and Anselin (2005, p. 148), we do this by implementing an empirical Bayes (EB) standardization as suggested by Assunção and Reis (1999). Also, longitudinal comparisons are inappropriate if the underlying structure of geographic units changes considerably over time (see, e.g., Darmofal, 2006, p. 131 n.6). This is not the case with Mexico's municipalities during this time frame. Values generated in GeoDa v1.4.0.

TABLE 2.2 *Global Moran's I Values for Homicide Rates in Mexico's Municipalities, 1995–2010*

year	Moran's I	z-value
2010	0.0940	7.63
2007–2009avg	0.1003	
2001–2006avg	0.1002	
1995–2000avg	0.1306	
1996	0.1720	13.97

support their findings based on state-level data that spatial clustering of violence appears to be decreasing over time in Mexico. While these substantive findings are compelling and merit further exploration, we focus instead on the methodological lessons that: (1) longitudinal comparisons of spatial clustering is appropriate if the underlying spatial/geographic structure among units is stable (see note 12); and (2) the decision to focus on municipalities or states, or any other level of analysis, is a critical consideration, and ultimately depends on one's research questions and existing theory.

In addition to global tests of spatial autocorrelation, another useful technique for exploratory analysis of spatial dependence, is the *local* Moran's *I*, or LISA (Anselin, 1995). A LISA statistic provides information about the correlation of an outcome of interest among a focal unit *i* and the units to which *i* is connected, *j* (e.g., *i*'s neighbors), whether the association is positive (i.e., similar values) or negative (i.e., dissimilar values), and whether the association is statistically significant (see Appendix on spatial weights). Thus, LISA statistics help identify local clusters or spatial patterns of an outcome of interest. To be clear, while the global Moran's *I* may suggest little overall spatial autocorrelation in the data, LISA values can help identify smaller geographic areas where positive or negative clustering occurs.[13]

LISA statistics can be analyzed on their own to detect extreme values, but visualizing these statistics – for example, with LISA cluster maps – can offer a quick and instructive way to proceed. Depending on the depth of one's knowledge of the subject at hand, LISA cluster maps and other visualizations can be very revealing and may even serve to test hypotheses. If deeper or broader contextual knowledge is absent, however, then any visualization exercise is purely exploratory.

Map 2.3 reports LISA cluster maps in two panels.[14] In both panels, blank areas indicate regions of spatial randomness in the distribution of violence,

[13] The global Moran's *I* is the mean of all LISA values (Anselin, 2005, p. 141).
[14] Color version is available from authors.

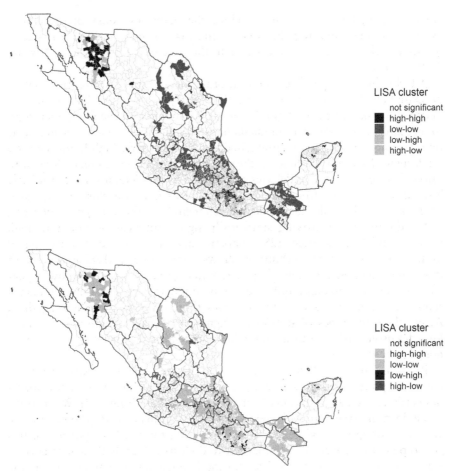

MAP 2.3 LISA Cluster Map of Homicide Rates

whereas shaded areas indicate nonrandom, statistically significant spatial clusters. All cluster associations are significant at least at the .05 level.[15] Note also that the shaded municipalities constitute the *core* of spatial clusters. That is, the shaded municipalities have a statistically significant relationship with the municipalities that border them, including those that

[15] All LISA statistics were generated using a conditional permutation approach (Anselin, 1995) with 999 permutations. Estimation was implemented in Python (version 3.5.2; Python Software Foundation, 2016) using the PySAL package (PySAL Developers, 2017; Rey & Anselin, 2007). All figures were generated in R (R Core Team, 2017), using ggplot package (Wickham, 2009).

are clear (i.e., have no shading). Thus, the outer boundary of the cluster extends into clear municipalities bordering shaded ones, and the true size of the spatial cluster is, in fact, larger than the shaded cores (see, e.g., Anselin, 2005, p. 146).

A LISA cluster map also contains information about the substantive content of spatial clusters. According to Anselin (2005, p. 140), this kind of map is "[a]rguably the most useful graph" in spatial analysis. In the first panel (top), for example, black identifies municipalities with higher-than-average homicide rates that are surrounded by municipalities with similarly high homicide rates (high-high). Medium shading, on the other hand, identifies municipalities with lower-than-average homicide rates surrounded by municipalities with similarly low rates (low-low). Other types of statistically significant clusters (discussed next) appear in light shading to distinguish them from the nonsignificant areas.

In addition to identifying statistically significant neighborhoods of high violence and low violence, LISA statistics also allow us to identify spatial outliers. The second panel (bottom) shows these outliers. Municipalities with low homicide rates, surrounded by ones with high rates (low-high) now appear with the darkest shading, and, conversely, municipalities with high homicide rates surrounded by ones with low rates (high-low) have medium shading. Again, the other types of statistically significant clusters (high-high and low-low, discussed earlier) appear in the lightest shading to distinguish them from non-significant areas.

Returning to the substantive issue of homicide rates in Mexico, the LISA cluster map presented in Map 2.3 provides strong evidence that complements our earlier, cursory evaluation of a map of the raw data (Map 2.2). Whereas we earlier identified the upper west coast of Mexico (from Nayarit to Sonora) as the clearest "hot spot" of violence, we now see that the northern portion of this geographic area constitutes the largest and clearest high-high spatial cluster. Adjacent to it, however, are less violent municipalities that do not fit the regional pattern and are therefore identified in the second panel as outliers, specifically as low-high clusters.

Additional insights can be gleaned by examining extreme values of LISA statistics – that is, by looking for the strongest, statistically significant positive and negative associations among focal and surrounding units. For instance, the five highest LISA values are all statistically significant: Four are from Oaxaca and one from Sonora, and all identify cores of high-high spatial clusters. Thus, from both the LISA cluster map and the examination of extreme LISA values, Sonora and Oaxaca would seem to be promising cases both for in-depth qualitative analysis and for more focused quantitative analysis. Moreover, visible clusters can also be seen that extend beyond state boundaries, including high-violence clusters in Coahuila and Nuevo León, and low-violence clusters across the country. These cases provide opportunities to explore whether formal state boundaries succeed (or fail) in containing violence. Notably, unlike the United States, where studies of homicide rates at the county level show that the south is a high-violence region and the northeast is a low-violence region (Land et al., 1990; Baller et al., 2001), no single region in Mexico can be similarly singled out.

Overall, mapping an outcome of interest in the ways illustrated here can generate valuable insights about its geographic distribution. This, in turn, provides a useful starting point for further qualitative and quantitative analysis.[16]

Spatial Regressions and Diagnostics

The techniques of exploratory analysis outlined in the previous paragraphs can generate a variety of insights about both the core research question and about case selection for further research. Depending on the question, these exploratory tools may even serve to test hypotheses about spatial patterns in the outcome of interest. Econometric techniques take the analysis several steps further, allowing us to examine key questions about the spatial nature of subnational politics.

Continuing with the example of homicide rates in Mexico, we offer a basic OLS regression analysis, diagnostics based on this regression, and then two core versions of spatial regressions that can be used to examine different underlying spatial dynamics: (1) a spatial error model; and (2) a spatial lag model. Only one of these – the spatial lag model – is related to diffusion, that is, the propagation-based spread of an outcome of interest from one place to another, and it is thus important to (a) distinguish between these two models and, (b) based on diagnostics of the basic OLS model, determine which model is most appropriate. Beyond these two core spatial models, we also identify several extensions of basic spatial regressions, including (a) a spatial Durbin model with a lagged dependent variable and lagged independent variables, (b) a geographically weighted regression that allows predictors of interest to vary in their effects across spatial units, (c) a spatio-temporal regression that includes temporal as well as spatial lags in order to analyze spatial processes longitudinally, and (d) spatial regression-discontinuity designs, in which a geographic boundary is treated as randomly separating a control area from a treatment area. There are other models we do not address, including multilevel models and models with complex forms of both spatial and network dependence. Disentangling the effects of different forms of dependence – separating the spatial component of an effect from a temporal, relational, or vertical (multilevel) component – is not a simple task, but there are feasible approaches. Multiple statistical models aim to do this, along with multiple estimation strategies for each model and diagnostics to facilitate interpretation (Franzese & Hays, 2008; Bivand & Piras, 2015; Darmofal,

---

[16] See Harbers and Ingram (2017a, 2017b) for specific strategies, including case selection strategies, using diagnostics of spatial regressions.

2015). Our goal here is not to provide an exhaustive assessment of all models and estimation strategies but to offer an introductory orientation to promising tools for exploring the spatial dimension of subnational politics.

Table 2.3 reports five models.[17] Drawing on existing research on the structural covariates of homicide rates in the United States (Land et al., 1990; Baller et al., 2001), the key independent variables in the models capture population pressures (total municipal population and proportion of the population that is male), socioeconomic pressures (average years of education, income per capita), and unemployment pressures (percent of the population that is *not* economically active). Following Graif and Sampson (2009), the models also capture migration pressures (proportion of the population that was born in another state), and building on conflict studies that find mountainous and other rough terrain is conducive to higher levels of violence (e.g., Fearon & Laitin, 2003), two variables capture elevation and the unevenness of the terrain (altitude and the standard deviation of altitude). The goal is not to provide the best specification of a model of homicide rates but instead to offer a reasonable approximation of such a model with the purpose of assessing the role of space in explaining patterns in this violence.

Across the models, the predictors of homicide rates are of less interest for our current purposes than determining the nature of spatial autocorrelation. The first model reports a basic OLS estimation (OLS1). Moran's *I* of the residuals measures remaining spatial autocorrelation unaccounted for by the variables in the model; the value of 0.0731 is highly statistically significant ($p<0.001$), strongly suggesting a positive spatial association not captured by the model. OLS2 reports an OLS model with a region dummy (0,1) where 1 captures states in Map 2.2 with high levels of violence (Chihuahua, Durango, Guerrero, Jalisco, Michoacán, Nuevo León, Sinaloa, Sonora, and Tamaulipas). That is, OLS2 reflects a common practice among researchers who attempt to account for regional effects by adding a simple dummy variable for a particular region or set of geographic units.[18]

However, diagnostics of the basic OLS model (OLS1) based on a classical Lagrange Multiplier (LM) test identify what kind of model may best capture the spatial dependence in the data. In other words, examination of the residuals helps test for spatial autocorrelation and determine which form of spatial dependence is present in the data. The LM test accomplishes this task, and two forms of the test distinguish between "spatial lag" and "spatial error" types of spatial dependence (Anselin, 1988; Baller et al., 2001, p. 590).[19]

---

[17] All models run in R (R Core Team, 2017); spatial statistics and models generated using package *spdep* (Bivand & Piras, 2015).

[18] A similar model with a dummy for all northern Mexican states bordering the United States, not reported here, showed no meaningful differences.

[19] Prior studies refer to the spatial error model also as a "spatial disturbance" model (see, e.g., Baller et al., 2001). Network analysts also refer to these models as "network effects" and "network disturbance" models (e.g., Dow, 2007).

TABLE 2.3 *Models of Municipal Homicide Rates in Mexico*[20]

y = homicide rate	OLS1	OLS2	SEM	SLM1	SLM2
(Intercept)	1.95**	1.91**	1.96**	1.83***	1.83***
	(0.66)	(0.66)	(0.69)	(0.49)	(0.65)
Population	-0.61***	-0.61***	-0.61***	-0.56***	-0.56***
	(0.01)	(0.01)	(0.02)	(0.02)	(0.02)
% male	-1.30	-1.25	-1.59	-0.48	-0.47
	(1.15)	(1.16)	(1.22)	(0.87)	(1.15)
% out of state	0.00	0.00	0.00	0.01	0.01
	(0.02)	(0.02)	(0.02)	(0.01)	(0.02)
Education	-0.07***	-0.07***	-0.07***	-0.07***	-0.07***
	(0.02)	(0.02)	(0.02)	(0.02)	(0.02)
Economic Inactivity	-0.52	-0.53	-0.54	-0.57	-0.57
	(0.38)	(0.38)	(0.39)	(0.36)	(0.37)
Income	0.45***	0.45***	0.45***	0.39***	0.39***
	(0.04)	(0.04)	(0.04)	(0.04)	(0.04)
Inequality (2005)	-1.25***	-1.25***	-1.18**	-1.07**	-1.07**
	(0.34)	(0.34)	(0.37)	(0.33)	(0.33)
Altitude	0.00	0.00	0.00	0.00	0.00
	(0.00)	(0.00)	(0.00)	(0.00)	(0.00)
Uneven terrain	-0.01	-0.01	-0.01	-0.02	-0.02
	(0.01)	(0.01)	(0.01)	(0.01)	(0.01)
Region		-0.02			
		(0.04)			
Lambda			0.17***		
			(0.03)		
Rho				0.16***	0.16***
				(0.02)	(0.03)
N	2455	2455	2455	2455	2455
RMSE	0.8163	0.8164	0.8076	0.8039	.8057
AIC	5982.26	5984.02	5954.19	5930.83	n/a
Moran's *I* (residuals)	0.0731	0.0733	-0.0057	-0.0068	-0.0076
Moran's *I* (p-value)	0.000	0.000	0.671	0.611	0.564

Note: *p<.05 **p<.01 ***p<.001

For all practical purposes, researchers need only consult the LM tests. Here, LM tests using a spatial weights matrix (W) based on simple rook-1 contiguity

[20] All measures are for 2010 unless otherwise noted. Population = total population, logged; % males = percentage of total population that is male; % out of state = percentage of total population that reported being born out of state; Education = average years of education; Economic Inactivity = % of total population classified as not economically active; Income = per capita income in 2005 in US dollars (logged); Inequality = Gini coefficient for 2005; Altitude = average altitude above sea level among localities in municipality; Uneven terrain = standard deviation of altitude among localities in a municipality.

(see Appendix) produced the following results: LMerror = 34.19, p<.001; robust LMerror = 0.34, p=0.559; LMlag = 57.82, p<.001; robust LMlag = 23.97; p<.001. The simple versions of the LMerror and LMlag tests provide an initial indication about whether spatial dependence exists in the data. Both are significant, suggesting both forms of spatial dependence are present. In these situations, we consult the robust forms of both (Anselin et al., 1995). Doing so reveals that only the robust LMlag is significant. This is good evidence that the spatial dependence follows a lag structure (i.e., Manski's "endogenous interaction") rather than an error or disturbance structure. This is also an indication that a diffusion or spillover process may be at work. Conversely, if the LMlag test were not significant, this would be a strong indication that there is no diffusion at work and that looking for diffusion may not be a fruitful avenue of further research. At the same time, the evidence we found of a spatial lag structure does not allow us to specify the exact nature of the diffusion process, because the LM test does not help identify the mechanisms of diffusion.

The next three models illustrate improvement in goodness of fit as the models capture the appropriate spatial dynamics. Although the spatial error model (SEM) was not the preferred model indicated by the LM tests, even this model improves the fit, reducing RMSE (or standard error of the regression), reducing AIC, and reducing Moran's I to the point that it is no longer statistically significant. Finally, the two spatial lag models (SLM1 employing maximum likelihood estimation, and SLM2 employing two-stage least squares) are the most indicated specifications and show further improvement in fit. Thus, even though LM tests indicate a spatial lag model (SLM) would be a better option, the SEM model turns out to be a better fit than either of the nonspatial models (i.e., OLS1 and OLS2), illustrating a point made by Franzese and Hays (2008a, p. 760) that, even if modest interdependence is present, any spatial model is better than a nonspatial one because, as they put it, "ignoring interdependence when appreciably present is usually far worse than imperfectly including it."[21]

Various extensions of the basic spatial models above (SEM and SLM) are possible, including a spatial Durbin model, geographically weighted regression (GWR; Fotheringham, Brunsdon, & Charlton, 2002), longitudinal models with a temporally lagged spatial lag (e.g., Franzese & Hays, 2008; Ward & Gleditsch, 2018), and geographic regression-discontinuity designs (Keele & Titiunik, 2015). Spatial Durbin models (SDM) incorporate a spatial lag of the dependent variable and also spatial lags of the independent variables (LeSage & Pace, 2010; Ellhorst, 2010; Yang et al., 2015). In this way, these models afford rich opportunities for exploring the spillover effect of the outcome of interest and of the dynamic local (direct) and neighbor (indirect) effect of explanatory variables. SDMs are thus considered the "state of the art" of spatial analysis

---

[21] Elsewhere, Franzese and Hays are more forceful: "Given any noticeable interdependence, then, nonspatial [least-squares] is an unmitigated disaster" (2008b, p. 6).

(Ellhorst, 2010; Yang et al., 2015). For an analysis of homicide in Mexico employing this technique, see Ingram (2014).

GWR offers a qualitatively different kind of analysis. Even when spatial lag or spatial error components of a model are significant, these models assume that the other covariates have a uniform effect across all units studied. That is, independent variables are assumed to have globally invariant or stationary effects. For instance, in the preceding analysis, education is assumed to have the same effect on violence across all Mexican municipalities. This assumption may be patently untenable in some situations, and it may be especially "inappropriate for modeling political behavior in a geopolitically diverse polity" (Darmofal, 2008, p. 957). GWR offers an alternative, allowing for "spatial variability of regression results across a region" so that "rather than [having to] accept one set of 'global' regression results, [researchers can produce] 'local' regression results from any point within the region so that the output from the analysis is a set of mappable statistics which denote local relationships" (Fotheringham, Charlton, & Brunsdon, 1998). Thus, where theory leads analysts to anticipate that the effect of a key explanatory variable may vary in significance or magnitude across spatial units or, alternatively, that interaction among key variables may produce different effects across space (e.g., Darmofal, 2008), a geographically weighted regression is appropriate. Ingram and Marchesini da Costa (2017) offer an analysis of homicide across Brazil's municipalities using this approach, and Harbers and Ingram (2017) provide comprehensive guidance for using GWR to inform case selection in mixed-methods research designs.[22]

Spatiotemporal models examine whether a spatial lag has a meaningful effect over time, offering spatial variants of the increasingly popular time-series cross-sectional analyses in research on subnational politics (Harbers, 2014; Giraudy, 2010; Ingram, 2013, 2016). A wide range of spatial panel or "space-time" models are available (e.g., Darmofal, 2015, chap. 8).

Finally, spatial or geographic regression-discontinuity designs (GRDs) rely on a geographic boundary that "splits units into treated and control areas and analysts make the case the division into treated and control areas occurs in an as-if random fashion" (Keele & Titiunik, 2015, p. 128), approximating randomized control trials, widely viewed as the "gold-standard" for causal inference. GRDs are thus a type of natural experiment that leverages the increasingly popular regression-discontinuity (RD) approach for causal identification, and the more convincing the case that the boundary occurred in an as-if random manner the more compelling the results. GRDs also resemble GWR in that GRDs estimate local effects on either side of a boundary whereas GWR estimate local effects for each unit (Keele & Titiunik, 2015, p. 152). To be

---

[22] GWR can be implemented in R with packages *spgwr* (Bivand & Yu, 2017), *gwrr* (Wheeler, 2013), or *GWmodel* (Gollini et al., 2013), or with a variety of standalone software packages (e.g., GWR4).

sure, GRDs are difficult to execute well, even more so than non-geographic RDs. Some of the assumptions of RDs are less likely to hold in a geographic context, and geographic boundaries often overlap with other bound and unbound phenomena, generating "compound treatments" which can make causal identification tricky (Keele & Titiunik, 2015, p. 133).[23]

Moreover, a tension exists between (a) GRD's emphasis on causal identification and (b) the goal of taking spatial interdependence seriously, as advocated throughout this chapter. Specifically, the experimental logic of GRDs rests on the assumption of the independence of units and also the stable unit treatment value assumption (SUTVA), which in part holds that there is no interference among units or, more precisely, that treatment in one unit does not affect outcomes in another unit. This assumption is violated if there is any feedback, spillover, transfer, or diffusion between units. Thus, the identification or anticipation of any spatial interdependence undermines the logic of GRDs. As Franzese and Hays observe succinctly regarding propensity-score matching techniques, "if interdependence, then not SUTVA" (2008a, p. 760). This tension between the goal of improving causal identification by using a quasi-experimental method like GRD, which assumes independence of units, on the one hand, and the goal of strengthening our understanding of how spatial dependence influences key phenomena of interest to social scientists, especially at subnational levels, on the other, suggests the fruitfulness of future research that focuses on how to combine GRD with MAUP (see Soifer's Chapter 3 in this volume), changing levels and scales of analysis, bound and unbound units, the nature of boundaries, the nature of spatial interaction, and GRD. Lastly, the effective use of GRDs in subnational research will also likely require strong local knowledge and substantive expertise (Keele & Titiunik, 2015, p. 128). This makes GRDs an especially promising tool for mixed-methods approaches that combine statistical analysis with in-depth fieldwork and also for collaborative research between GRD and substantive experts. As with many of the spatial econometric techniques presented here, their value and richness hinges on substantive knowledge of the subject matter and its spatial features.

2.4   CONCLUSION

This chapter develops a more self-conscious consideration of the role of space in the study of subnational politics, organizing the discussion across three core

---

[23] Keele and Titiunik use the example of media markets in the United States (citing Huber and Arceneaux [2007] and Krasno and Green [2008]), noting that the boundaries of these markets tend to overlap with county and, at times, state boundaries (Keele & Titiunik, 2015, p. 134). Researchers who want to examine the as-if random exposure to political ads from different media markets in the United States would thus need to consider the compound treatment of media market, county, and potentially state.

stages of research design. In the conceptualization stage, attention to space helps both to distinguish unbound from institutional phenomena and to select an appropriate subnational level of analysis. In the theorizing stage, attention to space helps clarify how structural dependence shapes outcomes and causal relationships of interest. Specifically, we distinguish between place-based and propagation-based processes to help clarify causal propositions about phenomena of interest. Lastly, in the analysis phase, a spatial perspective helps to identify spatial interdependence in the outcome of interest and also to differentiate among types of spatial dependence (e.g., spatial lag vs. spatial error). Summing up, taking space more seriously promises valuable insights for conceptualizing, theorizing, and analyzing subnational politics.

Although the spatial perspective arrived later in political science than in other social sciences, it is an exciting and welcome development because it explicitly addresses the dependent structure of the data which scholars in this field necessarily encounter. All data are embedded in some larger structure, which is why international relations scholars also find spatial analysis so useful. The spatial perspective is especially important in subnational research because the strength and density of the spatial dependence of observations is likely to be far stronger within a single country than across countries. Spatial tools and analysis thus hold great conceptual, theoretical, and empirical promise for subnational research in comparative politics.

APPENDIX

Constructing Spatial Weights Matrices and Spatial Lags

The operationalization of spatial weights is a key step in spatial analysis. Put simply, spatial weights capture the nature of connections among units. From a purely geographic standpoint, these weights capture the distance among units. So, for instance, a neighbor that is directly adjacent to unit A is deemed to be "contiguous."

Software packages for spatial analysis include various options for assessing contiguity or, more broadly, connectedness. Classic options include *rook contiguity* and *queen contiguity*. As the names imply, "rook" and "queen" are references to how these pieces can move in the game of chess. From the perspective of rook contiguity (Panel a in Figure 2.A1), unit 6 has four neighbors: 2, 5, 7, and 10. The weights matrix (Figure 2.A2) reflects these neighbors as 1s when reading across (or down) from 6. Note that units along boundaries have only three neighbors, and units in the corners have only two neighbors.

Queen contiguity (Panel b in Figure 2.A1) implies a more expansive definition of neighbors, including those units with which 6 shares only a vertex. Thus,

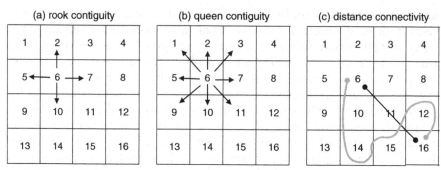

FIGURE 2.A1 Types of Contiguity in Spatial Analysis

	1	2	3	4	5	6	7	8	9	10	11	12	13	14	15	16
1	0	1	0	0	1	0	0	0	0	0	0	0	0	0	0	0
2	1	0	1	0	0	1	0	0	0	0	0	0	0	0	0	0
3	0	1	0	1	0	0	1	0	0	0	0	0	0	0	0	0
4	0	0	1	0	0	0	0	1	0	0	0	0	0	0	0	0
5	1	0	0	0	0	1	0	0	1	0	0	0	0	0	0	0
6	0	1	0	0	1	0	1	0	0	1	0	0	0	0	0	0
7	0	0	1	0	0	1	0	1	0	0	1	0	0	0	0	0
8	0	0	0	1	0	0	1	0	0	0	0	1	0	0	0	0
9	0	0	0	0	1	0	0	0	0	1	0	0	1	0	0	0
10	0	0	0	0	0	1	0	0	1	0	1	0	0	1	0	0
11	0	0	0	0	0	0	1	0	0	1	0	1	0	0	1	0
12	0	0	0	0	0	0	0	1	0	0	1	0	0	0	0	1
13	0	0	0	0	0	0	0	0	1	0	0	0	0	1	0	0
14	0	0	0	0	0	0	0	0	0	1	0	0	1	0	1	0
15	0	0	0	0	0	0	0	0	0	0	1	0	0	1	0	1
16	0	0	0	0	0	0	0	0	0	0	0	1	0	0	1	0

FIGURE 2.A2 Corresponding Spatial Weights Matrix (W) for Rook Contiguity

from the perspective of queen contiguity, unit 6 has eight neighbors: 1, 2, 3, 5, 7, 9, 10, and 11. Again, the corresponding weight matrix for queen continuity (not depicted here) reflects these units as 1s and all other units as 0s. Variations of both rook and queen contiguity can expand to include adjacent territorial units that may be two or more "neighbors" away. For instance, in Panel b of Figure 2. A1, rook contiguity-2 would add units 8 and 14 to the list of unit 6's neighbors.

Further, spatial weights matrices can also be specified using distance metrics. In these cases, the weights matrix is no longer binary but can include ordinal or continuous measures. One of the commonly used options is a spatial weights matrix based on Euclidean distance – the straight-line distance between units. Panel c in Figure 2.A1 illustrates this option as the straight line between units 6 and 16. Based on geographic coordinates (latitude and longitude), this distance is relatively straightforward to calculate. For very large spaces (e.g., regional or global analyses), calculations adjust for the curved surface of the earth to generate a more accurate measure of distance, the geodesic distance. Thus, both Euclidean and geodesic distances can be used to generate weight matrices different than those based on rook or queen contiguity. These distances can also be truncated at certain thresholds so that no effect is felt beyond a certain distance.

Yet another option raised in the measurement section is the possibility of generating additional spatial weights based on geographic features, georeferenced infrastructure, or other theoretically relevant aspects of the terrain. For instance, road infrastructure may be a more theoretically relevant way of measuring connectedness than either rook and queen contiguity or Euclidean (or geodesic) distance. This point is illustrated by the curving grey line in Panel c in Figure 2.A1, which represents a hypothetical road. Note that to get from unit 6 to 16 via the road, one must first pass through units 10, 14, 15, and 12. Several relevant implications flow from this fact. First, while queen contiguity and Euclidean distance would register unit 11 as being adjacent or close to unit 6, the road distance registers units 14 and 15 as closer than 11. Moreover, while queen contiguity and Euclidean distance would show unit 16 as the equivalent of two units away from unit 6, road distance shows these two units to be the equivalent of five units apart! Road networks are readily available in GIS format in many countries and can also be used to calculate travel time between observations. Further, other geographic features that are also readily available in GIS may be theoretically relevant depending on the research question (e.g., rivers and waterways, telecommunications infrastructure, sewage and other public utility infrastructure). For recent work employing a road network to construct spatial weights, see Zhukov (2012).

Regardless of how the spatial weights matrix is constructed, it is generally standardized by summing across each row and then dividing each element in the row by this row-sum. For instance, in the above rook contiguity matrix W, the sum of row 1 is 2. The row-standardized spatial weights matrix is then represented as follows in Figure 2.A3.

	row-standardized spatial weights matrix (W)																	Y		spatial lag (WY)
	1	2	3	4	5	6	7	8	9	10	11	12	13	14	15	16			
1	0	1/2	0	0	1/2	0	0	0	0	0	0	0	0	0	0	0		3	18.0
2	1/3	0	1/3	0	0	1/3	0	0	0	0	0	0	0	0	0	0		25	9.3
3	0	1/3	0	1/3	0	0	1/3	0	0	0	0	0	0	0	0	0		20	23.0
4	0	0	1/2	0	0	0	0	1/2	0	0	0	0	0	0	0	0		38	42.0
5	1/3	0	0	0	0	1/3	0	0	1/3	0	0	0	0	0	0	0		11	35.7
6	0	1/4	0	0	1/4	0	1/4	0	0	1/4	0	0	0	0	0	0		5	18.8
7	0	0	1/4	0	0	1/4	0	1/4	0	0	1/4	0	0	0	0	0		6	36.5
8	0	0	0	1/3	0	0	1/3	0	0	0	0	1/3	0	0	0	0	X	64	= 45.0
9	0	0	0	0	1/3	0	0	0	0	1/3	0	0	1/3	0	0	0		99	29.7
10	0	0	0	0	0	1/4	0	0	1/4	0	1/4	0	0	1/4	0	0		33	59.0
11	0	0	0	0	0	0	1/4	0	0	1/4	0	1/4	0	0	1/4	0		57	33.0
12	0	0	0	0	0	0	0	1/3	0	0	1/3	0	0	0	0	1/3		91	48.0
13	0	0	0	0	0	0	0	0	0	1/2	0	0	0	0	1/2	0		45	87.0
14	0	0	0	0	0	0	0	0	0	1/3	0	0	1/3	0	1/3	0		75	26.7
15	0	0	0	0	0	0	0	0	0	0	1/3	0	0	1/3	0	1/3		2	51.7
16	0	0	0	0	0	0	0	0	0	0	0	1/2	0	0	1/2	0		23	46.5

FIGURE 2.A3 Row-Standardized Spatial Weights Matrix (W) and Spatial Lags for Rook Contiguity

To generate the spatial lag for each observation, we then multiply the row-standardized matrix (16x16) by a vector Y (16x1) of a hypothetical outcome of interest in each relevant unit. Doing so for each observation (1–16) generates a vector of spatially weighted lags, or spatial lags (16x1). Note that the weight matrix and resulting spatial lags would look very different if the matrix were constructed based on queen contiguity, Euclidean distance, or road distance. How spatial closeness or proximity is conceptualized, and therefore how the spatial weights matrix is constructed, hinges ultimately on the research question and relevant theory. For an in-depth discussion of conceptualizing and constructing spatial weights, see Beck, Gleditsch, and Beardsley (2006), Darmofal (2015), and Neumayer and Plümper (2016)

BIBLIOGRAPHY

Anselin, Luc. (1988). *Spatial Econometrics: Methods and Models*. Dordrecht, Netherlands: Springer Science-Business Media.
Anselin, Luc. (1995). Local indicators of spatial association – LISA. *Geographical Analysis* 27(2), 93–115.

Anselin, Luc, & Bera, A. K. (1998). Spatial dependence in linear regression models with an introduction to spatial econometrics. In A. Ullah & D. E. A. Giles (Eds.), *Handbook of applied economic statistics*, pp. 237–289. New York, NY: Marcel Dekker.

Anselin, Luc. (2005). *Exploring spatial data with GeoDa: A workbook*. Available at: https://geodacenter.asu.edu/og_tutorials (last accessed April 2, 2013).

Assunção, R., & Reis, E. A. (1999). A new proposal to adjust Moran's I for population density. *Statistics in Medicine 18*(16), 2147–2161.

Baller, Robert D., Anselin, Luc, Messner, Steven F., Deane, Glenn, & Hawkins, Darnell F. (2001). Structural covariates of U.S. County homicide rates: Incorporating spatial effects. *Criminology 39*(3), 561–590.

Beck, Nathaniel, Gleditsch, Kristian Skrede, & Beardsley, Kyle. (2006). Space is more than geography: Using spatial econometrics in the study of political economy. *International Studies Quarterly 50*(1), 27–44.

Beck, Nathaniel L., & Katz, Jonathan N. (1996). Nuisance vs. substance: Specifying and estimating time-series-cross-section models. *Political Analysis 6*, 1–36.

Behrend, Jacqueline. (2011). The unevenness of democracy at the subnational level: Provincial closed games in Argentina. *Latin American Research Review 46*(1), 150–176.

Bivand, Roger, & Piras, Gianfranco. (2015). Comparing implementations of estimation methods for spatial econometrics. *Journal of Statistical Software 63*(18), 1–36.

Bivand, Roger, & Yu, Danlin. (2017). spgwr: Geographically Weighted Regression. R package version 0.6–31. Available at: https://CRAN.R-project.org/package=spgwr (last accessed December 7, 2018).

Cederman, Lars-Erik, & Gleditsch, Kristian Skrede. (2009). Introduction to special issue on "disaggregating civil war." *Journal of Conflict Resolution 53*(4), 487–495.

Cliff, A. D., & Ord, J. K. (1981). *Spatial Processes: Models and applications*. London, England: Pion Ltd.

Darmofal, David. (2006). The political geography of macro-level turnout in American political development. *Political Geography 25*(2), 123–150.

Darmofal, David. (2008). The political geography of the New Deal realignment. *American Politics Research 36*(6), 934–961.

Darmofal, David. (2015). *Spatial analysis for the social sciences*. New York, NY: Cambridge University Press.

Deane, Glenn, Messner, Steven F., Stucky, Thomas D., McGeever, Kelly, & Kubrin, Charis. (2008). Not "islands, entire of themselves": Exploring the spatial context of city-level robbery rates. *Journal of Quantitative Criminology 24*(4), 363–380.

Doreian, Patrick. (1980). Linear models with spatially distributed data: Spatial disturbances or spatial effects? *Sociological Methods & Research 9*(1), 29–60.

Doreian, Patrick. (1982). Maximum likelihood methods for linear models: Spatial effect and spatial disturbance terms. *Sociological Methods & Research 10*(3), 243–269.

Dow, Malcolm M. (2007). Galton's problem as multiple network autocorrelation effects. *Cross-Cultural Research 41*(4), 336–363.

Elhorst, J. Paul. (2010). Applied spatial econometrics: Raising the bar. *Spatial Economic Analysis 5*(1), 9–28.

Fearon, James D., & Laitin, David D. (2003). Ethnicity, insurgency, and civil war. *American Political Science Review 97*(1), 75–90.

Fotheringham, A. Stewart, Brunsdon, Chris, & Charlton, Martin. (2002). *Geographically weighted regression: The analysis of spatially varying relationships.* Chichester, England: Wiley and Sons.

Fotheringham, A. Stewart, Charlton, Martin, & Brunsdon, Chris. (1998). Geographically weighted regression: A natural evolution of the expansion method for spatial data analysis. *Environment and Planning A 30*(11), 1905–1927.

Franzese, Robert Jr., & Hays, Jude C. (2008a). Spatial interdependence in comparative politics: Substance, theory, empirics, substance. *Comparative Political Studies 41*(4/5), 742–780.

Franzese, Robert Jr., & Hays, Jude C. (2008b). Contagion, common exposure, and selection: Empirical modeling of theories and substance of interdependence in political science. *Concepts & Methods 4*(2), 2–8.

Gervasoni, Carlos. (2010). Measuring variance in subnational regimes: Results from an expert-based operationalization of democracy in the Argentine provinces. *Journal of Politics in Latin America 2*(2), 13–52.

Gibson, Edward L., & Suárez-Cao, Julieta. (2010). Federalized party systems and subnational party competition: Theory and an empirical application to Argentina. *Comparative Politics 43*(1), 21–39.

Giraudy, Agustina. (2010). The politics of subnational undemocratic regime reproduction in Argentina and Mexico. *Journal of Politics in Latin America 2*(2), 53–84.

Giraudy, Agustina. (2013). Varieties of subnational undemocratic regimes: Evidence from Argentina and Mexico. *Studies in Comparative International Development 48*(1), 1–30.

Gleditsch, Kristian Skrede, & Ward, Michael D. (2005). Visualization in international relations. In Alex Mintz & Bruce Russett (Eds.), *New directions for international relations: Confronting the method-of-analysis problem*, pp. 65–91. Lanham, MD: Lexington Books.

Gleditsch, Kristian Skrede, & Weidmann, Nils B. (2012). Richardson in the information age: Geographic information systems and spatial data in international studies. *Annual Review of Political Science 15*(1), 461–481.

Gleditsch, Kristian, & Ward, Michael. (2000). War and peace in time and space: The role of democratization. *International Studies Quarterly 44*(1), 1–29.

Goertz, Gary. (2006). *Social science concepts: A user's guide.* Princeton, NJ: Princeton University Press.

Gollini, Isabella, Lu, Binbin, Charlton, Martin, Brunsdon, Christopher, & Harris, Paul. (2013). GWmodel: An R package for exploring spatial heterogeneity using geographically weighted models. *arXiv:1306.0413.*

Griffith, Daniel A. (1987). *Spatial autocorrelation: A primer.* Washington DC: Association of American Geographers.

Hafner-Burton, Emilie M., Kahler, Miles, & Montgomery, Alexander H. (2009). Network analysis for international relations. *International Organization 63*(3), 559–592.

Harbers, Imke, & Ingram, Matthew C. (2014). Democratic institutions beyond the nation state: Measuring institutional dissimilarity in federal countries. *Government and Opposition 49*(1), 24–46.

Harbers, Imke, & Ingram, Matthew C. (2017a). Geo-nested analysis: Mixed-methods research with spatially dependent data. *Political Analysis 75*(3), 289–307.

Harbers, Imke, & Ingram, Matthew C. (2017b). Incorporating space in multimethod research: Combining spatial analysis with case-study research. *PS: Political Science & Politics 50*(4), 1032–1037.

Harbers, Imke. (2014). States and strategy in new federal democracies: Competitiveness and intra-party resource allocation in Mexico. *Party Politics 20*(6), 823–835.

Harbers, Imke. (2015). Taxation and the unequal reach of the state: Mapping state capacity in Ecuador. *Governance 28*(3), 373–391.

Hilgers, Tina. (2011). Clientelism and conceptual stretching: Differentiating among concepts and among analytical levels. *Theory and Society 40*(5), 567–588.

Hooghe, Liesbet, & Marks, Gary. (2016). *Community, scale and regional governance.* Oxford, England: Oxford University Press.

Huber, Gregory A., & Arceneaux, Kevin. (2007). Identifying the persuasive effects of presidential advertising. *American Journal of Political Science 51*(4), 957–977.

Huckfeldt, R. Robert, & Sprague, John. (1995). *Citizens, politics and social communication: Information and influence in an election campaign.* New York, NY: Cambridge University Press.

Ingram, Matthew C. (2013). Elections, ideology, or opposition? Assessing competing explanations of judicial spending in the Mexican states. *Journal of Law, Economics, and Organization 29*(1), 178–209.

Ingram, Matthew C. (2014). *The local educational and regional economic foundations of violence: A spatial analysis of homicide in Mexico's municipalities.* Mexico Institute Working Paper Series, Woodrow Wilson International Center for Scholars, Washington, DC.

Ingram, Matthew C. (2016). *Crafting courts in new democracies: The politics of subnational judicial reform in Brazil and Mexico.* Cambridge, England: Cambridge University Press.

Ingram, Matthew C., & da Costa, Marcelo Marchesini. (2017). A spatial analysis of homicide across Brazil's municipalities. *Homicide Studies 21*(2), 87–110.

Keele, Luke, & Titiunik, Rocio. (2015). Geographic boundaries as regression discontinuities. *Political Analysis 23*(1), 127–155.

King, Gary. (1997). *A solution to the ecological inference problem.* Princeton, NJ: Princeton University Press.

Kopstein, Jeffrey, & Reilly, David A. (2000). Geographic diffusion and the transformation of the postcommunist world. *World Politics 53*(1), 1–37.

Krasno, Jonathan S., & Green, Donald P. (2008). Do televised presidential ads increase voter turnout? Evidence from a natural experiment. *The Journal of Politics 70*(1), 245–261.

Land, Kenneth C., McCall, Patricia L., & Cohen, Lawrence E. (1990). Structural covariates of homicide rates: Are there any invariances across time and social space? *American Journal of Sociology 95*(4), 922–963.

Lankina, Tomila, & Getachew, Lullit. (2006). A geographic incremental theory of democratization: Territory, aid, and democracy in postcommunist regions. *World Politics 58*, 536–582.

LeSage, James P., & Pace, R. Kelley. (2010). Spatial econometric models. In Manred M. Fischer & Arthur Getis (Eds.). *Handbook of applied spatial analysis: Software tools, methods, and applications*, pp. 355–376. Berlin, Germany: Springer.

Logan, John R., Zhang, Weiwei, & Xu, Hongwei. (2010). Applying spatial thinking in social science research. *GeoJournal 75*(1), 15–27.

Manski, Charles F. (1993). Identification of endogenous social effects: The reflection problem. *The Review of Economic Studies 60*(3), 531–542.

Mears, Daniel P., & Bhati, Avitash S. (2006). No community is an island: The effects of resource deprivation on urban violence in spatially and socially proximate communities. *Criminology 44*(3), 509–548.

Messner, Steven F., Anselin, Luc, Baller, Robert D., Hawkins, Darnell F., Deane, Glenn, & Tolnay, S. E. (1999). The spatial patterning of county homicide rates: An application of exploratory spatial data analysis. *Journal of Quantitative Criminology 15*(4), 423–450.

Messner, Steven F., Teske, Jr., Raymond H.C., Baller, Robert D., & Thome, Helmut. (2011). Structural covariates of violent crime rates in Germany: Exploratory spatial analyses of Kreise. *Justice Quarterly, 30*(6), 1015–1041. doi:10.1080/07418825.2011.645862

Moncada, Eduardo, & Snyder, Richard. (2012). Subnational comparative research on democracy: Taking stock and looking forward. *Newsletter of the Comparative Democratization Section of the American Political Science Association 10*(1), 1–9.

Moran, Patrick Allen Pierce. (1948). The interpretation of statistical maps. *Journal of the Royal Statistical Society B, 10*, 243–251.

Neumayer, E., & Plümper, T. (2016). W. *Political Science Research and Methods 4*(1), 175–193.

O'Donnell, Guillermo. (1999). *Counterpoints: Selected essays on authoritarianism and democratization*. Notre Dame, CA: University of Notre Dame Press.

Parker, Robert Nash, & Asencio, Emily K. (2009). *GIS and spatial analysis for the social sciences: Coding, mapping and modeling*. New York, NY: Routledge.

PySAL Developers. (2017). PySAL—Python Spatial Analysis Library. Release 1.13.0 (May 2017). Available at: http://pysal.github.io/index.html (last accessed June 14, 2017).

Python Software Foundation. (2016). Python. Version 3.5.2. Available at: www.python.org/ (last accessed June 14, 2017).

R Core Team. (2017). R: A language and environment for statistical computing. R Foundation for Statistical Computing, Vienna, Austria. Available at: www.R-project.org/ (last accessed December 10, 2018).

Rey, S. J., & Anselin, L. (2007). PySAL: a python library of spatial analytical methods. *Review of Regional Studies 37*(1), 5–27.

Rodrigues-Silveira, Rodrigo. (2013). *The subnational method and social policy provision: Socioeconomic context, political institutions and spatial inequality*. Working Paper No. 36. desiguALdades.net, Berlin, Germany.

Rokkan, Stein. (1970). *Citizens, elections, parties*. Oslo, Norway: Universitetsforlaget.

Sampson, Robert J., & Graif, Corina. (2009). Neighborhood social capital as differential social organization: Resident and leadership dimensions. *American Behavioral Scientist 52*(11), 1579–1605.

Sartori, Giovanni. (1970). Concept misformation in comparative politics. *American Political Science Review 64*(4), 1033–1053.

Sartori, Giovanni. (2005 [1976]). *Parties and party systems: A framework for analysis*. Colchester, England: ECPR Press.

Schedler, Andreas. (2014). The criminal subversion of Mexican democracy. *Journal of Democracy 25*(1), 5–18.

Snyder, Richard. (2001). Scaling down: The subnational comparative method. *Studies in Comparative International Development* 36(1), 93–110.

Snyder, Richard, & Durán-Martínez, Angélica. (2009). Does illegality breed violence? Drug trafficking and state-sponsored protection rackets. *Crime, Law and Social Change* 52(3), 253–273.

Tollefsen, Andreas Forø, Strand, Håvard, & Buhaug, Halvard. (2012). PRIO-GRID: A unified spatial data structure. *Journal of Peace Research* 49(2), 363–374.

Trelles, Alejandro, & Carreras, Miguel. (2012). Bullets and votes: Violence and electoral participation in Mexico. *Journal of Politics in Latin America* 4(2), 89–123.

Ward, Michael, & Gleditsch, Kristian Skrede. (2018). *Spatial Regression Models*. 2nd ed. Thousand Oaks, CA: SAGE Publications.

Weidmann, Nils B., Kuse, Doreen, & Gleditsch, Kristian Skrede. (2010). The geography of the international system: The cshapes dataset. *International Interactions* 36(1), 86–106.

Wheeler, David. (2013). gwrr: Fits geographically weighted regression models with diagnostic tools. R package version 0.2–1. Available at: https://CRAN.R-project.org/package=gwrr (last accessed December 10, 2018).

Wickham, Hadley. (2009). *ggplot2: Elegant graphics for data analysis*. New York, NY: Springer-Verlag.

Yang, Tse-Chuan, Noah, Aggie J., & Shoff, Carla. (2015). Exploring geographic variation in S.S. mortality rates using a spatial durbin approach. *Population, Space, and Place* 21(1), 18–37.

Zhukov, Yuri M. (2012). Roads and the diffusion of insurgent violence: The logistics of conflict in Russia's North Caucasus. *Political Geography* 31(3), 144–156.

3

Units of Analysis in Subnational Research

Hillel David Soifer

The introduction to this volume shows there is a lively and growing body of scholarship that falls into the category of subnational research (SNR). As Snyder (2001a) argued in making the case for a turn to subnational comparison, "scaling down" opens up opportunities for higher-quality scholarship by allowing for better research design. Arguably, one way in which research design is improved is by giving scholars more freedom to choose the correct unit of analysis rather than limiting themselves to comparisons across countries. Yet, as Snyder (2001a) acknowledged, this increased choice has a risk: If scholars do not select the appropriate unit of analysis for their study, both descriptive and causal inferences generated will be seriously flawed. Thus, SNR needs some guidelines for selecting units of analysis so that scholars maximize the opportunities created by turning to subnational investigation while avoiding the pitfalls that come with flawed research design.

The introduction to this volume highlights the many strategies that one might take in SNR with multiple levels of analysis and the theoretically possible relationships among them, and Harbers and Ingram's Chapter 2 shows the payoffs from incorporating spatial processes that cut across units into our conceptual, analytical, and theoretical approaches to subnational research. This chapter focuses on the research setting where subnational units are treated as independent observations – what the introduction would call a "freestanding units" approach and Harbers and Ingram would call "place-based" processes – and explores in depth the stakes of choosing the right units of analysis, developing some guidelines for doing so.

I am grateful for comments on preliminary versions of this paper by participants at the two conferences for the edited volume, including Michael Coppedge, Thad Dunning, John Gerring, Edward Gibson, Kelly McMann, Lily Tsai, and Daniel Ziblatt. I also benefited from the suggestions of Vin Arceneaux, Sarah Sunn Bush, Gary Goertz, Melissa Lee, Rachel Riedl, and Prerna Singh, as well as audiences at APSA and the Princeton University Politics Department Qualitative Research Seminar, and notes from the editors of the volume and anonymous reviewers.

I analyze issues of unit selection with reference to the scholarship on patterns of subnational civil and ethnic violence. The political violence scholarship provides a useful context for exploring questions of research design because it has long focused on subnational comparison. It also is a propitious site for this exploration because it has approached the selection of units of analysis in many different ways. As we will see, scholars approach the study of ethnic violence by comparing patterns within a single country across subnational jurisdictions such as states (Wilkinson, 2004), cities (Varshney, 2002), and counties (Tolnay & Beck, 1995). Other scholars shift away from jurisdictions as the unit of analysis and instead approach the study of civil war through subnational comparison across countries (what Snyder [2001a] called "between-nation analysis") using various ways to divide up territory and identify zones of conflict (Buhaug & Rød, 2006; Buhau & Lujala, 2005). A third approach to the subnational study of conflict chooses as its unit of analysis the grid square, imposing a grid on the land area of a country or countries and making comparisons across square units (Gleditsch & Weidmann, 2012; Tollefsen et al., 2012). I use the various approaches to choosing the unit of analysis in the violence literature to identify a set of issues scholars engaging in SNR must take into consideration. Yet these issues are relevant to studies of other subnational phenomena as well.

I begin by discussing in Section 3.1 what geographers call the modifiable areal unit problem (MAUP), which makes it very likely that findings will change as they are measured across differently drawn spatial units, whether different in scale, or different in shape, that is, where the borders are drawn. Because of this characteristic of data generated from spatial units, the stakes of choosing the right unit are very high. Section 3.2 turns to the range of options; here I build on the discussion of institutional and unbound processes in Harbers and Ingram's Chapter 2. I distinguish between jurisdictional and non-jurisdictional units, giving examples of each and delineating some of the issues at stake in opting for one or the other, including the descriptive comparability of cases, the bundling of treatments that may characterize jurisdictional boundaries, whether borders are exogenous to the variables we wish to investigate, and whether borders can be defined in a precise, consistent, and replicable manner. Section 3.3 moves beyond the institutional/unbound or jurisdictional/non-jurisdictional distinction to the question of how to choose specific units of analysis, making the case that scholars should choose based on *theory*: They should opt for the level of analysis at which their proposed cause operates. I also point out the problems with choosing based on observed variation on the outcome of interest. Section 3.4 acknowledges the fact that theory does not always provide sufficient guidance to select the unit of analysis. Here, I identify several sources of theoretical ambiguity and suggest how they might be addressed. Section 3.5 makes the case for robustness checks, identifying several situations where they are particularly likely to be relevant and discussing what they might entail. Finally, Section 3.6 addresses issues of data availability, moving the discussion from the purely abstract realm of research design to more concrete guidelines for conducting research.

Before proceeding, it is worth defining the concept that lies at the heart of this paper. By "unit of analysis" or "level of analysis" I refer to what Gerring defined as "the sort of phenomena that constitute cases in a given research design" (2001, p. 160) or "the level of aggregation at which an analysis takes place" (2007, p. 214). The researcher selects the unit of analysis prior to identifying a population to study, selecting cases from that population, or collecting observations from those cases. For some research questions the unit is obvious: The political attitudes of individuals are studied, for example, by making comparisons across individuals, though these comparisons across individuals may then be stratified across some other set of collective categories. And inflation rates are studied by making comparisons across countries, though those countries may also be compared over time. Yet for other questions, the unit of analysis is far from clear: As Gerring (2007, p. 20) writes, "if one is studying terrorism, it may not be clear how the spatial unit of analysis should be understood." As will be discussed, scholars debate whether religious riots in India should be studied by comparisons across urban neighborhoods, across cities, or across Indian states. And, to name but one more example, it is unclear what unit of analysis should be used to study theories about lootable resources and civil war onset. The purpose of this chapter is to use the scholarship on subnational violence to develop guidelines for how scholars should make these choices.

3.1   THE MODIFIABLE AREAL UNIT PROBLEM (MAUP)

Studies based on territorial units are vulnerable to a particular problem, long recognized by geographers yet little addressed by existing subnational comparative analyses. Geographers have, for at least several decades, been aware of what is known as the modifiable areal unit problem or MAUP.[1] This problem derives from the fact that "statistical results can differ depending on the level of aggregation or size of the areal unit used to measure the data, as well as the zoning and specific partitions considered" (Gleditsch & Weidmann, 2012, p. 476). The MAUP is in fact composed of two logical sub-problems, as indicated in the quote in the previous sentence, though King (1997, chapter 3) shows that they are mathematically equivalent. One, known as the "zoning problem," stems from the borders drawn between units: Even holding the number of units constant, as borders are shifted the data generated from each unit on any variable of interest will change. This "zoning problem" is what is manipulated in the gerrymandering of electoral districts. The second sub-problem of the MAUP is the "scale effect" – changing the number of units, or

---

[1] See Amrhein (1995) and Openshaw (1984) for discussions of the history of the MAUP in the discipline of geography.

the resolution at which the data is collected, will generate "inconsistent analytical results from using data gathered at different spatial resolutions" (Wong, 2004, p. 571).

As the unit of analysis varies, so too will our results: Analysis based on geographic units will rarely be robust to scale and zoning changes. Relationships among variables – not just the sizes of effects but indeed the signs on correlations and regression coefficients – can change in dramatic and unpredictable ways as borders shift and as the scale of our analysis moves.[2] Results generated from an analysis at the state level, for example, can be wildly different than those generated from a municipality-level analysis, as seen in the top two panels of Figure 2.1 in Harbers and Ingram's Chapter 2. And results from a study based on 50x50 km grids can diverge from those generated from larger or smaller grid squares.

Though related to the ecological inference (EI) problem familiar to political scientists, the MAUP is distinct. In the classic EI situation, we have district level voting data and wish to know individual behavior. In other words, we know the unit at which the quantity of interest should be measured but do not have data disaggregated to that level. Ecological inference, in other words, is a data problem, and there are statistical techniques (King, 1997) said to mitigate it and allow the reconstruction of individual-level data from aggregates. By contrast, the MAUP is a *theoretical* problem: We are faced with the difficulty that our findings change as we analyze different data, and we do not know how to arbitrate among these contradictory findings.

Unless we have a reason to believe that one particular unit of analysis is "right" – that is, a reason to think that one set of data is more appropriate than another – we cannot move forward to data collection and analysis.[3] The only satisfying solution is to identify a compelling *a priori* reason to conduct our analysis with only one particular set of data, measured at a certain resolution and using a certain, precisely defined, set of borders among units. Only such a justification for a particular measurement strategy can help us avoid the MAUP, because it provides a credible rationale for considering only a single set of data and discarding all the rest. The stakes of choosing among the many options for possible units of analysis, under these circumstances, are very high. The remainder of this paper considers how we might make such a choice.

---

[2] Openshaw (1984, p. 22ff) shows that, by aggregating the same data into different sets of spatial units, he can generate correlations coefficients for the same pair of variables ranging from –0.93 to +0.99.

[3] King offers two proposals for solving the MAUP. One is to focus on "identifying or developing statistics that are invariant to the level of aggregation" though this is only useful (as he acknowledges) insofar as those statistics are meaningful in theoretical terms (King, 1997, p. 251). The second is to use the tools developed for ecological inference to transform data generated at one level into data measuring our quantity of interest at another level. But here, too, we need a justification for why the level we choose is the correct one.

3.2 JURISDICTIONAL AND NON-JURISDICTIONAL UNITS

SNR provides opportunities for better social science because it allows scholars to test their theoretical claims, where appropriate, at levels of analysis below the nation-state. As scholars design their research, they have the opportunity to choose from among a wide range of possible spatial units. A first set of possible units we might consider are what I call "jurisdictional" units. As discussed in the introduction, these include units of government administration and legal jurisdiction such as federal states; provinces or districts and other subnational units of governance; municipalities and other local governance units such as districts; school districts and other jurisdictions that exist to manage the provision of local public goods such as water; electoral jurisdictions of various sizes; and units at which information is agglomerated in public records such as census tracts. Other forms of governance also generate jurisdictional units; these include dioceses and other boundaries established by religious organizations, and boundaries established by non-state actors such as indigenous governance organizations.

Additionally, scholars might choose non-jurisdictional units for analysis – a point that the editors of this volume also discuss in the introduction. Possibilities include terrain-demarcated divisions – the classic jungle vs. mountains vs. coast divide in many South American countries, or the "hill" vs. "valley" distinction in Scott (2009), economic regions where certain kinds of economic activity dominate, regions where certain diseases are present, or regions that have a common history or cultural characteristic. Other non-jurisdictional units include urbanizations (which, as the urban studies literature has shown, can be defined in a way distinct from the administratively defined boundaries of a city), towns or villages, or neighborhoods.

Both jurisdictional and non-jurisdictional units are of theoretical relevance to political science. On the one hand, many of the questions central to comparative politics relate to the origins of political institutions and their effects on a wide range of aspects of political, social, and economic life; comparisons across subnational states, provinces, or municipalities (or other jurisdictions) can be used to isolate institutional variables of interest. For example, because Wilkinson (2004) argues that politicians are central to the onset and quelling of Hindu–Muslim violence in India, he analyzes its variation by making comparisons across cities and states.

On the other hand, many causal processes are "unbound" by political or administrative jurisdictions. Indeed, the two areas of research discussed in this chapter – civil war and communal violence – are often shaped by factors other than political institutions. Civil war may be the ultimate non-jurisdictional process, since battle lines, zones of control, and the determinants of victory or defeat often do not fall along jurisdictional lines. For this reason, in studies of civil war we see scholars defining the unit of analysis in various non-jurisdictional ways. One such approach defines the unit of analysis as the area where civil war fighting takes place, examining how conflict zones differ from non-conflict regions of the same country (Buhaug & Lujala, 2005; Buhaug & Rød, 2006).[4] The second, developed by Kalyvas (2006), uses the extent of control by armed actors to delineate boundaries that define units of comparison. A third approach, which I will discuss in more detail, defines the unit of analysis as equally sized squares in a grid covering all land area (Tollefsen et al., 2012). All of these approaches depart from the fact that civil war usually does not neatly follow administrative or political boundaries and that, for questions about the origins of conflict (in the former school) and its conduct in terms of violence against civilians (for Kalyvas [2006]), patterns across war zones, rather than across jurisdictional boundaries, reveal the true causal relationships.

It would be facile to try to make a general argument in favor of jurisdictional or non-jurisdictional units of analysis based on theoretical relevance. Still, for any given research question, theoretical relevance will point us toward one type of analysis or the other. In making this choice, several other implications of jurisdictional and non-jurisdictional analyses, raised by scholars in both traditions as they buttress their research design choices, are also worth considering. I begin with the question of whether units are comparable before turning to several issues relating to the nature of the borders of both kinds of units.[5]

The Comparability of Units

One concern often raised by skeptics of jurisdictional comparisons relates to the descriptive comparability of jurisdictional units. Most arguments in this vein focus on comparability across countries, stating that "the function and size of

---

[4] I set aside here a debate about how precisely to specify the conflict zone. Some scholars (i.e., Buhaug & Lujala, 2005) define conflict zones for each individual conflict event in a given civil war, whereas others (i.e., Buhaug & Rød, 2006, p. 322) instead define a conflict zone as the "polygon that encompassed all relevant battlefields for each conflict-year." The commonality between these approaches is their definition of units of analysis based on where conflict took place.

[5] If these issues were already not complex enough, scholars can also consider the possibility of going beyond the confines of SNR as defined in this volume and selecting *non-territorial* units, as in Dancygier (2010). To explain subnational patterns of immigrant conflict in England, France, and Germany, Dancygier emphasizes that variation in the nature and degree of conflict is shaped by characteristics of immigrant groups as well as by locality-specific characteristics. She argues that a similar density of immigrants in a particular subnational location will have contrasting political impact depending on *which* immigrants they are. By identifying these group-level factors, Dancygier can specify how much variation in conflict is and is not explained by characteristics of the local spatial context, as opposed to characteristics of immigrant communities. If the "subnational turn," in other words, has gotten us out of the "box" of only using countries as cases in comparative politics, we may also wish to explore the implications of breaking out of the territorial "box" to further explore non-territorial comparison.

regions vary extensively from country to country, so it might not be meaningful to divide all countries into smaller units" (Buhaug & Rød, 2006, p. 321). For example, the fact that "most of Niger's departments (first-order subnational units) are larger than Rwanda and Burundi combined" suggests that comparing them to subnational units in the latter countries might not be appropriate, at least for some research questions where the size of the unit matters (Buhaug & Lujala, 2005, p. 414).

Beyond size, one might also question the descriptive comparability of subnational units in countries with different territorial regimes, because the political attributes of those units can differ dramatically, with the result that they cannot be readily compared.[6] Gibson (2013, p. 18) pushes this line of argument to the within-country comparison, arguing that because the territorial regime in some federal countries can treat some units with more autonomy than others, comparison across administrative units even within a single country can be flawed if this is not taken into account.

The Nature of Borders

The nature of borders of subnational units raises several issues that must be taken into account in selecting an appropriate unit of analysis. Though many of these issues relate to jurisdictional borders in particular, the drawing of borders around non-jurisdictional units cannot be taken for granted either.

Bundling of Treatments

A central goal of comparisons across units in empirical analysis is to isolate a characteristic of those cases that might explain cross-case patterns on the outcome of interest. Yet when jurisdictional boundaries separate units, it is very hard to defend the claim that there is only a single difference between them. This is the *compound treatment problem* or the *bundled nature of treatment variables*. It is easiest to see at the national level: As Dunning (2012, p. 301) writes in discussing Daniel Posner's comparison of interethnic interactions in villages on opposite sides of the Zambia–Malawi border, "which aspect of being in Zambia as opposed to Malawi causes the difference in political and cultural attitudes?" But the difficulty of isolating a single difference between cases separated by a jurisdictional boundary also exists at the subnational level. As a result, concerns about the precise nature of the causal claim being tested can continue to lurk.

Non-jurisdictional units can, of course, be vulnerable to the same concern. It would be hard to claim that only a single difference exists, for example, between highland and coastal regions of Ecuador or Peru or that cotton-producing and sugar-producing regions of the US South are different in only

[6] I draw this language of descriptive comparability from Gerring (2001, pp. 174–175).

one way. Whereas scholarship on non-jurisdictional units (Berger, n.d.; Darden, in press; Dell, 2010) has explicitly grappled with these sorts of issues in depth, the more institutionalist arguments commonly tested using jurisdictional units of analysis have given less attention to questions about the compound treatment problem. If "specific institutional arrangements invariably have multiple effects," as Pierson (2004, p. 109) claimed, how do we pin down which effect of the institution is producing the variation we observe?

Drawing Precise, Consistent, and Replicable Borders

Another concern related to the borders of units involves the ability to draw them in a consistent, precise, and replicable manner. The issue of consistency arises for jurisdictional units when one considers the fact that the boundaries of political and administrative jurisdictions may change over time.[7] This in itself poses a problem for comparisons that require data collection across long time periods, since comparability is a real issue. Additionally, it suggests that we need to think carefully about the origins of border change, which I discuss further in Section 3.3.

Non-jurisdictional units are also subject to several concerns related to the drawing of their borders. These borders are difficult to define in several different ways that call into question the precision, consistency, and replicability of how these units of analysis are bounded. In terms of precision, it can, for example, be difficult to identify precisely where one neighborhood ends and the next begins or where to draw the line between "mountain" and "coastal" regions. Consistency is also an issue: For example, the threshold of population density used to identify city borders can vary, and even official data does not provide consistent definitions of these basic units across time and space. For all these reasons, scholars can fall short of providing fully replicable definitions of the subnational units they use. This, as discussed in Section 3.3, is one of the justifications for the turn to gridded datasets.

Exogeneity of Borders

Another concern about subnational jurisdictional comparisons relates to the exogeneity of the borders of subnational jurisdictions. Border change may not be independent of the political factors we seek to study in our subnational comparisons. This can be seen, for example, in a recent study of administrative unit proliferation or the rise in the number of subnational administrative units (Grossman & Lewis, 2014). The authors find that characteristics of local jurisdictions interact with national-level politics to

---

[7] This point is the central justification given by scholars who choose gridded datasets over subnational administrative units. See, for example, Buhaug and Rød (2006, pp. 321–322) and Tollefsen et al. (2012, p. 365).

affect the division of those jurisdictions into smaller administrative units. If borders are drawn in response to these local characteristics, then we risk serious error by treating them as exogenous – that is, as drawn independent of local factors. We might imagine that this concern is particularly serious where the borders of the units we seek to compare have been unstable over time and especially when they were redrawn co-temporally with the outcome under study.

A second aspect of the concern about the exogeneity of subnational jurisdictional divisions is that people choose where to live based on a range of characteristics of the locality. If movement across borders is large, and at all nonrandom, we might have reason to believe that there is a systematic logic to the relocation of people from one subnational unit to another. If that is the case, we cannot automatically treat characteristics of the populations of subnational units as independent of the institutions and context of those units themselves.[8] For example, a study that examined postindependence differences among villages on the two sides of the India–Pakistan border – a classic example of what Snyder (2001a) calls "between-nation comparison" – would be vulnerable to the criticism that people *chose* whether to locate in India or Pakistan, as seen in the massive population flows of the partition period.

In response to these threats to inference that are particularly likely to characterize research based on political and administrative jurisdictions, some scholars have turned to building spatial datasets with grid squares of various sizes as the unit of analysis. These scholars rest their research design principally on the exogeneity of this unit from any political or social process: As Tollefsen et al. (2012, p. 363) write, "Gridded data comprise inherently apolitical entities; the grid cells are fixed in time and space, they are insensitive to political boundaries and development, and they are completely exogenous to likely features of interest, such as civil war outbreak, ethnic settlement patterns, extreme weather events, or the spatial distribution of wealth." They also emphasize that gridded data provide a solution to the problems of precision, consistency, and replicability of border definition already discussed.

Another important response to these threats to inference represents one of the major currents of the subnational "turn" in comparative politics: the search for natural experiments. For all the reasons discussed in this section, scholars looking for natural experiments tend to avoid subnational jurisdictions as their units of analysis.[9] Instead, they seek subnational units divided by boundaries drawn arbitrarily and invested with as little contemporary meaning as possible.

---

[8] Experimental researchers describe this problem as "selection into treatment." It poses a problem not only for the study of spatial aggregates but also the study of individuals where location is taken as an outcome of the treatment under investigation.

[9] One exception to this tendency is scholarship on electoral institutions that uses regression discontinuity designs to explore the effect of district size thresholds as criteria for institutional assignment.

For example, Berger (n.d.) studies the effects of a British colonial administrative boundary drawn in 1900 (and erased in 1914) along 7°10' latitude, which "does not now and has not since formed an administrative boundary" (p. 4). By selecting this sort of border, Berger claims, his study can avoid concerns about the endogeneity of borders, selection onto sides of the border, and the bundled nature of administrative and political jurisdictions.

A third group of scholars, engaged in what we might consider traditional subnational comparison, responds to these threats to inference without abandoning the comparative study of subnational jurisdictions. Card and Krueger (1994), as discussed in the introduction to this volume, carefully design a comparison of New Jersey and Pennsylvania to explore the effects of an increase in the minimum wage that is sensitive to all the inferential concerns discussed here. And Snyder (2001b) compares the post-neoliberal political economy of four Mexican states and addresses these inferential concerns in the course of his detailed case studies.

3.3 THEORY-DRIVEN RESEARCH DESIGN

In addition to the task of distinguishing between these two broad types of units of analysis, subnational researchers face the further task of choosing a specific level at which research is to be conducted. In exploring these issues, this section builds on a shorter related discussion in Harbers and Ingram's Chapter 2. The first guideline for handling the task of unit selection is quite simple: The cause identified by the theory we have developed should guide the choice of unit of analysis.[10] King et al. (1994, p. 109) support this view, writing that, to select the unit of analysis, we should "select observations according to our explanatory variables." In other words, the unit of analysis should be identified based on our proposed explanation: The causal process we theorize should guide the selection of the units we will use to test whether that process is operating. A focus on the effects of a proposed independent variable is the dominant mode of research in quantitative political science and also characterizes much qualitative research (Goertz & Mahoney, 2012, table 17.1). When this sort of "effects of causes" research design is applied in subnational analysis, the theory in and of itself specifies either the appropriate unit of analysis or, as discussed in Section 3.4, the set of relevant units of analysis.

The Problem of Selecting Units of Analysis Based on Observed Variation

An alternative strategy often used is to select units of analysis based on observed variation on the outcome of interest. At first glance, this strategy seems to follow

---

[10] Note, once again, that selecting the unit of analysis is entirely distinct from selecting cases to compare. Thus, the large debate on case selection, which has centered around the relative merits of selecting on independent and dependent variables, is irrelevant to this discussion.

common research design guidance by ensuring that variation exists on the dependent variable. However, a number of problematic consequences can arise if we select the unit of analysis at which particularly salient variation across cases exists. Varshney (2002), for example, takes this approach in selecting the city as the unit of analysis for explaining variation in religious conflict in India. Based on a dataset compiled in collaboration with Steven Wilkinson of over 1,600 incidents of communal riots in India between 1950 and 1995, Varshney carries out what he describes as "a large-N analysis [that] can help us identify the spatial trends and allow us to choose the level at which variance is to be analyzed" (p. 6). He finds that although violence is clustered in certain states, "state-level aggregate data on deaths were simply artifacts of riots in a handful of cities" (p. 7). Based on this, he concludes that "the large-N analysis clearly establishes the town or city as the unit of analysis" (p. 7). Varshney, in other words, selects the city as the unit of analysis because dramatic variation on the dependent variable of interest exists when the violence data is disaggregated to this level.

Varshney's argument about the causes of riots in India, which emphasizes the nature of intercommunal social networks, has come to hold much credence in the field of conflict studies. My purpose here is not to challenge the empirical claim or to enter into a debate about the causes of riots. Instead, I focus on the logic used to select the units of analysis with which the theory is tested. There are two closely related threats to inference here, both of which relate to the selection of the unit of analysis based on observed variation in the dependent variable.

The first threat to inference involves causal processes operating at higher levels of aggregation. If we assume that some part of the cause of riots is explained by factors operating at a higher level of aggregation than the city – if Wilkinson (2004) for example is correct in arguing that state-level factors are also at work – then the selection for comparison of cities based on the level of riots they experience will lead to very misleading inferences. As Dunning (2012, p. 178) notes, in these situations Varshney's approach to unit selection will produce "overconfidence in conclusions about causal effects" and lead us to risk leaping too quickly to concluding that a city-level causal factor explains variation in riot proneness.[11] In other words, unless he can argue convincingly that supra-city level factors are irrelevant, Varshney is open to the criticism that his findings are not as convincing as he claims they are. The second problem is the logical opposite: What if the factors that make a particular location prone to riots operate at a level of analysis *smaller* than the city? In this case, analyzing variation across cities would understate the true size of the effect of city-level factors on riot proneness and thus bias toward the

---

[11] The problem here is the result of ignoring the possibility that causal factors can be assigned at the cluster rather than the individual level. Selecting a unit for analysis smaller than the level at which the treatment is applied will "produce a tendency to reject the null hypothesis even when there is no true effect" (Dunning, 2012, p. 178 n.21).

null hypothesis, meaning that we are less likely to find evidence supporting the effect of our proposed city-level cause.

While both problems can be addressed through some form of multilevel modeling or clustered analysis, this depends on the availability of information about the distribution of proposed causes and outcomes of interest at both the supra-city and sub-city levels. A better alternative is to avoid both problems if possible. The purpose of this chapter is to explore how we might do so, beginning from the guidance elaborated in this section that we should select units of analysis based on the causal process we propose to investigate.

3.4 UNIT SELECTION AND AMBIGUOUS THEORY

The previous section showed that the proposed cause should play a central role in identifying the unit of analysis at which a theory should be tested. But the theory a scholar intends to test does not always specify the choice of a single unit of analysis. The result is that the advice offered thus far – "let the theory guide the choice of unit" – is insufficient. The situations where this problem might arise yield further implications for research design.

One important source of ambiguity is the fact that some theories can operate equally well at more than one level of analysis. Take, for example, Varshney's (2002) argument that social networks, based most centrally on civic organizations that cut across religious lines, are necessary to prevent intercommunal violence in India. One can readily imagine that these networks exist to varying extents across a variety of levels of analysis. Still, there is an upper limit to where these network mechanisms could operate: The sorts of sustained and deep engagement that Varshney carefully shows are necessary for defusing conflict cannot exist at a national level or even at the state level in India, where states are as large in population as many countries. But the theory of intercommunal ties could operate at either the neighborhood or the city level, for example. Indeed, Varshney's case studies show that his theory operates at both levels, as seen in the differences across cities highlighted in most of his paired comparisons and also in the analysis of variation between neighborhoods within the city of Surat. Thus the theory in this instance does not provide enough information to specify a particular unit of analysis. There is no justification, based on the civil society theory of ethnic violence, for choosing between neighborhoods and cities as the unit of analysis.

By contrast, Wilkinson's (2004) argument about the role of state-level politicians in India in deploying the police to stop riots when their electoral incentives align with this response does point to one specific level of analysis at which the hypothesized electoral incentives should be assessed: the level at which the police are controlled.[12] The point here is not that Wilkinson's theory is better than Varshney's. I simply raise this comparison to highlight

---

[12] I set aside the local component of Wilkinson's argument to focus on the state-level component.

that some, but not all, theories lack sufficient information for choosing the best unit of analysis for testing them.

With regard to unit selection, three types of theories can be identified: (1) those that are *unit-independent* and can apply to any unit of analysis we might imagine; (2) those that are *unit-specific* to certain units of analysis; and (3) those that are *unit-limiting* in that they can be evaluated with certain units of analysis yet not others. Unit-independent theories are quite rare, because most causal claims are only applicable at certain levels of analysis. Wilkinson's theory discussed above is unit-specific: It can only be expected to account for subnational variation in riot proneness at the level of the jurisdiction that controls the coercive apparatus. By contrast, Varshney's theory is unit-limiting: It cannot be expected to apply across subnational units so large as to preclude the formation of social networks, nor in units so small that everyday ties connect all members of the community (pp. 50–51). Still nothing in this theory itself tells us whether it is best tested at a particular level between those extremes.

In response to this variation in the amount of guidance provided by theories, I suggest it can be useful to spell out explicitly the full range of possible levels of analysis at which a theory might apply, so that one can choose from among them in a strategic manner while explicitly ruling out levels of analysis at which the theory cannot be expected to apply.[13] This exercise helps identify the extent to which the unit of analysis is determined by the theory itself, as opposed to other considerations.

Other important sources of theoretical ambiguity also affect the research process. Two closely related ones are of particular note. First, theory might not provide sufficient guidance for identifying the best unit of analysis because the concepts of interest in the relevant area of research are insufficiently precise. Many scholars proposing a variety of theories for the onset or character of domestic conflict, for example, point to characteristics of the "local environment" or the "neighborhood" or the "region" or the "community." These concepts, however, are open to different interpretations, which, in turn, imply distinct operational definitions. Yet one struggles to find scholarly literature about how one should define these concepts and how they should be operationalized. Under these circumstances, a panoply of possible units of analysis seem equally appropriate ways to operationalize the comparative study of "neighborhoods" or "communities" or "regions."

Another source of ambiguity is related but analytically distinct: If our theories about why characteristics of "neighborhood" or "region" are relevant for domestic conflict operate through people's perceptions of their community, then we should also consider that people may perceive the boundaries of their community (or region or neighborhood, etc.) in very

---

[13] Again, the task here is distinct from ruling out cases to which the theory cannot be expected to apply – it is distinct from identifying either the possibility principle or the relevant scope conditions (Mahoney & Goertz, 2004).

different ways. Here, the problem is not that a theory may be appropriately tested at multiple levels of analysis or that we lack a precise definition of key concepts but that we need to figure out how our subjects define these concepts (see Arjona's Chapter 7 in this volume). There may be variation here across localities, and across individuals. In terms of the former, as Lynch (1960) showed, people's understanding of the cities in which they live can be mapped in very different ways. Thus, not only can "local contexts" that are said to shape people's attitudes and actions not be matched neatly to an administrative or political jurisdiction, but the very boundaries of "local contexts" are defined by different spatial features in different communities.[14] Moreover, theories that operate through contextual effects face what Wong et al. (2012) call the "pseudo-environment" problem: that local context is a psychological construct that varies across individuals.[15]

Yet these types of ambiguity need not lead us into anarchy. Instead, one should engage in a considered and careful choice from among the available options. An important way to do so is by explicitly engaging with context-specific evidence about where the "joints" of social and political life, and people's perceptions thereof, are found in a particular research setting.

An informative example of how to choose from among the many options generated by these two forms of ambiguity in theories of racial violence is Tolnay and Beck's *A Festival of Violence*. Tolnay and Beck (1995) seek to explain the determinants of lynching in the US South in the post-Reconstruction era (1882–1930), and they offer an explicit and detailed defense of their choice of *county* as the core unit of analysis.[16] Their justification has five distinct components. Two relate to issues of data availability (which I discuss in Section 3.6), but the other three defend the choice of county as the unit of analysis on theoretical grounds. First, Tolnay and Beck write that "counties historically have been important units for governmental administration, including law enforcement and criminal justice, within the South" (p. 39). This is crucial because one of the explanations they seek to test is that lynchings operated as a form of "popular justice" in which perpetrators responded to perceived failings of the formal criminal justice system. Thus, the county is the

---

[14] A thornier problem with operationalizing "local context" arguments is that the independent variable is a psychological context that varies across individuals. I set this individual level variation aside to focus on variation across time and space. One way to justify this simplification is to rely on scholarship that follows Lynch (1960) in finding robust and stable patterns of mapping across individuals in a given city and that such mapping rules vary sharply across cities even within a single country.

[15] Wong et al. (2012) address this concern by asking survey respondents to draw maps of their communities, which can then be used as the context for which contextual effects are evaluated for that individual. Though its utility may be limited to certain kinds of research, this is a promising approach to addressing many of the concerns noted in this chapter.

[16] In describing county as Tolnay and Becks's "core" unit of analysis, I refer to the fact that, while they use state, month, and year as units of analysis for the purposes of exploring variation, they use county data alone for hypothesis testing.

appropriate level of analysis for testing the claim that formal justice and other elements of government administration operated at the county level.

Second, Tolnay and Beck claim that "people, especially in the rural South, tended to identify closely with their county of origin or residence" (p. 39) Thus their choice of the county as the unit of analysis reflects the fact that people (presumably, whites) form their perceptions of political and economic conditions based on their evaluation of the county in which they are born or reside. Arguments about both economic and political threat as the reason for lynchings incorporate claims about how whites evaluated threats to their "privileged access to society's scarce resources" (p. 166). But this evaluation could, in theory be based on whites' perceptions at many levels – the neighborhood, the town, the county, the state, or even the South as a whole. As discussed in Section 3.3, this is an instance in which the theory of "perceived threat" does not specify a level of analysis. In choosing how to assess this explanation, then, Tolnay and Beck rely on the claim cited above that whites "tended to identify closely with their county."

This gives us a clear way forward and is a model that scholars should follow: to identify the level of analysis at which actors form their perceptions of relevant aspects of context in a particular setting. Still, it is worth noting that Tolnay and Beck provide no evidence to support this claim – it is simply stated that the county is the appropriate unit of analysis and that (quoting Charles S. Johnson) "the county appears to be a community in itself" (p. 39). The more evidence scholars can give to support this sort of claim, the stronger the defense of their research design will be.

The third justification for using the county as the unit of analysis is that the dominant form of economic activity in the county shapes social organization in fundamental ways. The claim is that it makes sense to talk about "cotton counties" and "non-cotton counties" and, in turn, to use the county as the unit of analysis to study how conditions in the cotton trade affected patterns of lynching. The argument that a dominant crop shapes social relations, of course, resonates with mode-of-production arguments made by many other scholars. But why do the causal processes underlying this relationship operate at the county level in the US South, whereas scholars like Kurtz (2013) and Shafer (1994) claim that sectoral effects on social relations operate at the national level? Here, Tolnay and Beck (p. 39) again quote Charles S. Johnson, who writes, "Although every county may have some variation within its borders, the type of underlying economy that dominates tends to enforce itself throughout the county and to be reflected in the characteristics of social organization." This seems persuasive until we notice that Johnson is the author of a statistical atlas of Southern counties from which the quote is drawn. One wonders whether Johnson's claim should be taken as fact rather than as historiographic interpretation.[17]

---

[17] This concern about selection of historical texts as evidence is carefully elaborated in Lustick (1996).

What can we take away from Tolnay and Beck's discussion of why they chose county as the unit of analysis? First, Tolnay and Beck center their defense of the county on the theoretical place of the county in each of the explanations they seek to test. By contrast, much other scholarship focuses the discussion of the choice of the unit of analysis on data availability. Data concerns are, of course, important, and Tolnay and Beck discuss them as well, but theory comes prior to data because it identifies the set of possible levels of analysis we should consider based on other factors, including data quality. Second, it is striking that this core issue of research design is addressed in just two paragraphs, even in this particularly careful accounting. While much ink is spilled on issues of case selection, discussions of the choice of unit of analysis are often strikingly thin, even in classic exemplars of subnational scholarship.

Because the options are manifold, and because the stakes of the choice are so high, scholars would be well advised to elaborate more carefully the logic underlying their choice of unit of analysis. Such a justification should include a discussion about the presence of the various sources of theoretical ambiguity discussed in this section in their particular research context, as well as an explicit elaboration of the reasoning used to move from what are often contested and murky theoretical concepts to operationalization.

3.5 THE IMPORTANCE OF ROBUSTNESS CHECKS

Because of the modifiable unit areal problem, we know that findings based on spatially demarcated sub-units (whether jurisdictional or not) are likely to be fragile. This has important implications when our theory does not clearly and explicitly specify the unit of analysis to be used. Because we have reason to believe that findings are dependent on how the unit of analysis is chosen, a way to reassure skeptics and increase confidence in results is to show that the finding also holds when tested using other theory-appropriate units of analysis. In any situation where the choice of unit of analysis is not fully determined by theory, scholars can strengthen their arguments by showing that the findings are robust across the range of units of analysis to which the theory can be applied. This could involve using multiple operationalizations of single concepts like "local" or "neighborhood" or "community" or by testing the same theory for multiple types of (appropriate) units. For example, the fact that Varshney demonstrates that his social network argument accounts for variation in riot proneness at both the city and neighborhood levels helps to increase confidence in the claims he advances. By contrast, a scholar who only finds support for the theory being tested at one of the possible levels of analysis can use this information to further refine claims about the scope of the theory being tested.

These robustness checks are especially important for scholars using the gridded non-jurisdictional data discussed above. Because the main advantage of gridded data is that its borders are exogenous to any social or economic or political phenomenon, there are no theoretical grounds on which to justify the use of one grid mapping over another. Beyond reasons related to data availability, scholars who choose to use gridded data can say very little about why they have chosen a particular unit size for their analysis. Confidence in findings generated from grid-based datasets cannot, then, rest on the theoretical logic for a particular grid mapping. For these kinds of studies, robustness checks can be especially important in making findings persuasive.[18] To the extent that a researcher can show that the finding is not an artifact of a particular unit of analysis, and that the modifiable areal unit problem discussed above does not affect the findings, the claims made will be more persuasive.[19]

3.6 DATA AVAILABILITY

Thus far, the discussion has been based on the implications of theory for research design. In practice, however, other considerations are also relevant. As discussed in the concluding Chapter 11 in this volume, even as new and rich sources of subnational data become increasingly common, scholars often face the problem that data is not available for the proposed indicator at the level of analysis at which they wish to conduct their research. Jurisdictional units often have an advantage in terms of data availability: Many measures of the quantities of interest to social scientists are generated by official government agencies, and the data is aggregated at various jurisdictional levels. This is true not only for electoral data but also for economic and demographic information. Data availability is an important concern for non-jurisdictional approaches: To study greed and grievance theories of civil war, for example, scholars have had to turn to proxies like satellite images of electric light as a measure of wealth (Gleditsch & Weidmann, 2012) and have struggled to compile data about the control exercised by armed actors (Kalyvas, 2006). Gridded data becomes especially scarce when one moves beyond very recent events, because satellite imagery and other sources are not available. This places important bounds on the utility of research designs using gridded units of analysis. Where data availability is a concern, I see four possible responses.

First, scholars can shift the chosen indicator for the quantity of interest to one for which data is available. For example, Buhaug and Rød (2006, p. 319) seek to assess whether poverty is associated with domestic armed conflict, yet they lack socioeconomic data at the grid level. Thus, they write, "we cannot test this conjecture directly." Instead, they turn to studying how local road density shapes conflict patterns, arguing that this taps "the nexus between another

[18] Buhaug and Rød (2006, p. 322) note, "Ultimately we might want to test various resolutions and compare the results," but neither they nor other researchers using grids have taken this step.

[19] Yet there is a deep problem here concerning how to evaluate these robustness checks: We lack a standard for interpreting mixed findings across them, and, even worse, we lack information on the distribution of results for all possible units of analysis that we might consider. For a parallel discussion about the lack of standards for evaluating mixed results in what he calls large-N qualitative testing, see Goertz (2017), chap. 7.

aspect of development and domestic armed conflict." Their response to the lack of data is to identify a proxy for the quantity of interest that is available for the chosen unit of analysis. This, of course, is common: Scholars interested in assessing relationships between certain objects of interest and committed to proceeding at a certain level of analysis must find a way to measure those objects of interest. Yet the cost introduced here is some slippage between indicator and underlying concept: In this case, we might wonder whether road density really serves as a good measure of level of development.

Two other solutions to this problem depart from skepticism about choosing sub-optimal indicators for the object of interest and seek instead to generate data for the preferred indicator at the chosen level of analysis. One way to do so is to assemble new data at the preferred level of analysis. Here, of course, there are obvious costs, and scholars are often reluctant to take this step, especially for research projects that cover subnational units in multiple countries or over long periods of time (Herrera & Kapur, 2007). The other data generating solution is to turn to King's (1997) strategy for solving the ecological inference problem by reconstructing data at one level of analysis from available data at a more aggregated level. Yet this is only possible where systematic (quantitative) data exists at the more aggregated level and where we have information about the bounds that the value of our quantity of interest can take in each disaggregated unit. Thus, while both of these proposed solutions to problems of data availability are plausible, in practice they are only likely to be applied under certain limited circumstances.

Given the important costs associated with these first three responses, a fourth possibility is to consider data availability as a criterion for selecting the level of analysis. In addition to the theory-based justifications of the choice of county as the unit of analysis that were discussed in Section 3.4, Tolnay and Beck (1995, p. 39) explain that their choice of unit of analysis was restricted in part because they were able to code the state and county where lynchings occurred yet lacked sufficient data to assign lynchings to smaller spatial sub-units like towns. Here, then, we have moved away from the purely methodological injunction to choose the unit of analysis based on the proposed independent variable to a strategy that also considers data availability.

Scholars, of course, often proceed in this manner and consider data availability when selecting the level of analysis. Still, it can be useful to spell out which of the choices about units of analysis are made on theoretical grounds and which are made for reasons of data availability. This is important not only for reasons of analytical transparency but also because it makes it easier to assess any threats to inference introduced by choices made. It is also a valuable practice because scholars who are not limited by the same constraints of data availability – whether because of new data collection or, alternatively, the extension of a theory to a new context where better data is available – need not make the same compromises. The result will be that imperfect tests of a theory can be refined over time – the very definition of knowledge accumulation.[20]

3.7 CONCLUSION

Snyder's (2001) article opened a robust agenda for subnational comparison. The empirical chapters in this edited volume, as well as the rich literature on which they build, show that SNR has allowed scholars both to ask new questions and to ask old questions at different, and more apt, levels of analysis. SNR has made possible better measurement and more accurate coding of core phenomena of interest in political science research. Still, if subnational research is to achieve its potential, it must leverage to the greatest extent possible the opportunities opened by the multitude of possible levels of analysis by choosing units of analysis in an optimal manner. This chapter presents guidelines for best practices as scholars seek to do so.

The choice of levels of analysis, as I have argued, should begin with theory – that is, with the causal claim one intends to evaluate. The issues raised by scholars debating the relative merits of jurisdictional and non-jurisdictional analyses, including debates about the nature of borders and the comparability of units, are important, but they should not be the primary determinants of the level of analysis. Instead, they should be considered only within the broader context of a research design guided by the goal of testing the specific causal claim being advanced.

But moving from theory to research design is not as easy as we might expect: For a variety of reasons detailed in the chapter, theories can provide insufficiently concrete implications for research design. One source of ambiguity is that theory can apply to multiple levels of analysis. Here, scholars should identify the multiple levels where it is possible to test their theory, as Varshney (2002) does in exploring both city-level and neighborhood-level variation in riot proneness. Sometimes the problem is conceptual: Many theories underpinning subnational research center on concepts that are too vague, fundamentally contested, or require additional contextual knowledge to operationalize in any given setting. Here, scholars need to spell out explicitly the steps taken in moving from theory to research design. This will allow the development of standard practices that can be considered across cases. It will also promote the collection of information about how to operationalize systematically a core concept in a particular research setting. Where appropriate, scholars should carry out robustness checks either at different levels of analysis or with different operationalizations of the same concepts. And finally, while scholars must grapple with issues of data availability, it is valuable to be clear about which choices are made for theoretical reasons and to

---

[20] I draw here on the inclusion of iterated hypothesis testing as a core element of knowledge accumulation, as stipulated by Mahoney (2003).

specify where data availability does and does not shape research design, so that scholars working on similar research questions with different data can effectively build on existing research.

BIBLIOGRAPHY

Amrhein, Carl G. (1995). Searching for the elusive aggregation effect: Evidence from statistical simulations. *Environment and Planning A* 27(1), 105–119.

Berger, Daniel. (n.d.). *Taxes, institutions, and local governance: Evidence from a natural experiment in colonial Nigeria.* Unpublished working paper. Essex University Department of Government.

Buhaug, Halvard, & Lujala, Päivi. (2005). Accounting for scale: Measuring geography in quantitative studies of civil war. *Political Geography* 24(4), 399–418.

Buhaug, Halvard, & Rød, Jan Ketil. (2006). Local determinants of African civil wars 1970–2001. *Political Geography* 25(3), 315–335.

Card, David, & Krueger, Alan B. (1994). Minimum wages and employment: A case study of the fast-food industry in New Jersey and Pennsylvania. *American Economic Review 84*, 772–793.

Dancygier, Rafaela. (2010). *Immigration and conflict in Europe.* Cambridge, England: Cambridge University Press.

Darden, Keith. (in press). *Resisting occupation in Eurasia.* Cambridge, England: Cambridge University Press.

Dell, Melissa. (2010). The persistent effects of Peru's mining mita. *Econometrica* 78(6), 1863–1903.

Dunning, Thad. (2012). *Natural experiments in the social sciences: A design-based approach.* Cambridge, England: Cambridge University Press.

Gerring, John. (2001). *Social science methodology: A criterial framework.* Cambridge, England: Cambridge University Press.

Gerring, John. (2007). *Case study research: Principles and practices.* Cambridge, England: Cambridge University Press.

Gibson, Edward L. (2013). *Boundary control: Subnational authoritarianism in federal democracies.* Cambridge, England: Cambridge University Press.

Gleditsch, Kristian Skrede, & Weidmann, Nils B. (2012). Richardson in the information age: Geographic information systems and spatial data in international studies. *Annual Review of Political Science 15*, 461–481.

Goertz, Gary. (2017). *Multimethod research, causal mechanisms, and case studies: An integrated approach.* Princeton, NJ: Princeton University Press.

Goertz, Gary, & Mahoney, James. (2012). *A tale of two cultures: Qualitative and quantitative research in the social sciences.* Princeton, NJ: Princeton University Press.

Grossman, Guy, & Lewis, Janet. (2014). Administrative unit proliferation. *American Political Science Review* 108(1), 196–217.

Herrera, Yoshiko M., & Kapur, Devesh. (2007). Improving data quality: Actors, incentives, and capabilities. *Political Analysis* 15(4), 365–386.

Kalyvas, Stathis N. (2006). *The logic of violence in civil war.* Cambridge, England: Cambridge University Press.

King, Gary. (1997). *A solution to the ecological inference problem: Reconstructing individual behavior from aggregate data.* Princeton, NJ: Princeton University Press.

King, Gary, Keohane, Robert O., & Verba, Sidney. (1994). *Designing social inquiry: Scientific inference in qualitative research.* Princeton, NJ: Princeton University Press.

Kurtz, Marcus. (2013). *Social foundations of institutional order.* Cambridge, England: Cambridge University Press.

Lustick, Ian S. (1996). History, historiography, and political science: Multiple historical records and the problem of selection bias. *American Political Science Review 90*(3), 605–618.

Lynch, Kevin. (1960). *The image of the city.* Cambridge, MA: MIT Press.

Mahoney, James. (2003). Knowledge accumulation in comparative historical research: The case of democracy and authoritarianism. In James Mahoney & Dietrich Rueschemeyer (Eds.), *Comparative historical analysis in the social sciences,* pp. 131–174. Cambridge, England: Cambridge University Press.

Mahoney, James, & Goertz, Gary. (2004). The possibility principle: Choosing negative cases in comparative research. *American Political Science Review 98*(4), 653–669.

Openshaw, Stan S. (1984). *The modifiable areal unit problem.* Working paper series on Concepts and Techniques in Modern Geography, Institute of British Geographers, No. 38.

Pierson, Paul. (2011). *Politics in time: History, institutions, and social analysis.* Princeton, NJ: Princeton University Press.

Scott, James (2009). *The art of not being governed: An anarchist history of upland Southeast Asia.* New Haven, CT: Yale University Press.

Shafer, D. Michael. (1994). *Winners and losers: How sectors shape the developmental prospects of states.* Ithaca, NY: Cornell University Press.

Snyder, Richard. (2001a). Scaling down: The subnational comparative method. *Studies in Comparative International Development 36*(1), 93–110.

Snyder, Richard. (2001b). *Politics after neoliberalism: Reregulation in Mexico.* Cambridge, England: Cambridge University Press.

Tollefsen, Andreas Forø, Strand, Havard, & Buhaug, Halvard. (2012). PRIO-GRID: A unified spatial data structure. *Journal of Peace Research 49*(2), 363–374.

Tolnay, Stewart, & Beck, E. M. (1995). *A festival of violence: An analysis of southern lynchings, 1882–1930.* Champaign: University of Illinois Press.

Varshney, Ashutosh. (2002). *Ethnic conflict and civic life: Hindus and Muslims in India.* New Haven, CT: Yale University Press.

Wilkinson, Steven. (2004). *Votes and violence: Electoral competition and ethnic riots in India.* Cambridge, England: Cambridge University Press.

Wong, Cara, Bowers, Jake, Williams, Tarah, & Drake Simmons, Katherine. (2012). Bringing the person back in: Boundaries, perceptions, and the measurement of racial context. *Journal of Politics 74*(4), 1153–1170.

Wong, David W. S. (2004). The modifiable areal unit problem. In Donald G. Janelle, Barney Warf, & Kathy Hansen (Eds.), *Worldminds: Geographical perspectives on 100 problems,* pp. 571–575. Dordrecht, Netherlands: Kluwer Academic Publishers.

PART II

REGIMES AND REPRESENTATION

4

Politics in the Provinces: Subnational Regimes in Russia, 1992–2005

Gavril Bilev

The central argument of this chapter is that regime trajectories at the subnational level are not simply a subset of national-level politics and therefore warrant a closer look. Specifically, analysis of executive–legislative relations – an important element of regime trajectories – and a related aspect, executive contestation, reveals both a wealth of variation inside countries and significant differences in the processes that produce outcomes between the capital and the periphery. The focus here is on institution-building, specifically the creation of subnational legislatures. The literature on regime transitions features a rich body of scholarship on parliaments and presidents, constitutions, and the inter-branch balance of power.[1] There is a near-universal consensus on the need for strong institutions to make a variety of important national-level outcomes possible – such as, for example, accountability and democratic consolidation. Until recently, however, the vast majority of this literature ignored subnational polities and implicitly or explicitly assumed isomorphism across subnational units mirroring the national-level setup.[2] While much of the existing body of theory is portable to the subnational level, some modifications and additions are necessary to shed light on the patterns of subnational inter-branch relations. This chapter lays the foundation for theorizing distinct provincial inter-branch politics by focusing on the different set of incentives and constraints that subnational actors face.

---

[1] Pioneering work by Linz emphasized the risks that the structural rigidities of presidentialism pose for nascent democracies (Linz, 1990a, 1990b; Linz & Valenzuela, 1994). More specifically, Linz and many of his followers identified the incentive structure embedded in winner-take-all electoral competition as a crucial culprit in democratic breakdowns. In the postcommunist context, Fish has been most forceful in attributing democratic failures to legislative weakness and unrestrained executive authority, particularly in the paradigmatic case of Russia (Fish, 2005, 2006).

[2] It is worth mentioning that a nascent but growing branch of scholarship focusing on subnational regimes, often situated in Latin America, has emerged recently (Gibson, 2005; Garvasoni, 2010; Benton, 2012; Giraudy, 2015). There is still a dearth of scholarship on subnational legislatures outside of established democracies.

The empirical contribution of the chapter is to substantiate the claim that subnational jurisdictions do not mirror national-level patterns. A closer look at inter-branch relations and executive contestation in the periphery demonstrates that conventional socioeconomic factors such as development and geography do not play the same decisive role in shaping regime trajectories. Simply put, the explanatory power of the usual democracy predictors diminishes when we scale down, buttressing the warning against "theory stretching" that the editors of this volume make in Chapter 1. A quick look at one measure of legislative strength and three measures of contestation uncovers support for this claim, based on data from the expansive and heterogeneous Russian Federation, 1992–2005, with its 89 (at the time) federal sub-units.[3] The inclusion of executive contestation here is intentional, as this indicator of democratization is strongly associated with parliamentary strength – autonomous legislatures are far less likely in polities with little to no contestation.

Drawing on a controlled comparison of two extremely similar provinces, I identify conditions that can lead to the emergence of strong subnational legislatures or, alternatively, produce rubber-stamp bodies. The devil of parliamentary strength is found in the details of the first constitutions, particularly the seemingly minute rules governing who is permitted to run for a deputy seat and who is prohibited from doing so. Eligibility rules shape composition, which in turn drives strength. Executive influence during the institutional formation stage is crucial in formulating the particular eligibility rules in place. Once set up, however, legislative composition displays strong status quo-preserving tendencies and quickly becomes "sticky" due to the self-interested behavior of deputies who are quick to lock into the regional charter the particular rules of the game that give them advantages.[4]

The chapter proceeds as follows. First, a theoretical framework section identifies the points of difference between national and subnational inter-branch relations and describes a strategy, peculiar to the subnational level, for reining in assemblies. A quick look at the broader pattern of subnational

---

[3] Regional political dynamics deserve to be studied in their own right. Indeed, Russia's unusually large number of subnational regions and enormous diversity within has pushed many students of politics to leave the borders of the capital (Ross, 2002; Stoner-Weiss, 2002; Gorenburg, 2003; Hale, 2003; Golosov, 2004; McMann, 2006; Sharafutdinova, 2006; Remington, 2011). Moreover, the outcome of the distributional struggle at the subnational level can have potentially greater consequences for the lives of the vast majority of the population than the political game played in the center. In the case of Russia this is best exemplified by welfare provision, an area where much responsibility is delegated to regional governments (Cook, 2007). Broadly, this tendency is common for most federal states, as the average citizen has more direct and frequent interactions with the unit of government that is located in closer proximity. Yet most of the existing democratization studies focus predominantly on politics at the national level. This form of scholarly bias, what Snyder calls a "center-centered perspective," leads to an underestimation of the importance of regional politics and a dearth of studies on this topic (Snyder, 2001, p. 101).

[4] The conventional assumption in the existing literature is that officeholders, in this case sitting deputies and governors, are primarily motivated by the desire to retain their office.

outcomes in terms of contestation and legislative strength follows to substantiate the claim that different patterns are in place in the periphery and to situate the two regions in the Russian Federation. Then, I briefly outline a puzzling pair of subnational cases and set up a controlled comparison to highlight the role of the assembly in each. Finally, I explain the empirical puzzle in the controlled pair with a critical juncture during the institutional formation period and examine the subsequent evolution of the two regime trajectories.

4.1 THEORIZING SUBNATIONAL EXECUTIVE–LEGISLATIVE RELATIONS IN COMPETITIVE-AUTHORITARIAN REGIMES

Competitive-authoritarian systems are polities in which the principal means of obtaining political authority are formal institutions, yet incumbents violate rules to such an extent that the regime cannot be classified as fully democratic (Levitsky & Way, 2002). Importantly, the opposition in such regimes faces an uneven playing field that significantly complicates its efforts to bring down the government. Competitive authoritarian systems are of interest to students of democracy in part because of their in-between status: It is possible that these polities will further consolidate their democracy or, conversely, backslide into full authoritarianism. Due to its prevalence, scholars have identified and conceptualized one particular form of the latter scenario under the label "electoral authoritarianism" (Schedler, 2006). Such polities hold regular elections, yet violations of democratic norms and rules are so pervasive that effectively elections become a means of further entrenching rulers instead of holding them accountable.

The political regime of the Russian Federation at the national level for the period 1992–2005 meets the criteria for a competitive-authoritarian regime. The same can be said of many of its subnational polities, referred to here as "regions". A great number of them, however, could be classified as electoral-authoritarian, as Section 4.4 on executive contestation across the federation details. A large and heterogeneous federation, Russia contains an unusually high number of subnational polities, making it an ideal case of studying the dynamics of hybrid systems and illustrating the diversity of regimes at the subnational level.[5]

Understanding subnational inter-branch relations, as with any other aspect of a political regime, requires that we take federalism seriously, since the entities of interest are subnational units located inside a larger polity. The larger entity exerts a variety of important effects on the smaller ones, ranging from legal constraints to economic dependence and, occasionally, even direct political interventions. Consistent with the overarching theme of this volume, the implications for subnational politics occupy a central place in the analysis.

---

[5] Examples of similar large, federal competitive-authoritarian systems include, at different moments in their history, Mexico, Ukraine, Argentina, Brazil, and India.

The functioning of legislative bodies at the subnational level has been a subject of interest among students of American politics for decades. One of the main lines of inquiry focuses on the level of professionalization of legislatures, a concept that encompasses three measures: salary, meeting times, and staff resources (Squire, 1992). When explaining the considerable amount of variation between the 50 states, scholars find that professionalization results in higher levels of overall effectiveness measured as the amount of legislation produced, greater levels of attentiveness to constituents, and, crucially, more independence from both party leadership and governor (Squire, 1998, 2005; King, 2000; Kousser, 2005; Harden, 2013). They also document a rising level of professionalization over time across the United States, in part due to increasing spending by states (Malhotra, 2006).

The argument developed in this section is broadly consistent with this focus on professionalization and its effect on the functioning of subnational legislatures. However, the setting and, consequently, the stakes are vastly different. As an established, advanced industrialized democracy, the United States has a long history of legislative activity at the subnational (state) level, older than the American Republic itself in some states. As a result, the range of outcomes at the subnational level in the modern period is relatively narrow, due to, among other factors, tradition, an established and functioning legal system, and the high level of economic development. In contrast, subnational politics in a competitive-authoritarian federation, such as Russia for the period under study, are the product of a very recent set of experiments in institutional formation and democratization without much prior history and, for the most part, without side rails. While it would be unfortunate for an American state to end up with an inefficient legislature, in Russia the range of realistic outcomes includes fully authoritarian polities, in which rubber-stamp bodies enable the maintenance of personalistic rule by local strongmen permanently occupying the governor's office.

To understand subnational politics in competitive-authoritarian regimes like Russia's, we begin by tracing the effect of several differences that exist between the national and provincial levels. These cannot be ignored, because they alter the behavior of actors and shape outcomes. First, while politicians in both national and subnational polities operate under external constraints, the latter are further limited by legal imperatives, in the form of federal laws, the national constitution, and the threat of federal prosecution. Consequently, the menu of options and strategies outside of the capital differ, though is not necessarily shorter. Assuming institutional isomorphism across units leads to committing a dual fallacy. Not only do we ignore crucial variation in the implementation of national rules across subnational polities; more importantly, we miss the institutional innovations that subnational politicians devise to advance their interests, in turn producing politics markedly different from the federal center. Even something as important as the rules governing the election of the top post in a province – the governor's – can be manipulated to the advantage or disadvantage of the incumbent. Surprisingly, actors operating in the periphery can sometimes get away with more while acting within federally imposed legal constraints. As Gibson observes with respect to Argentina and the southern United States immediately after Reconstruction, subnational authoritarianism is attainable when provincial authorities have high regime autonomy in a perfectly legal fashion – institutionalized and legally sanctioned in the provincial constitution (Gibson, 2013, p. 162).[6]

Second, at the national level assemblies are nearly always full-time, salaried professional bodies. Outside of the capital, however, this is frequently not the case, thus opening possibilities for arrangements that blur the boundary between the two branches and circumvent accountability to the electorate. Following from this, the career ambitions of subnational politicians are likely to differ from those of national politicians.[7] Provincial legislators may combine their representative office with additional private or public engagement, thus being more vulnerable to outside influence and conflicts of interest. Also, given the lack of compensation for serving as a deputy, legislators may opt to serve the administration on the floor in hopes of being "promoted" to a full-time paid position in the administration. In contrast to the classical assumption that legislators are solely motivated by the need to ensure reelection, provincial lawmakers face a mixed incentive structure. This is an important point of departure for explaining their behavior.

Third, national legislators have great latitude in dividing the national budget, whereas their provincial counterparts are often constrained by the size of the fiscal proceeds they receive from above. The enormity of fiscal transfers from the center relative to the size of the local economy can further amplify this effect in poorer peripheries. Furthermore, governors who can claim to bring in a greater share of the pie from the capital are likely to wield more influence at home – the same is generally not true for national-level executives. Gervasoni makes this argument with evidence from subnational variation in Argentina – "fiscal federalism rents" enable incumbent governors to limit contestation in poorer regions (Gervasoni, 2010). Moraski demonstrates that Russian governors who manage to establish stable patronage networks, powered by fiscal proceeds, reap substantial electoral rewards (Moraski, 2006).

Fourth, it is incorrect to assume that the subnational branches of national parties behave in the same way as they do in the capital. More importantly, the

---

[6] If we were to apply the framework of the four territorial regimes that Gibson presents to post-Soviet Russia, it would have to be classified as a hybrid between decentralized and centralized federalism – due to the variable over time and contingent on issue area and the level of regime autonomy available to provincial authorities. This is why, consistent with the expectations laid out in Gibson's argument, we observe both informal and formal strategies for power consolidation at the subnational level.

[7] Another important difference in career tracks and ambition is that prominent governors have a choice to make between setting their sights on the national stage or further consolidating power locally.

TABLE 4.1 *Differences Between National and Subnational Levels*

	National	Subnational
Legal constraints	Internal	External and internal
Full-time deputies	All	Some
Budget latitude	Complete control	Partial control
Political party presence in assembly	Universal	Contingent

relevance of parties in subnational units cannot be assumed even when the federal arena features relatively well-organized parties. Sometimes no national parties manage to penetrate the local political arena. This can be largely due to the strategies and behavior of key subnational actors. Moraski (2006) argues persuasively that the use of patronage by governors is one of the main causes of the low level of penetration of national parties at the subnational level. The case of Novgorod, presented in Section 4.4, fits this pattern as a powerful governor shied away from party affiliation while managing to almost completely crowd out national parties in his region. Even when national parties are present, their local branches are more likely to ignore ideological considerations when pursuing local, parochial goals. Table 4.1 summarizes the differences.

How do these differences combine to produce distinct subnational politics and what portions of existing national-level theory travel to the provinces? It is easy to conceive of a number of incentives that executives at any level, once elected to office, face that would lead them to strive to curtail legislative power, pursue an aggressive legislative agenda; increase the ease with which budget policy can be manipulated as sticks and carrots; punish disobedience and reward loyalty; bend electoral rules in their own favor; thwart the rise of potential challengers through the legislature; deny the visibility of a public platform to political opponents; and, most obviously, prevent the introduction of term limits and overturn or loosen existing ones. Indeed, it is difficult to imagine a scenario in which an executive in a presidential system would not prefer a cooperative if not compliant legislature. In competitive-authoritarian systems like Russia's, where the nature of the political regime is fundamentally ambiguous and major institutions are frequently in a state of flux, executives face even-greater-than-usual incentives to rein in the assembly and reduce the uncertainty associated with it (Levitsky & Way, 2002).

If these executives also happen to be in office during the period of constitution writing and institutional creation, it is clear from this logic that they will seek ways to minimize the influence of the legislature through any means available to them. At the very least, the possibility of political opponents capturing a majority or plurality of seats in the new parliament is enough to warrant caution about the role of the new body. In contrast, as Elster notes, legislators that serve in the constitution-drafting assembly have an incentive to promote parliamentary power at the expense of executive authority, due to the expectation that they may serve in the future legislature (Elster, 1993; Elster et al., 1998). Consequently, one straightforward expectation is that the greater the influence of the executive branch at the time of institutional formation, the more the balance of power between the two branches will be skewed in favor of the executive. Lijphart refers to this as influence at the negotiation table, Elster labels it the extent of presidential involvement in the constitution drafting process, while for Frye it is the "bargaining power" of the electoral favorite (Lijphart, 1992; Elster et al., 1998; Elster, 1993; Frye, 1997). Following Elster's institutional self-interest logic, the converse expectation is, of course, that, in cases where executives are incapable of influencing the institutional design process, the legislature will expand or fortify its powers.

Institutional formation can be positioned on a continuum ranging from a constitutional crafting process dominated by an executive incumbent to factional or multiparty negotiations and compromises that only minimally involve the executive branch. Ambitious executives can seize the opportunity to devise the new constitution or to set the conditions for the constitution drafting process so as to maximize the levers of power against the future legislature and tilt the playing field in their own favor. Unsurprisingly, as the body of national-level theory on this subject concludes, in the absence of constraints such situations produce executive-dominated constitutional frameworks – ambitious executives cement their power by institutionalizing legislative weakness. However, what happens when subnational politicians face external and internal constraints, as is very often the case at the provincial level?

In subnational cases, external constraints can take the form of articles of the national constitution, federal laws, or presidential decrees that place certain powers, such as budget approval, squarely within the purview of regional legislatures. International pressure from advanced democracies and the presence of robust civil society can play a similar, though generally weaker, constraining role at the national level. Internal constraints, on the other hand, can be posed by rival subnational political elites, independent media, the courts, and civil society organizations – political actors that are able to pass judgment on the executive's actions and on the democratic quality of the new rules.

If setting up a completely imbalanced constitutional framework with an appendage legislature is impossible due to legal limitations, what strategies can subnational executives employ in order to keep legislators in check? How do provincial executives ensure that the personal ambitions of deputies or their collective institutional interests as elected members of the assembly do not pose obstacles to the executive agenda? The next best alternative for an ambitious governor is to adjust the mode of selection and eligibility rules of the future representative body with the aim of populating it with loyalists or, in other words, *packing the assembly*. When implemented successfully, the packing strategy produces a "rubber-stamp" assembly with a consistent majority or plurality of legislators loyal to the executive.

Legislative strength is defined here as the extent of insulation of the vast majority of deputies in the assembly from the direct and formal or semiformal influence of the governor.[8] While total insulation of the assembly would be extremely rare in democratizing polities, the degree of insulation should be inversely related to the ability of the governor to deploy negative inducements or punish disobedience against individual legislators. Negative inducements include removing parliamentary deputies from other positions of power they covet, expelling them from a party or faction that is instrumental to their reelection, and withholding budgetary proceeds from their legislative district. Although this definition of legislative strength focuses on negative inducements, it does not exclude the use of positive inducements. Indeed, when subnational executives rely mainly on positive inducements – for example, policy concessions, graft, and partisan benefits – in exchange for votes on key bills, this may be a sign of executive weakness relative to the legislature. Moreover, it is useful to distinguish between formal and informal links of dependence of assembly deputies. Governors prefer legislatures that are compliant because of dependence and loyalty, since this reduces the need to make costly policy concessions and minimizes the risk of a stalled agenda.[9]

In settings where outright manipulation of the future assembly's formal powers is impossible, subnational executives can resort to a less obvious yet equally effective strategy for subduing the legislature: packing the assembly with loyal and obedient supporters. One way for governors to achieve this is by sponsoring lower-level, subprovincial executives, such as town mayors, as candidates for the provincial legislature. In Russia, provincial legislators are allowed to hold joint appointments as both deputies *and* mayors. Even if subprovincial executives (i.e., mayors) are elected in competitive elections, their dual role in two distinct branches of government (i.e., the executive and legislative) breeds trouble for parliamentary strength in relation to the

---

[8] A working definition of legislative strength as employed here relies primarily on formal, and consequently observable, indicators – that the legislative body functions as an autonomous entity, functionally separate from the executive branch, and that the majority of deputies in parliament are not directly dependent on the executive through formal or informal channels of influence. Indicators include the ease of passage of the annual budget bills, amendments to the charter (constitution) that modify enumerated powers of either branch of government, important changes to election laws, and the affiliation of the current speaker (chairperson).

[9] One could argue that informal ties and corruption could be equally instrumental in subjugating a legislature. This is not always true due to the differing levels of reliability of control and the visibility of the vote buying. When unable to employ negative inducements, governors are forced to resort to buying votes through bribes. However, the informality of control breeds uncertainty about its reliability and duration. If deputies sell their votes to the governor, it is possible that they would also sell to challengers to the governor or to opposing groups. This has the effect of making the assembly as a whole far less predictable. Some votes come at a very high cost, and it is precisely the strength of the legislature that increases the value of a legislative vote.

provincial governor. On the one hand, as provincial legislators they represent the interests of the electorate of their legislative district. On the other hand, as mayors, they serve the interests of the constituency of their executive district. The former role potentially pits them *against* the governor in order to carry out the constitutionally mandated "checking" function entrusted to the assembly. The latter role drives them to seek the cooperation of the provincial executive in order to both ensure the smooth functioning of their mayoral administrations and bring pork to their district. Consequently, when these "mayor-deputies" face a choice among competing responsibilities stemming from their split roles, they will prioritize the demands linked to the more prestigious and better compensated of the two positions.

A consequential institutional caveat lurks in this story. For an individual to serve simultaneously as a mayor and a provincial legislator, one of the two positions must be part-time. Governors thus face strong incentives to manipulate provincial political institutions in ways that elevate the position of mayor above the position of provincial deputy, because it is mayors, not legislators, whom governors are more able to control. Governors have multiple ways available to them to reduce the prestige and privileges of holding a legislative seat, including undercutting the professionalism of the assembly by ensuring that the vast majority of deputies receive little or no remuneration and that legislative sessions are short, with few if any legal or material benefits tied to service in the assembly. Consequently, the mayor-deputies face a strong incentive to prioritize the imperatives of their executive obligations over their legislative ones. This strategy of packing the assembly requires a de-professionalization of the legislature, a far more difficult task to achieve at the national level, where assemblies are full-time, professional bodies.

In practice, both positions of the mayor-deputies may be tied to serving the same master. They are elected to the assembly in part on the basis of their proximity to the chief executive. They make an implicit or explicit promise to the electorate that their dual links to the governor will enable them to serve the region better – by bringing in more pork in the form of infrastructure projects and direct budget proceeds. There exists, of course, a threat that the mayor-legislator will elicit negative inducements Governors can also pressure mayor-legislators through negative inducements administrative punishment in the form of refusing or delaying much needed fiscal transfers to the lower-level administration. Furthermore, the chief executive can support the candidacy of lower-level officials for the assembly by offering them financial and administrative support during campaigns, either through illicit cash contributions or through explicit spending in the district funded by the upper level of government. Careful micromanagement of legislative elections can produce pluralities or even majorities of mayor-deputies loyal to the incumbent chief executive governor.

The analysis to this point has focused on the crucial period of institutional formation. Yet, to build the case for the importance of eligibility rules as a means by which governors subdue legislators, we must address the possibility of simply changing the rules after the initial period. For the early institutional creation period, 1992–1994, to meet the criteria for a "critical juncture," it must profoundly affect the strength of these new bodies and alter the trajectory of the regimes they are located in. Demonstrating this will complete the list of components of a historical legacy that Collier and Collier outline – mechanisms of production, mechanics of reproduction, and a stable set of core attributes (Collier & Collier, 2002, pp. 30–31). What are the "mechanisms of reproduction" that make this institutional choice stick?

Explaining the durability of the new rules for subnational legislatures, born in the heat of a relatively brief and unique moment, requires a deeper look at the incentives of individual legislators. Rules about the composition of a representative body that votes on its own constitution exhibit a strong lock-in effect, because in addition to having the power to determine their own powers, assemblies also have the power to determine their own mode of selection – the rules according to which legislators are elected, the duration of their term, and their own privileges (Elster, 1996). This is a crucial insight from the national-level literature that we can extend to the provinces – it is very difficult to get deputies to consent to diminishing the prestige of their own post or to disqualify themselves from occupying it in the future. Furthermore, sitting deputies are typically the beneficiaries of the particularities of the existing mode of selection – election rules, district boundaries, and eligibility requirements. If they were not, it is likely they would not have gotten elected in the first place.

Another insight from studies of institutional effects at the national level is that even though initial institutional design is typically endogenous – that is, determined by the present distribution of power among relevant actors – it gradually becomes a fixed constraint on the behavior of actors in an exogenous manner (Remington, 2001). Actors, notably governors, are constrained to operate under it. The analysis here elaborates on the status quo-preserving tendencies of legislatures that amplify the effects of initial institutional design. Any significant change to these rules imperils the reelection prospects of incumbent legislators – either by making it easier for potential rivals to win under different rules or by opening the door to previously disqualified individuals.[10]

The scope of the present argument should not be overstated. First, the assembly-packing strategy, because it hinges on the fusing of the roles and responsibilities of mayors and deputies, is only possible in subnational polities in which the boundaries of administrative units and legislative electoral districts coincide. Second, the assembly-packing strategy would be harder to implement in a federation where disciplined, ideologically coherent, and well-organized national political parties have gained a foothold in the provinces. Post-Soviet

---

[10] This explains why, even in the sea of institutional changes that took place during the first decade of provincial legislative activity in Russia, the rules governing parliamentary composition remained fixed in the two provinces studied here following the institutional formation period.

Russia, like many competitive-authoritarian regimes, does not feature a mature party system, a weakness that many governors across the federation both exploited and exacerbated.[11]

Third, even though economic development is certainly not destiny, as both the controlled comparison and the large-N analysis in Section 4.4 will show, the strategy of assembly packing is probably more likely to succeed if implemented in poor peripheries. As some students of the Russian regions have already noted, the economic dynamism and diversity of more developed and economically self-sustaining polities, coupled with a more robust civil society, predisposed them toward an inherently more pluralistic and contentious political arena (McMann, 2006). Importantly for the purposes of this argument, such polities would not easily accommodate a docile and unrepresentative legislative body. In poorer economic settings, however, the packed assembly strategy is a viable option. A relatively anemic civil society combined with an economy chronically dependent on transfers from the center, much of which are left to the discretion of the chief executive to distribute, provide the governor with far greater latitude.

4.2   CASE SELECTION AND PERIODIZATION

The methodology I employ relies on a mixed-method approach following the logic of nested analysis (Lieberman, 2005). Quantitative exploratory analysis of a larger set of cases complements an in-depth qualitative account built on a controlled comparison of two provinces selected so that they match across a range of characteristics. The pair feature remarkable similarity of starting conditions while exhibiting tremendous differences in terms of outcomes. Pskov consistently displays a higher level of both legislative strength and executive contestation, while Novgorod demonstrates a trajectory of unmistakable authoritarian backsliding. A large-N exploration of the two aspects of regime trajectories across the entire federation demonstrates the limited reach of macrosocial prerequisites explanations and provides context for these two cases.

Historical legacies, structural preconditions, and the political situation at the federal center in Russia during the early 1990s certainly did not create a hospitable environment for parliamentary strength in the provinces.[12] Yet,

---

[11] Dedicated assessments of the development of parties in post-Soviet Russia at both the national and regional levels universally conclude that the party system is severely underdeveloped (Golosov, 2004; Hale, 2006; McFaul, 2001a). One of the frequently cited explanations is the institutionalized weakness of the country's legislature vis-à-vis the president – lowering the incentives for potential party builders to pursue legislative majorities. A possible and at best partial exception to the overall pattern is CPRF, the communist party which is relatively stable and would meet most classical definitions of a party.

[12] Post-Soviet Russia is a challenging venue for institutional arguments in general and parliamentary strength in particular. After centuries of monarchical absolutism, followed by the totalitarian Soviet state of the twentieth century, the country is hardly an exemplar of powerful formal

as the case of Pskov demonstrates, such outcomes did occur, even if they were not the norm. The chapter also examines the competitiveness for executive office of each political system, a distinct but related metric of democratization and institution building. Students of democracy have long considered contestation as a timely and relevant indicator of progress in terms of democratic consolidation – simultaneously a benchmark and an essential prerequisite.[13] Executive contestation can be considered a strong correlate of legislative strength, because the successful consolidation of power by executives usually involves gaining and maintaining a firm grip on the regional legislature. The inability of governors to control their constitutional counter-weights, that is, legislatures, often imperils their own political survival – a dynamic visible in the case of Pskov province, as explained in Section 4.4.

The selection of the historical period, 1992–2005, reflects the objective of studying provinces in a de facto federation. Russia's regions offer useful cases of subnational polities only if most major developments in the political arena are not simply dictated from above. Virtually all of the new regional legislatures were formed in early 1994 though the relevant period of their creation extends back to 1992 – the starting point of this study. While selecting the point of departure is easy, simply the beginning period in which the liberalization of the entire federation began, drawing a finish line is harder. As virtually all observers today agree, Russia is neither a democracy nor a de facto federation; however, disagreement exists on the exact date or event that marked the end of the liberal episode. The implications for the argument here are large – the moment the country ceases to be a federation is the moment that regional political units cease to be useful cases for studying regime trajectories broadly and executive-legislative relations in particular. After that point, political outcomes across the provinces are driven mainly by the Kremlin's policy of provincial administration.

Thus, the objective is to select the end point so as to utilize all of the available information without looking into the recentralization period when democratic experimentation was aborted from above. I chose the symbolically important abolition of gubernatorial elections that formally went into effect at the beginning of 2005. This roughly coincides with the rapid rise and spread of the pro-Putin United Russia party, commonly seen as a vehicle for disseminating Moscow's dictates across the federation, through the majority of provincial parliaments. The combination of appointed, not elected, governors and party-dominated

institutions and parliamentary strength. Historical legacies predispose toward unchecked executive authority, further validated by the executive-dominated constitution passed under President Yeltsin, only to be followed by the reliably authoritarian President Putin. As explained subsequently, in the early 1990s then-President Yeltsin had reasons to be weary of empowering local councils and instead preferred to stack the deck in favor of regional executives, almost all of whom were directly appointed by him at the time.

[13] The term is used here in the same way as by Dahl and follows from the minimalist Schumpeterian definition, defended by Przeworski (Dahl, 1971; Przeworski, 1991).

legislatures in the recentralization period effectively rendered the regions far too dependent on the center to be useful cases for studying subnational regime trajectories and institution-building.

4.3   SUBNATIONAL PATTERNS OF EXECUTIVE CONTESTATION AND LEGISLATIVE STRENGTH ACROSS RUSSIA

A brief look at the nature of subnational political regimes in the Russian Federation for the period under study highlights three trends. First, there is considerable variation in terms of both executive contestation and legislative strength: an uneven subnational terrain of democratic progress and authoritarian back-sliding. In spite of the preponderance of factors working against a democratic deepening across Russia's vast expanse, the democratization process unfolded extremely unevenly within the country and advanced far in some provinces. Even regions with very similar starting conditions in 1992 experienced a wide range of outcomes by 2005 – from successful power consolidation projects under local strongmen to balanced institutional designs with plenty of political contestation. Contrary to conventional wisdom, democratic flowers did indeed blossom in the supposedly inhospitable Russian soil. The range of contrasting outcomes highlights the positive role that institutional arrangements can play in counteracting antidemocratic legacies and curtailing authoritarian ambition. Nevertheless, plenty of the subnational regimes display the features of electoral authoritarianism.

Second, traditional predictors of democratic progress, namely the macro-social prerequisites commonly employed in the transitions literature, do not fare as well at subnational levels of analysis and leave much unexplained variation. Third, in contrast to the strong geographic clustering patterns observed at the national level and well documented in the democratization literature, subnational regimes in Russia exhibit no detectable spatial dependencies.[14]

In line with the existing literature, I use executive contestation to explore variation in the extent of democratic progress. I rely on several measures of competitiveness based on the results of gubernatorial elections that took place in all of Russia's 89 regions, 1993–2005 – spanning more than 230 gubernatorial contests in the 87 federal units that held elections over this 11-year period. To capture the concept of contestation within such a short time period (a decade), the analysis relies on three distinct measures: effective number of candidates for governor; the number of times an incumbent lost; and the margin of vote share against the incumbent.

The focus on executive contestation, in particular gubernatorial contests, is warranted by the importance of this post. For the period under consideration,

---

[14] Notable examples include O'Loughlin et al. (1998); Mainwaring and Pérez-Liñán (2005); Elkink (2011).

1992–2005, the Russian Federation consisted of 89 federal territorial units belonging to several types, all of them referred to here as "regions," headed by chief executives referred to as "governors." Russian governors during the period under study commanded a vast array of institutional resources – ranging from extensive influence over the region's budget (shared with the assembly) and resource distribution, dealings with the center, the composition of cabinet, and the large number of public employees under their direct authority. In terms of prestige, the position was extremely high in the state hierarchy, making it roughly comparable to US governors (with the additional similarity of the often invoked analogy with mini-presidents). Most would prefer it over a Duma or Federal Council seat (lower and upper chambers of the national legislature).

The first measure of competitiveness reflects the effective number of gubernatorial candidates in a given election – ENC. It is analogous to the commonly used effective number of parliamentary parties.[15] ENC essentially weighs the number of candidates for the gubernatorial post by their vote share – producing a highly sensitive, continuous estimate of the amount of competition present in the election – ranging from 1 to infinity. Substantively, an ENC of 1 represents an election with only one candidate (no contestation). A score of 2 or greater reflects instances when either two or more contenders are evenly matched or no candidate captures an overwhelming majority of the vote. A score of 3 or 4 indicates three or four evenly matched candidates each accounting for, respectively, a third or a quarter of the electorate. I collected data on the measure for each gubernatorial election, both the first round and the runoff round when present, for all gubernatorial contests that took place in postcommunist Russia. Map 4.1 presents a choropleth map of the variable across the regions of the federation.

The second measure, incumbent loss, represents the number of times a gubernatorial incumbent lost an election. It is equivalent to the traditional turnover variable in democratization studies. Higher count indicates a more contested polity. This is a relatively conservative measure of contestation. Even though the period during which there were elections in the regions of the Russian Federation was relatively brief – barely more than a decade (1994–2005) – the variation on this measure is not small, ranging from regions where no turnover ever took place (35 regions) to a single governor

---

[15] The formula is:

$$N = \frac{1}{\sum_{i=1}^{n} p_i^2},$$

where n is the number of candidates in the gubernatorial election and p_i^2 is the square of each candidate's proportion of all votes cast (Laakso & Taagepera, 1979). Konitzer uses the same measure on a more limited set of Russian gubernatorial contests in order to assess the extent of accountability in the federation during roughly the same period in time (Konitzer, 2005).

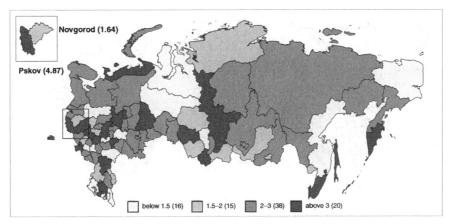

MAP 4.1 Effective Number of Candidates for Governor, 1993–2005, Average, All Russian Regions

losing (39) to two or more incumbent losses (15) (Mean = .78; σ=.72).[16] Note that even "zero" does not necessarily indicate that only one officeholder occupied the gubernatorial post for the entire period under study, as transfers of power occasionally occurred without elections. At times, governors willingly resigned from a position, were forced out of office, or died.

The third measure of executive contestation, margin, captures the difference between incumbent and top challenger (both on first rounds and during runoffs; plot omitted for brevity). The variable is equal to the incumbent percent share of the vote minus the top vote getter percent share. The greater the difference, the lesser the level of contestation in the region. A negative margin implies more competition, as the incumbent has garnered a smaller share of the vote than the top challenger.

This bird's-eye view of contestation in the federation illustrates a diversity of political outcomes. At one end of the competitiveness spectrum, a large number of regions did not feature a significant amount of executive contestation. More than a third of the provinces had an ENC score of 2 or less indicating dominance by a single candidate, of course almost always the incumbent. Similarly, 35 regions never witnessed even a single gubernatorial loss (Map 4.2). It is reasonable to assume that the vast majority of these regions would fall under the rubric of electoral authoritarianism. On the opposite end of the spectrum, 20 provinces averaged ENC scores greater than 3, while in 15 governors lost elections more than once. These are the competitive polities where elections had uncertain outcomes and incumbents had reason to worry. Finally, the remaining regions, slightly less than half of the total, fall somewhere in between these two groups.

---

[16] In two regions there were, remarkably, three incumbent losses.

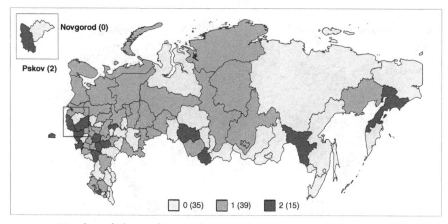

MAP 4.2 Number of Electoral Losses by Incumbent Governors in Russia, 1993–2005

Legislative ratio is a proxy measure of legislative strength, more specifically the amount of resources available to provincial legislatures. It is the ratio of legislative staff members to the number of legislators in a parliament.[17] The measure captures the same concept as the staff resources measure used in the study of professionalism in American state legislatures (Squire, 2007). For the vast majority of regions, legislative ratio ranges from roughly half a staff member per legislator to 2.5. (Mean = 2.1; σ = 1.7)[18] Map 4.3 presents a choropleth map of the variable, illustrating wide variation across the entire federation. At the bottom of the legislative capability distribution, a dozen provinces averaged less than one staff member per deputy, which would indicate a very weak or non-functional legislature. Conversely, more than a third of the regions hired more than two staff members, on average, for every deputy in the legislature. While a high ratio does not guarantee legislative strength, it does suggest the potential of these assemblies to function independently. Russia's regional parliaments, in short, were not all made of the same mold.

What are the factors that explain this wide range of outcomes? When exploring patterns of contestation and legislative strength at the subnational level, it is evident that macro-social preconditions lack the explanatory power they display in cross-national research. Figure 4.1 juxtaposes two of the measures of contestation, ENC and margin, with two standard measures of

---

[17] I wish to thank Dan Epstein for pointing out the relevant data buried in an obscure part of the annual yearbook released by the Russian State Statistical Service (ROSSTAT, formerly GOSKOMSTAT) – Regionni Rossii 2004. The journal presented data on the total number of legislative staff in each region. The number of legislators is extracted from Kseniya Punina's doctoral thesis in the Perm' State University Department of Political Science – generously provided by the author. The data are only for 2003, but this is the best estimate available to date.

[18] There is one significant exceptional case: the federal capital Moscow, with a ratio of over 12. In general, Moscow is an outlier in almost every respect.

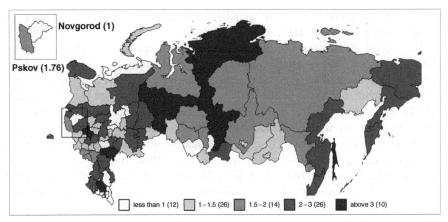

MAP 4.3 Ratio of Legislative Staff to Deputies in Russia's Regional Parliaments, 2003

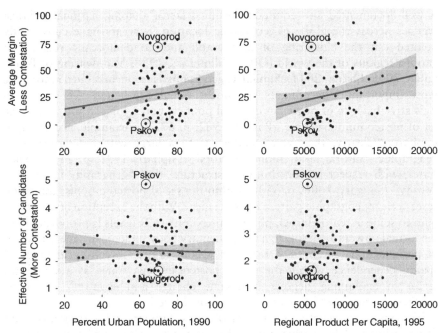

FIGURE 4.1 Margin of Victory, Effective Number of Candidates (ENC), and Socioeconomic Conditions in Russia's Gubernatorial Elections, 1994–2005

socioeconomic development – gross regional product per capita (the subnational equivalent to GDPpc) and percent urban population for a region. Black dots represent regions, the straight lines plot a simple bivariate regression line and the shaded regions indicate the bootstrapped 95 percent confidence interval at any given level of the predictor variable. Note that higher levels of margin indicate less contestation.

The figure illustrates the limited explanatory power of socioeconomic preconditions. While urbanization could potentially serve as a robust predictor of subnational regime trajectories once all of the appropriate additional controls are introduced in a multivariate model, as Remington (2011) argues, there is certainly a lot of residual variation. As seen in the two bivariate plots on the left, these bare-bones models fail to reach statistical significance when predicting either indicator of contestation. Regional product, the equivalent of the omnipotent GDPpc predictor in national studies, exhibits a flat regression line. In other words, the most powerful predictor of democracy at the national level has little traction at the subnational level within this large and diverse federation.[19]

Spatial Dependence?

A well-documented and commonly studied factor shaping national political regimes across the globe is geographic location. Scholars have consistently pointed out the clustering of democratic and nondemocratic regimes in various regions of the world (O'Loughlin et al., 1998; Mainwaring & Pérez-Liñán, 2005; Elkink, 2011). Similarly, geography is frequently cited among the most important determinants of constitutional types and the executive-legislative balance of power in national polities, both globally and within the set of postcommunist cases. (Powell, 1982, p. 67) For example, according to Lijphart: "Clearly, the overall pattern is to a large extent determined by geographic, cultural, and colonial factors" (Lijphart, 1991, p. 74). Shugart states, with respect to constitutional structure, that "geography is virtually destiny" (Shugart, 2006, p. 350). Within the set of postcommunist transition cases, a clear geographic pattern is also evident. With the exception of Mongolia (and to some extent Belarus), physical proximity to Brussels is proportional to the formal powers available to a parliamentary body under Fish's measurement of parliamentary strength.[20] Kopstein (2000) argues forcefully in favor of spatial dependence within the set of postcommunist states as a significant factor in explaining degrees of regime change and economic openness. Do these patterns hold true at the subnational level?

The answer is negative in this set of cases. Subnational variation of both contestation and legislative power does not necessarily mirror the patterns observed at the national level. Specifically, geography does not seem to have played a role in determining Russian provincial regime trajectories. A visual inspection of the geographic distribution of contestation confirms the absence

---

[19] For the association between democracy and economic development, see Lipset (1959); Rustow (1970); Przeworski et al. (2000); and Boix et al. (2003).

[20] Fish's Parliamentary Powers Index (Fish, 2005, p. 206).

of a clearly discernible pattern of clustering among either similar or dissimilar values. Maps 4.1 and 4.2 contain no obvious geographic pattern that would indicate clustering or spatial dependence. Regions with higher levels of contestation are not more likely to be located in any particular part of the country or to cluster together. A plot of the margin contestation measure, omitted for brevity, also supports this conclusion. The same conclusion holds true for legislative ratio, the variation of which cannot be explained by either geographic clustering or the conventional preconditions explanation (Map 4.3).

Formal quantitative tests for spatial dependence under various specifications of contiguity reveal no significant spatial autocorrelation for the contestation measures or for the proxy measure of legislative strength. I used a polygon map of the Russian administrative units (89 regions), accurate for the period under study. Global Moran's I values under "queen" contiguity for the main contestation measures, average ENC, average margin, and incumbent losses are, respectively, -.14 with a p-value of .98; -.04 with a p-value of .69; .03 with a p-value of .25. Similarly, the value for legislative ratio of .05 does not meet the conventional level of statistical significance with a p-value of over .12.[21] The lack of a discernible pattern of similarity or dissimilarity in regime type among adjacent units points to the absence of the clustering, diffusion, or neighborhood effects often observed with national-level regime measures. Simply put, subnational regime dynamics in Russia operate differently than a straightforward extrapolation of the regime studies literature would lead us to expect.

An important implication of this lack of spatial dependence is worth noting. Chapter 2 by Harbers and Ingram in this volume rightly places the burden of proof on researchers who claim, or tacitly assume, independence between subnational units to provide evidence for it. Since many processes of change of interest to social scientists more often than not move unevenly through space, clustering and spatial dependence among units are highly likely. While there is a real danger in ignoring their warning, the analysis of regime patterns in Russia presented here, highlights the converse pitfall: that is, the presence of spatial dependence should not be simply assumed either. Ultimately, whether or not spatial dependence exists is an empirical question that should be answered with data.

4.4   THE CASES: NOVGOROD AND PSKOV

Novgorod and Pskov are small, adjacent provinces in the northwestern part of the Russian Federation, nearly indistinguishable on the socioeconomic variables traditionally identified in the democratization literature as driving political regime outcomes – economic development, ethnic makeup, cultural

---

[21] Different specifications of contiguity ("rook"), ways of calculating the spatial weight matrix, and graph-based neighbor algorithms – such as triangulation, sphere of influence graph, and relative neighbor graph – also did not reveal any evidence of spatial dependence. Tests were performed in R, using the **spdep** R package. For more information, see Bivand (2014).

TABLE 4.2 *Novgorod and Pskov, Select Indicators*

	Novgorod Region	Pskov Region
Percent urban population, 1990	69.90	63.50
Percent ethnic Russian, 1979	96.26	95.86
Regional product per capita, 1995, millions of rubles	5857.40	5380.70
Industrial product, 1990, millions of rubles	2.50	2.40

legacies, and natural resources. The two regions are also similar in population size, composition of the economy between industry and agriculture, status vis-à-vis the federal budget (both are recipient regions, heavily dependent on federal government subsidies), old regime legacies, World War II history (both were occupied and nearly completely destroyed), and even medieval period history (ancient city-states). Table 4.2 reports select indicators for the two provinces, illustrating the high level of similarity.[22] The location of the two regions is shown in inset mini-plots in the left-hand corner of Maps 4.1, 4.2, and 4.3, along with the values for each of the four measures in brackets.

Despite the commonalities highlighted in Table 4.2, during the first decade of their existence following the collapse of communism and the creation of the new Russian state, the newly formed legislative bodies in the two provinces could not have behaved more differently. From the first day of its existence in 1994, the Novgorod Duma (Council) behaved as a classic rubber-stamp body, a mere appendage of the gubernatorial administration. Deputies would typically vote on a resolution after less than five minutes of deliberation and pass it unanimously. Agendas consisting of over 30 items would be rushed through two-hour sessions while budget bills, the most important piece of legislation each year, would be approved swiftly with purely cosmetic revisions. The body can hardly be taken seriously as a parliament. In contrast, the Pskov *Zakonodatel'noe Sobranie* (Legislative Assembly) consistently displayed a degree of strength vis-à-vis gubernatorial administrations that often came close to checks and balances.[23]

[22] Compiled from multiple annual statistical yearbooks, Regionni Rossii. Published by the Federal State Statistics Service, Russian Federation, Moscow. Regioni Rossii, 1997–2005. Socio-Economic Indicators. Rosstat.

[23] The balance of power between executives and legislatures is difficult to measure, a problem that has resulted in a scarcity of cross-national data. At the subnational level, it is even harder to find valid indicators that successfully capture the strength or weakness of parliaments. Much of the data behind the conclusions presented here comes from process tracing based on thousands of newspaper articles as well as select interviews with local experts collected during a year of fieldwork in Russia, 2008–2009. The information-rich accounts of each legislative session from regional newspapers provide a detailed picture of how regional bodies conducted their

TABLE 4.3 *Novgorod and Pskov, Measures in Context of All Russian Regions*

	Novgorod	Pskov	Min	Max	Mean	Std. Dev.
Avg. ENC	1.64	4.87	1.00	5.63	2.40	0.89
Incumbent losses	0	2	0	2	0.78	0.72
Avg. margin (lower means more competitive)	70.50	1.09	−59.30	92.70	23.00	28.19
Legislative ratio	1.00	1.76	0.63	12.20	2.13	1.67

This puzzling contrast does not end with parliamentary behavior. The divergence in outcomes between the two regions extends to political contestation. In Novgorod, Governor Mikhail Prussak reigned virtually unchallenged for over 15 years, cruising to victory in three gubernatorial elections with no real competition. By 2005, the regime in the province fit the description of electoral authoritarianism. Pskov, on the other hand, stands out from the rest of the regions due to the unusually high levels of political competition. On two separate occasions gubernatorial heads rolled, with executive incumbents failing to attract even a third of the vote.

Table 4.3 presents the values for the contestation measures for the two provinces and the mean and standard deviation for all regions where the available data exist. Notably, Pskov stands out with its average ENC, while Novgorod represents a far more typical case, closer to the national average. The rightmost two columns report the mean and standard deviation for each measure across the entire federation. In terms of contestation, Novgorod ranks lower than an average region, while Pskov is unusually competitive. (In terms of incumbent loss, the province is close to two standard deviations above the mean.) Still, Novgorod is by no means an exception, since roughly a third of all regions never witness an electoral loss by an incumbent governor.

The notorious ubiquity and prevalence of informal institutions, crony capitalism, and patronage during the post-Soviet period hardly make for an environment conducive to establishing and maintaining a robust democratic order.[24] The conventional wisdom about subnational regimes in the Russian federation is that the majority of constitutions/charters mirrored the balance of power stipulated in the federal constitution – what has been labeled "super-presidentialism" after the rise of Vladimir Putin. This depiction is largely based on single-case studies and anecdotal evidence (often pointing to some of the more authoritarian ethnic republics.) For

business during the period under study. Information from interviews with local political experts, journalists, and politicians largely corroborated the newspaper accounts.

[24] See, for example, Ledeneva (2006); Fish (2005); McFaul (2001b); and Blasi et al. (1997).

example, Fish (2005) points to the cases of Bashkortostan and Chechnya as examples of coercion where local omnipotent governors (holding the official title of "president") can deliver almost any electoral result Moscow expects. While accurate, this depiction paints an overly simplistic picture of the balance of power between legislatures and executives across the entire federation, because it is based on two highly unrepresentative cases. Golosov (2004) presents a more nuanced, in-depth look in a study of formal powers extending to almost all regions. He concludes that, contrary to existing belief, significant variation exists between regions in terms of the strength of the legislative assembly vis-à-vis the governor.

4.5 DESIGNING SUBNATIONAL POLITICAL INSTITUTIONS: RUSSIA 1991–1994

If macro-social preconditions and geography do not explain the dramatic divergence between Novgorod and Pskov, then what does? This section traces the process of institutional creation of the new legislatures in the two regions with emphasis on the power of relevant actors at crucial points in time. Paradoxically, the same external stimulus, a second crisis at the center, led to a divergence of trajectories in the periphery. As such, this is an instance of a multilevel explanation with heterogeneous top-down effects, following the classification developed in Chapter 1 of this volume.

Differences in the texts of regional constitutions have their origins in events at the national level. The background conditions in which the institutional formation of the new representative bodies in Russian regions took place were marked by the fallout from two dramatic conflicts at the national level. The first of these pitted the pro-reform, newly elected President Yeltsin (elected in June of 1991) against remnants of the old-guard communist party elite during a failed coup attempt – the August putsch of 1991. The second resulted in a standoff between the president and a faction of parliamentary opponents elected to the Russian Supreme Council (*Verhovnii Soviet*). Table 4.4 lists major events in chronological order and refers to the consequences of each event for the regions.

In the aftermath of the failed 1991 coup attempt, President Yeltsin took control over the entire executive branch, including authority over provincial administration. Through the use of executive decrees, he reformed the structure of regional governance by abolishing the Communist Party executive committees (*ispolkom*) and replacing them with a newly created position of governor (*glava administratsii*, or administrative heads) which he rapidly appointed throughout the federation's regions with the mission of carrying out his major economic reforms. The goal of these reforms was to dismantle the planned economy of state socialism and transition to a market-driven model as quickly as possible. Yeltsin and the people around him justified the de facto usurpation of authority as necessary to prevent further attempts by former

TABLE 4.4 *Institutional Formation Timeline*

Time	Event	Consequences for regions
August 1991	First national crisis, failed coup (*putsch*). President Yeltsin abolishes the Communist Party, assumes authority, and soon ends the Soviet Union.	Provincial councils forced to choose a side in a situation of great uncertainty; responses vary.
September–October 1991	President Yeltsin appoints governors across Russia.	Executive authority in the provinces is transferred from Communist Party officials to appointees (governors). Within months, governors appoint town mayors throughout their provinces.
October 1993	Second national crisis; constitutional standoff between President Yeltsin and Supreme Council resolved through violence. Yeltsin prevails.	Provincial councils again forced to choose a side in a situation of uncertainty. Based on their public statements, Yeltsin dismisses some seen as sympathetic to the Supreme Council and allows others to continue their existence until the end of 1993.
October–December 1993	President Yeltsin issues a series of decrees reorganizing the structure of provincial governments across the federation.	Elections for newly formed legislative bodies set to take place between January and March of 1994. Appointed governors, in conjunction with regional councils *wherever present*, create temporary charters detailing the functioning and composition of the new regional parliaments.
January–March 1994	Regional legislative elections are held.	New legislatures begin functioning.

(*continued*)

TABLE 4.4 (continued)

Time	Event	Consequences for regions
April–June 1994	Newly formed legislatures approve regional charters.	Regional legislatures codify the rules of the provincial regime, including election laws for legislative and executive elections, within the limits set by federal laws and presidential decrees.
December 1995–June 1996	Gubernatorial elections held across almost regions. Town mayors also elected for the first time.	First round of gubernatorial elections – some appointees remain, while others do not.

communist elites to stall and reverse the course of democratization in Russia. A basic separation of powers arrangement was set up between these new regional chief executives and the existing communist-era regional councils (*oblsoviet*), with the councils having budgetary oversight while all executive functions were the sole responsibility of the governors.

In many provinces, the old councils (*soviets*) were far from subdued and often worked hard to counter the reform efforts of the new presidential appointees due to the fact that a major portion of these bodies consisted of the old Communist Party *nomenklatura*, the functionaries of the dying party-state. The majority of soviets across the federation were seen as sympathetic to the Supreme Soviet and antagonistic toward Yeltsin, especially in the late spring and summer of 1993, when the executive-legislative conflict at the federal level intensified. In terms of ideological placement, many of these soviets sought to weaken or obstruct the economic liberalization to which the president and his regional emissaries (the governors) were committed.

In Novgorod and Pskov, the chairs of the last regional soviets were also the former chairs of the Communist Party executive committee. This fact explains to some extent why these bodies, which followed in the Soviet-era tradition of being dominated by a chairperson, were relatively active in resisting the authority of the new governor. The uneasy relationship between appointees and regional councils would come to a halt soon after the second major crisis at the federal level, in early October of 1993. In the constitutional crisis in late September and early October of 1993, Yeltsin and an opposing faction leading what remained of the national legislature (*Verhovnii Soviet*, or Supreme Council) entered the final stages of a standoff that was ultimately resolved through armed assault on the building where the parliament was housed.

After the crisis, the victorious President Yeltsin viewed the regional councils as reactionary bodies, since a majority had supported the Supreme Soviet during the conflict. Through several executive decrees Yeltsin stipulated a short timetable for their dissolution and replacement by new regional representative bodies, whose formative elections would take place in the first three months of 1994.

However, reactions by the regional soviets to the constitutional crisis of 1993 were not uniform, as some were more tenuous in their support of the Supreme Council. Some of the old assemblies were more objectionable to the Kremlin than others and, consequently, were ordered to dissolve immediately. In late September of 1993 the controlling committees of the regional councils in the provinces (*malyi soviet*) met to discuss their response to the crisis. On September 21, 1993, they received a cable from Moscow informing them of Yeltsin's decree #1400 ordering the dissolution of the Supreme Council. With little time to react in a situation of high uncertainty, they were forced to choose between siding with the president or with the parliament – a public pronouncement that would be published in the official regional newspaper.

While the Pskov and Novgorod councils passed very similar resolutions, declaring the presidential decree unconstitutional and calling for elections of both the president and the Supreme Council, the statement publicized by the Pskov council was far more balanced and neutral. Unlike the analogous measure in Novgorod, it also declared the actions of the national parliament unconstitutional and called for a restitution of the pre-crisis status quo. Additionally, the resolution was accompanied by another statement calling on the population to keep calm and respect the law that was signed jointly by the chairman of the regional council and the new governor, whose allegiance to the president as an appointee was clear. In contrast to these measured, carefully calibrated responses, the Novgorod resolution bluntly blamed the president's actions for the crisis, which resulted in the swift dissolution of the Novgorod council via presidential decree.

What explains the consequential difference in responses at this critical juncture? In short, lessons learned from the previous national constitutional crisis. During the failed *putsch* of 1991, provincial councils were also forced to take sides in a dramatic conflict at the national level that pitted the newly elected president of Russia against several key members of the Soviet upper echelon who tried to take over power in order to save the Communist Party and the Soviet Union in a coup. At the time, the leader of the Pskov council, an experienced chairman by the name of Vitalii Pushkarev, did not denounce the coup attempt early and decisively as so many other provincial leaders did but instead adopted a "wait and see" approach. After the crisis passed and Yeltsin emerged victorious, many inside and outside of Pskov province blamed Pushkarev for failing to denounce the coup early and called for his resignation. In spite of the criticisms, he stayed in power and continued to dominate the regional council.

When the second national crisis struck in September of 1993, a chastised Pushkarev responded quickly. Well aware of the possibility that the president could prevail again, the Pskov regional council chairman was careful not to blame Yeltsin for the crisis and enlisted the support of the regional governor, a presidential appointee, in a show of unity. As a result, the Pskov council was allowed to continue its existence and participated in the constitutional drafting process, profoundly altering the trajectory of the region. Ironically, the actions of a communist-era apparatchik shielded the institutional design process from executive influence and ultimately resulted in a strong and independent regional assembly.

The sequencing of events is crucial to understanding the repercussions of the standoff for the regions. Soon after the resolution of the crisis, the presidential administration issued another decree that named several regions, the legislatures of which had actively supported the Supreme Council, and ordered them to dissolve immediately. The Novgorod Council (*oblsoviet*) was among them, and the dissolution took place relatively early – on October 20, 1993, transferring all of its powers and staff to the administration. Consequently, the temporary charter for the region (*vremenoe polozhenie*), analogous to a constitution, as well as the rules governing eligibility for deputies in the first legislature, elections, and even the number of seats in the new assembly would all be determined solely by the appointed governor.

Governor Mikhail Prussak was in no rush to set up a new legislative body. He set the assembly election for late March of 1994, the latest allowed under presidential decree. Thus, for a period of six months all power in the province was concentrated in the hands of its chief executive. The governor used the opportunity presented by this six-month window to allow town mayors to serve on the body responsible for oversight of his administration. It should be noted that these mayors were at the time also directly appointed by the governor to their posts, as municipal elections would not be held until December of 1995. In other words, Governor Prussak staffed the first legislature with direct subordinates.

The scenario played out differently in Pskov. Given the more balanced response of the regional assembly to the national executive-legislative crisis, the council chairman rebuffed calls to dissolve the body, which in any case were not coming from Moscow, and held sessions until late December of 1993, the latest possible date under presidential decree. All of the key documents for the election of the new legislature were created by a joint commission of members of both the controlling committees of the regional councils and the governor's administration subject to the approval of the full council. Crucially, the commission established a strict line of separation between the executive and legislative branches. No assembly member could simultaneously serve on the legislature and hold a post in the executive branch at either the provincial or municipal level. The temporary charter, and the subsequent ratified permanent charter, contained an article that expressly prohibited members of the executive branch at any level of government from serving on the assembly. This article proved crucial for preserving the institutional autonomy of the assembly because it effectively blocked the governor of Pskov from deploying a potent tool for packing the assembly: the election of appointed mayors to serve as legislative deputies. In Novgorod, by contrast, the regional charter contained no such prohibition. This in turn rendered the legislature vulnerable to the governor's efforts to control it by sponsoring the candidacies for legislative seats of mayors who were directly accountable to him.

Whereas Pskov emerged from the institutional formation period with a relatively autonomous legislature, events took a different course in Novgorod where the governor relied heavily on his power to appoint town mayors as a way to capture the legislature. For the first two years of legislative activity, the mayor-deputies in Novgorod could be fired at any time from their primary job as mayors by the governor. When the first round of municipal elections occurred in December of 1995, the mayor-deputies in Novgorod had an advantage in terms of prominence and name recognition that gave them an edge as assembly candidates. With the assistance of the executive in the form of pork they consistently won a plurality in the assembly, sealing its fate as a mere appendage of the administration.

The governor's use of pork to prop assembly candidates was no secret. In newspaper interviews, mayor-deputies in Novgorod shamelessly bragged about pet projects and claimed credit for bringing them to their district. In early February of 1995, a journalist from the official regional newspaper asked deputy Valentin Ob'iedkov, mayor of Staraya Russ' district, what had given him the decisive edge over other candidates during the campaign. Ob'iedkov was quick to point to a water supply problem in one of the towns of the district, an issue resolved soon after the election through the construction of a new water conduit.[25] Similarly, deputy Nikolay Renkas, mayor of Krestetsky district, emphasized the fact that, thanks to him, the district got a 100-apartment housing complex, a new school, and a health center.[26] It was obvious to most in the province at the time that it was the governor who allocated funds for all of these projects.

The Novgorod legislature (*Duma*) was almost entirely a nonprofessional body, with only the speaker, a close associate of the governor's, serving as a paid, full-time employee. Moreover, it met infrequently for short sessions, typically less than four hours in total. Furthermore, the body had almost no legislative staff for most of the first decade of its existence, crippling its ability to draft bills and perform monitoring functions. In contrast, the Pskov assembly

---

[25] "Slovo Deputatu: 'Rossiya vistoit blagodarya provintsii.' Valentin Obe'dkov." *Novgorodskie Vedomosti.* February 8, 1995. (A word from the deputy: "Russia will survive because of the provinces.")

[26] "U menya – svoya pozitsiya." *Novgorodskie Vedomosti.* January 5, 1995. (I have a position of my own.)

immediately used the maximum number of full-time professional deputies allowed under presidential decrees, hired permanent staff to assist both the speaker and the deputies, and held long sessions occasionally spanning several days.

A pertinent question emerges regarding the possibility of demonstration effects between the two neighboring regions. Why were the Pskov draft writers so vigilant about the separation between the executive and legislative branches for the future, yet-unformed, assembly? Did they simply observe its effect in neighboring Novgorod and proactively preempt the possibility of a mayor-dominated assembly? A partial answer to this question lies in the fact that both assemblies opposed the appointed governors in the provinces, imposed on them by Moscow, and sought ways to minimize their influence. These appointments were part of President Yeltsin's broader campaign against the old communist guard, and as such they were intended to limit the power of the local political and economic elites across the federation. This fact was not lost on most councils. Had the Novgorod council survived for a few more months, it would have insisted on establishing a strict separation line between the two branches as well.

Careful sequencing of events contains the remainder of the answer. The timeline of the crucial institutional formation period simply did not allow for any horizontal learning, instead forcing constitution drafters to make assumptions about the new legislative bodies. The two temporary charters, which set the rules for the formation and election of the new regional parliaments, were finished by the end of 1993, and elections for the new parliaments in Pskov and Novgorod were held within six weeks of each other in the spring of 1994. In other words, institutional formation in the two provinces occurred simultaneously. Prior to the creation of the temporary charter in both provinces, no region in Russia had yet elected an assembly under the new system set up by presidential decrees. This meant that it was unclear what role the new bodies would play vis-à-vis regional governors or what factors would drive legislative elections. Members of the Pskov regional council along with its dominant chairperson simply assumed that they would have the best chance of making it into the new legislature if they would not have to compete against the new town mayors, recently appointed by the governor, or any other administration officials. They guessed correctly – several council members did indeed make it into the new chamber. Their counterparts in Novgorod had no such luck, however, because they were sent home before they could have any impact on the temporary charter. Figure 4.2 presents an outline of the argument.

Having described the circumstances surrounding the period of institutional formation in the two regions, I now move to the resulting balance of power between executives and legislatures during the first decade after the collapse of the Soviet Union. Did the initial institutional configuration "stick"? In Novgorod, where the executive had manipulated the body's mode of

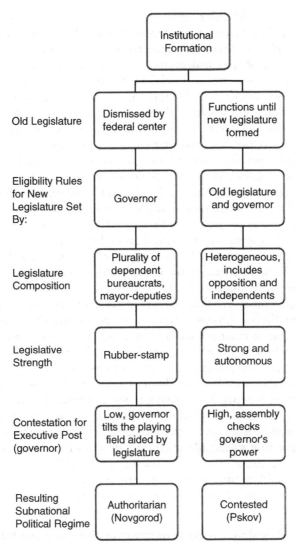

FIGURE 4.2 The Process of Subnational Regime Formation in Novgorod and Pskov

selection to elicit compliance, there was no shortage of calls for change. Every time any amendments to the constitution were on the agenda, there were initiatives, usually by civil society organizations, to abolish the practice of mayors serving as deputies, especially intense during the regional charter writing period in mid-1994 but also in the latter part of the 1990s. All of them were ignored, often with the humorous counterargument that nobody was more knowledgeable about the districts than the municipal mayors and therefore nobody could better represent them. Naturally, the mayor-deputies in the assembly had no incentive to change the eligibility rules, because doing so would have resulted in their self-imposed disqualification.

The perception of mayor-deputies in Novgorod, as reported in the local press, was that they were simply members of the "governor's team" (*"komanda gubernatora"*). A TV interview, reported in the official regional newspaper, with one of the mayor-deputies in January of 1995 presents a telling illustration of their position. A journalist at one of the regional TV channels criticized the legislature for passing everything that the governor introduces. Deputy Leonid Apel'sinov replied that the bills are carefully scrutinized in committee and therefore their passage does not require much deliberation by the full body. The journalist then probed further by asking whether it is possible that people place too much faith in deputies, even though in the eyes of voters they are seen mostly as paper pushers or stampers (*"tolkach"*). Apel'sinov, clearly annoyed, responded by saying that he likes no party, and the roles of "politician" and "manager" (*"khozyastvenik"*) do not interfere with each other, implicitly acknowledging the unusual nature of his dual appointment.[27]

The autonomous legislature in Pskov successfully resisted numerous attempts by governors to allow mayors to serve on the assembly. As already mentioned, to thwart similar advances in the future, the assembly passed provisions in the permanent charter expressly prohibiting members of the executive branch at any level from serving, which the governor in the region reluctantly signed. The institutionalization of this eligibility requirement is not surprising: Had the incumbent legislators assented to the removal of the barrier preventing sitting mayors from serving in the assembly they would have been inviting strong potential competitors in their next district reelection races. This would have been an extremely risky move, especially for legislators who were openly in opposition to the administration or unaffiliated with it. They could reasonably expect the governor to throw logistical and financial support behind mayors who would, in turn, have an incentive to side with him for the prospect of broadening their portfolio to include an assembly seat.

The Executive–Legislative Balance of Power in Novgorod and Pskov, 1994–2004

Within the context of the two case studies, I rely on three main indicators to assess the position of the legislature vis-à-vis the governor: (1) the ease of passage of the annual budget bills; (2) formal powers amendments to the charter and gubernatorial election law; and (3) the affiliation of the speaker (chairperson). Each indicator provides a stream of observations that shed light

---

[27] "Ta politika, ot kotoroi stanovit'sya luchshe." *Novgorodskie Vedomosti.* January 5, 1995. Interview with Leonid Apel'sinov, mayor of Okulovsky district. (The type of politics that makes us better off is best.)

on the functioning of the assembly as it performs some of its most important duties. Budget bills and regional charter amendments are of particular importance to the executive branch. The manner in which they pass or do not pass through the legislature reveals quite a lot about the degree to which governors get their way. These are the occasions when the "rubber" of executive ambition meets the "road" of legislators' interests.

With regard to the budgetary process, I focus on the extent to which governors got what they sought from legislatures fiscally and also how the process of passing the budget transpired. This negotiation takes place at least once every year (in reality more often, due to budget amendments) and is a good indicator of the strength of the regional assembly. Budgets are typically the most important single piece of legislation each year. Furthermore, in the context of the executive–legislative relationship, they constitute one of the most important levers that an assembly has at its disposal – what is often referred to in the study of US politics as the "power of the purse."[28] The cases range from almost routine rejection of the governor's bills (1994–1998, Pskov) to nearly every budget bill passing unanimously in the very first session it was introduced (1998–2004, Novgorod).

The second indicator rests on the formal dimensions of power. The first decade under the new Russian constitution (1994–2004) saw incessant institutional fiddling at the regional level across the federation. In all cases, gubernatorial election laws were changed prior to every election. While most of the changes were minor and technical, many were not. They concerned such fundamental issues as eligibility requirements for gubernatorial candidates, the number of rounds of voting necessary to win, and term limits. A similar pattern applies to regional charters – many underwent major reforms, with amendments that changed the responsibilities of governors and legislatures, the budget process, and the number of cabinet-member or mayoral appointments subject to assembly consent. The tug-of-war between the executive and legislative branches left many traces in the form of major and minor institutional changes.

Finally, my focus on the affiliation of the speaker reflects both the enormous influence that the position offers in most regional legislatures and the fact that control of this position is a good indicator of the number of deputies loyal to the executive. Dramatic changes in the proportion of seats the governor controls frequently led to a change of speaker, since a simple majority could impose its preference on the chamber by electing a new speaker.

---

[28] I use newspaper reports to establish how the budget bill introduced by the regional administration passed (or did not pass) through the legislature: what kind of objections were raised if any, over what items deputies and representatives of the governor clashed, and in whose favor were disputes resolved; how did the final round of voting on the entire budget bill go; how many sessions did it take to resolve differences and pass the budget; and how much time elapsed between introduction and passage?

TABLE 4.5 *Share of Mayor-Deputies in Novgorod Duma*

Novgorod Duma	Total Deputies	Mayor-Deputies	Share
I. (April 1994–December 1995)	19	8	42%
II. (December 1995–March 1997)	27	8	30%
III. (October 1997–October 2001)	26	12	46%
IV. (October 2001–October 2006)	26	10	38%

The Novgorod *Duma* epitomized a classic rubber-stamp body from the first day of its creation, existing as a mere appendage to the gubernatorial administration over the entire period of study. The assembly was populated by consistent pluralities of mayors who performed loyal service to the governor and guaranteed smooth and seamless passage of bills. Table 4.5 shows the proportion of mayor-deputies serving in the four legislative sessions during the period of study. Deputies typically voted on resolutions after less than five minutes of deliberation and passed them unanimously. Agendas consisting of over 30 items were rushed through two-hour sessions, while budget bills, the most important piece of legislation each year, passed smoothly, with only occasional cosmetic revisions.

The shares of mayor-deputies displayed in Table 4.5 could lead us to question whether this was indeed the most important element to controlling the assembly, since their numbers never reached a simple majority and were instead limited to a consistent plurality. Two additional considerations are necessary to fully appreciate the impact of the mayor-deputies, whose influence was greater than their numbers would suggest. First, these deputies come in addition to the other openly pro-gubernatorial deputies that were elected. In Novgorod province, as in most of the rest of the federation, governors were essentially guaranteed at least few seats in the legislature, typically about three to four. They would strategically place candidates in districts considered sympathetic to the governor, give them financial support, and, often, publicly endorse them.[29] In Novgorod, this was the case for three deputies, two of whom worked directly for the governor prior to running for the assembly. The one and only speaker of the Novgorod assembly, Anatolii Boytsev, who served for two years as deputy-governor under Prussak (1992–1994), fits that category, as does the deputy-speaker. Together with the mayor-deputies, they formed a cohesive voting block with a simple majority most of the time.

The second consideration is that the presence of the mayor-deputy group greatly reduced the incentives to organize an opposition in order to capture the

---

[29] A similarly sized group was usually present in the Pskov legislature as well; however, they were marginalized and isolated frequently throughout the period under study.

assembly. If the Novgorod governor was certain to capture a near-majority of the chamber, then what could an opposition faction accomplish? At best, they could only hope for a stalemate, assuming they banded together and won every seat that the governor did not hold. A successful veto override, for example, was unattainable. Per presidential decree, all of the legislatures across the federation were initially set up with a two-thirds veto override requirement. In other words, a supermajority of two-thirds of the deputies was necessary to truly force the governor's hand. Unsurprisingly, there were never any vetoes or veto overrides in Novgorod, in contrast to neighboring Pskov, where veto overrides occurred at least once per year in the first five years. The permanent presence of the mayor-deputies in the chamber simply limited the space for a viable opposition.

The remainder of the seats belonged to a few representatives who were connected to the administration and a group of directors of mixed-ownership and private companies, which gradually increased in size. With almost no exceptions they, too, behaved acquiescently. The single exception was a generally unruly deputy, who was also the only party-affiliated candidate to make it into the chamber for the entire first decade – a testament to the success of the strategy of packing the assembly in suppressing party development.

Other assembly members were "promoted" to serve as senior administration officials – repayment for loyal service on the assembly floor. Since Governor Prussak considered the legislature a part of his administration, he also used it as a cadre reserve, especially the mayor-deputy group. Given the fact that the mayor-deputies received no remuneration for their service as representatives, they would consider being hired to work full-time as a member of the gubernatorial administration to be a promotion. A position in the regional government was also seen as a step up from serving as a town mayor for a rural district, in terms of both salary and prestige.

The legislature in the adjacent Pskov province operated quite differently, methodically opposing the governor's initiatives. The assembly consistently displayed a degree of strength vis-à-vis gubernatorial administrations that often came close to a checks-and-balances arrangement. Particularly during the first assembly (1994–1998), lawmakers successfully completed veto overrides, questioned and criticized senior administration officials on spending, rejected or significantly amended budget bills, and rebuffed attempts by the governor to expand formal powers or centralize regional tax revenues. Political elites and electorates in the province took the assembly seriously and actively participated in the elections for the body. Turnout for legislative elections was always higher in Pskov, as the importance of the legislature was not lost on voters.

The composition of the legislatures was far more diverse in Pskov than in Novgorod. The first and most powerful assembly vis-à-vis the executive branch assembly (1994–1998), included several experienced jurists, one of whom had been responsible for drafting the temporary charter for the old council, while another would later be appointed prosecutor for the region by the federal justice ministry. The deputies elected from the city of Pskov consisted of several representatives loyal to the mayor (who was in conflict with the governor), three doctors from city hospitals, and a university professor. The most aggressive opponent of the appointed governor was a deputy from a rural district, Genadii Bubnov, a former state farm manager who nominally ran as an independent but was assumed to be opposed to governor Vladislav Tumanov. Bubnov held the second most important post in the assembly – chair of the budget committee.

During the entire period under study the Pskov assembly remained a relatively autonomous and powerful legislature with heterogeneous composition and a permanent presence of at least several deputies openly opposed to the chief executive. Notably, the chamber was home to two different opposition factions – a group of communist party deputies affiliated with a regional chapter of the national Communist Party of the Russian Federation (CPRF) and a local faction of several prominent politicians opposed to the governor. From the very beginning and until almost the end of the first decade of legislative activity, the assembly was led by a widely respected and genuinely independent speaker, Iurii Shmatov, who kept the governor at an arm's length.

Executive Contestation in Novgorod and Pskov

The pair of case studies presented here pose a puzzle for existing studies of democratization – extremely similar polities located in close proximity to each other that experience widely divergent levels of contestation. In Novgorod, Governor Prussak reigned virtually unchallenged from early 1992, when he was appointed by President Yeltsin, until 2007, cruising to victory in three gubernatorial elections with suspiciously high levels of support. For example, as seen in Table 4.6, he collected 92 percent of the vote in September of 1999. If Novgorod had been a sovereign state instead of a federal sub-unit, it could plausibly be classified as an electoral authoritarian regime, in light of the results of its gubernatorial elections past the first cycle in 1995.

Pskov, by contrast, stands as an outlier within the Russian federation in terms of political contestation. On two occasions gubernatorial heads rolled. The second time was clearly an anomaly in relation to the gradual drift toward authoritarianism seen across the country, as it occurred in early 2005 when an incumbent governor, officially supported by the pro-presidential United Russia party, lost in a rare defeat for the Kremlin. Incumbent governors in Pskov failed to muster even a third of the vote in the first round, a stark contrast to adjacent Novgorod.

The divergence across the two provinces can be attributed partly to the successful strategy of packing the assembly implemented by the governor in Novgorod. In the first two years of their existence, assemblies in most Russian regions were charged with devising the laws regulating gubernatorial elections.

TABLE 4.6 *Gubernatorial Contests in Novgorod and Pskov*

Incumbent First-Round Vote Share	Novgorod	Pskov
1995/1996	56%	31%
Incumbent reelected	Yes	No
1999/2000	92%	28%
Incumbent reelected	Yes	Yes
2003/2004	79%	30%
Incumbent reelected	Yes	No

One of the most pressing and immediate reasons for any incumbent governor to attempt to bring a legislature under control was to ensure, within the confines of federal law, that every procedural opportunity to tilt the playing field in his favor would be implemented. Predictably, docile legislatures often created electoral rules favoring incumbent governors. They also did not perform their budget monitoring functions, which enabled executive incumbents to move money around freely and engage in patronage.

One important way to create an advantage for the incumbent was to have the gubernatorial seat be decided in a single-round election; that is, eliminating the runoff round altogether. This improved a sitting governor's chances of reelection by raising the bar for potential challengers. Under a two-round election, opposition candidates who failed to reach the second stage could throw their support behind the runner-up. Therefore, runoff rounds served the dual function of identifying the most viable challenger and providing opposition candidates with an incentive to build an electoral alliance against the incumbent – typically the only way to unseat a governor. With a single-round election, on the other hand, only a highly unsuccessful and tremendously unpopular governor could lose, and that was likely to happen only if another candidate emerged who could match him in name recognition and campaign resources.[30]

Since the subservient Novgorod Duma secured the guarantee of a single-round election for the governor soon after the collapse of the Soviet Union, the combination of the certainty of executive reelection, which was virtually ensured by the single round election law, and the lack of budget oversight led to a vicious cycle of self-reinforcing expectations. The Novgorod Duma deputies, both those serving simultaneously as municipal mayors and others, became increasingly dependent on the governor, in turn, further weakening the assembly. At the heart of this dependence was the implicit, yet credible, dual

[30] It should be noted that a single-round election for provincial governors in Russia went against the precedent in place at the federal level (presidential elections) and municipal level (mayoral elections).

claim by the governor – that he would not only continue to be around for the foreseeable future but also remain the sole source of pork. The fiscal proceeds that he directed with no oversight were desperately needed, particularly in the poorer, rural districts where most of the deputy-mayors came from. In large part due to the docile nature of the legislature, no significant challengers emerged during the entire period of study and the incumbent governor's victory margins continued to increase over time.

In contrast, the appointed governor of neighboring Pskov lost in 1996 in large part because the regional assembly refused to eliminate the runoff electoral round. His successor eventually suffered a similar fate in 2004, although he managed to win reelection in 2000 by buying enough deputy votes in order to change the electoral law to a single-round election. Unfortunately for him, the combination of public outcry against the blatant corruption coupled with the fact that, unlike his Novgorod counterpart, he was unable to suppress the rise of opposition factions in the legislature, eventually led to his electoral demise in 2004. The loss occurred even though the incumbent was endorsed by the Kremlin and the pro-presidential United Russia party at a time when pro-Kremlin candidates across the country were virtually guaranteed a win.

The role of the mayor-deputies helps explain why a personalistic and uncompetitive regime emerged in Novgorod yet not in Pskov. In Novgorod, the governor's strategy of controlling the regional assembly by packing it with mayor-deputies formalized their position as vassals of the governor serving in the legislature. Among the members of the assembly in Novgorod, the near-certainty of gubernatorial reelection meant that there were few incentives to be disloyal to the governor. Moreover, despite the de jure oversight of the assembly, the governor enjoyed de facto discretionary control over how to spend much of revenue transferred by the federal government. As a result, pork for a legislator's district could only be secured with the governor's blessing. Whereas the governors in Pskov were limited in their ability to move money around due to the strength of the legislature, the governor of Novgorod faced no such constraint.

In Pskov, most of the municipal mayors were openly critical of the governor after their post became popularly elected. Instead of supporting the governor, they would use the assembly as a platform for demanding protection from executive maltreatment and also the fair distribution of fiscal transfers from the federal government. Deputies in Pskov closely monitored spending bills and modified them, in the process criticizing the chief of the provincial Department of Finance.

Over time, the regimes of these two very similar provinces moved in opposite directions, one closely resembling electoral authoritarianism and the other being remarkably contested. By the end of the first decade of legislative activity, executive elections in Novgorod had become yet another means of reinforcing the authority of the one and only governor, whose every decision was reliably rubber-stamped by a docile legislature. Meanwhile in neighboring

Pskov, a strong and independent assembly tied the hands of multiple governors and prevented them from tilting the playing field.

4.6 CONCLUSION

Subnational politics in competitive authoritarian regimes like Russia's is shaped by institutions and processes that diverge from those operating at the national level. The controlled comparison between Pskov and Novgorod featured in this chapter shows that otherwise similar subnational polities can experience widely divergent political outcomes, especially with regard to patterns of executive-legislative relations and levels of contestation. Moreover, as both the qualitative and descriptive quantitative analysis presented in this chapter show, subnational variation in political regimes in Russia is not easily explained with standard national-level predictors and socioeconomic "prerequisites" of democracy, nor can it be explained with geography. Consequently, explaining subnational regime trajectories in Russia requires a distinct theoretical framework, one that focuses on the contrasting incentives and constraints that drove the behavior of subnational politicians across the provinces.

Russia's provinces differed in their formal constitutional rules concerning matters such as the eligibility requirements for serving in the assembly, especially whether mayors appointed by the governor could simultaneously hold elected office in the regional assembly and whether gubernatorial elections would be decided in single round or, alternatively, in a runoff if no candidate won at least half the votes. These institutional differences, in turn, had consequences for subnational regimes. As seen in Novgorod, permissive eligibility requirements that allowed the governor to stack the assembly with compliant "mayor-deputies," together with single-round elections, contributed to the emergence and maintenance of personalistic and uncompetitive regimes dominated by the governor. By contrast, as seen in Pskov, tighter eligibility requirements that shielded the assembly from executive penetration by prohibiting its members from holding executive branch offices, coupled with two-round gubernatorial elections, effectively blocked governors from consolidating their power and contributed to the maintenance of competitive politics.

Moreover, these institutional differences were no accident: They were deliberately designed to serve either the interests of subnational executives seeking to centralize power, or, alternatively, of subnational legislatures aiming to prevent executive dominance. Whether the new rules favored executives or assemblies depended largely on the balance of power at the provincial level between the two branches at the onset of the period of subnational institutional design at the beginning of the 1990s. This provincial balance of power, in turn, was determined largely by national-level factors, namely the outcome of two national political crises in the early 1990s. In provinces like Novgorod, where the provincial assembly supported the losing side in the violent executive–legislative conflict between President Yeltsin and the national assembly in September of 1993, President Yeltsin subsequently intervened to strengthen the hand of the provincial executive by immediately dissolving the legislature. By contrast, in provinces where assemblies maintained a neutral stance, as in Pskov, the victorious national executive permitted the legislature to continue to exist. These contrasting national interventions set these two quite similar subnational political units on remarkably different paths. To trace these heterogeneous subnational effects of national-level causes, the chapter thus deploys what the editors of this volume label a "top-down" multilevel perspective.

As the case of Pskov's assertive legislature shows, subnational institutions have the remarkable ability to produce and sustain outcomes that differ markedly from the national trend. Subnational political actors are not passive recipients of dictates from the national capital but are instead active agents with considerable potential influence over outcomes. Importantly, as this chapter has shown, the behavior and strategies of subnational actors do not simply mirror those available to their counterparts at the national level. Politics in the periphery is a distinct and curious phenomenon that deserves further study.

BIBLIOGRAPHY

Benton, Allyson Lucinda. (2012). Bottom-up challenges to national democracy: Mexico's (legal) subnational authoritarian enclaves. *Comparative Politics* 44(3), 253–271.

Bivand, Roger. (2014). spdep: Spatial dependence: weighting schemes, statistics and models. R package version 0.5–77.

Blasi, Joseph R., Kroumova, Maya, & Kruse, Douglas. (1997). *Kremlin capitalism: The privatization of the Russian economy*. Ithaca, NY: Cornell University Press.

Boix, Carles, & Stokes, Susan C. (2003). Endogenous democratization. *World Politics* 55(4), 517–549.

Collier, Ruth Berins, & Collier, David. (2002). *Shaping the political arena: Critical junctures, the labor movement, and regime dynamics in Latin America*. Notre Dame, IN: University of Notre Dame Press.

Cook, Linda. (2007). Negotiating welfare in postcommunist states. *Comparative Politics* 40(1), 41–62.

Dahl, Robert Alan. (1971). *Polyarchy: Participation and opposition*. New Haven, CT: Yale University Press.

Elkink, Johan A. (2011). The international diffusion of democracy. *Comparative Political Studies* 44(12), 1651–1674.

Elster, Jon. (1993). Bargaining over the presidency. *East European Constitutional Review* 2(4), 95–98.

Elster, Jon. (1996). The role of institutional interest in East European constitution-making. *East European Constitutional Review* 5(1), 63–65.

Elster, Jon, Claus Offe, & Preuss, Ulrich K. (1998). *Institutional design in post-communist societies: Rebuilding the ship at sea*. Cambridge, England: Cambridge University Press.

Fish, M. Steven. (2005). *Democracy derailed in Russia: The failure of open politics.* Cambridge, England: Cambridge University Press.

Fish, M. Steven. (2006). Stronger legislatures, stronger democracies. *Journal of Democracy* 17(1), 5–20.

Frye, Timothy. (1997). A politics of institutional choice: Post-communist presidencies. *Comparative Political Studies* 30(5), 523–552.

Gervasoni, Carlos. (2010). A rentier theory of subnational regimes: Fiscal federalism, democracy, and authoritarianism in the argentine provinces. *World Politics* 62(2), 302–340.

Gibson, Edward L. (2005). Boundary control: Subnational authoritarianism in democratic countries. *World Politics* 58(1), 101–132.

Gibson, Edward L. (2013). *Boundary control: Subnational authoritarianism in federal democracies.* Cambridge, England: Cambridge University Press.

Giraudy, Agustina. (2015). *Democrats and autocrats: Pathways of subnational undemocratic regime continuity within democratic countries.* Oxford, England: Oxford University Press.

Golosov, Grigorii. (2004). *Political parties in the regions of Russia: Democracy unclaimed.* Boulder, CO: Lynne Rienner Publishers.

Gorenburg, Dmitry P. (2003). *Minority ethnic mobilization in the Russian Federation.* Cambridge, England: Cambridge University Press.

Hale, Henry E. (2003). Explaining machine politics in Russia's regions: Economy, ethnicity, and legacy. *Post-Soviet Affairs* 19(3), 228–263.

Hale, Henry E. (2006). *Why not parties in Russia? Democracy, federalism, and the state.* Cambridge, England: Cambridge University Press.

Harden, Jeffrey J. (2013). Multidimensional Responsiveness: The Determinants of Legislators' Representational Priorities. *Legislative Studies Quarterly* 38(2), 155–184.

King, James D. (2000). Changes in professionalism in U.S. state legislatures. *Legislative Studies Quarterly* 25(2), 327–343.

Kousser, Thad. (2005). *Term limits and the dismantling of state legislative professionalism.* Cambridge, England: Cambridge University Press.

Konitzer, Andrew. (2005). *Voting for Russia's governors: Regional elections and accountability under Yeltsin and Putin.* Baltimore, MD: Johns Hopkins University Press.

Kopstein, Jeffrey S., & Reilly, David A. (2000). Geographic diffusion and the transformation of the postcommunist world. *World Politics* 53(1), 1–37.

Laakso, Markku, & Taagepera, Rein. (1979). Effective number of parties: A measure with application to West Europe. *Comparative Political Studies* 12(1), 3–27.

Ledeneva, Alena V. (2006). *How Russia really works: The informal practices that shaped post-Soviet politics and business.* Ithaca, NY: Cornell University Press.

Levitsky, Steven, & Way, Lucan. (2002). The rise of competitive authoritarianism. *Journal of Democracy* 13(2), 51–65.

Lieberman, Evan S. (2005). Nested analysis as a mixed-method strategy for comparative research. *American Political Science Review* 99(03), 435–452.

Lijphart, Arend. (1991). Constitutional choices for new democracies. *Journal of Democracy* 2(1), 72–84.

Lijphart, Arend. (1992). Democratization and constitutional choices in Czecho-Slovakia, Hungary and Poland 1989–91. *Journal of Theoretical Politics* 4(2), 207–223.

Linz, Juan J. (1990a). The perils of presidentialism. *Journal of Democracy* 1(1), 51–69.

Linz, Juan J. (1990b). The virtues of parliamentarism. *Journal of Democracy* 1(2), 84–91.

Linz, Juan J., & Valenzuela, Arturo (Eds.). (1994). *The failure of presidential democracy: Comparative perspectives.* Baltimore, MD: Johns Hopkins University Press.

Lipset, Seymour Martin. (1959). Some social requisites of democracy: Economic development and political legitimacy. *American Political Science Review* 53(1), 69–105.

Mainwaring, Scott, & Pérez-Liñán, Aníbal. (2007). Why regions of the world are important: Regional specificities and region-wide diffusion of democracy. In Gerardo L. Munck (Ed.), *Regimes and democracy in Latin America: Theories and methods*, pp. 199–229. New York, NY: Oxford University Press.

Malhotra, Neil. (2006). Government growth and professionalism in U.S. state legislatures. *Legislative Studies Quarterly* 31(4), 563–584.

McFaul, Michael. (2001a). Explaining party formation and nonformation in Russia: Actors, institutions, and chance. *Comparative Political Studies* 34(10), 1159–1187.

McFaul, Michael. (2001b). *Russia's unfinished revolution: Political change from Gorbachev to Putin.* Ithaca, NY: Cornell University Press.

McMann, Kelly M. (2006). *Economic autonomy and democracy: Hybrid regimes in Russia and Kyrgyzstan.* Cambridge, England: Cambridge University Press.

Moraski, Bryan. (2006). *Elections by design: Parties and patronage in Russia's regions.* DeKalb: Northern Illinois University Press.

O'loughlin, John, Ward, Michael D., Lofdahl, Corey L., Cohen, Jordin S., Brown, David S., Reilly, David, Gleditsch, Kristian S., & Shin, Michael. (1998). The diffusion of democracy, 1946–1994. *Annals of the Association of American Geographers* 88(4), 545–574.

Powell, Bingham G. (1982). *Contemporary democracies: Participation, stability, and violence.* Cambridge, MA: Harvard University Press.

Przeworski, Adam. (1991). *Democracy and the market: Political and economic reforms in Eastern Europe and Latin America.* Cambridge, England: Cambridge University Press.

Przeworski, Adam. (2000). *Democracy and development: Political institutions and well-being in the world, 1950–1990.* Cambridge, England: Cambridge University Press.

Remington, Thomas F. (2001). *The Russian parliament: Institutional evolution in a transitional regime, 1989–1999.* New Haven, CT: Yale University Press.

Remington, Thomas F. (2011). *The politics of inequality in Russia.* Cambridge, England: Cambridge University Press.

Ross, Cameron. (2002). *Federalism and democratization in Russia.* Manchester, England: Manchester University Press.

Rustow, Dankwart A. (1970). Transitions to democracy: Toward a dynamic model. *Comparative Politics* 2(3), 337–363.

Schedler, Andreas (Ed.). (2006). *Electoral authoritarianism: The dynamics of unfree competition.* Boulder, CO: Lynne Rienner Publishers.

Sharafutdinova, Gulnaz. (2006). When do elites compete? The determinants of political competition in Russian regions. *Comparative Politics* 38(3), 273–293.

Shugart, Matthew Soberg. (2006). Comparative executive-legislative relations. In R. A. W. Rhodes, Sarah Binder, & Bert Rockman, *The Oxford Handbook of Political Institutions*, pp. 344–365. Oxford: Oxford University Press.

Snyder, Richard. (2001). Scaling down: The subnational comparative method. *Studies in Comparative International Development 36*(1), 93–110.

Squire, Peverill. (1992). Legislative professionalization and membership diversity in state legislatures. *Legislative Studies Quarterly 17*(1), 69–79.

Squire, Peverill. (1998). Membership turnover and the efficient processing of legislation. *Legislative Studies Quarterly 23*(1), 23–32.

Squire, Peverill. (2005). The Evolution of American Colonial Assemblies as Legislative Organizations. *Congress & the Presidency 32*(2), 109–131.

Squire, Peverill. (2007). Measuring state legislative professionalism: The Squire index revisited. *State Politics & Policy Quarterly 7*(2), 211–227.

Stoner-Weiss, Katherine. (2002). *Local heroes: The political economy of Russian regional governance.* Princeton, NJ: Princeton University Press.

5

Multilevel Causation in Gender Policy: Abortion and Violence against Women Laws in the Mexican States

Caroline Beer

As multiparty democracy was institutionalized in Mexico during the early 2000s, gender-equality policies emerged as central political issues across the country. State governments debated and reformed abortion and violence-against-women (VAW) laws. But while similar VAW laws diffused throughout the country, with every state adopting new legislation between 2006 and 2010, Mexico City's 2007 law to liberalize abortion was not replicated anywhere else. In fact, Mexico City's abortion law faced a challenge in the Supreme Court, and then backlash legislation further criminalized abortion in over half the states. Explaining variation in patterns of policy adoption within countries requires a multilevel approach that considers causal factors at various levels of analysis. My main argument is that patterns of policy adoption vary depending upon issue characteristics. Different policies will have different patterns of adoption, based on the level of national and international consensus on the issue and the strength of the organized opposition to policy reform. The increasing attention to gender-equality policies since Mexico's transition to multiparty democracy shows how the voices of all Mexicans are increasingly joining public policy debates.

This chapter compares the patterns of policy adoption for abortion and VAW policies across the states in Mexico. A complete explanation of subnational policymaking requires the incorporation of subnational, national, and international factors. In both cases subnational feminist activism inspired national engagement with the policy issue when the "loser" of the local political game appealed to higher-level authorities, but national and international factors played a much more important role in VAW policy than in abortion policy. When there was no national or international consensus, and there was a strong, well-financed opposition, as in the case of abortion, we see a diversity

Many thanks to Catalina Smulovitz for her comments and suggestions on an earlier version of this manuscript. Thank you to Mike Ballard for his help with the graphics. This research was funded by a grant from the Rakin Foundation at the University of Vermont.

of policy outcomes at the state level, reflecting internal differences among the states. In contrast, when there was an international norm with strong national agreement and no organized opposition, as in the case of VAW laws, we see replication across the country. Differences in international norms, national public opinion, and organized opposition resulted in different patterns of policy adoption. Subnational political characteristics are most important in determining subnational legislative decisions when there is no national or international consensus on the issue. When there is national or international consensus on an issue, national and international factors will have more influence on subnational policymaking. The analysis shows how multilevel theory as part of SNR, and, as outlined in the introduction to this volume, can play an important role in advancing our understanding of the politics and important consequences of gender policy.

This chapter analyzes policies that are formally under the purview of the state government. The criminal codes that regulate both abortion and VAW are part of the state governments' jurisdiction in Mexico. The outcome of interest is a state-level variable (adoption of new gender policy), though the main dependent variable in this study is the *pattern* of policy adoption in states across the entire country: Does policy innovation in one state lead to replication across the country or, alternatively, to heterogeneous outcomes? In the introduction to this volume, the editors outline seven distinct strategies for SNR based on the number of levels of analysis and the type of causal relationships that exist among levels of analysis. This chapter assesses the capacity of these strategies to produce hypothesized causal paths that can explain the different patterns of policy adoption for abortion and VAW legislation in the Mexican states. The first potential causal path is state-level characteristics driving state-level policy adoption (that is, subnational units are autonomous, or what the editors call "freestanding units"). The second potential causal path is horizontal influence whereby some states influence other states. This is the classic "diffusion" hypothesis prominent in studies of US federalism. The third and fourth potential causal paths focus on how top-down influence from national and international forces influence state-level policy adoption. Finally, I examine reciprocal causality whereby subnational activism or policy innovation activates national or international institutions, which in turn exert top-down pressure on other states to adopt new policy. The chapter analyzes which of these causal paths best represents the policymaking process for gender policy in Mexico.

5.1 THEORETICAL CONSIDERATIONS

The most straightforward answer to the question of which level of government is most important for making policy is the level of government that has the formal institutional prerogative to make laws and regulations. These institutional rules vary across policy areas and countries (Smulovitz, 2015).

For example, Argentina and Brazil each have one national penal code, whereas the Mexican states each have their own penal code. Thus, we should expect subnational factors to drive policy outcomes to a greater extent under Mexican federalism (Lopreite, 2014; Haussman, 2005; MacDonald & Mills, 2010). Similarly, marriage laws also vary in different federal systems. Marriage laws are under the jurisdiction of state governments in Mexico and the United States but under the purview of the national government in Argentina and Canada (Díez, 2015). Thus, following the institutional argument, we would expect state-level factors to dominate in policymaking related to marriage equality in the United States and Mexico, whereas national-level factors would be central for Argentina and Canada (Beer & Cruz-Aceves, 2018). But even when subnational governments have the formal power to legislate, national-level factors may constrain subnational policy options through judicial action or federal legislation. International-level variables may also influence subnational politics. The level of government where policy decisions are made is a constant focal point for political conflict. The institutional framework sets the parameters, but these parameters can change as losers seek advantage over policy outcomes by moving decision-making arenas to different levels of government, in what is often referred to as "venue-shopping" (Baumgartner & Jones, 1993). Therefore, a static formal institutional explanation may not be sufficient to determine which level of government is most influential in subnational policymaking, and multilevel analysis may provide more theoretical leverage. Following the strategies for subnational research outlined in the introduction to this volume, I examine five potential causal paths for explaining subnational policy adoption.

The first potential causal path is one where subnational governments operate as if they were autonomous or "freestanding units." Therefore, policies vary across subnational units primarily as a result of factors internal to each subnational unit. This reflects the classic rationale for federalism wherein local governments can have diverse policies to reflect the preferences of their constituents more closely. If subnational units are autonomous, they may function similarly to national polities and provide useful opportunities to test cross-national theories of comparative politics, though as discussed in Soifer's Chapter 3 in this volume, the modifiable areal unit problem (MAUP) may result in different findings at different levels of analysis. If subnational governments are freestanding units, then we would predict heterogeneous subnational policy outcomes determined by subnational characteristics. In the case of gender policy, we would expect states with strong feminist movements (Mazur, 2002; Weldon, 2002), more women in government (Childs & Krook, 2008; Schwindt-Bayer, 2010), and a less influential Catholic Church (Loaeza, 2013; Htun, 2003; Blofield, 2006) to be more likely to adopt gender-equality policies.

The second possible causal path is horizontal causality, whereby subnational units influence other subnational units at the same level. For example, a policy innovation in one state influences other states, possibly through policy learning, backlash, or competition among states (for prestige, tax revenue, investment, etc.). Thus, under this scenario, subnational governments are not treated as autonomous, as in the freestanding units approach, but rather are influenced by other units at the same level of government. The classic policy learning diffusion model from studies of US federalism offers a well-known example of horizontal causation among subnational units (Karch, 2007; Gray, 1973; Walker, 1969). In this model, one state experiments with a policy innovation. If it is successful, other states learn from this experiment and replicate successful policies. Horizontal influence can also include backlash whereby states adopt opposing legislation to forestall the replication of innovative reforms in another jurisdiction (Haider-Markel, 2001). Horizontal causality would predict variation based on the level of interaction among the states. If there is horizontal influence, states with close geographic proximity and states connected by networks of professionals or activists would be more likely to have similar policies (Sugiyama, 2008).

A third causal path is top-down pressure from forces located at a higher scale for subnational policy change. Tools that national governments might use to exert top-down pressure include financial incentives, threats to withdraw transfers or other benefits, national legislation, or judicial action. The traditional understanding of Mexican policymaking, sometimes referred to as "hyper-presidentialism," in which national elites make policy decisions that subnational political leaders are expected to implement in a process sometimes referred to "harmonization," exemplifies the top-down model (Hernández-Rodríguez, 2003; Weldon, 1997). This causal path would predict similar policy across subnational units, though some subnational units may be more vulnerable to national pressure than others. States governed by the same party as the national government may be more vulnerable to political pressure exerted by national authorities. Poorer states might be more vulnerable to threats by the national government to withdraw transfers or other financial benefits. The case of abortion policy in Salta, Argentina, provides an interesting example of national influence. A 2012 Supreme Court ruling required all states to adopt regulations to provide abortions in the cases permitted in the penal code. The governor of Salta publicly refused to enact the new abortion regulations after the Supreme Court ruling, but, after widespread public shaming in the national press, Salta ironically became the first province to adopt the regulations (Smulovitz, 2017).

Top-down pressure for subnational policy change can also come from international institutions. Act 28 of the Inter-American Convention on Human Rights, for example, requires subnational jurisdictions in federal systems to fulfill their country's international treaty obligations (Dulitzky, 2006). International organizations may influence subnational polities through public shaming or financial incentives. Top-down international pressure would predict similar policies across subnational units, though subnational units that are more deeply embedded in world policy networks may be more likely to follow international norms (Levitsky & Way, 2006).

The final causal path is reciprocal causation among subnational, national, and international levels. This causal path resembles Keck and Sikkink's (1999, pp. 93–94) "boomerang pattern," whereby national actors who are unsuccessful having their demands met appeal to international allies to bring outside pressure on their governments. Keck and Sikkink see this pattern as relying on transnational advocacy networks. Following O'Brien (2013), the reciprocal model here adds a subnational level to Keck and Sikkink's "boomerang pattern," such that subnational actors may seek allies at the national level *or* the international level when they are unsuccessful at the subnational level. Keck and Sikkink argue that issue characteristics and actor characteristics such as international salience, strength of networks, and ability for leverage are important for understanding the influence of international pressure. They argue that issues that involve "bodily harm to vulnerable individuals" are more likely to resonate internationally (Keck & Sikkink, 1999, p. 98). This suggests that violence-against-women policies may have more international resonance than abortion policies. Organized opposition is likely to be stronger for issues that conflict with central tenets of a community's dominant religion (such as abortion and the Catholic Church) (Htun & Weldon, 2010). Because of greater opposition from the Catholic Church, we would expect less reciprocal causation for abortion liberalization than for VAW laws. Sugiyama (2012) finds reciprocal causation in the policy adoption of conditional cash transfer programs in Brazil. In this case, policy innovation emerged in subnational units and was emulated at higher levels of government, and then top-down pressure promoted policy adoption in other subnational units. Hughes, Krook, and Paxton (2015) examine reciprocal causation in the adoption of national gender quotas, but they find a negative interaction between global pressures and domestic transnational organizing.

A multilevel approach incorporates multiple potential causal paths to explain complex patterns of subnational, national, and international interaction. Outcomes depend upon the issue characteristics and relative influence of competing policy advocates. I find that patterns of policy adoption follow different causal paths depending on the issue. For issues where there are strong international norms, weak opposition, and strong agreement in national public opinion, such as violence against women, there will be reciprocal causality, more national and international influence, and more homogenous outcomes across subnational units. Without international norms, where there is influential opposition and divided public opinion, there will be less top-down pressure, subnational units will be more autonomous, and outcomes will be more heterogeneous, reflecting subnational differences.

5.2   GENDER POLICY ADOPTION IN MEXICO: ABORTION AND VAW

Mexico's transition to democracy in the late 1990s brought new vigorous debates about gender policy. Because many gender policies divided the constituencies of the former ruling Institutional Revolutionary Party (PRI), during one-party rule the PRI attempted to quell public debate on gender policy. With the advent of multiparty competition, and with the growing influence of both a secular left party (the Party of the Democratic Revolution, or PRD) that embraced feminist goals and a Catholic right party (the National Action Party, or PAN) that opposed feminist goals, conflicts over gender equality grew dramatically. In addition to the domestic political transition, international pressure for countries to protect women from gender violence increased in the 1990s. The Inter-American Convention on the Prevention, Punishment, and Eradication of Violence against Women (also known at the Belém do Pará Convention) was adopted in 1994. Mexico ratified the convention in 1998.

The most recent wave of policy reform for abortion started when local feminist political activism produced subnational policy innovation in Mexico City in 2007. The new policy decriminalized abortion during the first 12 weeks of gestation. Opponents of the local policy innovation sought to "nationalize" the abortion policy debate by challenging the new law in the Supreme Court. When the Supreme Court upheld the Mexico City law, abortion opponents organized a widespread subnational backlash to promote antiabortion legislation. There was neither national legislation nor national judicial constraint on subnational policy, and limited international involvement. Consequently, the key causal factors for abortion policy were subnational factors: localized feminist activism and organized opposition. The pattern of abortion policy adoption fits the expectations of freestanding units and horizontal causality: Local characteristics and horizontal influence from other states were most important, as shown in the visual representation of the pattern of abortion policy adoption in Figure 5.1. The first step is state policy innovation (1), followed by unsuccessful efforts to nationalize the issue by appealing to the Supreme Court (2), and then horizontal influence as the original state policy innovation leads to attempts at replication in some states and backlash in other states (3). International factors did not come into play.

The pattern of policy adoption for VAW laws also began with local political activism, when human rights groups organized to demand accountability for the extreme levels of violence against women in Ciudad Juárez, in the northern state of Chihuahua. When the state government failed to respond, activists appealed to both national and international institutions. New national legislation in 2007 and a ruling from the Inter-American Court of Human Rights in 2009 led to near-universal replication of new VAW laws, overseen by international institutions. The most important factors that account for VAW policy adoption were subnational activism, national legislation, and international institutions. There was interaction among the levels, as local activists appealed to national and international institutions, which then exerted pressure on subnational governments. As seen in Figure 5.2, the pattern of VAW policy adoption thus follows a complex reciprocal pattern of subnational, national,

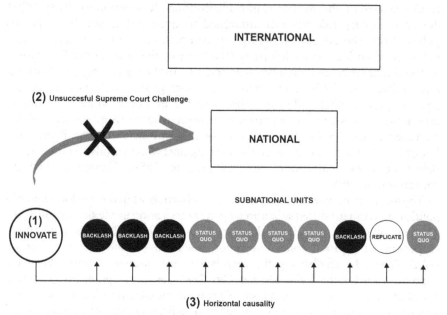

FIGURE 5.1 Causal Paths for Abortion Legislation in Mexico: Policy Divergence

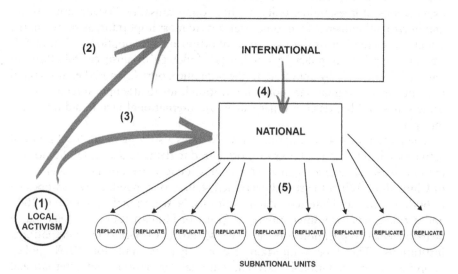

FIGURE 5.2 Causal Paths for Violence against Women Legislation in Mexico: Policy Convergence

and international interactions. The policy cycle started with local activism and unsuccessful efforts at policy innovation (1), followed by activist appeals to international institutions (2) and the national legislature (3) to intervene. International institutions then put pressure on the national government (4), which passed new legislation and pressured states to pass new VAW laws (5).

5.3 POLICY DIVERGENCE: ABORTION LAWS IN THE MEXICAN STATES

Local feminist activism in Mexico City brought about local abortion policy innovation. The most important activist group was Grupo de Información en Reproducción Elegida (Group for Information on Selected Reproduction, or GIRE), founded in 1992 by Marta Lamas, along with Patricia Mercado, Sara Sefchovich, Maria Consuelo Mejía, and Lucero González.[1] Pressure from feminist groups first resulted in the "Ley Robles" in Mexico City in 2001. This law widened the set of circumstances under which abortion was legal and created a regulatory framework to guarantee access to abortion when permitted by law. In 2007 the Mexico City legislature passed a new law to decriminalize all abortion during the first 12 weeks of gestation. This law also established regulations to provide free abortions in government clinics (Lamas, 2009).

Abortion opponents from the PAN, the conservative Catholic party that governed at the national level, attempted unsuccessfully to nationalize the issue with a Supreme Court challenge to the new law. The National Commission of Human Rights (CNDH) and the Attorney General's Office (PGR), both controlled by the PAN, challenged the constitutionality of the Mexico City law in the Supreme Court. In 2008 the Supreme Court allowed the Mexico City law to stand. The attempt by the "losers" of the subnational political game – that is, the antiabortion forces – to overturn the subnational policy by nationalizing the issue failed. The national government did not exert top-down pressure on the subnational governments, and the national legislature did not weigh in with any national legislation (Beer, 2017b).

Although there was limited vertical influence on abortion policies at the state level, there was horizontal influence. Policy innovation in Mexico City inspired well-financed and organized abortion opponents to promote a wave of backlash legislation in which 18 states passed constitutional amendments specifying that life begins at the moment of conception. Giving fetuses the legal rights of personhood had significant legal consequences, including possibly criminalizing emergency contraception, intra-uterine devices, and reproductive technologies. It also made abortion legally equivalent to murder. National and international actors were clearly involved in the policy debate – the Mexican antiabortion movement is supported by the Catholic Church and the international pro-life movement – but

[1] https://gire.org.mx/

neither the national government nor any international agreements were used to exert top-down pressure on the states. A variety of groups, such as CitizenGo, SíVida, and Red Familiar make up the pro-life movement in Mexico. All of these groups have ties to the Catholic Church, and some also have ties to evangelical churches. The most influential and best-funded organization promoting the antiabortion constitutional amendments was Incluyendo Mexico. Vicente Segu Marcos and Luis Guillermo Zazueta Domínguez founded the organization in April 2007, the same month the government of Mexico City decriminalized abortion. Before founding Incluyendo Mexico, Segu Marcos had been the director of Red Familiar, a network of organizations promoting Catholic values. Incluyendo Mexico received almost 10 million US dollars of donations in 2016, and 46 million US dollars since 2009. It is the fourth-wealthiest NGO in Mexico, following only the Red Cross and two corporate foundations, Fundación BBVA and Fundación TV Azteca. Its biggest contributors are business leaders with close ties to the Catholic Church (Beauregard, 2017).

After the wave of backlash legislation, there was another attempt to nationalize the issue by appealing again to the Supreme Court. This time, however, the losers of the subnational political game were the feminist activists hoping to liberalize abortion laws across the country. Activists challenged the state constitutional reforms in Baja California and San Luis Potosí that specified life begins at the moment of conception. In 2011 the Supreme Court upheld the fetal life amendments, again refusing to nationalize the abortion issue. While the majority of the Supreme Court voted (7–4) to strike down the Baja California constitutional reforms, the reforms were allowed to stand because the Mexican Constitution requires a two-thirds super-majority vote by the justices to strike down state laws (Pou Jiménez, 2009, Madrazo & Vela, 2011). Map 5.1 provides a map of Mexico highlighting Baja California and San Luis Potosí, along with the other states discussed below.

There is no international consensus or international norm on abortion; rather, there are conflicting global frames (Boyle, Longhofer, & Minzee, 2015). Abortion has been a central conflict in international women's meetings. Article 4 of the Inter-American Convention on Human Rights, known as the Pact of San José, protects life from the moment of conception. Thus international agreements could be used to oppose efforts to liberalize abortion laws. But in 2012, the Inter-American Court of Human Rights ruled against Costa Rica's ban on in vitro fertilization, potentially laying the groundwork for a more extensive ruling in favor of reproductive rights. The 2012 decision, which is binding on all 22 member countries, found that the protection of an embryo is not absolute and must be weighed against the reproductive rights of women.[2]

National public opinion in Mexico is divided on abortion, with about half of the population opposed to abortion under any circumstances and half of the

[2] www.oas.org/en/iachr/media_center/preleases/2016/013.asp

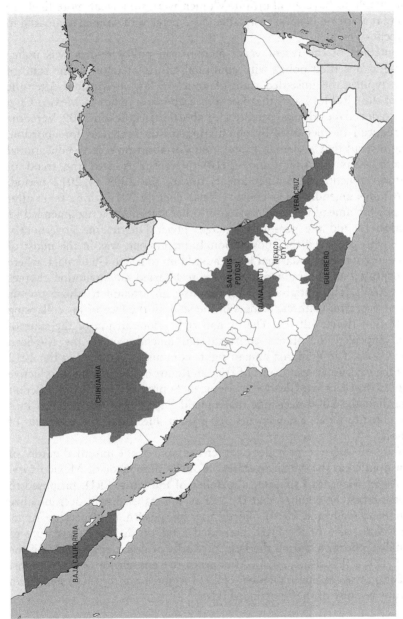

MAP 5.1 States in Mexico Selected for Analysis

population supportive of abortion under some circumstances. According to the 2005 World Values survey, 51.9 percent of respondents in Mexico said it is never justifiable to have an abortion. Women were somewhat more likely to respond that abortion is never justifiable (53.2 percent of women compared to 50.5 percent of men).[3]

The outcome of the recent wave of abortion policy reform was policy diversity and unsettled policy with continual efforts at reform. The state of Veracruz typifies the unsettled state of abortion law in Mexico. After the passage of the "Robles Law" that liberalized abortion policy in Mexico City, Veracruz reduced the criminal penalties for abortion in 2003. In 2009, Veracruz further reduced the penalties by eliminating prison sentences for abortion, requiring instead that a woman found guilty of abortion receive educational and health training (Altamirano, 2016). Veracruz resisted the trend of antiabortion constitutional amendments during the 2009 to 2012 period, when 16 states amended their constitutions. Then in 2016, three years after the last pro-life amendment had passed in other states, Veracruz amended its constitution to add the pro-life language. Javier Duarte, the governor of Veracruz who proposed the constitutional amendment, was in the midst of a massive corruption scandal that later caused him to flee to Guatemala, where he was captured and extradited to Mexico to be tried on corruption charges (Semple, 2017). The antiabortion reform was an attempt to shore up the support of powerful Catholic leaders in the state in the face of his collapsing administration (Reina, 2016). The human rights commission of the state of Veracruz appealed the state's constitutional amendment to the Mexican Supreme Court. The Veracruz human rights commission hopes that the 2012 ruling of the Inter American Court of Human Rights in the case of reproductive rights in Costa Rica will lead the Mexican Supreme Court to a different outcome than the 2009 decisions that upheld Baja California and San Luis Potosí's constitutional amendments to protect life from the moment of conception.

The state of Guerrero provides another example of the unsettled nature of abortion politics in the Mexican states. In 2014 the mayor of Mexico City, Miguel Ángel Mancera Espinosa, a member of the leftist PRD, proposed to governors across the country that the rest of the states should decriminalize abortion (Pérez Courtade, 2014). Shortly after, the governor of Guerrero, Ángel Aguirre Rivero, also of the PRD, presented a bill to the state legislature to decriminalize abortion during the first 12 weeks of gestation, replicating the Mexico City law (Excelsior, 2014). After pressure from religious organizations, the legislation was tabled. In October of 2014 Aguirre was forced to step down as governor because of the Ayotzinapa crisis.[4]

---

[3] Question V204. www.worldvaluessurvey.org/WVSOnline.jsp

[4] In 2014, 43 students of the Ayotzinapa Rural Teachers College were massacred in Iguala, Guerrero. Local police and federal forces have been implicated in the murders.

In Mexico there is no national agreement about abortion. Moreover, there are no international norms about abortion, and there is a well-organized and well-funded opposition to abortion liberalization. As a result, there is policy heterogeneity based on state characteristics following the freestanding units causal path. State characteristics have been most important in determining state policies: States that are more conservative are more likely to pass conservative restrictions on abortion, whereas states that are more liberal are more likely to liberalize abortion. Horizontal influence also played a role in that policy innovation in Mexico City inspired unsuccessful attempts at replication in some states and successful backlash initiatives in other states. Without the threat of legal abortion spreading across the country, it seems unlikely that antiabortion constitutional amendments would have passed in so many states. Abortion policy has followed the causal paths of freestanding units and horizontal causality.

5.4 POLICY CONVERGENCE: VIOLENCE-AGAINST-WOMEN LAWS IN THE MEXICAN STATES

In the case of violence against women, local activism did not initially result in state policy innovation but rather the state government largely ignored the demands of local activists. Since the early 1990s, a distressingly large number of young women were murdered or disappeared in Ciudad Juárez, Chihuahua, in what became known as "femicide." In one of the most disturbing instances, known as the "Cotton Fields Case," the bodies of eight women were found in a cotton field in 2001 (Washington Valdez, 2006). The government of the state of Chihuahua failed to seriously investigate and prosecute the crimes. The families of the victims, together with local human rights activists, sought justice by appealing to national and international institutions.

In 2002 the families of the victims filed a complaint with the Inter-American Human Rights Commission. In 2007 the Commission issued a number of recommendations to the Mexican government. When the government did not adequately respond, the Commission submitted the case to the Inter-American Court of Human Rights. The Court recognized 379 cases of gender violence in Ciudad Juárez from 1993 to 2005. In 2009 the Court ruled, "The insufficient answers and indifferent attitudes of authorities in the investigation of these crimes seem to have allowed the perpetual violence against women in Ciudad Juárez." The court ordered the Mexican government to investigate and prosecute the murders and punish public officials involved in the cases, improve its response to violence against women, and create a database to help find missing people and keep track of violence against women.[5]

---

[5] Wikileaks 10Mexico75, created January 25, 2010, released January 28, 2011. www.corteidh.or.cr/docs/casos/articulos/seriec_205_esp.pdf.
www.cladem.org/programas/litigio/litigios-internacionales/12-litigios-internacionales-oea/22-caso-campo-algodonero-mexico-femicidio-feminicidio.

In the face of this international pressure and attention, in 2003 the federal Senate created a special commission to study femicide. Marcela Lagarde, a highly respected feminist anthropologist, was chosen to lead the Senate Commission. Based on the Commission's recommendations, the federal government passed national legislation to address violence against women in 2007, the *Ley General de Acceso de las Mujeres a una Vida Libre de Violencia* (General Law of Access for Women to a Life Free from Violence, or LGAMVLV). The federal law required the state governments to pass similar laws (Cabrales Lucio, 2016). The state of Chihuahua had already passed a comprehensive VAW law in 2006. The Instituto Nacional de las Mujeres (National Institute for Women, or INMUJERES) circulated a template of a comprehensive VAW law for the states to adopt. Between 2006 and 2010 all states adopted some version of the new VAW law. The Organization of American States (OAS) monitored compliance with the Belém do Pará Convention on Violence against Women, further pressuring state governments to adopt the new VAW legislation. The OAS created the Follow-up Mechanism to the Belém do Pará Convention (MESECVI) to enforce the implementation of the convention. MESECVI prepared and published reports to evaluate each country's compliance with the convention. The outcome of the wave of VAW policy reform in Mexico was near policy homogeneity across subnational units. Still, it is important to note that while all states ultimately passed new VAW laws, some states dragged their feet and the content of the laws varied somewhat across the states (Beer, 2017a).

Guanajuato presents an especially interesting case. According to the federal LGAMVLV, the states were required to start legislative changes to harmonize state laws within six months. In July 2007 feminist activists submitted a proposal to the Guanajuato state legislature for a new gender-violence law. The legislative leaders refused to put the proposal on the legislative agenda (Diego Rodriguez, 2007). In March 2009, the state legislature of Guanajuato passed a new anti-violence law proposed by the PAN governor, Juan Manual Oliva. Not only did this bill not directly address gender violence, it also eliminated state-financed shelters for victims of domestic violence. In September 2009, the state legislature rejected three different bills for a gender violence law. The PRD proposed one bill, the PRI another, and Mayra Enríquez Vanderkam, a member of the majority PAN and president of the Gender Commission, proposed the third bill. A legislative statement approved by the PAN majority declared that a gender-violence bill was not necessary because of the recently passed general violence law. This left Guanajuato as the only state in the country without a gender-violence law (García & Chávez, 2009). In March 2010, deputies from Convergencia and the PRD presented another gender-violence bill, citing the national law and the requirement that states create their own laws (El Universal, 2010).[6] Again, the PAN took no action.

---

[6] *Convergencia* (Convergence) was a center-left, social democratic party founded in 1999. In 2011 it changed its name to *Movimiento Ciudadano* (Citizen's Movement).

Luz María Ramírez Villalpando, director of the Guanajuato State Women's Institute (Instituto de la Mujer Guanajuatense, a government agency established to promote women's rights) under Governor Oliva (2006–2012) from the PAN, led the opposition to the gender-violence proposal. Ramírez Villalpando was appointed to the position by her brother-in-law, the ultra-conservative secretary of government and director of the gubernatorial transition Gerardo Mosqueda Martínez. She was known for her ultra-conservative views on gender, including suggesting that women should tolerate domestic violence "in the name of God and the family." Ramírez Villalpando has also publicly claimed that women have a biological defense mechanism that prevents pregnancy during a rape (Guardiola, 2015). After taking control of the Women's Institute, she fired the professional staff that ran programs to promote women's rights (Diego Rodriguez, 2006).

In November 2010, Guanajuato finally passed a gender-violence law to harmonize the state's laws with federal law. A representative of the United Nations Office of the High Commission of Human Rights had visited Guanajuato in August 2010, at the request of local feminist organizations. The UN Representative declared that in Guanajuato "a climate of worrisome violence against women, including sexual violence, predominated." She called on the governor to send a bill to the state legislature to comply with the national gender-violence legislation. A few days later the governor presented a bill to the legislature, and it was passed in November 2010 (Proceso, 2010). The case of Guanajuato offers a clear example of reciprocal causation and top-down pressure from international institutions. Local feminist activists brought in the representative of the UN Commission on Human Rights, who then publicly shamed the governor. Just days after this public shaming, the governor proposed a gender-violence bill, after four years of blocking all efforts at reform. Cheryl O'Brien (2013) shows a similar pattern of interaction between subnational activists and international institutions in the states of Jalisco and Oaxaca.

A central difference between abortion and VAW concerns the strong international norm recognizing VAW as a human rights violation. This strong norm was marked by the 1994 adoption of the Inter-American Convention on the Prevention, Punishment and Eradication of Violence against Women (known as the Belém do Pará Convention), which Mexico ratified in 1998. In 2004 the Organization of American States created MESECVI, the Follow-up Mechanism to the Belém do Pará Convention, to evaluate the implementation of the convention. Also, in contrast to abortion, there was no strongly organized opposition to gender violence laws. Many state governments were reluctant to treat violence against women as a serious problem, but there was no organized opposition. There are also important differences in public opinion related to abortion and VAW. Whereas public opinion on abortion in Mexico is divided, a strong majority of Mexicans agree that it is never justifiable for a man to beat his wife. In the 2005 World Values Survey, 74.4 percent of respondents said it was never justifiable for a man to beat his wife, though 4.4 percent of respondents say it is always justifiable, and over 20 percent of respondents believed it was justifiable under some circumstances. The responses of men and women were very similar.[7]

In contrast to the pattern of policy adoption for abortion, in the case of VAW reciprocal causation was evident in the appeals local activists made to national and international institutions, which then exerted top-down pressure for reform. The pattern of VAW policy adoption was marked by a complex pattern of subnational, national, and international interactions in which subnational activists initially lost at the local level then successfully elicited the support of national and international actors, which in turn exerted top-down pressure. Ultimately, all Mexican states adopted new gender-violence legislation during the 2006–2010 period.

5.5 STATISTICAL EVIDENCE

In addition to the case studies in Sections 5.3 and 5.4 that illustrate the contrasting patterns of policy adoption for abortion and gender-violence legislation, this section provides an event history analysis of the causes of policy adoption for each issue. The statistical evidence supports the argument that local political characteristics were more important for the adoption of new abortion laws than VAW laws. We will see from the results in Table 5.1 that both the party of the governor and the influence of the Catholic Church are significant in determining the adoption of abortion laws, whereas the state's wealth (gross state product per capita) and geographic proximity are significant in the VAW model.

The causal path in which states are understood to operate as autonomous, freestanding units suggests that state characteristics determine state policy outcomes. Thus, we would expect to find state-level variables such as the party in power, the strength of the women's movement, and the influence of the Catholic Church to be associated with policy reform. The model includes a dummy variable for a governor from the rightist PAN and a governor from the centrist PRI. The base category is a governor from the leftist PRD.

A second variable, strength of the women's movement, is measured as the number of NGOs in each state that name gender equality as one of their major goals. The list comes from the "Directorio Nacional de Organizaciones de la Sociedad Civil" (National Directory of Civil Society Organizations) published by the Mexican government's Secretaría de Gobernación (Secretariat of Government, or SEGOB). The directory lists each organization, the activities it carries out, and the date it was founded. I calculated a time-varying indicator based on these data, counting the number of organizations listed in the directory that include gender equality as one of their activities. While there are certainly

---

[7] Question V208. www.worldvaluessurvey.org/WVSOnline.jsp.

TABLE 5.1 *Results of Event History Analysis*

Variables	Model 1 Abortion		Model 2 VAW	
	Coef.	Std. Err.	Coef.	Std. Err.
PAN governor	1.344	2.016	0.700	1.346
PRI governor	9.330^t	4.922	2.481	2.673
GDP per capita	–0.037	0.024	0.011**	0.004
% women in legislature	0.024	0.029	0.005	0.022
Number of women orgs	–0.003	0.007	0.000	0.002
Influence of Catholic Church	1.446*	0.654	0.106	0.410
Geographic diffusion	–0.273	0.290	0.263^t	0.148
Chi-squared	15.4*		12.53^t	
Number of subjects	31		32	
Number of failures	16		32	
Time at risk	21812		16101	

^{t} p<0.1, * p<0.05, ** p<0.01

organizations that are not listed in this directory, organizations have important incentives to register with SEGOB in order to gain access to resources provided by the federal government.[8]

I operationalized the influence of the Catholic Church by measuring the state means of Question 3 k from the Epemex Survey (Loza & Méndez, 2014). The survey asks local political experts from each state to rank the influence of the Catholic Church on public policies, from 0 = None to 4 = A lot.[9] I also include a variable for the percentage of women in the state legislature.

If the subnational policy outcomes result from a horizontal causal path, where the dominant factors are influence across states, then I expect to find geographic proximity to be important. Following the literature on diffusion in the United States (Berry & Berry, 1990; Karch, 2007; Boushey, 2010), I measure geographic proximity for each state by the number of neighboring states that had adopted the policy at time "t." Alternatively, if the outcomes

---

[8] The directory is available at www.organizacionessociales.segob.gob.mx/en/Organizaciones_Sociales/Directorio_de_OSC. In some cases we might worry about endogeneity for a measure like this, because the effort to further criminalize abortion might encourage the formation of new women's groups. Such endogeneity is unlikely in this case because the antiabortion reforms to state constitutions took place just a few months after the Supreme Court ruling. The new groups would thus not have had enough time to form and make it onto the government's list of civil society organizations.

[9] The survey was carried out in late 2012 and early 2013. Experts were asked to evaluate local politics from 2001 to 2012 (Gervasoni, Loza, & Mendéz, 2016). While it is possible that the conflict over abortion influenced the expert evaluations, this measurement is closely correlated with a number of other historical measures of the strength of the Catholic Church, suggesting that the Church's strength does not vary dramatically over time (Beer, 2016).

result from top-down causal paths, where pressure from national and international forces determine subnational policy outcomes, I expect to find policy homogeneity across states and also that state-level characteristics are not important. Still, GDP per capita may be important if wealthier states are less vulnerable to top-down pressure than poorer states or if wealthier states are more deeply engaged in the international economy and therefore more supportive of international norms. Because top-down pressure ultimately determines policy outcomes in the reciprocal causation model (though top-down pressure requires bottom-up activation), I would expect the same statistical results as those predicted for top-down models.

In Model 1, the dependent variable is the adoption of an antiabortion fetal life amendment. Sixteen states adopted this constitutional amendment between 2008 and 2015.[10] States with a governor from the centrist PRI were more likely to adopt the antiabortion amendment than states governed by the leftist PRD. States governed by the rightist PAN were also more likely to adopt the antiabortion amendment than states governed by the PRD, but the difference is not statistically significant at standard levels of confidence. Neither the number of women's organizations nor the number of women in the legislature is significant. The more influence the Catholic Church has on local politics, the more likely the state was to adopt the antiabortion constitutional amendment.

In Model 2, the dependent variable is adoption of VAW laws between 2006 and 2012. As hypothesized, top-down pressure led to the universal adoption of the new VAW laws. Because every state adopted a similar law during this period, the only variation to explain in the event history analysis is the speed of adoption. As predicted by the top-down causal path, none of the local political variables is significant. The only state-level characteristic that is statistically significant is the state gross product per capita. Wealthier states were quicker to adopt the new VAW legislation than states with a lower standard of living. The geographic proximity variable is also significant (with 90 percent confidence) in the VAW model. This provides some support for the hypothesis that horizontal influence from other states was important for the adoption of VAW policy.

These statistical results provide evidence to support my main argument that state-level political characteristics were more important in determining subnational abortion policy, whereas national and international factors were more important in determining VAW policy. Two of the local political characteristics, PRI party control and the influence of the Catholic Church, are both significant in explaining abortion but not VAW. Neither the number of women in the legislature nor the number of women's organizations is significant. States where women were more powerful were expected to be less likely to approve the antiabortion reforms. Because of the role of gender quotas in the selection of state legislators, there is not a lot of variation in the number of

---

[10] Chihuahua adopted the amendment in 1994, long before the policy wave analyzed here, and Veracruz adopted the amendment in 2016.

female legislators across the states, which may explain why the variable is not significant. It is more troubling that the measure for women's organizations is not significant in the abortion model. Evidence from the case studies shows that local feminist groups were, in fact, central to reforms of both abortion and VAW policies. It is very difficult to measure the strength of the women's movement, and it may be that the measure used here is not effective. While the number of local registered NGOs that consider gender equality central to their mission may seem like a good measure, it may be that some states have many small and weak organizations, whereas other states have only a few organizations but they are much more powerful.

GDP per capita and geographic diffusion are significant for VAW policy but not for abortion. Wealthier states passed new VAW laws more quickly than less prosperous states. I had mixed expectations for this variable. On the one hand, poorer states may be more vulnerable to top-down pressure than wealthier states because they are likely to be more dependent on financial transfers from the central government. On the other hand, wealthier states may be better connected with the international economy and therefore more likely to value international norms. Following the logic of Inglehart and Norris, a wealthier polity with a larger middle class may be more influenced by "post-material" values (Inglehart & Norris, 2003). In the case of VAW laws in Mexico, wealthier states were quicker than less prosperous states to make policy changes that aligned with international norms. The geographic diffusion variable is not significant for abortion, suggesting that the horizontal influence of the backlash did not have a geographic component. The diffusion variable is significant for the VAW laws, which means that a state was more likely to adopt a new VAW law at time "t" if more of its neighbors had already adopted the reform.

The statistical results are consistent with the explanation provided in the case study analysis. Both the case studies and the statistical analysis suggest that abortion policy resulted from a causal path in which subnational units are autonomous and local political characteristics are the most important causes of policy adoption. Local political characteristics were not as important for the adoption of VAW laws. Instead, VAW laws resulted from a complex pattern of reciprocal causation.

5.6 CONCLUSION

This chapter compares the policy process of two gender policies in Mexico to evaluate different causal paths for subnational policymaking. It draws on the multilevel strategies for subnational analysis proposed by the editors in the introduction to this volume. This chapter finds that when there are no international norms, divided national public opinion, and a strong opposition, subnational units will be more autonomous and local political conditions will determine the outcome of policy debates. This was the case for abortion law in

Mexico from 2007 to 2016. By contrast, when there are strong international norms and weak opposition, we instead see reciprocal causation, as local activists seek support from national and international allies, who in turn exert top-down pressure on other subnational units. This was the case for VAW laws in Mexico from 2001 to 2010.

The research provides important insights for the study of subnational politics. It shows that even in cases where formal institutions are the same; the subnational policymaking process can vary dramatically across policy issues. As underscored in the introduction to this book, the findings presented in this chapter show that multilevel theoretical frameworks that encompass national and international forces can provide stronger explanations of subnational policy outcomes. National and international variables such as international norms and national consensus can have important consequences for subnational policymaking. These variables will have different effects on different types of policies.

This chapter also opens new perspectives for the study of gender policy. Most comparative work on gender policy has been cross-national, but in political systems where subnational governments have authority to make or implement policy decisions it is critical to include a focus on subnational variance. The example of abortion laws in Mexico shows that intra-country variance can be as large as cross-national variance: Mexico City permits abortion for any reason and provides abortion free in government clinics, whereas in other states a fetus has the same legal rights as a person and abortion is therefore legally equivalent to murder. National averages or aggregates of indicators that are unevenly distributed are likely to produce inaccurate findings. This study draws attention to the value of comparative subnational analysis for identifying important variation in critical outcomes of interest, such as gender policy diffusion, in ways a national focus simply does not allow.

Future research should aim to clarify further the patterns of multilevel causation that drive subnational politics by examining other policy areas and other federal systems. Comparing subnational policy processes in different federal systems is likely to be especially productive. Scholars also need to find better ways to measure important phenomena, such as the strength of the women's movement.

BIBLIOGRAPHY

Altamirano, Claudia. (2016, January 25). El Congreso de Veracruz aprueba una reforma antiabortista del Gobernador. *El País*. Available at: https://elpais.com/internacional/2016/01/25/mexico/1453688213_930974.html?rel=mas (last accessed December 16, 2018).

Baumgartner, Frank R., & Jones, Bryan D. (1993). *Agendas and instability in American politics. American politics and political economy series.* Chicago, IL: University of Chicago Press.

Beauregard, Luis Pablo. (2017, February 16). La millionaria asociación provida que mueve los hilos de la ultraderecha en México. *El País.* Available at: https://elpais.com/internacional/2017/02/16/mexico/1487209541_075721.html (last accessed: December 16, 2018).

Beer, Caroline. (2016). La Iglesia Católica y la igualdad de género en los estados Mexicanos. In Irma Mendéz & Nicolás Loza (Eds.), *Poderes y democracias: La política subnacional en Mexico*, pp. 283–302. Mexico City, Mexico: FLACSCO-Mexico and Instituto Electoral del Distrito Federal.

Beer, Caroline. (2017a). Left parties and violence against women legislation in Mexico. *Social Politics* 24(4), 511–537.

Beer, Caroline. (2017b). Making abortion laws in Mexico: Salience and autonomy in the policymaking process. *Comparative Politics* 50(1), 41–59.

Beer, Caroline, & Cruz-Aceves, Victor. (2018). Extending rights to marginalized minorities: Same-sex relationship recognition in Mexico and the United States. *State Politics & Policy Quarterly* 18(1), 3–26.

Berry, Frances Stokes, & Berry, William D. (1990). State lottery adoptions as policy innovations: An event history analysis. *American Political Science Review* 84(2), 395–415.

Blofield, Merike. (2006). *The politics of moral sin: Abortion and divorce in Spain, Chile and Argentina.* New York, NY: Routledge.

Boushey, Graeme. (2010). *Policy diffusion dynamics in America.* New York, NY: Cambridge University Press.

Boyle, Elizabeth H., Longhofer, Wesley, & Minzee, Kim. (2015). Abortion liberalization in world society, 1960–2009. *American Journal of Sociology* 121(3), 882–913.

Cabrales Lucio, Josés Miguel. (2016). Análisis jurídico (en perspectiva de derechos humanos) de la Ley para prevenir, atender, sancionar, y erradicar la violencia contra las mujeres para la entidad federativa de Tamaulipas y algunas propuestas para su operatividad. In Teresa De Jesús Guzmán Acuña & Josefina Guzmán Acuña (Eds.), *Género, universidad, y sociedad*, pp. 13–26. Mexico City, Mexico: Universidad Autónoma de Tamaulipas, Miguel Ángel Porrúa.

Childs, Sarah, & Krook, Mona Lena. (2008). Critical mass theory and women's political representation. *Political Studies* 56(3), 725–736.

Diego Rodríguez, Martín. (2006, December 10). Despiden a equipo de defensa de los derechos de la mujer en Guanajuato. *La Jornada.* Available at: www.jornada.unam.mx/2006/12/10/index.php?section=estados&article=034n1est (last accessed: December 16, 2018).

Diego Rodríguez, Martín. (2007, July 9). Guanajuato: Piden ONG ley contra violencia a mujeres. *La Jornada.* Available at: www.jornada.unam.mx/2007/07/09/index.php?section=estados&article=040n1est (last accessed: December 16, 2018).

Díez, Jordi. (2015). *The politics of gay marriage in Latin America: Argentina, Chile, and Mexico.* New York, NY: Cambridge University Press.

Dulitzky, Ariel. (2006). Federalismo y derechos humanos: El caso de la convención Americana sobre derechos humanos y la República Argentina. *Anuario Mexicano de Derecho Internacional* VI, 199–249.

El *Universal*. (2010, March 5). Piden en Guanajuato ley vs violencia a mujeres. *El Universal*. Available at: http://archivo.eluniversal.com.mx/notas/663618.html (last accessed July 16, 2014).

Excelsior. (2014, May 6). Aguirre presenta iniciativa para despenalizar el aborto en Guerrero. *Excelsior*. Available at: www.excelsior.com.mx/nacional/2014/05/06/957754 (last accessed December 16, 2018).

García, Carlos, & Chávez, Mariana. (2009, September 18). Guanajuato desecha ley contra violencia de género y Querétaro aprueba normas contra el aborto. *La Jornada*. Available at: www.jornada.unam.mx/2009/09/18/index.php?section=estados&article=032n2est (last accessed December 16, 2018).

Gervasoni, Carlos, Loza, Nicolás, & Mendéz, Irma. (2016). Introducción. In Nicolás Loza & Irma Mendéz (Eds.), *Poderes y democracias: La política subnacional en Mexico*, pp. 15–42. Mexico City: FLACSO Mexico.

Gray, Virginia. (1973). Innovation in the states: A diffusion study. *American Political Science Review* 67(4), 1174–1185.

Guardiola, Andrés. (2015, April 5). Política polémica va por alcaldía en León. *Excelsior*. Available at: www.excelsior.com.mx/nacional/2015/04/05/1017186 (last accessed: December 16, 2018).

Haider-Markel, Donald P. (2001). Policy diffusion as a geographic expansion of the scope of political conflict: Same-sex marriage bans in the 1990s. *State Politics and Policy Quarterly* 1(5), 5–26.

Haussman, Melissa. (2005). *Abortion politics in North America*. Boulder, CO: Lynne Rienner Publishers.

Hernández-Rodríguez, Rogelio. (2003). The renovation of old institutions: State governors and the political transition in Mexico. *Latin American Politics & Society* 45(4), 97–127.

Htun, Mala. (2003). *Sex and the state: Abortion, divorce, and the family under Latin American dictatorships and democracies*. Cambridge, England: Cambridge University Press.

Htun, Mala, & Weldon, S. Laurel. (2010). When do governments promote women's rights? A framework for the comparative analysis of sex equality policy. *Perspectives on Politics* 8(01), 207–216.

Hughes, Melanie M., Krook, Mona Lena, & Paxton, Pamela. (2015). Transnational women's activism and the global diffusion of gender quotas. *International Studies Quarterly* 59(2), 357–372.

Inglehart, Ronald, & Norris, Pippa. (2003). *Rising tide: Gender equality and cultural change around the world*. Cambridge, England: Cambridge University Press.

Karch, Andrew. (2007). *Democratic laboratories: Policy diffusion among the American states*. Ann Arbor: University of Michigan Press.

Keck, Margaret E., & Sikkink, Kathryn. (1999). Transnational advocacy networks in international and regional politics. *International Social Science Journal* 51(159), 89–101.

Lamas, Marta. (2009). La despenalización del aborto en México. *Nueva Sociedad* 220 (March/April), 154–172.

Levitsky, Steven, & Way, Lucan A. (2006). Linkage versus leverage. *Comparative Politics 38*(4), 379–400.

Loaeza, Soledad. (2013). *La restauración de la Iglesia católica en la transición Mexicana.* Mexico City: El Colegio de México.

Lopreite, Debora. (2014). Explaining policy outcomes in federal contexts: The politics of reproductive rights in Argentina and Mexico. *Bulletin of Latin American Research 33*(4), 389–404.

Loza, Nicolás, & Méndez, Irma. (2014). *Encuesta a expertos en política estatal en México 2001–2012.* Edited by PNUD FLACSO, y CONACYT. Available at: http://podesualflacso.wordpress.com (last accessed December 16, 2018).

MacDonald, Laura, & Mills, Lisa. (2010). Gender, democracy and federalism in Mexico: Implications for reproductive rights and social policy. In Melissa Haussman, Marian Sawer, & Jill Vickers (Eds.), *Federalism, feminism, and multilevel governance*, pp. 187–198. Burlington, VT: Ashgate.

Madrazo, Alejandro, & Vela, Estefanía. (2011). The Mexican supreme court's (sexual) revolution? *Texas Law Review 89*(7), 1863–1893.

Mazur, Amy. (2002). *Theorizing feminist policy.* Oxford: Oxford University Press.

O'Brien, Cheryl M. (2013). Beyond the national: Transnational influences on (subnational) state responsiveness to an international norms on violence against women. (Doctoral dissertation). Purdue University, West Lafayette, IN.

Pérez Courtade, Luis. (2014, April 24). Propondrá Mancera despenalización del aborto en el resto del país. *Excelsior.* Available at: www.excelsior.com.mx/comunidad/2014/04/24/955612 (last accessed December 16, 2018).

Pou Jiménez, Francisca. (2009). El aborto en México: El debate en la Suprema Corte sobre la normativa del Distrito Federal. *Anuario de Derechos Humanos 5*, 137–152.

Proceso. (2010, November 25). Aprueban en Guanajuato ley de acceso a vida libre de violencia. *Proceso.* Available at: www.proceso.com.mx/98666/aprueban-en-guanajuato-ley-de-acceso-a-vida-libre-de-violencia (last accessed December 16, 2018).

Reina, Elena. (2016, July 29). Veracruz abre la vía para que el aborto sea considerado como un homocidio. *El País.* Available at: https://elpais.com/internacional/2016/07/29/mexico/1469810266_277274.html (last accessed December 16, 2018).

Schwindt-Bayer, Leslie A. (2010). *Political power and women's representation in Latin America.* Oxford, England: Oxford University Press.

Semple, Kirk. (2017, April 17). Javier Duarte, Mexican ex-governor accused of diverting money, is captured. *The New York Times.* Available at: www.nytimes.com/2017/04/16/world/americas/mexico-javier-duarte-captured.html?_r=0 (last accessed December 16, 2018).

Smulovitz, Catalina. (2015). Legal inequality and federalism: Domestic violence laws in the Argentine provinces. *Latin American Politics & Society 57*(3), 1–26.

Smulovitz, Catalina. (2017, June 20–23). *The transnational and sub-national study of abortion lawfare.* Paper presented at the International Meeting on Law and Society, Mexico City, Mexico.

Sugiyama, Natasha Borges. (2008). Theories of policy diffusion: Social sector reform in Brazil. *Comparative Political Studies 41*(2), 193–216.

Sugiyama, Natasha Borges. (2012). Bottom-up policy diffusion: National emulation of a conditional cash transfer program in Brazil. *Publius: The Journal of Federalism 42*(1), 25–51.

Walker, Jack L. (1969). The diffusion of innovations among the American states. *American Political Science Review* 63(3), 880–899.

Washington Valdez, Diana. (2006). *The killing fields: Harvest of women – The truth about Mexico's bloody border legacy.* Los Angeles, CA: Peace at the Border.

Weldon, Jeffrey. (1997). Political sources of presidencialismo in Mexico. In Scott Mainwaring & Matthew Soberg Shugart (Eds.), *Presidentialism and democracy in Latin America,* pp. 225–258. Cambridge, England: Cambridge University Press.

Weldon, S. Laurel. (2002). *Protest, policy, and the problem of violence against women: A cross-national comparison.* Pittsburgh, PA: University of Pittsburgh Press.

PART III

STATES AND SECURITY

6

Multilevel Partisan Conflict and Drug Violence in Mexico

When Do Criminal Organizations Attack Subnational Elected Officials?

Guillermo Trejo
Sandra Ley

One of the most important and often understudied features of organized crime is that criminal groups need the complicity of state actors to operate illegal markets. To successfully operate drug trafficking routes, for example, drug cartels need protection from the security forces in charge of policing roads, private airports, and ports and from law enforcement agents in charge of investigating, prosecuting, and punishing crime. These operational needs lead cartels to try to infiltrate governments and develop informal networks of protection (Bailey & Taylor, 2009; Snyder & Durán-Martínez, 2009; Trejo & Ley, 2018). Because the drug trafficking industry is a global chain of local operations, drug lords often seek to infiltrate *subnational* governments and law enforcement agencies.

To infiltrate local governments and develop informal networks of protection, cartels can use bribes or coercion. Although a few exemplary executions of local authorities can help cartels establish a reputation for toughness, drug lords have powerful incentives to favor bribes over coercion. Kidnapping or murdering public officials expose criminal groups to the public domain and make them vulnerable to government encroachment. In co-opting authorities to protect crime, bribes are cheaper (Dal Bó et al., 2006; Lessing, 2015).

In this chapter we analyze a surprising wave of 364 lethal attacks perpetrated by drug cartels and their criminal associates against Mexican government authorities, political candidates, and party activists over the course of 17 years of inter-cartel wars, from 1995 to 2012. Lethal attacks include kidnapping, death threats, assassination attempts, and murders. Although inter-cartel wars in Mexico broke out in the mid-1990s (Blancornelas, 2002;

We are grateful to Todd Eisenstadt, Agustina Giraudy, Eduardo Moncada, and Richard Snyder for their insightful advice and to participants at the Brown and Harvard workshops for useful suggestions. The chapter benefited greatly from the feedback of two anonymous reviewers and from the editorial work of Caroline Domingo. We thank Magdalena Guzmán and Elizabeth Orozco for superb research assistance.

Grillo, 2012; Trejo & Ley, 2018), it was not until a decade into these conflicts that government officials and politicians became targets of lethal criminal violence. One of the most conspicuous features of this wave of attacks is that municipal authorities and local political candidates – rather than national authorities and political leaders – became the main targets of criminal violence in Mexico's federal system.[1]

Why did Mexican cartels and their criminal associates start killing local officials and politicians when they had secured their cooperation through bribes for more than a decade? Why did drug lords adopt a subnational strategy and systematically target municipal and city-level authorities but only occasionally attack state-level and federal authorities? Are criminal attacks random events, or are authorities and candidates from specific political parties at greater risk of criminal attacks?

Understanding the motivations and patterns of criminal attacks against local government authorities and party candidates is crucial because this new form of violence marks an inflection point in almost two decades of drug wars in Mexico. It represents a radical transformation in the forms of engagement of criminal organizations with state authorities and a new mechanism by which organized crime has begun to reinvent Mexico's local political orders. Although drug cartels and their criminal associates have no stated political ambitions or clear ideological preferences, their decision to begin murdering local government officials and party candidates has had dramatic effects on local governance – that is, on who rules, the policies local authorities adopt, and the levels and quality of citizen participation in local politics.

We argue that the wave of criminal attacks against local authorities and politicians, which began in 2006, was the result of two intertwined conflicts: (1) the dramatic intensification of inter-cartel competition and violence following a major federal military intervention in Mexico's most conflictive subnational regions; and (2) intense intergovernmental partisan conflict between conservative federal authorities and leftist subnational authorities after the polarized 2006 Mexican presidential election.

We suggest that a major federal intervention, by which the Mexican government deployed thousands of army troops to the country's most conflictive areas to fight drug cartels and capture their leaders, had the unintended consequence of increasing levels of inter-cartel competition and violence, forcing cartels to extend their grip into new illicit markets to finance their turf wars. We claim that the cartels and their criminal associates identified two lucrative illicit markets that placed municipalities and local authorities at the center of operations: extortion and kidnapping for ransom. Cartels and their criminal associates saw in the municipalities' fiscal revenues and in local taxpayers two attractive sources of income. Acting as racketeers, through the use of targeted violence against local authorities, cartels could charge a criminal

---

[1] For the period under analysis here, Mexico was divided into 31 states and 2,448 municipalities.

tax to municipal authorities. They could also gain access to the local property-tax registry and use this privileged information to extort local businesses and undertake kidnapping-for-ransom operations.

Whether local officials were able to resist or became victims of targeted lethal attacks depended partly on the protection they received from federal authorities. In a context of acute national political polarization following the 2006 presidential election, in which the leftist candidate refused to concede defeat in favor of the conservative winner, we suggest that the president systematically assisted his rightist co-partisans when they faced threats from organized crime but kept his leftist political enemies unprotected and sought to expose them as inept and corrupt. Cartels took advantage of intergovernmental partisan conflict to gain de facto control over municipal governments in leftist states where mayors and local party candidates were purposefully unprotected by the federal government.

We use quantitative and qualitative evidence to test our propositions. Based on statistical analyses of criminal attacks across 2,018 municipalities[2] from 2007 to 2012, we show that violence against local authorities was more common in municipalities experiencing the most intense levels of inter-cartel violence, where cartels were engaged in bitter conflicts over drug trafficking routes and in need of fresh resources to finance turf wars. We also show that local authorities in states ruled by leftist governors were four to seven times more likely to become targets of criminal attacks than local authorities in states ruled by the president's conservative co-partisans. We interpret this as strong evidence of the lethal consequences of politicizing law enforcement in the context of wars against criminal organizations.

Using techniques of spatial analysis allows us to explore in greater detail the endogenous dynamics of criminal attacks against local authorities. By assessing how lethal attacks against local authorities in one municipality affect its neighbors, we are able to show the existence of important diffusion effects across localities and reveal the modus operandi of the attacks: Cartels and their criminal associates chose some cities as focal points for criminal attacks – municipalities in leftist states – and then coerced neighboring municipalities to gain control over entire regions.

To further explore why local authorities and politicians became targets of criminal attacks in conflictive regions where mayors were unprotected by the federal government for partisan reasons – and why attacks proceeded from one focal point to neighboring municipalities – we analyze criminal attacks in municipalities in Guerrero, a state governed by the leftist Party of the Democratic Revolution (PRD). We complement this analysis with information about criminal attacks in municipalities in Baja California – a state governed by the rightist National Action Party (PAN).

---

[2] We exclude 418 municipalities from Oaxaca that select their mayors through indigenous customary practices and where political parties do not participate in municipal elections. Mexico's Federal District, which had a special administrative status up until 2016, is also excluded from the analysis.

The chapter is divided into four sections. We first discuss why cartels and their criminal associates need subnational government protection and outline conditions that would lead them to coerce and kill, rather than simply bribe, local authorities. After outlining our hypotheses, in the second section we discuss the main features of the wave of attacks against public officials and party candidates. We then present the results of the statistical analysis showing the likely impact of inter-cartel violence and intergovernmental partisan conflicts on the lethal targeting of local authorities and political leaders. In the fourth section we offer case studies that show how the targeting of local authorities is remaking local political orders in Mexico's most conflictive regions. The conclusion reflects on the importance of a subnational lens for understanding the operation of organized crime as well as the value of a multilevel perspective that highlights interactions between national and subnational politics for explaining criminal wars.

6.1   THE SUBNATIONAL POLITICS OF ORGANIZED CRIME: BRIBES AND VIOLENCE

Bribes and Threats as Mechanisms to Co-opt Local Authorities

Controlling the criminal underworld largely depends on the ability of organized criminal groups to count on the implicit or explicit cooperation of law enforcement agents. In the specific case of the drug trafficking industry, drug lords need the complicity of security forces charged with policing highways, private airports, ports, and borders. If their associates are arrested in spite of police protection, drug lords need contacts in the justice system and the public prosecutor's office to derail criminal investigations. In the event they are indicted, they need contacts in the prison system who can enable them to continue conducting business from prison or to escape.

Because the transshipment of drugs across countries is a global chain of *local* operations, cartels seek to recruit subnational authorities, security forces, and law enforcement agents to create informal networks of government protection.[3] The multi-billion-dollar nature of the drug trafficking industry provides drug lords with unparalleled resources with which to bribe subnational authorities and officials into looking the other way or actively participating in protecting the transshipment of drugs. But when cartels develop their own private militias to defend themselves against rival groups or against national government attacks, they can also rely on coercion to force local government authorities to provide protection. In developing government protection networks, drug lords have the choice of using bribes or punishment – *plata* (i.e., silver, as in money) or *plomo* (i.e., lead, as in bullets).

---

[3] This does not exclude the possibility of seeking protection from national-level security officials.

Even though punishment may be a mechanism to enlist government cooperation in the criminal underworld, cartels have few incentives to rely on violence against public authorities. Bribes are their preferred mechanism for co-optation because this method allows them to maintain the secrecy required for the successful operation of the criminal underworld.[4] Kidnapping or killing government officials exposes cartels to the public realm and can result in unwelcome public scrutiny and government investigations. While a few random assassinations of meaningful political figures can be an effective signaling device for creating a reputation that persuades authorities to cooperate with them in the future, drug lords will always prefer to use bribes and *threats* of coercion over the actual use of systematic violence against government authorities. This preference for bribes and coercive threats over violence differentiates drug cartels from armed rebel groups (Lessing, 2015; Trejo & Ley, 2018), who are not interested in infiltrating governments and influencing their policy actions but, rather, in removing them from power and installing a new political regime.

From Bribery and Threats to Murder and Extortion

In his influential theory of order and power, Mancur Olson introduced the important distinction between stationary and roving bandits (Olson, 2000). Stationary bandits are criminals who establish their residence in places where they are able to monopolize crime and violence. In these contexts, bandits develop long-term encompassing interests in the welfare of the community where they live, charge moderate criminal taxes in exchange for protection, and become public good providers – they invest in public infrastructure to make the community more productive. In contrast, roving bandits are criminals with no residential ties who simply loot communities as they move from one place to another. Roving bandits do not develop long-term and encompassing interests but narrow short-term interests that lead them to plunder as much wealth as possible from their victims.

We suggest that when cartels have a monopoly over drug trafficking routes and can count on the complicity of local governments and civilians to operate their illegal trade without any major challenge, they are more likely to behave like stationary bandits and restrain from coercing government authorities and civilians in their place of residence. However, when government protection networks break down, the relationship between criminal organizations and governments and civilians rapidly transforms. This is a situation that can quickly unleash turf wars, as rival cartels enter into their now unprotected territory and drug lords begin to act like roving bandits.

Turf wars tend to be protracted conflicts. As inter-cartel wars become increasingly expensive to finance, both the "home" cartel and the outside

---

[4] On the importance of secrecy, see Gambetta (2010).

"challengers" will have incentives to seek new sources of income. As Charles Tilly observed, taxing the local population can be an important source of revenue for criminals to finance wars (Tilly, 1985). For drug cartels and other criminal groups, taxing usually takes the form of extortion or kidnapping for ransom, and victims include local government officials and local taxpayers. In a context of widespread competition for territorial control, all cartels and their criminal associates have incentives to engage in extractive activities.

While scholars in conflict studies have underscored the ability of armed rebel groups and paramilitaries to loot natural resources to finance wars, some recent studies have shown that non-state armed actors can also loot local governments. For example, in the case of Colombia, following a major decentralization that transferred political power and fiscal revenues from the center to the periphery, armed groups began targeting local governments and authorities to capture their fiscal resources (Eaton, 2006; Chacón, 2014). Following this literature, we suggest that cartels and their criminal associates can target local governments for extortion. Because cartels do not want to attract the attention of national authorities, who may closely oversee the use of federal transfers by local governments, they are more likely to target municipalities with an autonomous tax base. Looting local governments can take the form of a monthly criminal tax that mayors or local authorities pay to criminal organizations.

Besides local governments, local citizens can also be important sources of revenue for cartels. While extortion and kidnapping can affect the entire population, it is usually more profitable for organized criminal groups to tax local businesses (i.e., restaurants, hotels, shops, rich farmers, factory owners, etc.). In order to find out who is rich enough to pay and how much to demand, cartels need access to privileged local information such as the local property tax registry.[5] Because city and municipal authorities control or have direct access to these important sources of financial information, they become crucial actors in these new criminal markets. Local authorities serve a dual purpose for criminal organizations: They can make direct payments from the government tax revenues and give access to privileged information about local businesses.

Surrendering local tax revenues to organized crime and giving criminals access to information about local businesses and property owners can be politically very costly for municipal authorities because it makes them complicit in civilian victimization. Whereas the provision of protection for cartels only entails that local authorities refrain from enforcing the law, a move which inflicts no direct harm on civilians, surrendering local tax

---

[5] Even though local governments in countries like Mexico have a weak taxing capacity, they nonetheless have access to important information about local property. Because property owners care about property rights, they have incentives to have their assets registered in the local land registry (*catastro*). This information can be a crucial starting point for criminal groups to understand the territories they attempt to control, their characteristics, and areas with greatest affluence and profitability.

revenues and giving access to citizens' financial information to facilitate extortion or kidnapping can permanently damage government officials' bonds with their constituencies. To use Olson's conceptual language, municipal authorities and local party candidates are stationary actors who wish to live and govern their constituencies for the long run. Becoming part of extortion rackets could signify the end of their political careers. Hence, they will resist giving out this sensitive information to organized crime or agree to sell it only in exchange for unusually high bribes.

When cartels are impelled to raise money to finance protracted and expensive turf wars, however, it is unlikely that they will have resources to spare to buy off local authorities. Instead, as Lessing suggests, cartels resort to violence as a mechanism to reduce the cost of bribery (Lessing, 2015). Thus, to gain access to local governments' tax revenues and financial records, cartels will prefer to coerce, rather than simply bribe, local officials and party candidates. Through the use of violence, criminal organizations create a reputation for themselves as ruthless tax enforcers and define the penalty for noncompliance in lethal terms. This turns incumbent officials (mayors) and future officials (political candidates) into targets of criminal attacks.

We derive two propositions from this discussion:

H1. Local officials and politicians are more likely to become targets of criminal attacks in municipalities experiencing the most intense levels of inter-cartel competition and violence, where cartels and their criminal associates are expanding their illegal activities into extortion and kidnapping-for-ransom to finance war against rival cartels.

H2. Local officials who have access to greater local tax revenues are more likely to become targets of lethal criminal attacks than authorities from municipalities that are highly dependent on national fiscal transfers.

Protecting Local Authorities from Criminal Attacks: The Politics of Law Enforcement in Federal Systems

In federal systems, when lower-level authorities (e.g., mayors) face especially violent situations, higher-level authorities (e.g., governors and presidents) can potentially come to their rescue. Assisting lower-level authorities, however, is not simply a technical decision but a political one. As scholars of social conflict have recently shown, electoral incentives often drive policing decisions in federations (Wilkinson, 2005; Auyero, 2006). Intergovernmental cooperation – whether initiated "from above" by higher-level authorities or "from below" by lower-level ones – often depends on partisanship and electoral strategies.

In his important study of religious riots in India, Wilkinson shows that state-level authorities more actively deployed police forces to stop Hindus from attacking Muslim neighborhoods in electoral districts where Muslims could become pivotal voters and decide the outcome of elections (Wilkinson, 2005). In contrast, where Muslim voters were not a decisive electoral force, state-level authorities allowed Hindu gangs to break into Muslim neighborhoods and victimize them. Similarly, in his influential study of poor people's urban riots following a major macroeconomic collapse in Argentina, Auyero shows that opposition subnational provincial authorities associated with the Justice Party (PJ) ordered local police forces to prevent looting in areas where their business constituents would be affected but allowed looting where businesses were associated with the incumbent party (Auyero, 2006).

Following Auyero and Wilkinson, we suggest that in a context of acute political polarization, where the logic of friends and foes invades the body polity, intergovernmental cooperation to deal with major waves of criminal violence becomes a function of partisanship. Higher-level authorities are more likely to assist lower-level authorities in resisting violent criminal threats when they are members of the same party or belong to the same electoral coalition because, under such conditions, higher-level authorities want their subnational co-partisan colleagues to succeed. In contrast, higher-level authorities will provide little assistance to subnational political rivals facing similar dangers. To put it more precisely, in a context of acute political polarization, the vertical fragmentation of political power, or the juxtaposition of authorities from different political parties at different levels of government, can be a crucial determinant of intergovernmental cooperation in confronting major criminal threats.

Let us return to the situation described earlier in this chapter in which multiple cartels become involved in intense turf wars and start taxing the population via extortion and kidnapping to finance their ongoing conflicts. In this attempt to expand the criminal underworld, local authorities with access to greater tax revenues and the financial records of local businesses become targets of attacks. Whether local authorities are able to resist or, alternatively, become victims of organized crime largely depends on the cooperation of state- and national-level authorities. In most Latin American countries, municipal governments do not have the policing capacity to resist attacks from cartels – they thus need assistance from more powerful security forces. In a context of acute ideological polarization between different political parties, we would expect that:

H3. Local authorities are more likely to become targets of criminal attacks in subnational regions where political power is more vertically fragmented – i.e., where a mayor belongs to a different party from the governor and the governor from the president – than where power is unified and all three executive authorities belong to the same party.

While H1 suggests that in contexts of more intense inter-cartel violence, where criminal organizations transform themselves into racketeers, local authorities are at greater risk of criminal attacks, especially in fiscally autonomous municipalities (H2), H3 claims that different patterns of intergovernmental conflict or cooperation will determine whether local authorities can reduce the risks of criminal attacks and thus avoid becoming victims of criminal wars. In the following sections, we test these hypotheses using original data on criminal attacks against local officials in Mexico.

6.2 WHAT THE DATA SHOW ABOUT THE WAVE OF CRIMINAL ATTACKS ON LOCAL GOVERNMENT AUTHORITIES

Although Mexican drug producers were important suppliers of marijuana and poppy seeds for US markets for most of the twentieth century, it was only in the early 1980s, when the US government successfully closed the cocaine traffic route from the Andes to Miami via the Caribbean, that Mexican cartels became major players in the transshipment of illegal drugs from South America into the United States (Bagley, 2012). Mexican cartels rose to prominence in the international transshipment of drugs under the informal protection of Mexican federal and subnational security and military authorities linked to the Dirección Federal de Seguridad (DFS) – Mexico's security agency in charge of policing political dissent in the era of one-party rule (Aguayo, 2001; Astorga & Shirk, 2010). After the dissolution of the DFS in the mid-1980s, political policing was decentralized to subnational state-level police forces. Officers from the state police and municipal agencies became the key actors in the development of informal networks of government protection for Mexico's four major drug cartels (Trejo & Ley, 2018): Tijuana, Juárez, Sinaloa, and the Gulf.

As we have shown in previous research (Trejo & Ley, 2018), the spread of subnational party alternation and the rotation of parties in gubernatorial power in the 1990s led to the breakdown or renegotiation of these informal networks of subnational government protection for cartels. To cope with the uncertainty of having no effective protection and to defend themselves against external attacks from rival cartels and from federal authorities, drug lords developed their own private militias. The spread of subnational party alternation and the proliferation of private armies led to the onset of multiple inter-cartel wars. When Mexico's federal government launched a major military offensive against cartels in 2007, inter-cartel violence dramatically increased and inter-cartel wars spread to almost one-half of the country's territory.

Based on the Criminal Aggression against Political Actors in Mexico (CAPAM) dataset – an original newspaper-based data bank that we constructed – we examine 364 lethal criminal attacks on government officials, political candidates, and party activists from 1995 to 2012. Information from CAPAM is drawn from eight national newspapers, 18 subnational newspapers, and two weekly magazines specializing in drug trafficking and organized crime.[6]

Unlike other datasets on political violence that are confined to lethal attacks against municipal presidents (Ríos, 2012), we focus on executive authorities, political candidates, and party activists. This distinction is important because cartels and their criminal associates seek to influence incumbent authorities and future political leaders (candidates) and their political associates (party activists). Whereas most datasets on political violence against public authorities focus exclusively on murders, we collect data on a wide variety of coercive actions, ranging from kidnapping, death threats, and assassination attempts to murder. An exclusive focus on murders would yield two sources of bias: It would underestimate the extent of violence by assuming that murders are the only means of coercion available to criminal organizations; and it would exclude cases in which criminal groups try but fail to murder their targets.

Information from the CAPAM dataset reveals five features of this wave of criminal violence against public officials and political leaders in Mexico. First, the criminal attacks are lethal (or potentially lethal): Two-thirds of all acts of aggression involved lethal attacks (53 percent murders and 12 percent assassination attempts). The remaining one-fourth involved lethal threats (25 percent assassination threats[7]) and coercion (9 percent kidnapping cases) but did not result in murder.[8] This information suggests that when drug cartels and their criminal associates decided to target public officials and politicians for coercion, their goal was to murder them. Our records show that cartels and their criminal associates murdered 156 mayors and other municipal-level officials, candidates, and party activists between 1995 and 2012.

Second, local actors are the main target of criminal attacks: 80 percent of attacks on government officials were directed at members of municipal

---

[6] We used the national daily *Reforma* as our primary source of information. *Reforma* has become the most specialized source of media information on drug trafficking and organized crime in Mexico. We supplemented all the information with seven other national newspapers and a weekly magazine (*Proceso*). For detailed information on all cases and for a follow-up on government investigations we supplemented our dataset with information from 18 subnational (state-level) newspapers and a weekly magazine (*Zeta de Tijuana*).

[7] We only included death threats when at least one of the following conditions was met: 1) authorities or political candidates received threatening messages signed by a specific criminal group; 2) public authorities resigned or left the municipality after receiving a threat by a criminal group; 3) political candidates resigned from participating in elections after receiving a threat; and 4) political parties publicly admitted that they were unable to appoint candidates because they had received explicit warnings from organized crime.

[8] To identify cases of criminal kidnapping, assassination attempts, and murders we relied on the naming of the cartel or the criminal group by the newspaper report. When none of the 19 local sources reported a name of a cartel or the criminal group involved, we relied on three indicators to decide whether or not this was actually a case of organized crime: 1) the use of assault weapons for killing; 2) signs of torture and brutal violence (e.g., bodies wrapped in a rug or mutilated); and 3) written messages left on the bodies.

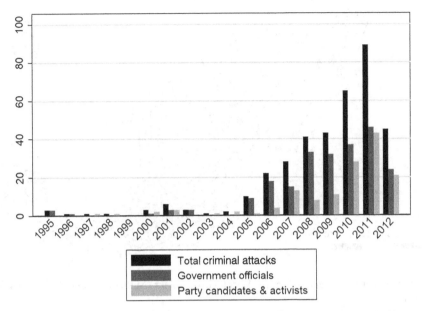

FIGURE 6.1 Time Series of Criminal Attacks in Mexico by Target (1995–2012)

governments (mostly mayors but also members of the local councils, mayors' advisers, local services directors, and bureaucrats), and 83 percent of attacks on political candidates and party activists were directed at municipal actors. These data unambiguously show that the wave of criminal attacks against public authorities and political leaders was a municipal phenomenon – one that involved incumbent mayors and municipal government officials and future mayors (political candidates) and their associates (political activists). If we adopted a national lens and only looked at national-level figures – as most cross-national studies currently do – we would thus be missing out on more than four-fifths of criminal attacks against government officials.

Third, the wave of criminal attacks followed, rather than preceded, the federal intervention launched in 2007. Figure 6.1 presents the time series of all attacks, distinguished by criminal target – government authorities and party members (candidates and activists) – for the 1995–2012 period. The information shows that while some attacks against government authorities had begun one year before President Calderón declared a war on cartels and deployed the Mexican army throughout the country's main conflict areas, the number of attacks had more than doubled four years after the federal government intervention in 2007. Moreover, in the case of attacks against party candidates and political activists, the time series shows that such attacks actually began after the federal intervention. Taken together (see the black bar), the aggregate information

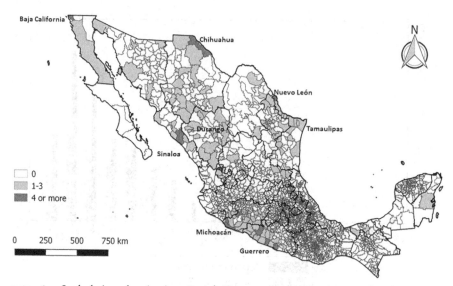

MAP 6.1 Lethal Attacks Against Local Government Authorities and Politicians in Mexico

strongly suggests that the wave of attacks against municipal authorities and local political leaders followed the federal intervention.

Fourth, attacks are geographically clustered in violent regions. Map 6.1 illustrates the geographic spread of lethal attacks against local government authorities and politicians. It shows that attacks were clustered in specific regions, suggesting that cartels and their criminal associates did not simply target one municipality at a time but entire regions. Note that in most cases there is a focal point of intense violence surrounded by lower levels of violence. The map identifies three clusters of criminal attacks: (1) northwest in the states of Baja California, Chihuahua, Sinaloa, and Durango; (2) northeast in the states of Nuevo León and Tamaulipas; and (3) southwest in the states of Michoacán and Guerrero. These three regions are major battlefields of inter-cartel wars for the control of drug trafficking routes.

Fifth, attacks against local authorities did not affect political parties equally. In absolute terms, the largest number of attacks affected PRI members (43 percent), followed by members of the leftist PRD (30 percent) and the conservative PAN (20 percent).[9] In relative terms, however, local government officials and party candidates linked to the leftist PRD were disproportionately punished by criminal organizations – the PRD governed

---

[9] PRI = Institutional Revolutionary Party; PRD = Party of the Democratic Revolution; PAN = National Action Party.

16 percent of the country's municipalities yet contributed 32 percent of victims. Both the PRI and the federal incumbent PAN were less commonly targeted than leftist officials. These results suggest that the attacks were not politically neutral. The question is whether leftist officials were particularly vulnerable to attacks because drug lords purposefully wanted to eliminate local leftist authorities and candidates or simply because they were purposefully unprotected from the federal government. As we have argued, cartels do not have discernable ideological preferences. This leaves us with one option for testing: Leftist mayors might have been attacked because they were politically unprotected.

6.3   WHAT MAKES A LOCAL AUTHORITY A LIKELY TARGET OF CRIMINAL ATTACKS? STATISTICAL ANALYSIS OF RISK FACTORS

We draw on information from the CAPAM dataset to test our three hypotheses about lethal criminal attacks against government officials and party candidates. We use the municipality as our spatial unit of analysis because (1) the drug trafficking industry is a global chain of *local* operations, (2) drug cartels fight turf wars to control municipal sites (or plazas), and (3) 80 percent of victims are linked to municipal politics. We assess the annual evolution of violence across 2,018 municipalities[10] during the 2007–2012 period, when the Mexican federal government declared war on cartels and deployed the Mexican army throughout the country's territory.

The total count of criminal attacks against government officials, political candidates and party activists is our key dependent variable. CA_{it} expresses the count of attacks in municipality i in year t. The mean of CA is 0.026 and the standard deviation is 0.185.

Our first theoretical proposition, H1, suggested that government officials and party candidates would be at greater risk of criminal attacks in subnational regions experiencing the most intense levels of inter-cartel competition and violence, where cartels were diversifying their activities into extortion and kidnapping for ransom. Because the municipality offers important opportunities for the development of these criminal markets, local officials and other local political actors become target of attacks.

We draw on the Criminal Violence in Mexico (CVM) dataset,[11] which aggregates murders committed by cartels and organized criminal groups, on the basis of reports in the Mexican daily *Reforma*. We transform the

---

[10] There are 2,448 municipalities in Mexico, but we exclude Mexico's Federal District and municipalities elected under indigenous customary law in Oaxaca, where political parties are banned from competing for office by the state's law.

[11] For more information about CVM, see Trejo and Ley (2016, 2018).

count of murders and executions into *Drug-related murder rate per 1,000 population.*[12]

Our second theoretical proposition, H2, claimed that local authorities and party candidates would be more likely to become targets of criminal attacks in municipalities with greater tax revenues, where mayors could make discretionary use of the municipality's fiscal resources without federal oversight. Drawing from official Mexican statistics, we use the proportion of a municipality's total income that comes from local taxes as a measure of local tax revenues. Mexico is a centralized and uneven federation (Díaz-Cayeros, 2006) in which only 4 percent of the mean municipal income comes from local taxes. Yet governments in large cities such as Tijuana, Ciudad Juárez, Acapulco, or Lázaro Cárdenas and in the state capitals can raise up to 40 percent of their income through local taxes. To explore whether cartels were attracted to fiscally wealthier – not just fiscally autonomous – municipalities, we also test for the impact of the per capita log of local tax revenues.

Our third proposition, H3, suggested that government authorities and political actors would be at greater risk of criminal attacks in subnational regions where they had little support from higher-level authorities to confront organized crime. We claimed that attacks against local officials and politicians would be more likely in areas where power was more fragmented vertically; that is, in municipalities where mayors were from a different party than governors and governors in turn were from a different party than the president.

Mexico's party system has three major political parties (PAN, PRI, and PRD) which compete for office at three levels of government (federal, state, and municipal).[13] During the 2007–2012 period, the conservative PAN held the presidency but gubernatorial and municipal powers were dispersed across the three major parties. As illustrated in Table 6.1, we test for nine different combinations of juxtaposition or power dispersion, where the party identified on the first row in the brackets is the party in presidential power, the second is the party in the gubernatorial office, and the third is the party ruling the municipality. As the information on the table's last column shows, political power in Mexico's federation was considerably fragmented vertically.[14] For purposes of statistical analysis we use unified governance (PAN-PAN-PAN) as the reference category.

---

[12] Instead of using 100,000 people as the population base to measure the homicide rate, we use the murder rate per 1,000 inhabitants because the demographic density at the municipal level is significantly lower than national aggregates.

[13] Four small parties played important political roles during this period. Because all except for one party fielded candidates for office in coalition with the three big parties, we subsumed the small parties into the three major ones (e.g., the Green Party under the PRI and the Workers' Party under the PRD).

[14] For the pioneering analysis on "juxtaposition" or vertically fragmented power in the Mexican federation, see Remes (1999). For analyses of subnational democratization in Mexico, see Beer (2003), Gibson (2012), and Giraudy (2015).

TABLE 6.1 *Layering of Parties in Mexico's Three Levels of Government, 2007–2012*

Party Labels	Percentage of Municipalities
PAN-PAN-PAN	11.30
PAN-PAN-PRI	9.92
PAN-PAN-PRD	2.34
PAN-PRI-PAN	14.26
PAN-PRI-PRI	36.24
PAN-PRI-PRD	8.29
PAN-PRD-PAN	3.29
PAN-PRD-PRI	8.27
PAN-PRD-PRD	6.11

Notes: The party in the first cell is the president's; the second is the governor's; and the third is the mayor's. PAN-PAN-PAN is the reference category. PAN = national incumbent (conservative); PRI = opposition (center); PRD = opposition (Left).

We introduce a series of political controls, including the impact of *municipal* and *state alternation* as well as *municipal* and *state electoral competition*, because previous studies have found an association between alternation (Trejo & Ley, 2018) and competition (Villarreal, 2002; Dube et al., 2013) and increases in violence. We also include important sociodemographic controls: the log of population (to test for city size), poverty (measured as a composite index of access to public goods and services), and a series of regional controls, including *North, North-center, Center, Pacific, Gulf, South,* and *Southeast.* Note that due to a significantly high correlation among the municipal tax revenues, population, and poverty, we only test for taxes.

For purposes of statistical testing we use negative binomial regression models. We rely on random effects instead of fixed effects models because some of our key political variables (e.g., the juxtaposition variables) remain unchanged for a number of years. Because the attacks are geographically clustered within eight states, we ran additional models with lagged spatial controls.[15]

Results

The results, summarized in Table 6.2, show that local authorities and political leaders were more likely to become targets of criminal attacks in contexts of

---

[15] We test for a one-year lag of criminal attacks against local authorities in neighboring municipalities. We define neighboring municipalities as the most-immediate adjacent neighbors that share geographic borders.

TABLE 6.2 *Negative Binomial Models of Criminal Attacks against Subnational Authorities and Political Actors by Mexican Municipality, 2007–2012 (Random Effects)*

	Model 1		Model 2		Model 3	
Inter-cartel wars	Coeff.	IRR	Coeff.	IRR	Coeff.	IRR
Drug-related murder rate per 1,000 pop.	0.267*** [0.071]	1.307	0.252*** [0.071]	1.286	0.245*** [0.065]	1.278
Fiscal revenues from local taxes (%)	0.051*** [0.012]	1.053			0.047*** [0.012]	1.048
Local tax revenues per capita (ln)			0.269*** [0.071]	1.309		
Intergovernmental partisan conflict						
PAN-PAN-PRI	0.367 [0.462]	1.444	0.370 [0.464]	1.448	0.357 [0.460]	1.428
PAN-PAN-PRD	–0.069 [1.079]	0.933	–0.017 [1.079]	0.983	–0.089 [1.074]	0.914
PAN-PRI-PAN	0.514 [0.417]	1.672	0.558 [0.418]	1.747	0.492 [0.413]	1.635
PAN-PRI-PRI	0.770** [0.383]	2.159	0.786** [0.385]	2.194	0.745** [0.379]	2.107
PAN-PRI-PRD	0.461 [0.518]	1.585	0.520 [0.520]	1.681	0.447 [0.513]	1.564
PAN-PRD-PAN	1.567*** [0.531]	4.791	1.592*** [0.535]	4.914	1.468*** [0.528]	4.340
PAN-PRD-PRI	2.019*** [0.428]	7.532	2.031*** [0.429]	7.619	1.828*** [0.428]	6.223
PAN-PRD-PRD	2.080*** [0.427]	8.001	2.105*** [0.429]	8.207	1.977*** [0.423]	7.220
Spatial diffusion						
Attacks in adjacent neighbors t-1					0.312*** [0.068]	1.366
Electoral controls						
Mun. alternation	0.062 [0.157]	1.064	0.017 [0.158]	1.017	0.067 [0.155]	1.069
St. alternation	–0.052 [0.197]	0.950	–0.004 [0.197]	0.996	–0.067 [0.197]	0.935
Mun. electoral competition	–0.328** [0.131]	0.720	–0.338** [0.133]	0.713	–0.309** [0.129]	0.734
St. electoral competition	0.050 [0.312]	1.051	0.138 [0.316]	1.148	0.032 [0.307]	1.032

TABLE 6.2 (*continued*)

	Model 1	Model 2	Model 3
Demographic & geographic controls	YES	YES	YES
Constant	−2.244***	−2.885***	−2.441***
	[0.799]	[0.870]	[0.785]
Observations	9,853	9,719	9,853
Number of municipalities	1,995	1,985	1,995
Log-likelihood	−1074.082	−1068.353	−1065.375
BIC	2368.856	2357.071	2360.639

*** p<0.01, ** p<0.05, * p<0.10.
Standard errors in brackets
The party in the first cell is the president's; the second one is the governor's; and the third is the mayor's. PAN - PAN - PAN is the reference category. PAN = national incumbent (conservative); PRI = opposition (center); PRD = opposition (Left).

greater inter-cartel competition and violence. As shown in Model 1, for every additional murder per 1,000 population resulting from inter-cartel wars, the odds of government authorities and political leaders becoming targets of criminal attacks increases by 31 percent (IRR = 1.307).[16]

It is important to recall that in our argument, the intensification of inter-cartel competition and violence leads cartels to expand their activities into extortion and kidnapping in search of additional resources to finance war. Municipal authorities and local political actors become targets of criminal attacks because the municipality is a key institution in the expansion of the criminal underworld – as a new potential source of criminal revenues but also as a source of information for extorting local businesses. We will use case studies to illustrate this chain of interrelated events.

The results in Table 6.2 show that local authorities and political leaders were at greater risk of attack in municipalities with a larger local tax base. As shown in Model 1, for every additional percentage point of a municipality's total income that comes from local tax revenues, the probability of a criminal attack against the local authority increases by 5.3 percent (IRR = 1.053). This means that if we take two nearly identical municipalities, with the only difference that in one of them the share of the government's income from local taxes is greater by 10 percent, the odds of local authorities becoming

---

[16] Using a database that only includes murders of Mexican mayors, Ríos (2012) reports that inter-cartel violence is also a positive predictor of the odds of local authorities becoming targets of criminal murder.

targets of criminal attacks increases by 53 percent in the municipality with more local fiscal resources. Additional results in Model 2 show that attacks took place not only in municipalities with greater fiscal capacity but also in municipalities with greater per capita tax revenues.

While the positive impact of inter-cartel violence on criminal attacks suggests that cartels were more likely to murder local officials in contexts of intense inter-cartel violence, the impact of the tax revenue variables on criminal attacks suggests a motive: Criminal organizations used coercion to impose criminal taxes on those local authorities with discretionary access to local sources of income and with a larger local tax base. In a context of war, cartels and their criminal associates were in search of new resources, and mayors in municipalities with greater fiscal capacity became targets of extortion and attacks. Mayors were relevant because they had access to income (via taxation) but also to information that would facilitate extortion and kidnapping of local business owners and citizens.

But local authorities and political actors became targets of criminal attacks not only in municipalities with large fiscal resources but also in municipalities that were unprotected from organized crime. The results in Table 6.2 show that intergovernmental partisan conflict made local opposition authorities more vulnerable to criminal attacks. As shown in Model 1, compared to a situation of unified vertical governance in which the president's co-partisans ruled at the gubernatorial and municipal levels, when vertical governance was not unified local opposition authorities and politicians were significantly more vulnerable to criminal attacks, particularly when the state governor was affiliated to the leftist PRD – the party that had been directly in opposition to the president and his conservative party since the 2006 election. In fact, compared to a situation of unified governance, in which the president, governor, and mayor belonged to the incumbent party (PAN, PAN, PAN), results in Model 1 show that criminal attacks more commonly took place in municipalities in states ruled by the Left. If we focus only on cases of juxtaposition in cities from states ruled by governors from the leftist PRD (where the PRD appears as the second category in Table 6.2), results show that municipal authorities and party candidates in leftist states were between 379 percent (IRR = 4.791) and 700 percent (IRR = 8.001) more likely to become targets of attack than officials in states where the president's conservative co-partisans ruled. Within leftist states, partisanship continued to matter: PRI and PRD local officials were more likely to be target of criminal attacks than PAN officials.

This evidence confirms that not all local authorities and political actors faced the same risks of becoming targets of criminal attacks. Our results unambiguously show that partisanship mattered: Opposition mayors and local political candidates were significantly more likely to become targets of criminal aggression when they were located in states ruled by leftist governors who had been in direct opposition to the president since the polarized 2006 election, when the leftist presidential candidate failed to concede defeat and accept President Felipe Calderón as Mexico's legitimate president. In this story of intergovernmental partisan conflict, the relationship between the president and the governors is crucial.

Governors play a key role in Mexico. Because the country experienced a federalist transition to democracy, by which opposition victories in municipal and state elections paved the way for the national defeat of the PRI in the 2000 presidential elections, the dynamics of democratization led to a process of economic decentralization. Yet, although political power and public resources were transferred from the federal government to the states, governors devolved little power to the municipalities. In fact, governors became Mexico's new power brokers. Coordination between federal authorities and governors became a crucial factor for successful policymaking, but potential for political conflict between the center and the periphery grew exponentially after the 2006 polarizing election and the federal intervention in the War on Drugs.

According to Mexican laws, drug-trafficking and organized criminal violence are considered federal crimes. But since drug trafficking is a global chain of local operations, subnational authorities – particularly the state's attorney, the state-level police, and mayors – can play a key role in law enforcement against the cartels or, alternatively, in the provision of informal protection to them. If subnational authorities decide to work in favor of law enforcement, however, they lack the legal capacities or the policing power to confront the cartels and their private militias. They need the protection of federal authorities as much as federal authorities need the subnational authorities' access to potentially finer local-level information. When cooperation between the federal government and the states breaks down and the governors are left unprotected, they are rendered incapable of effectively assisting municipal level officials and coordinating security strategies across municipalities.

Contrary to the widespread argument that during the War on Drugs a lack of technical *coordination* between the federal government and opposition governors prevented successful joint military and civilian operations against cartels and resulted in greater violence (Urrusti, 2012; Ríos, 2013), our findings suggest that intergovernmental partisan *conflict* between President Calderón and the leftist opposition party explains why local authorities and politicians became particularly vulnerable to criminal attacks in states ruled by leftist governors. The crucial question is whether lethal attacks against opposition PRI and PRD mayors and local politicians resulted from the federal government's strategic decision to politicize law enforcement and leave states ruled by leftist governors unprotected or from the unwillingness of leftist governors to work with the president. We address this question in the case studies.

The results in Model 3 show that our findings are robust to the inclusion of spatial controls. The lagged spatial variable provides new important information. It shows that for every criminal attack against local authorities in neighboring municipalities, the odds that a municipal authority becomes a target of attacks increases by 37 percent (IRR=1.366).[17] This finding suggests the modus operandi of the criminal organizations: Cartels and their criminal associates selected their victims based on the fiscal capacity of the municipality and on the level of federal political protection and then subsequently attacked their neighbors. This means that criminal organizations do not seek to control a single municipality but entire regions, which would enable them to exercise more effective controls over drug trafficking routes and over new criminal industries, including extortion, kidnapping for ransom, and the looting of natural resources (minerals and forests).

6.4 WHY CRIMINAL LORDS ATTACK SUBNATIONAL AUTHORITIES: CASE STUDIES

Although the statistical analysis provides valuable information about the correlates of criminal attacks against local authorities, we are still missing a more complete account of the causal chain that connects inter-cartel competition and partisan intergovernmental conflict to criminal attacks against local authorities and party candidates.

To explore in greater detail this causal chain, we focus on attacks in municipalities in the southern state of Guerrero – a leftist state that experienced a major spike of inter-cartel violence between 2005 and 2012, in which dozens of mayors and party candidates, mainly from the centrist PRI and the leftist PRD, became targets of lethal criminal attacks. These attacks took place in municipalities with high inter-cartel violence and high partisan fragmentation (PAN-PRD-opposition), where cartels and their criminal associates were more likely to use targeted lethal violence against local authorities and party candidates in order to capture new financial resources required to remain competitive in the turf wars. These targeted criminal attacks were possible in a state ruled by the Left, like Guerrero, because municipal authorities and local party candidates were purposefully unprotected by a conservative federal government that used security policy to punish their subnational (leftist) political rivals.

Throughout this section, we supplement the information from Guerrero with evidence from other leftist states, including Michoacán. We close the section with a brief discussion of a contrasting state, Baja California, where the PAN federal government worked closely with a PAN governor and PAN mayors, and this co-partisan cooperation, in turn, contained a major outbreak of inter-cartel war, thereby keeping lethal attacks against local authorities and politicians to a minimum.

---

[17] See Harbers and Ingram (Chapter 2 in this volume) for an insightful discussion of spatial analysis crime.

The Federal Intervention and the Transformation of the Drug Industry

For much of the 1990s and into the early 2000s, the drug production and trafficking industries in Guerrero, a major producer of marijuana and poppy, were under the monopolistic control of the Sinaloa Cartel and its private militia led by the Beltrán-Leyva brothers. After the PRI lost the state's gubernatorial seat in 2005, and the Sinaloans temporarily lost access to the informal protection they had enjoyed from state authorities, the rival Gulf Cartel sought to capitalize on this opportunity by sending their powerful private militia, the Zetas, to Guerrero to challenge the Sinaloans' control over the state (Trejo & Ley, 2018). The breakdown of the Sinaloa cartel's drug monopoly in Guerrero led to the outbreak of fierce turf wars between the Beltrán-Levya brothers (the armed branch of the Sinaloans) and the Zetas (the armed branch of the Gulf Cartel). These conflicts had first erupted in other parts of the country, such as Baja California, Chihuahua, Jalisco, Nuevo León, and Tamaulipas, throughout the 1990s and early 2000s.

Although inter-cartel wars in Guerrero broke out in 2005, the state experienced a dramatic increase in drug violence and a major transformation in the drug industry only after the 2006–2007 federal intervention. Scholars of drug trafficking in Mexico have shown that the federal intervention in Mexico's inter-cartel wars and the deployment of the military in the country's most conflictive war zones between 2006 and 2012 led to (1) a dramatic increase in inter-cartel violence; (2) the fragmentation of some of Mexico's leading cartels into dozens of smaller organized criminal groups; and (3) the expansion of cartels and their criminal associates into new industries, most notably extortion and kidnapping for ransom (Guerrero, 2011a; Ríos, 2013; Bailey, 2014). Security analysts interpret these changes as the unintended consequence of the success of Mexico's security forces in "decapitating" the leadership of Mexico's dominant drug cartels via incarceration or murder (Guerrero, 2011a; Calderón et al., 2015; Phillips, 2015).

The federal policy of cartel decapitation pursued throughout the country had a dramatic impact in Guerrero. The state plunged into a major inter-cartel war when one of the Beltrán-Leyva brothers was arrested and another murdered. Suspicions that the leaders of the Sinaloa Cartel had facilitated Alfredo Beltrán-Leyva's arrest first led the Beltrán-Leyva Organization (BLO) to break from the Sinaloans. And Arturo Beltrán-Leyva's subsequent murder led to the fragmentation of BLO. Many of the BLO local plaza chiefs – the BLO commanders who controlled specific cities or towns – created their own independent criminal organizations and engaged in fierce wars for control of Guerrero's criminal underworld (Kyle, 2015). Security experts' estimates suggest that by 2016, 25 different organized criminal groups – from large drug cartels to regional criminal organizations to local gangs – operated in the state (Guerrero, 2016).

Two important transformations in the criminal underworld resulted from the decapitation of cartels and their criminal associates. First, following the arrest or assassination of a major drug lord, paramilitary groups and private militias such as the Beltrán-Leyva Organization, which had operated as the security arms of the Gulf and Sinaloa cartels, became independent and transformed themselves into new drug cartels. Second, the government's success in decapitating cartels and arresting or killing the chiefs of private militias weakened internal controls in these criminal organizations, which allowed a significant number of their plaza chiefs and street gangs – whose members had worked as foot soldiers for private militias – to become relatively independent. A local observer of crime in Acapulco – Guerrero's largest city and a major tourist destination – effectively captured this dynamic: "After Arturo Beltrán-Leyva [head of the Beltrán-Leyva Organization] was killed in December 2009, inter-cartel violence skyrocketed in Acapulco and new local leaders heading a multiplicity of criminal groups emerged in the region. These groups specialized in criminal activities hitherto unknown in the state, including extortion, car robbery, and kidnapping-for-ransom" (Guerrea, 2013).

As Guerrero's criminal underworld moved from criminal monopoly to dyadic conflict to multi-front wars, the drive for new financial resources to fight these wars led organized crime groups (OCGs) to expand into new criminal markets, particularly extortion and kidnapping for ransom. Initially, OCGs developed extortion and kidnapping rings in Guerrero's main urban centers, including Chilpancingo, the state capital, and Acapulco, one of Mexico's leading tourist resorts. They subcontracted local gangs to gain local territorial control in peripheral impoverished neighborhoods and used these places as bases of operation (Kyle, 2015). Although they first targeted wealthy businesses (e.g., hotels and construction companies), beginning in 2008 they added small enterprises (e.g., restaurants, tortilla retail shops, and pharmacies) and social service providers (e.g., teachers, doctors, and priests). OCG's also rapidly expanded from the state's main urban centers to the countryside, particularly the state's east–west mountain chain. In these regions, they worked with local caciques (Kyle, 2015) to gain control over Guerrero's rich natural resources – minerals and forests – and over drug production, particularly marijuana and poppy, as well as over drug trafficking routes connecting the Pacific Ocean with central and northern Mexico.

The proliferation and independence of multiple criminal groups in Guerrero's criminal underworld led to the development of new illegal markets to finance turf wars.[18] One of the most surprising outcomes of this transformation is that, as cartels expanded into new illegal activities beyond drug trafficking, municipal governments became crucial instruments in the cartels' pursuit of new resources to finance their turf wars.

---

[18] On the proliferation of criminal groups throughout the country, see Guerrero (2011b) and Ríos (2013).

Murdering Local Authorities to Loot Municipal Governments and Local Economies

As municipalities became a primary source of new revenues for the cartels' criminal ambitions, mayors and local party candidates became primary targets of criminal attacks. Cartels and their criminal associates used targeted coercive violence to extract two types of resources: the municipalities' local revenues and information about private property.

According to the National Federation of Mexican Municipalities (FENAAM) – a network of mayors linked to the PRI – by 2013, 40 percent of the country's municipal presidents – that is, 983 out of Mexico's 2,457 mayors – had received death threats from organized crime (SinEmbargo staff, 2013b). The Mexican Network of Local Authorities (AALMAC) – an organization of leftist mayors – reports that by 2013, 250 mayors from 10 states had received death threats and had been bullied by criminal organizations. AALMAC's list of 10 states matches perfectly with the geography of criminal attacks against local authorities reported in Map 6.1.[19]

Cartels and their criminal associates used death threats against local authorities to secure access to municipal resources and murdered them when they resisted or failed to pay "protection" fees. As an AALMAC representative put it, "After criminal organizations gain access to the municipality's annual budget, they demand that mayors divert a significant proportion of their budget for public works to pay criminal fees and sometimes even ask that companies on their payroll become contractors" (SinEmbargo staff, 2013b). A former mayor from AALMAC thus described this process: "The cartel's plaza chiefs ask mayors to pay a 'security fee' if they want to be safe and left alone. Mayors from small municipalities are asked to pay monthly fees of up to [8,000 dollars] while medium and large municipalities have to make monthly payments of up to [16,000 dollars]."[20]

In the region of Tierra Caliente in the western part of Guerrero, mayors have reported being coerced into paying criminal fees to different cartels. With a long history of attacks since 2006, local authorities from Coyuca de Catalán (six attacks), Arcelia (one attack), and Pungarabato (one attack) report that, because of the lack of protection from the federal government, they have been forced for several years to surrender part of their budget to the drug lords. Moreover, these local officials report great difficulty resisting the cartels' demand that they appoint cartel members as directors of the municipal treasury (Herrera & López, 2016; Aristegui Noticias, 2015). While these municipalities' own history of high-profile attacks shapes mayors' and local candidates' behavior, attacks in neighboring municipalities and in the region

---

[19] The states are: Michoacán, Tamaulipas, Coahuila, Durango, Chihuahua, San Luis Potosí, Zacatecas, Guerrero, Mexico State, and Veracruz. See Irizar (2013).

[20] Personal interview.

also influence their actions. When mayors from Coyuca, Arcelia, and Pungarabato describe pressures from cartels and their criminal associates, they also have in mind the long history of attacks in other municipalities from the region, including San Miguel Totolapan (one attack) and Zirándaro (three attacks). As our statistical results reveal, an attack in one municipality increases the odds of attacks in a neighboring municipality by 37 percent.

In the Tierra Caliente region in the neighboring state of Michoacán, also ruled by a leftist governor, mayors report similar dynamics of criminal extortion. Guillermo Valencia, a PRI mayor from Tepalcatepec elected in 2011, is explicit about the dynamics of looting by criminal organizations: "Under life threat, I was forced to surrender 10 percent of my budget to the Templars[21] ... You simply couldn't say 'no' to them ... Paying the criminal fee was my life insurance" (Calderón & Chouza, 2014). Valencia's neighboring mayors from Michoacán's Tierra Caliente region confirmed they were similarly coerced by threats into paying criminal fees and surrendering their budgets for public works (Maerker, 2014).

Cartels and their criminal associates targeted local authorities not only to extract resources from the municipal coffers but also to infiltrate local governments and gain access to privileged administrative positions and information that allow them to gain control over the local economies and loot local businesses and households. The case of the tourist resort of Acapulco, on Guerrero's Pacific Coast, is typical of the criminals' demands for local information. A few weeks after taking office in Acapulco in 2012, leftist municipal authorities faced a wave of death threats from local criminal groups. Local gangs, which had become racketeers since the assassination of Arturo Beltrán Leyva, the head of the Beltrán-Leyva cartel, demanded that the new authorities give them access to the municipal property tax registry, where they knew they could find detailed information about thousands of homeowners and hotels, restaurants, retail stores, and other local businesses. The gangs' goal was to become more efficient in levying criminal taxes and in conducting kidnapping-for-ransom operations. Because local authorities resisted, within a few weeks into the new government two municipal officials from the property tax office were murdered (Maerker, 2014). Following these murders, the property office director[22] resigned, and the position remained vacant for the rest of the administration.

Having access to accurate local information is absolutely crucial for criminal organizations seeking new resources through extortion and kidnapping-for-ransom. As a prominent Catholic priest from Acapulco put it, "Criminal organizations want to infiltrate municipal institutions such as the property tax office or the local business regulatory office because they want access to Acapulco's largest and most important databases. [With this information they

---

[21] The Knights Templar was the dominant cartel in the state of Michoacán around 2011.
[22] *Dirección del Catastro e Impuesto Predial.*

are able to charge criminal fees to] restaurant, hotel and shop-owners ... but also to private health clinics, law and accounting firms" (Guerrea, 2013). Data from the 2014 National Business Victimization Survey (ENVE)[23] substantiates the clergyman's description: 30 percent of Guerrero's small and medium enterprises – from tortilla retail stores to restaurants to pharmacies – report having been victims of criminal extortion in the previous year. Largely as a result of such rising insecurity, more than 300 small and medium-sized bars and restaurants have closed down operations in Acapulco (Juárez, 2016).

Murdering Politically Unprotected Local Authorities and Party Candidates

While quantitative and qualitative data show that cartels and their criminal associates targeted local authorities in cities with autonomous fiscal resources and wealthy tax payers, our information shows that criminal organizations also targeted municipalities that were unprotected for political reasons by the federal government. As our statistical results show, municipal authorities and local party candidates were particularly vulnerable to criminal attacks in cities located in states ruled by the Left and where leftist governors and President Calderón's conservative party, PAN, had been engaged in a bitter conflict from the first days of his administration, when the federal government's War on Drugs was launched.

Was criminal violence against municipal authorities and political candidates more common in leftist states because leftist governors and mayors did not want to receive federal aid from – or coordinate their actions with – a government they perceived to be "illegitimate"? Or did the federal government purposefully launch ineffective operations and weak military deployments in states ruled by leftist governors and mayors?

There is extensive public evidence of leftist subnational authorities demanding federal protection after receiving death threats from organized crime – even if they had previously declined to publicly accept President Calderón as Mexico's legitimate president. For example, Governor Lázaro Cárdenas Batel from Michoacán did not hesitate to demand military assistance in 2006 when conflicts between La Familia Michoacana[24] and the Zetas escalated to unprecedented levels. The response was a poorly coordinated federal program.

We also know that the leftist mayor of Santa Ana Maya, Michoacán, Ygnacio López Mendoza, who was brutally murdered in 2013, had been demanding federal protection for years. As a prominent leader from AALMAC, the network of leftist mayors, declared after López's assassination: "[President Calderón] was perfectly aware of the death threats that mayors ...

---

[23] The ENVE is a large-scale survey on victimization of Mexican business owners conducted by the National Institute of Statistics and Geography (INEGI) on a biannual basis since 2012.

[24] Mexican drug cartel based in the state of Michoacán, precursor of the Knights Templar.

like López … were receiving, but he was never willing to meet with us [AALMAC] when we asked for help" (SinEmbargo staff, 2013a). Mayor Valencia, from the PRI, faced a similar situation in his hometown of Tepalcatepec, Michoacán. After criminal organizations first approached him for criminal fees and after receiving his first death threat in 2011, Valencia reports that he insistently demanded "federal protection and the presence of the army." But he "did not receive any response."

Based on information from national and subnational newspaper reports and from hundreds of press releases and speeches made by military zone commanders, as well as interviews with national security officials from the Calderón administration and former opposition governors, in previous work we found that "joint operations" conducted during the Calderón administration, involving the army, navy, federal police, and state and municipal police forces, were not designed and implemented uniformly across states (Trejo & Ley, 2016). In states ruled by the opposition, particularly the Left (e.g., Guerrero, Michoacán, and Zacatecas), operations were not joint, because they only involved the army and the federal police, and were limited to some but not all of the states' conflict zones. By contrast, operations in states ruled by the president's PAN co-partisans (e.g., Baja California) involved a high degree of communication and coordinated efforts across federal, state, and local governments.

The parallel experiences of local authorities from the central/southern states of Guerrero and Michoacán – two leftist strongholds – highlight the effect of partisan intergovernmental conflict during the War on Drugs.

In Guerrero, after receiving several death threats from organized criminal groups throughout 2006, including a decapitated human head in his office, the leftist mayor of Acapulco, Félix Salgado, demanded federal protection for himself and federal intervention to confront a major wave of criminal violence in his city (Flores & Guerrero, 2006; Herrera, 2007; *La Jornada Guerrero*, 2007). Although the federal government did deploy the military to Acapulco, President Calderón's Secretary of Public Security, instead of offering protection to Mayor Salgado, declared on national television that his office was investigating alleged linkages between the mayor and the state's cartels. The secretary later retracted his tendentious statement; he had, however, already triggered a smear campaign against Salgado that made the mayor and his team increasingly vulnerable to criminal attacks. According to local leftist leaders, the fact that Salgado had denounced Calderón's election as fraudulent explained the reluctance of federal authorities to protect the mayor's life (*La Jornada Guerrero*, 2007).

Over the next six years, organized criminal groups took advantage of partisan intergovernmental conflicts between the federal government and the Left in Guerrero to coerce local authorities and to expand their illegal actions into extortion and kidnapping among a wide range of social and economic groups in Acapulco. Guerrero became Mexico's second most lethal state for mayors and local political leaders, after Michoacán.

The experience of local authorities in Michoacán – a state ruled by the Left from 2001 to 2012 – is also instructive of the partisan nature of the federal intervention in the War on Drugs. As PRI and leftist mayors systematically complained about criminal violence, the military rarely came to their rescue when they received death threats and faced major spikes of violence. Rather than assist and work with them, during the first three years of the War on Drugs – when the federal intervention had a high citizen approval rate – President Calderón launched a media campaign contrasting his iron-fist policies with, on the one hand, the long history of corruption during the seven decades of PRI rule and, on the other hand, alleged collusion between leftist state and local authorities and organized crime. A few hours before the beginning of the 2009 midterm legislative election campaign, the president and his attorney general conducted a large-scale arrest of 24 leftist state-level officials and 12 mayors in Michoacán. Although all but one of the arrested officials were released a year later, this mass arrest allowed the federal government to launch a major smear campaign against the leftist state government and prime the electorate to view the Left as partners of organized crime. After the strong showing of the Left in the 2006 elections, in which the leftist presidential candidate Andrés Manuel López Obrador lost by a razor-thin margin, President Calderón was determined to prevent a strong leftist showing in the midterm elections.

Over the course of the following months and years, as intergovernmental partisan conflict between Left and Right deepened, Michoacán became one of Mexico's most lethal battlefields for organized crime and the most dangerous Mexican state for extortion and kidnapping-for-ransom. As criminal organizations learned that the federal government had strategically decided to leave local officials in leftist states relatively unprotected, mayors and political candidates in states like Michoacán became easy prey for criminal coercion.

WHY CARTELS DID NOT MURDER PROTECTED AUTHORITIES IN CONFLICTIVE REGIONS

In contrast to the experiences of local authorities in Guerrero and Michoacán, in states such as Baja California – where the PAN had held the gubernatorial seat since 1989 – the federal intervention against organized crime was designed to assist, cooperate with, and protect mayors, especially those affiliated with the PAN (Sabet, 2012).

The city of Mexicali, where PANista federal, state, and municipal authorities worked together to reduce levels of violence associated with major turf wars between the Tijuana Cartel and the Sinaloa Cartel, is emblematic of partisan cooperation. Despite experiencing levels of inter-cartel violence similar to those in Guerrero's largest cities (e.g., Acapulco) in 2007, Mexicali did not suffer a single criminal attack against local authorities during the Calderón administration (2006–2012).

The city of Tijuana, home of the Tijuana Cartel and also ruled by the PAN, experienced a major outbreak of inter-cartel conflict in 2008, but intergovernmental cooperation allowed local authorities to contain violence. Although Tijuana did experience five attacks against local authorities and party candidates between 2006 and 2012, this is a relatively low number given the unprecedented level of inter-cartel competition and violence. Together, a decisive federal intervention that deployed the military in Tijuana in coordination with the governor and the mayor; a coordinated purge of the local police; and a coordinated policy intervention that funneled new public resources for focalized social projects worked to contain violence (Sabet, 2012; Durán-Martínez, 2015; Trejo & Ley, 2016).

While intergovernmental coordination was neither automatic nor unproblematic in Mexicali and Tijuana,[25] shared electoral incentives motivated co-partisans from different levels of governments to work together effectively and to recover the state's authority over territories previously controlled by drug cartels. Unlike in leftist Guerrero and Michoacán, in Baja California aligned partisan incentives led conservative national and subnational authorities to collaborate, and their coordinated actions discouraged the cartels from attacking local government officials and party candidates.

6.5 CONCLUSIONS

One of the most important lessons we have learned in the past decade from the study of political violence is that the interests, strategies, and identities of non-state armed actors change throughout the course of protracted conflicts (Kalyvas, 2006). Focusing on Mexico's criminal wars, we analyzed a dramatic transformation in the forms of engagement of drug cartels with subnational authorities after almost two decades of inter-cartel wars. Even though cartels had successfully obtained informal government protection via bribes and had not systematically murdered government authorities during 12 years of criminal wars, between 2007 and 2012 more than 300 municipal officials and local political candidates became targets of lethal criminal attacks.

We have provided extensive empirical evidence showing that this wave of criminal attacks was the result of two intertwined conflicts: (1) the dramatic intensification of inter-cartel violence following a federal intervention intended to contain the cartels' turf wars; and (2) intense intergovernmental partisan

---

[25] The federal intervention in Baja California experienced an initial crisis when high-ranking military officials deployed in the state accused PAN local officials of corruption and collusion with criminal organizations. See Trejo and Ley (2016) for a detailed discussion of this case.

conflict between conservative federal authorities and leftist subnational authorities following the polarized 2006 presidential election.

We showed that the intensification of inter-cartel violence after the federal intervention and the resulting need for additional resources to finance ongoing wars led drug cartels and their criminal associates to expand operations into new criminal markets, including extortion and kidnapping for ransom. Municipal authorities became targets of criminals when they had discretionary access to local tax revenues and information about the tax records of wealthy individuals and local businesses. Whether local officials were able to resist or, alternatively, became victims of lethal attacks depended partly on whether they received effective protection from federal authorities. Our evidence shows that in an overarching context of acute elite polarization between Left and Right, the conservative federal government more often provided effective protection to subnational authorities in states where the president's party ruled yet failed to protect local authorities facing major criminal threats in states ruled by opposition forces, particularly the Left, the president's political nemesis.

Our study has two important theoretical implications for future research on the subnational politics of organized crime and large-scale criminal violence.

First, although Mexican drug cartels and their criminal associates do not seek to take over national governments but simply to infiltrate subnational institutions in order to facilitate the operation of illegal industries, their expansion into extortion and kidnapping and their attacks against local authorities and candidates are redefining local political orders. By using lethal violence to impose criminal taxes on local authorities, businesses, and citizens, criminal organizations are radically changing the dynamics of local governance in conflict zones. Under the threat of the gun, mayors in wealthy and politically unprotected municipalities have lost control over a significant share of government resources, and criminal organizations have gained de facto control over key financial decisions. Under the rule of *plomo*, citizens are victims of dual criminal taxation: They pay direct fees to criminals, and a proportion of their local taxes also end up in criminal hands. Criminal monopoly of violence and control over local tax revenues have turned Mexican cartels and their criminal associates into de facto authorities in conflict zones.

While a national-level focus would make it hard to conclude that Mexico is a failed state, applying a subnational lens has enabled us to identify important subnational regions where local state authorities no longer perform a state's most basic function – the provision of security in exchange for taxes. In these regions, cartels and their criminal associates are increasingly monopolizing violence, security, and taxation and are remaking local political orders. This finding has important theoretical implications. It strongly suggests the need to unpack organized crime and the state geographically in order to understand spatial variation in subnational political orders.

Second, while most studies of drug trafficking and organized crime focus on the actions of national governments or on neighborhood dynamics, in this chapter we show the crucial role that domestic intergovernmental relations between national and subnational authorities can play in driving the evolution of criminal markets and of drug violence and in redefining local political orders. Looking at the inter-relationship between multiple layers of government has a major advantage over national-level studies. Whereas a focus on national actors would led us to concentrate on a technical assessment of federal security policies in the War on Drugs, our focus on intergovernmental relations made it easier to see that partisanship was a defining element of Mexico's federal intervention.[26] Observing vertical relations among national, state, and local governments sheds light on the long-term impact that the politicization of law enforcement has had on local governance in Mexico's most conflict-ridden criminal zones.

Our findings about the politicization of law enforcement in the War on Drugs would lead us to question established theories of the state. Contrary to the widely held Weberian assumption that state authorities will always seek to monopolize violence, we find that multilevel partisan conflict drove Mexican federal authorities to leave their subnational political rivals unprotected in the struggle against the country's powerful cartels – even if this meant that in some subnational regions the state would probably contain epidemics of violence and protect local authorities, whereas in others it would fail to contain all forms of violence. By unpacking the state and policymaking processes into its multiple territorial and political dimensions, one of the most surprising lessons from our analysis is that, in contexts of acute ideological polarization, state actors do not always take actions that are conducive to the development of strong and capable states and to the construction of peaceful local political orders.

BIBLIOGRAPHY

Aguayo, Sergio. (2001). *La charola: Una historia de los servicios de inteligencia en México*. Mexico City: Grijalbo.
Arias, Enrique Desmond. (2017). *Criminal enterprises and governance in Latin America and the Caribbean*. Cambridge: Cambridge University Press.
Aristegui Noticias. (2015, December 3). Gobierno federal simula seguridad en la Tierra Caliente de Guerrero. *Aristegui Noticias*. Available at: http://aristeguinoticias.com/0312/mexico/gobierno-federal-simula-seguridad-en-la-tierra-caliente-de-guerrero-parte-i/ (last accessed December 17, 2018).
Arjona, Ana M. (2016). *Rebelocracy: Social order in the Colombian civil war*. Cambridge, England: Cambridge University Press.
Astorga, Luis, & Shirk, David. (2010). *Drug trafficking organizations and counter-drug strategies in the U.S.–Mexico context*. USMEX Working Paper 1.

---

[26] On the importance of a multilevel approach for studying crime, see Moncada (2013).

Auyero, Javier. (2006). The political makings of the 2001 lootings in Argentina. *Journal of Latin American Studies 38*(2), 241–265.

Bagley, Bruce. (2012). *Drug trafficking and organized crime in the Americas: Major trends in the twenty-first century.* Latin American Program, Woodrow Wilson International Center for Scholars, Washington, DC.

Bailey, John. (2014). *The politics of crime in Mexico.* Boulder, CO: Lynne Rienner.

Bailey, John, & Taylor, Mathew. (2009). Evade, corrupt, or confront? Organized crime and the state in Brazil and Mexico. *Journal of Politics in Latin America 1*(2), 3–29.

Beer, Caroline. (2003). *Electoral competition and institutional change in Mexico.* Notre Dame, IN: University of Notre Dame Press.

Blancornelas, Jesús. (2002). *El cartel.* Mexico City, Mexico: Plaza & Janés.

Calderón, Verónica, & Chouza, Paula. (2014, March 14). El narco cobraba el 10% del dinero federal enviado a Michoacán. *El País.*

Calderón, Gabriela, Robles, Gustavo, Díaz-Cayeros, Alberto, & Magaloni, Beatriz. (2015). The beheading of criminal organizations and the dynamics of violence in Mexico. *Journal of Conflict Resolution 59*(8), 1455–1485.

Chacón, Mario. (2014). *In the line of fire: Political violence and decentralization in Colombia.* Typescript, New York University, New York, NY.

Dal Bó, Ernesto, Dal Bó, Pedro, & Di Tella, Rafael. (2006). "Plata o plomo?" Bribe and punishment in a theory of political influence. *American Political Science Review 100* (1), 41–53.

Díaz-Cayeros, Alberto. (2006). *Federalism, fiscal authority, and centralization in Latin America.* Cambridge, England: Cambridge University Press.

Dube, A., Dube, O., & García-Ponce, O. 2013. Cross-border spillover: US gun laws and violence in Mexico. *American Political Science Review 107*(3), 397–417.

Durán-Martínez, Angélica. (2015). To kill and tell? State power, criminal competition, and drug violence. *Journal of Conflict Resolution 59*(8), 1377–1402.

Eaton, Kent. (2006). The downside of decentralization: Armed clientelism in Colombia. *Security Studies 15*(4), 533–562.

Flores, Sergio, & Guerrero, J. (2006, July 1). No soy 'Rambo', revira Salgado. *Reforma.*

Gambetta, Diego. (1993). *The sicilian mafia.* Boston, MA: Harvard University Press.

Gambetta, Diego. (2010). *Codes of the underworld: How criminals communicate.* Princeton, NJ: Princeton University Press.

Gibson, Edward L. (2012). *Boundary control: Subnational authoritarianism in federal democracies.* Cambridge, England: Cambridge University Press.

Giraudy, Agustina. (2015). *Democrats and autocrats: Pathways of subnational undemocratic regime continuity within democratic countries.* Oxford, England: Oxford University Press.

Grillo, Ioan. (2012). *El narco: Inside Mexico's criminal insurgency.* London, England: Bloomsbury Press.

Guerrea, José Antonio. (2013, March 11). Acapulco tiene miedo; hasta las autoridades renuncian. *El Financiero.*

Guerrero, Eduardo. (2011a). *Security, drugs, and violence in Mexico: A survey.* Paper presented at the 7th North American Forum, Washington, DC.

Guerrero, Eduardo. (2011b, January 1). La raíz de la violencia. *Nexos.*

Guerrero, Eduardo. (2016, June 1). La inseguridad 2013–2015. *Nexos.*

Herrera, Rolando. (2007, January 25). Enfrenta Félix Salgado amenazas del narco. *Reforma.*

Herrera, Rolando, & López, Mayolo. (2016, July 7). Pidieron a alcalde hasta apagar la luz. *Reforma*.

Irizar, Guadalupe. (2013, November 9). Amenaza crimen a 250 alcaldes. *Reforma*.

Juárez, Alfonso. (2016, March 29). Cierran restaurantes en Acapulco por crimen. *Reforma*, p. 1.

Kalyvas, Stathis. (2006). *The logic of violence in civil war*. Cambridge, England: Cambridge University Press.

Kyle, Chris. (2015). Violence and Insecurity in Guerrero. In *Building resilient communities in Mexico: Civic responses to crime and violence*. Briefing Paper Series, Woodrow Wilson Center, Washington, DC.

La Jornada Guerrero. (2007, February 11). Diputados perredistas critican amenazas de muerte contra Salgado Macedonio. *La Jornada Guerrero*.

Lessing, Benjamin. (2015). The logic of violence in criminal war. *Journal of Conflict Resolution* 59(8), 1486–1516.

Maerker, Denise. (2014, April 1). Auxilio: ¿dónde está el estado? *Nexos*.

Moncada, Eduardo. (2013). The politics of urban violence: Challenges for development in the global south. *Studies in Comparative International Development* 48(3), 217–239.

Olson, Mancur. (2000). *Power and prosperity: Outgrowing communist and capitalist dictatorships*. New York, NY: Basic Books.

Phillips, Brian J. (2015). How does leadership decapitation affect violence? The case of drug trafficking organizations in Mexico. *Journal of Politics* 77(2), 324–336.

Reforma staff. (2012, October 30). Niega base de datos y crimen lo ejecuta. *Reforma*.

Remes, Alain. (1999). Gobiernos yuxtapuestos en México: Hacia un marco analítico para el estudio de las elecciones municipales. *Política y Gobierno* 6(1), 225–253.

Ríos, Viridiana. (2012). Tendencias y explicaciones al asesinato de periodistas y alcaldes en México: El crimen organizado y la violencia de alto perfil. In José Antonio Aguilar Rivera (Coord.), *Las Bases Sociales del Crimen Organizado y la Violencia en México*, pp. 275–308. Mexico City, Mexico: Secretaría de Seguridad Pública.

Ríos, Viridiana. (2013). Why did Mexico become so violent? A self-reinforcing violent equilibrium caused by competition and enforcement. *Trends in Organized Crime* 16 (2), 138–155.

Sabet, Daniel M. (2012). *Police reform in Mexico*. Palo Alto, CA: Stanford University Press.

SinEmbargo staff. (2013a, November 8). FCH es oportunista, ahora tuitea peri ni nos recibió … *SinEmbargo*.

SinEmbargo staff. (2013b, November 16). La extorsión generalizada alcanza a los alcaldes; ya no es asunto de ciudadanos, comerciantes y agricultores. *SinEmbargo*.

Snyder, Richard, & Durán-Martínez, Angélica. (2009). Does illegality breed violence? Drug trafficking and state-sponsored protection rackets. *Crime, Law and Social Change* 52(3), 253–273.

Tilly, Charles. (1985). War making and state making as organized crime. In Peter Evans, Dietrich Rueschemeyer, & Theda Skocpol (Eds.), *Bringing the State Back In*, pp. 169–191. Cambridge, England: Cambridge University Press.

Trejo, Guillermo, & Ley, Sandra. (2016). Federalism, drugs, and violence: Why intergovernmental partisan conflict stimulated inter-cartel violence in Mexico. *Política y Gobierno* 23(1), 9–52.

Trejo, Guillermo, & Ley, Sandra. (2018)."Why did drug cartels go to war in Mexico? Subnational party alternation, the breakdown of criminal protection, and the onset of large-scale violence. *Comparative Political Studies* 51(7), 900–937.

Urrusti, Sinaia. (2012). La violencia como consecuencia de la falta de coordinación política. In J. A. Aguilar (Coord.), *Las Bases Sociales del Crimen Organizado y la Violencia en México*, pp. 337–370. Mexico City, Mexico: Secretaría de Seguridad Pública.

Villarreal, Andrés. (2002). Political competition and violence in Mexico: Hierarchical social control in local patronage structures. *American Sociological Review* 67(4), 477–498.

Wilkinson, Steven. (2005). *Votes and violence: Electoral competition and ethnic riots in India*. Cambridge, England: Cambridge University Press.

7

Subnational Units, the Locus of Choice, and Concept Formation

Conceptualizing Civilian Behavior in Contexts of Civil War

Ana Arjona

Scholars in the field of social science have referred to concepts as indispensable tools of science (Weber, 2015), "the building blocks of all inferences" (Gerring, 1999), and "the elements of a theoretical system" (Sartori, 1970, p. 1039). Scholars have also described concepts as "data containers" (Sartori, 1970, p. 1039) and the guides for "the acquisition of empirical data" (Goertz, 2006, p. 62). From the questions we ask to the theories we develop and the empirical evidence we gather, work on concept formation and methodology demonstrates that concepts shape the entire research process.[1]

One of the ways that concepts matter is by influencing unit and case selection – that is, the level at which the analysis is conducted, and the specific cases that are studied.[2] As several scholars have argued (e.g., Gerring, 2007; Goertz, 2006; Gschwend & Schimmelfennig, 2007; Soifer, Chapter 2 in this volume), unit and case selection should be informed by theory – and since theories are built on concepts, concepts are quite consequential. Scholars have also debated whether, and how, the level of analysis actually affects concept formation and what the conditions are under which concepts developed at one level can be applied to other units.[3] What is seldom recognized is that another type of unit selection shapes the content of concepts – the unit in which we situate the actors whose behavior we seek to understand. This is important because many of the theories we develop in the social sciences aim to explain the

I thank the editors of this volume, Agustina Giraudy, Richard Snyder, and Eduardo Moncada, as well as participants at two conferences organized for this volume and two anonymous reviewers for their valuable feedback. I am grateful to Nicholas Blake and Emma Kupor for their research assistance.

[1] See Schedler (2011) for a brief discussion of the importance of concepts for social science research.

[2] More formally, the unit of analysis is "the abstract entity that we study" (e.g., states, institutions, decisions) and *cases* are "the specific units of analysis that we choose to analyze" (e.g., Germany, congress, voting) (Gschwend & Schimmelfennig, 2007, p. 5). Throughout the chapter I use the term *unit* when referring to the type of unit or level of analysis, not a specific *case*.

[3] See Harbers and Ingram's Chapter 2 in this volume.

decisions of specific actors.[4] Theories of phenomena such as consumer behavior, voting, corruption, and war-making often consist of propositions about why consumers, voters, rulers, or rebels make one choice over another.

Scholars in the social sciences recognize that explaining individual behavior requires taking into account the context in which individuals are embedded, as contextual factors can affect the decision-making process in multiple ways.[5] What tends to be overlooked, however, is that our choices as researchers in situating actors in particular units also impacts our conceptualization of the behaviors we seek to explain.

In a literal sense, every decision-making process takes place within multiple units such as a neighborhood, city, region, or country. Yet, whenever we conceptualize a phenomenon that consists of an individual actor's choice – like voting, joining a gang, or paying taxes – we do not consider all the units in which the actor is embedded. We also do not consider the decision-making process in a vacuum. Rather, we focus on the unit that we deem relevant for that particular decision – say, the county for voting, the neighborhood for joining a gang, or the country for tax-paying. I use the term "locus of choice" (hereafter LOC) to refer to the unit(s) that, either implicitly or explicitly, we consider to be the relevant spatial context of the decision-making processes.

Subnational research (SNR) has made important contributions to theory development and empirical research by, among other things, increasing the menu of units available to researchers (Snyder, 2001; Introduction, this volume). At the same time – as discussed by Snyder (2001) and various chapters in this volume[6] – the subnational approach also poses new challenges because researchers must carefully select the appropriate unit of analysis when forming concepts, building theories, or making causal and descriptive inferences. In this chapter I argue that another type of unit selection is quite consequential for concept formation: the unit in which we situate actors whose decisions we seek to explain – that is, their LOC.

I identify three specific ways that our selection of a LOC for a decision-making process influences our concepts. First, selection impacts how we understand the ontology of the phenomenon under study.[7] There are multiple

---

[4] The terms *individual decision, choice*, and *behavior* are often used differently across fields. In this chapter, I use them to denote a person's decision to act in a specific way.

[5] Studying individual behavior in economics, sociology, political science, and psychology usually involves identifying contextual factors that impact individuals' constraints, opportunities, incentives, values, beliefs, identities, or emotions, to name a few, which in turn affect individuals' choices. To be sure, social scientists may disagree on what type of contextual factors matter the most, as well as on what are the underlying mechanisms; but they tend to agree on the importance of considering some kind of contextual factors to explain human behavior. For a discussion of social science explanations of human behavior, see Elster (2007).

[6] See the Introduction as well as Chapter 3 by Sofier and Chapter 2 by Harbers and Ingram.

[7] There are multiple definitions of the term "ontology." I follow a common approach, according to which ontology "is concerned with the (specific) set of assumptions made about the nature,

ways to conceptualize a phenomenon, and our focus on a given LOC affects which aspects we consider to be more salient. Second, the unit we select informs what we consider the phenomenon *not* to be, and distinguishing instances of a phenomenon from non-instances is crucial for a concept to be applicable. The unit we select as the LOC informs our criteria to determine what elements are included and excluded in the concept. And third, the LOC informs our classificatory systems for both the concept in question and neighboring concepts.[8] The LOC we as researchers choose affects which specific acts we recognize as belonging to the phenomenon under study. In addition, the LOC influences our identification of the menu of alternatives available to the decision-maker, which is in turn a key conceptual step in building an explanation of a specific choice.

Carefully considering the unit in which we situate actors is therefore quite consequential for concept formation and, thus, for the entire research process. I illustrate this argument by discussing how our conceptualization of civilian support for rebel groups has changed as SNR has advanced our understanding of localities in conflict zones.[9] When civil war scholars adopted a subnational focus, tremendous progress was made in this field: the quality of evidence improved; theoretical accounts started to rely on more realistic assumptions; the microfoundations and causal mechanisms of conflict received greater attention; new evidence led to new research questions; innovative research designs that exploited subnational variation allowed for better causal inference; and, as a consequence, our understanding of the causes, dynamics, and consequences of civil war improved substantially (Kalyvas, 2008b; Blattman & Miguel, 2010; Cederman & Gleditsch, 2009). Among these contributions is the identification of the locality as both a crucial unit of analysis and the relevant context for understanding civilian behavior.

I rely on three seminal contributions to the study of civil war by Petersen (2001), Wood (2003), and Kalyvas (2006) to illustrate how SNR has advanced the conceptualization of civilian support. Despite being considered a determinant of the conduct, duration, and termination of civil war, civilian support had been poorly conceptualized in the literature prior to these studies: The term was rarely defined, and its alternatives were rarely specified. I show how the turn to the locality as the locus of civilian choice led to a substantial improvement in the conceptualization of civilian support and of civilian behavior in conflict zones more generally.

---

essence, and characteristics (in short, the reality) of an object or set of objects of analytical inquiry" (Hay, 2006, p. 3).

[8] Neighboring concepts are those that share multiple attributes with each other but also differ in important ways (Gerring, 2007, p. 42).

[9] By locality, I mean small territorial units such as neighborhoods, villages, and hamlets in both urban and rural areas, where community members "interact directly, frequently, and in multi-faceted ways" (Bowles & Gintis, 2002, p. 420).

I further argue that delving even deeper into the dynamics of the localities in conflict zones can lead to more nuanced and sophisticated conceptualizations of the choices that civilians make. Relying on my previous and ongoing work, I argue that taking into account the existence of different forms of social order at the local level reveals important aspects of civilian behavior in conflict zones. In particular, I demonstrate that obedience is a central form of cooperation that is often ignored, and that civilian resistance against armed actors – which was until recently largely overlooked – is likely to arise in conflict zones. Incorporating obedience and resistance into our conceptualization of civilian support, and into our typologies of civilians' choices more generally, can help advance our understanding of civilian, rebel, and counterinsurgent behavior in conflict zones.[10]

In Section 7.1, I argue that the unit we as scholars select as the locus of a given choice, and what we know about it, shapes our conceptualization of the phenomenon under study. In Section 7.2 I introduce the phenomenon of civilian support for rebels and explain the significance of the *locality* as the LOC for civilians in wartime. In this section I also show how the progression of research on the subnational dynamics of civil war has improved the study of civilian decision-making, with scholars increasingly considering the locality as the LOC. In Section 7.3, I draw on both my previous and ongoing research to show that a more nuanced understanding of local conditions in conflict zones can further refine our conceptualization of civilian choice during wartime. I illustrate my arguments with original evidence on individuals and communities in conflict zones throughout Colombia. I conclude in Section 7.4 with a discussion of how a better conceptualization of the LOC can improve concept formation in comparative politics more broadly.

7.1 THE LOCUS OF CHOICE AND THEORY BUILDING

Concept formation often involves an iterative process. Sometimes the process starts with a selection of an already established concept. We then look for applicable facts and data, perhaps realizing in the process that we need to refine the concept in order to better capture the observed facts. Alternatively, we may start by first observing empirical evidence and then creating a concept to capture its salient attributes. As we work on the concept, we may realize that we must return to the facts and reexamine them, paying closer attention to traits we had previously ignored. In this refining process, the context in which we situate the phenomenon matters. We seldom consider facts in purely abstract terms; rather, we approach them within a particular situation. This is an important

---

[10] The discussion of how civilian support has been conceptualized in civil war studies builds on Arjona (2017), where I propose a typology of civilian cooperation and noncooperation with non-state armed groups.

finding in the research on human cognition, which suggests that the mind conceptualizes objects or events differently when considering them within different contexts. Indeed, as Yee et al. (2016, p. 1016) note, "no one would deny that context influences conceptual processing." Some researchers even contend that, in the mind, "*the concepts themselves are inextricably linked to the contexts in which they appear*" (ibid.; emphasis in original).[11]

When it comes to studying individual behavior, the unit in which we consider the decision-making process to take place can be especially consequential. As the introduction to this volume explains, subnational spatial units are often characterized by distinct social, political, economic, and physical environments.[12] Even though individuals make decisions while embedded in multiple subnational units, when we consider a specific action we usually do so within the context of a particular type (or types of) unit(s). I use the term "locus of choice" (LOC) to refer to the type of spatial units that, either implicitly or explicitly, we consider to be the relevant context in which a given decision is made. The unit we select as the LOC – and what we know about it – influences our conceptualization of the behavior of the actors we study in three important ways.

First, our decisions as researchers about the relevant unit(s) in which actors are situated (their LOC) shape how we understand the ontology of the phenomenon in question. Following Goertz (2006, p. 5), "concepts are theories about ontology: they are theories about the fundamental constitutive elements of a phenomenon." In this sense, "to develop a concept is more than providing a definition: it is deciding what is important about an entity" (Goertz, 2006, p. 27). How do we decide what a phenomenon's core attributes are? One of the criteria for determining these core attributes is that they are important for explaining the causes or consequences of the phenomenon. Goertz's example on the concept of democracy is illustrative: One of the reasons why the ability to replace leaders via election is often seen as a fundamental attribute of democracy is because it has important effects on other phenomena. The democratic peace theory, for example, contends that democracies avoid fighting wars because, among other reasons, voters can penalize leaders for war losses.

I argue that the LOC is crucial as we identify the core attributes of a phenomenon. Both the unit we select – say, the province or neighborhood – and what we know about it influence our selection of attributes. This is the case

---

[11] For a useful review of studies of cognition on how "context" influences conceptual processing, see Yee et al. (2016).

[12] Following the definition of subnational research presented in the Introduction to this volume, subnational spatial units can be formal/jurisdictional or informal/non-jurisdictional. The former "have clearly demarcated, legally-constituted boundaries," whereas the latter "are not legally constituted and typically lack crisp boundaries, although actors with local knowledge may be able to identify them" (see Introduction, this volume).

because some aspects of a phenomenon only become visible when considered within a specific unit. Moreover, as we consider which elements of the phenomenon could play an important role in theories about its causes and consequences, the unit or units in which we situate the actor can be decisive.[13]

Consider James C. Scott's work on hidden resistance. As he points out in his preface to *Weapons of the Weak* (Scott, 1985, p. xv), "most subordinate classes throughout most of history have rarely been afforded the luxury of open, organized political activity." Based on his research in a Malaysian village, Scott conceptualizes a series of daily behaviors of peasants as "everyday forms of resistance." In *Domination and the Arts of Resistance* (1990), he further analyzes the ways in which subordinates resist. Rather than focusing on a single village, he considers various contexts characterized by severe conditions of subordination and dependency. In both books, his focus on specific units in which these behaviors took place is essential for his analysis. As he puts it, "we are led to examine the social sites where this resistance can germinate" (Scott, 1990, p. xii). Without a focus on the plantation, the village, or the factory, it is hardly possible to come to see *resistance* as a key attribute of acts as dissimilar as foot-dragging, gossiping, or mockery.

A second way that our selection of the relevant LOC influences concept formation is through informing what the phenomenon is *not*. Specifying when the phenomenon does not occur or is not present is an essential task in concept formation (Sartori, 1970; Goertz, 2006; Collier & Gerring, 2009; Schedler, 2011). A good concept of democracy, for example, has to make clear what democracy is not. Careful stipulation of the relevant units in which our subjects operate – that is, their LOC – can foster good concept formation by helping limit the attributes we focus on for conceptualizing the phenomenon.

The third way our decisions about the relevant LOC drive our concepts is through influencing our classificatory systems. Conceptualizing a phenomenon involves defining its genus – the overarching category, group or class to which the phenomenon belongs – and identifying other species within that genus – the other phenomena that belong to the same category or class (Sartori, 1970). Because our conceptualization of a phenomenon shapes our understanding of the ontology of that phenomenon, how we specify the LOC drives our placement of that phenomenon within a particular genus. Moreover, by influencing which attributes of the phenomenon we regard as

---

[13] One could wonder whether the opposite is true – to wit, that our ontological views drive our selection of the LOC. Yet, where would those ontological views come from? We know that our theories (about causal relations) are driven by the unit of analysis we focus on (see the Introduction to this volume as well as Soifer's Chapter 3 and Harbers and Ingram's Chapter 2 for a discussion). If our ontological views come from our theoretical priors about the causes or consequences of the phenomenon, then such views are also driven by the units that we focus on.

salient, our specification of the LOC informs the identification of the phenomenon's specific types. These classificatory systems, in turn, guide the entire research process from the dimensions of the phenomenon on which we focus to the data we collect to the explanations we build.

How we specify the LOC also affects another classificatory task that emerges when building theories to explain the decisions of individuals: identifying the menu of options available to them. This entails listing and often classifying a set of actions that share similar attributes. Our understanding of both the ontology of the phenomenon and the LOC informs which attributes to focus on, as well as which alternative actions to include among an actor's options. What we know about the place or places in which an actor is embedded, and what aspects of those places we focus on, influences how we identify the menu of options the actor can consider. This menu is, in turn, quite consequential for our explanations. As a large literature shows, the set of available options can influence behavior by constraining actors' choices, shaping their desires or preferences, or altering their beliefs (Elster, 2007). Our explanations for an actor's behavior, and our understanding of their choices among those available alternatives, depend on how we specify their LOC.

Scholars are increasingly aware that the unit of analysis matters for theoretical and empirical work (Snyder, 2001; see also Soifer, Chapter 3, and Harbers & Ingram, Chapter 4, in this volume). Still, as emphasized in the editors' concluding Chapter 11 as well as in Soifer's Chapter 3 and Harbers and Ingram's Chapter 2, researchers seldom discuss why they focus on one spatial unit over another. This is also the case when it comes to the unit we select as the LOC when studying individual behavior: Researchers rarely specify which spatial unit or units – and what information about them – inform their conceptualizations. Carefully specifying the LOC and clearly stating our assumptions about it is likely to improve not only the quality of our concepts but also the collective production of knowledge. In making it easier to assess the unit's value for specific research goals, we can improve on previous conceptualizations and identify some of the reasons why concepts, theories, and findings addressing the same phenomenon tend to differ significantly.

As the introduction to this volume shows, by producing novel theoretical accounts and new empirical evidence, SNR has collectively enhanced our understanding of specific territorial units and the actors that live within them. This knowledge can guide our selection of the LOC for the behaviors we wish to study and strengthen concept formation in the ways discussed in the preceding paragraphs. In Section 7.2, I illustrate these ideas by discussing how the conceptualization of civilian support for insurgents has improved as SNR continues to enhance our understanding of civil war and scholars focus more on the locality as the locus of civilian choice.

7.2   CONCEPTUALIZING CIVILIAN SUPPORT IN CIVIL WAR STUDIES

Studies of civil war often view civilian support as one of the most important determinants of a conflict's conduct and eventual outcome.[14] The patterns of civilian support for a rebel group can, for example, influence the latter's use of violence (Kalyvas, 2006; Weinstein, 2007); its internal organization (Cohen, 2013; Weinstein, 2007); and whether and how it governs civilians (Mampilly, 2011; Arjona et al., 2015; Wickham-Crowley, 1987; Arjona, 2016). The extent of civilian support for insurgents or counterinsurgents can also determine the efficacy of specific military strategies (Beath et al., 2011; Lyall & Wilson, 2009; Lyall, 2009, 2010) as well as which sides wins the war (e.g., Galula, 1964; Packwood, 2009; Benhabib et al., 2007; Trinquier, 2006). Not surprisingly, many books and articles on civil war rely on the assumption that civilian support has an important impact on the conduct of war.[15]

Yet, the term "civilian support" is seldom defined. Scholars and policymakers alike often use the words "collaboration," "support," and "participation" to refer to civilians' backing of a warring group. However, what such terms entail tends to be at best vaguely identified. These terms usually imply the existence of positive attitudes toward an armed group, although in a few cases they refer to specific acts.[16] In addition, there is little discussion about what does not constitute "civilian support" and what the available alternatives are to this support. The common assumption that the alternatives to supporting a rebel group are either doing nothing or actively supporting the opposing side ignore the complexity of civilian choice; civilians seldom face these simple dichotomies, as they can engage in multiple forms of support, they can flee, or they can resist (Arjona, 2009, 2017; Barter, 2014; Masullo, 2017). Insofar as people make choices while considering the alternatives available to them, identifying the range of those options is an essential step in theory building. It is precisely here where a subnational approach, which brings into focus the LOC, can help advance our understanding of the options available to civilians in wartime settings and, in

---

[14] By "civilians" and "locals" I mean all persons in a conflict zone who do not participate in hostilities and are not full-time members of any state or non-state armed organization, including regular civilians and public officials.

[15] As an illustration, a search in Google Scholar of the terms "civil war" and "popular support" combined led to about 39,800 results in January of 2014. The pattern is far from changing, as the same search almost four years later, in October of 2017, produced about 64,900 results.

[16] Military historians and early studies of guerrilla warfare tended to be more precise than the civil war literature developed since the 2000s. Johnson (1962, p. 654), for example, provided several examples of French, British, and American studies of military doctrine that clearly identified specific acts that were crucial for the success of guerrilla tactics: "The providing of food, shelter, communications, stretcher bearers, labor for mine-laying, and the like by the civilian population all go to make up that ubiquitous word of guerrilla catechism: mobility." Military historians also highlighted the importance of intelligence provided by civilians.

turn, the factors that explain their decisions in response to armed groups with whom they interact.[17]

The conceptualization of civilian support for rebel groups is improving substantially as scholars increasingly adopt a subnational approach and begin to pay attention to the locality as the locus of civilian choice during wartime. In the coming paragraphs I show that our understanding of civilian support – and of civilians' choices vis-à-vis armed actors more generally – has advanced as scholars have employed a subnational approach to develop a deeper understanding of the local context in which civilians live.

Conceptualizing Civilian Support with the Locality as the Locus of Choice: The Value of a Subnational Approach

The majority of civil wars are fought between irregular non-state armed groups and the armed forces of a state (Kalyvas & Balcells, 2010). Such irregular groups do not attempt to confront the state on an open battlefield but seek instead to exercise military control over local territories: The larger the portion of the country under rebel control, the greater the challenge to the state. Insurgents' key strategic goals are to seize and maintain control of a locality, as controlling local territories is necessary for the success of a rebellion (e.g., Kalyvas, 2006, p. 88; McColl, 1969; Thompson, 1983). The state, for its part, tries to recover territories controlled by rebel forces as well as prevent them from expanding to new places. This competition leads to the fragmentation of territory, whereby the country is divided into pockets either under the dispute of or controlled by one of the warring sides.[18] This means that, in countries enduring civil war, there is large subnational variation both in whether or not there is military confrontation and in each warring side's level of military control.

Scholars who take a subnational approach have found that many other dynamics of civil war also vary substantially at the local level, including violence against noncombatants (e.g., Balcells, 2010; Kalyvas, 2006); displacement of civilians (e.g., Steele, 2017; Ibánez & Moya, 2010); resistance against occupation (Petersen, 2001); wartime institutions (Arjona, 2016); the effects of counterinsurgency (e.g., Lyall & Wilson, 2009; Lyall et al., 2013); and

---

[17] The misconceptions regarding the range of choices available to civilians is perhaps explained by the fact that, for the most part, civilian support was not the object of study but either an independent variable or a mechanism explaining how some causal factor leads to an outcome. In the large literature on civil war duration and termination, for example, whether or not civilians support rebels is often considered a crucial factor explaining the continuation of war. Yet, most studies of war duration fail to define the terms "support" and "participation," and many do not even distinguish between recruitment and enlistment, implicitly assuming that they are either the same thing or caused by the same factors.

[18] See Kalyvas (2006) for an extensive discussion of how civil war fragments space and for examples of multiple conflicts around the globe.

responses to peacekeeping (e.g., Dorussen & Gizelis, 2013). These studies suggest that civilians experience war – and therefore decide how to act – within drastically different *local* realities. It should thus be no surprise that the conceptualization of civilian support, and civilian choice more generally, improves as scholars pay greater attention to the locality as the LOC.

Roger Petersen (2001) aims to explain why individuals decide to carry out resistance in his work on civilian participation in rebellions against foreign occupation in Eastern Europe. He identifies the local community as the locus of civilian choice and focuses on the different social structures that exist across communities. With regard to the Merkine region in Lithuania, for instance, he states: "Relatively small differences in community structure can create different signals for potential rebels that, in turn, produce different rebellion dynamics" (p. 10). This emphasis on the community level allows Petersen to question the simplistic view of civilian support according to which people either rebel or not. Instead, he finds that there are several roles civilians can elect to play within their communities, such as that of "collaborators, neutrals, locally-based rebels, [and] mobile fighters," as well as those roles that exist as "gradations in between" (p. 8). He thus proposes a spectrum of roles that individuals can play in a rebellion ranging from –3 to +3, where 0 is complete neutrality; +1 is unarmed and unorganized opposition to the regime; +2 is direct support or participation in locally based, armed organizations; +3 is membership in a guerrilla unit or rebel army; and –3, –2, and –1 are the equivalent forms of support for the occupying regime. In Petersen's conceptualization, participating in rebellion is therefore about undertaking specific acts that either support or oppose the occupying power. The ontology of the phenomenon is thus quite different from what is commonly implied in the literature on civil war. It is not about holding positive attitudes or preferences for a rebellion or a rebel group but about taking certain actions and performing specific behaviors that contribute in some way to the rebellion.

Petersen's focus on communities in subnational locales with varying social structure influences his views on the ontology of the phenomenon of civilian support, his definition of what does and does not constitute support, and his framework for classifying civilian behavior during wartime. Moreover, Petersen's specification of the locale as the appropriate spatial context for understanding civilian behavior leads him to examine why an individual decides to play a specific role in a rebellion – moving from one point on the spectrum to another – and why communities tend to develop their own "equilibria" rather than focusing solely on *why* an individual chooses to rebel (pp. 9, 13). The impact of Petersen's conceptualization of civilian support is also evident both in his theory, which stresses the role of local social networks in driving individual decision-making, and in his data collection, which focuses on gathering evidence of a variety of acts that can help a rebellion within distinct community structures.

In her study of peasant support for the insurgency in El Salvador, Elisabeth Wood (2003) similarly considers the locality as the key LOC for civilians. Wood's work focuses on a particular type of locality: those in contested areas where insurgents and state forces actively compete for control over territory. In those areas, the risks faced by an individual supporting the rebels were much higher than elsewhere in the country, as "covert death squads and regular military forces carried out assassinations and disappearances with impunity" (p. 5). This clear identification of the locus of civilian choice provides the grounds for Wood's conceptualization of civilian support.

As in Petersen's study, Wood views the ontology of civilian support through a focus on specific acts rather than on vague ideas about civilian preferences and attitudes. Abandoning the traditional dichotomous view of rebels and non-rebels, she proposes a new classificatory system that differentiates between nonparticipants (or noninsurgents), full-time members of the guerilla movement, and insurgent *campesinos* (or civilian supporters of the insurgency). Focusing on the latter, Wood defines support for the insurgency as "the provision to the insurgents of information and supplies beyond the contribution necessary to remain in contested areas, and the refusal to give information and supplies to government forces beyond the necessary contribution" (p. 17). By paying close attention to the LOC, Wood is able to delineate when support does not exist – in her account, this is when civilians are only helping insurgents in order to remain in that territory. This is the case because offering support requires taking risks, as enemy sides can punish collaborators. Although she does not say it explicitly, her conceptualization suggests that neutrality is often not an option.

Rather than simply asking why people rebel, Wood asks a different question: "Why do civilians become *insurgent campesinos* in contested localities?" Wood's focus on risky behavior by civilians to aid rebels leads her to examine important factors that had not been previously taken into account, such as the role of moral principles and what she calls the "pleasure of agency." Likewise, Wood's novel conceptualization of civilian behaviors drives her overall empirical strategy: The empirical evidence she collects reflects her conceptualization of civilian support; for example, her study provides detailed accounts of the risks peasants take in order to help the rebels.

Finally, although Kalyvas (2006) aims to explain armed groups' use of violence against noncombatants, he pays careful attention to civilian support for armed actors. In his theory, armed groups kill civilians in order to create incentives for locals to avoid aiding enemy forces. Whereas in Petersen's and Wood's work civilian support is the main outcome of interest, for Kalyvas the dependent variable is violence and civilian support is part of the causal mechanism. Kalyvas's approach also focuses on the locality as the LOC for both civilians and combatants; while Wood focuses only on contested areas, Kalyvas also considers localities under full control of either the state or the rebel group.

Like Petersen and Wood, Kalyvas focuses on actions rather than "mental states" such as attitudes, beliefs, and preferences.[19] He centers on one form of

---

[19] In fact, Kalyvas has a detailed discussion of the difference between the two (Kalyvas, 2006, p. 92).

support – the denunciation of, or provision of information to an armed actor about other civilians who are collaborating with enemy forces – while clearly stating what support is not: defection. In fact, rather than identifying different types of support, he proposes a classification of defection, identifying three types: noncomplying, informing, and switching sides. Noncomplying includes different forms of opposition such as shirking and fleeing; informing entails supplying information about one side to its rival; and switching sides consists of openly collaborating with the enemy.

As with the other two studies, Kalyvas' grounded conceptualization of civilian support permeates his theory. His focus on civilian denunciations as a form of support (and defection) is essential to his overarching argument because armed groups' use of violence is understood to depend on their demand for information as well as on their expectations that civilians will supply that information. His focus on denunciations also drives his search for detailed evidence on civilian support, which centers on how private matters can motivate civilians to denounce neighbors as collaborators of enemy forces.

By adopting a subnational approach and focusing on the locality as the LOC, these three studies improve previous conceptualizations of civilian support in two ways. First, they clearly define what support entails by focusing on observable acts rather than unobservable preferences, dispositions, or beliefs, resulting in a clearer and more useful conceptualization of civilian support.[20] Second, these authors provide a more nuanced typology of support that differentiates among opposition, neutrality, support, and enlistment and identifies specific acts of collaboration. This is an important improvement: Whereas almost every study of insurgency and counterinsurgency mentions civilian support as a crucial explanatory factor, very few explicitly identify a menu of alternatives to collaboration. In reality, civilians are not confronted by the simple dichotomy of either offering full support or none at all. The nuanced conceptualizations offered by Petersen, Wood, and Kalyvas compel us to explain not only why civilians support the rebels but also why they support them in one way rather than another. This illustrates how SNR can play an important role in refining our concepts in ways that improve the content of our explanations, the questions that we ask, and the theories we build to answer them.

7.3 WARTIME SOCIAL ORDER, THE LOCUS OF CHOICE, AND CIVILIAN BEHAVIOR IN CONFLICT ZONES

In Sections 7.1 and 7.2 I demonstrated how the conceptualization of civilian support improved when researchers shifted their focus to the locality as the locus of civilian choice. In this section I build upon my previous and ongoing

---

[20] To be sure, a definition that focuses on preferences or beliefs would also be valid (despite the fact that observing "support" would be more difficult). The point is that concepts need to be clearly defined, and a careful consideration of the locus of decision-making can facilitate that task.

research to argue that delving even deeper into the attributes of localities can further strengthen our conceptualization of civilian support and of civilian decision-making during wartime more generally. I illustrate my arguments with original data on civilians and communities in conflict zones throughout Colombia.

Social Order in Conflict Zones

Understanding civilians' choices in conflict zones requires a deeper engagement with the many ways that war transforms local life. Although the presence and behavior of armed groups often create disorder, they also create *new* forms of order where institutions – understood as the formal or informal rules that structure human interaction (North, 1991) – regulate the behavior of both civilians and combatants (Arjona, 2016). Because institutions have a great power to influence the economic, political, and social life of society, the institutions that operate in conflict zones need to be incorporated in our analyses of wartime civilian choice (Arjona, 2014).

Rebels, state agents, and civilians can establish institutions that structure life in conflict zones. In previous works, I provided original, systematic evidence from Colombia to identify and analyze variation in the extent to which armed actors influence these institutional arrangements across localities (Arjona, 2014, 2016). The growing literature on rebel and criminal governance also demonstrates that both rebel and criminal groups often carry out different governance functions in the areas where they operate, influencing civilians' lives in a myriad of ways.[21] To illustrate how deeply war can transform local life – not only by bringing disorder and chaos but also by creating new forms of order – I present descriptive data on the Colombian conflict in Figures 7.1 and 7.2. I collected the data in 2010 and 2012 in two random samples of 74 localities where guerrillas or paramilitaries operated between 1970 and 2012. Map 7.1 shows the localities included in the sample.

The evidence on social order under rebel and paramilitary rule comes from memory workshops and individual surveys with local experts.[22] In the data that I present, the unit of analysis is the community-armed group dyad per year. The data describe the institutions that armed groups established, or failed to establish, in the communities where they operated.[23] Figure 7.1 shows the variation in the existence of clear institutions – whether or not there was an established order in the locality. In the former case, civilians knew the rules that

---

[21] On rebel governance, see for example Arjona et al. (2015); Mampilly (2011); Metelits (2010); Weinstein (2007); Kasfir (2004); Wickham-Crowley (1987). On criminal governance, see Gambetta (1993); Varese (2001); Skarbek (2011); Lilyblad (2014); Arias (2009); Wolff (2015); Arias (2006); Grillo (2012); Cockayne (2016); Davis (2009); Harbers et al. (2016).

[22] For a detailed description of the sampling process and data gathering methods see Arjona (2014, 2016).

[23] All figures include sampling weights.

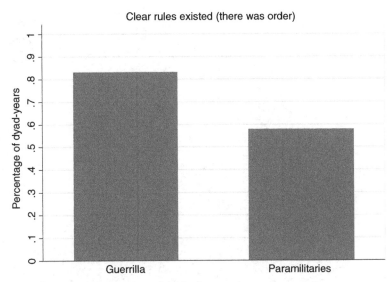

FIGURE 7.1 Presence or Absence of Order by Locality

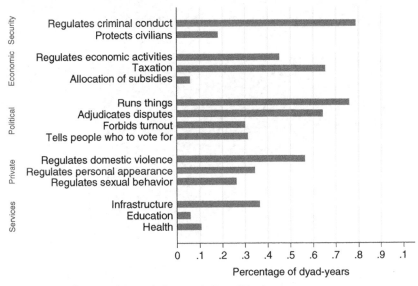

FIGURE 7.2 Influence of Armed Groups in Local Institutions

were in place and were able to form expectations based on these rules in their daily lives; in the latter case, civilians faced high levels of uncertainty. As the data suggest, in about 73 percent of the cases clear rules did exist and uncertainty was low; however, many localities also endured disorder, especially in situations

MAP 7.1 Colombian Localities Included in the Sample

where paramilitary groups were present. This difference is likely to be explained by the fact that paramilitaries often expanded into territories where guerrillas operated, thus making paramilitary presence correlate with active competition between the two types of armed actors.

In Figure 7.2 I turn to the kinds of institutions that allow a new form of order to emerge[24], showing how armed groups influenced several institutional arrangements that operated in conflict zones. Starting with security, in most cases (79 percent) armed groups established rules to maintain public order – that is, forbidding crimes like robbery and rape. In about 1 out of 5 cases, the group protected civilians from other armed actors.

Moreover, armed groups' influence also extended to the economic sphere: In 46 percent of all dyad-years, these organizations established rules to regulate a myriad of activities such as fishing, mining, and coca cultivation and transportation. In 66 percent of all observations, the groups collected "taxes" in either money or kind. Armed actors also intervened in the allocation of state subsidies in a few of the places where they operated (6 percent of cases).

Politically, armed groups became the most important actor in the locality in 76 percent of the cases. This is measured with answers provided to the survey question "Who used to run things (or be in charge) in the locality?"[25] Another unequivocal signal of their political power is the fact that people turned to them to adjudicate disputes in 64 percent of the cases. As Arjona and Boucoyannis (2017) argue, this is a central instrument for consolidating political rule. Armed groups also directly intervened to regulate the political behavior of local residents in several ways. For example, in 31 percent of the cases they told people who to vote for in elections, and in 30 percent they banned voting altogether.

Armed groups also established institutions to regulate private conduct. In 56 percent of the cases studied, they established rules against forms of domestic violence; in 34 percent, they established rules on personal appearance, such as banning short skirts in women and long hair in men; and in 26 percent of the cases, they regulated sexual conduct in some form, such as imposing rules on prostitution or banning homosexual relationships. Finally, these armed organizations intervened in the provision of public goods, either directly or by influencing (or coercing) public officials: In 36 percent of the cases, they did so to build or maintain infrastructure, including roads the group would benefit from; in a few cases (11 percent), they intervened in the provision of health services, and in fewer (6 percent) in the provision of education.

These figures capture both variation in a single community over time and across communities under the presence of the same armed actor. Institutions

---

[24] The data in Figure 7.2 include only observations where there was order (i.e., where there were clear rules of behavior).

[25] The Spanish wording captures in a clear way that this is about who is the de facto ruler: "Quién mandaba?"

also vary within a single district or municipality at a given point in time. Clearly, civilians may live within very different wartime institutional arrangements. Moreover, in many cases the relationship between armed actors and local residents is one of ruler and ruled. It is in settings such as these that civilians in the midst of war live, interact with both rebels and insurgents, and make choices regarding their relations with armed actors. As we will see in the next section, taking this fact into account has important implications for our conceptualization of civilian support and, more generally, of civilians' choices in conflict zones.

Wartime Order and Civilian Choice in Conflict Zones: A New Typology

In a previous work, I proposed a typology of civilian cooperation and non-cooperation with non-state armed groups (NSAGs) that takes into account the local transformation of institutions as well as the consolidation of different forms of order across localities in conflict zones (Arjona, 2017).[26] I present my typology here and discuss how it builds on a refined understanding of how localities function in conflict zones.[27]

First, I propose to use the term *cooperation* rather than support, participation, or collaboration. "Support" and "participation" are often used to denote positive attitudes or endorsement for a given group, thereby excluding cases in which civilians reluctantly help armed actors. The term "collaboration" is similarly confusing, as it can also suggest a moral condemnation reminiscent of civilian involvement with the Nazis and the Axis powers during World War II. I therefore use the term "cooperation" instead, defining it as *an act performed by a civilian that directly benefits an armed group.*[28] I consider cooperation as one of several options available to civilians regarding their behavior towards armed actors. These options are depicted in Figure 7.3.

I identify three forms of cooperation that vary depending on their level of engagement (Figure 7.3).[29] First there is *enlistment,* which entails joining the armed organization as a full-time member without having received the order to do so. Next, there is *spontaneous support,* which includes volunteering to do specific tasks that favor the armed group short of joining, without the armed group having given the civilian, either explicitly or implicitly, the order to do so. Examples include expressing endorsement or approval, offering information,

---

[26] I use the term "non-state armed groups" to refer to different types of armed organizations that are not directly linked to state forces, such as rebels, paramilitaries, and militias. See Arjona (2017).

[27] Segments of this section were published previously (Arjona, 2017).

[28] I emphasize that the act has to benefit the group "directly" in order to differentiate acts that are intended to benefit the group – like providing intelligence or food – from those that accidentally end up aiding the group. For example, if a civilian decides not to go to work for some personal reason, this is not an act of cooperation even if it ends up aiding the rebels in some way.

[29] This typology builds on the typology introduced in Arjona (2017).

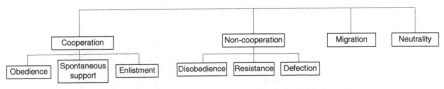

FIGURE 7.3 A Typology of Civilian Behaviors toward Armed Actors

and volunteering to be a lookout. Note that neither definition concerns civilians' motivations.

Whereas previous conceptualizations distinguish between support and full-time participation, I add a third alternative: *obedience*. I define obedience as any action a civilian commits after an armed group has ordered him or her to do so, either directly or by establishing a general rule. Under this definition, the provision of food to a combatant after she or he has demanded it and obeying a curfew are instances of obedience to an armed group.

The importance of obedience becomes apparent when we consider the existence of new forms of order in conflict zones and the role NSAGs play as local rulers. NSAGs strive to create order and rule local communities because creating clear rules of conduct facilitates monitoring and punishing defection (Arjona, 2016). In addition, by ruling, NSAGs can regulate economic, political, and social behavior in ways that render valuable benefits, such as obtaining resources, accessing political and social networks, putting into practice their ideology, and gaining the recognition and reciprocity of local residents (Arjona, 2016; Förster, 2015; Mampilly, 2011). Yet, for all these benefits to materialize, civilians have to obey. Such obedience entails not only avoiding helping enemy forces – which scholars have long emphasized (e.g., Kalyvas, 2006) – but also following many other regulations that are essential for the form of local order that NSAGs prefer to be consolidated and endure. Obedience is, therefore, an important form of civilian cooperation, and it is different from voluntary support.

Data on Colombian localities show that obedience to the rules established by both guerrillas and paramilitaries tended to be quite high: In most locality-years, most people obeyed (Figure 7.4).[30] At the same time, the data suggest that civilians' have some leeway, as most civilians did not obey the rules in about 20 percent of all locality-years. Moreover, levels of obedience varied depending on the rule in question. As Figure 7.5 shows, civilians were more likely to obey some rules, like those forbidding crimes, than others, for example those on sexual conduct. A subnational approach proves fundamental for our ability to

---

[30] The question used in the survey to gather this evidence is the following: "In general, did people [in the community] obey the rules established by [the armed group]?" (*En general, la gente obedecía las normas que establecía [el grupo]?*)

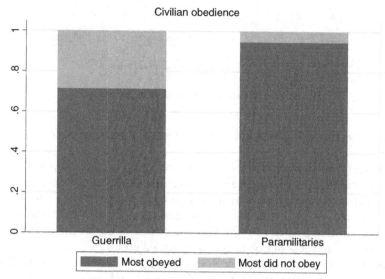

FIGURE 7.4 Civilian Obedience to the Rules of Armed Actors

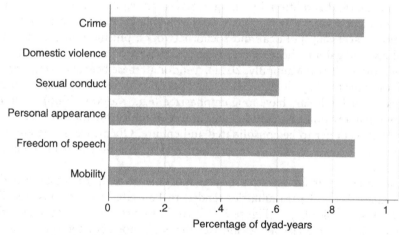

FIGURE 7.5 Levels of Civilian Obedience to Armed Actors, by Rules

disaggregate behavior in order to more accurately conceptualize and measure civilian cooperation with an armed group.[31]

---

[31] The wording of the questions is as follows. The survey asked about rules to regulate different kinds of conducts: "Illegal rules like stealing or rape" (*conductas ilegales como robar o violar*); "domestic violence" (*violencia doméstica*); "sexual behavior, for example prostitution or homosexual relations" (*comportamiento sexual como prostitución o relaciones homosexuales*);

What could we gain by distinguishing between obedience and spontaneous support? First, insofar as NSAGs need massive obedience and only some spontaneous support, differentiating between the two can improve our theories of rebel behavior toward civilians. Second, the decision by civilians to offer spontaneous support entails a different choice than deciding to obey a rule or command. These options can entail very different consequences, and civilians can consider them within different menus of alternatives. Separating the concept of obedience from that of support thus helps not only to bring clarity to the phenomenon under study but also to improve the quality of our explanations: Even though it is obvious that obeying a rule involves a markedly different choice from volunteering to offer help, we cannot provide distinct explanations for these phenomena unless we first differentiate them conceptually – a task made easier by carefully identifying the LOC.

As I have discussed, most accounts of civilian support either fail to identify what the alternative to that support is or identify neutrality and defection as the only other alternatives.[32] Yet, taking into account the role that NSAGs play as rulers reveals that civilians can also opt for many forms of non-cooperation. This is the case because even the most repressive regimes have fissures through which subjects can express their grievances and disagreements (Scott, 1985). In addition, armed groups often learn that allowing for some expression of dissent can help them to maintain control over the territory and the population, as a regime that is based solely on coercion is likely to be short-lived (Mampilly, 2011; Arjona, 2016). Moreover, several studies show that civilians sometimes come together to resist the presence and behavior of armed actors collectively (e.g., Arjona, 2015, 2016; Mampilly, 2011; Kaplan, 2013; Barter, 2014; Masullo, 2017; Mouly et al., 2015).

I define non-cooperation as any act that directly harms the armed group, and I identify three forms of non-cooperation depending on its level. Disobedience entails failing to follow an order given by an armed group or a rule established by it. Examples include denying help to a wounded combatant who demands it or violating a curfew. Resistance entails opposing or attacking the group in any way, and defection entails aiding the enemy, either by offering it spontaneous support or enlisting in the enemy group as a full-time member.

Figures 7.6 and 7.7 show data that I gathered with an individual-level survey conducted in 2016 in most of the localities sampled in 2012.[33] The evidence

---

"personal appearance like long hair, earrings or skirts" (*imagen personal como pelo largo, aretes o faldas*); "what people could and could not talk about" (*lo que se podía o no se podía decir*); and "mobility, like where people could go and when" (*movilidad, como a dónde se podía ir o a qué hora*). For each type of rule, the following questions were asked: "Did [armed group] establish rules about [type of rule]?" And, "Were these norms obeyed by most people [in the community]?"

[32] Arjona (2009), Barter (2014), and Masullo (2017) are important exceptions.

[33] The survey was conducted with a random sample of about 1900 civilians in 53 of the 58 communities sampled in 2012.

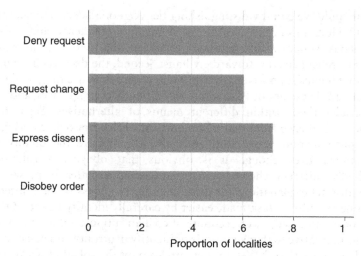

FIGURE 7.6 Forms of Individual Civilian Resistance in Colombian Localities

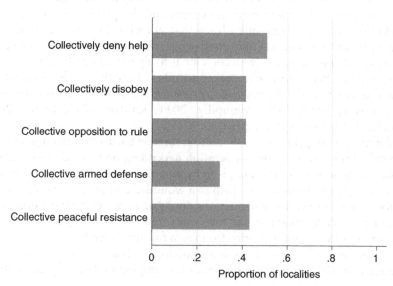

FIGURE 7.7 Forms of Collective Civilian Resistance in Colombian Localities

shows that resistance is indeed more common than is often assumed and can take many forms. The survey asked the following question: "When [armed actor] was present in the locality, did you do any of the following? Not doing something the armed group had asked you to do; talked to a combatant or commander in order to ask him to change his behavior; expressed your disagreement with the group about something; and disobeyed a specific rule or order given by the group."[34] Figure 7.6 shows the percentage of localities in which at least one person reported having engaged in each of these forms of resistance. Overall, each type of individual resistance took place at least once in more than 60 percent of the sampled localities, and some form of individual resistance was reported in 85 percent of all localities.

The survey also asked the following question about *collective* non-cooperation: "When [armed actor] was present in the locality, did the community get together to ... deny help to the armed group; disobey its commands; oppose its rule; engage in armed resistance; and peacefully oppose the presence of the armed actor in the territory?" Figure 7.7 shows that between 30 percent and 51 percent of localities engaged in each form of collective non-cooperation at least once. Overall, there was at least one event of collective non-cooperation in 60 percent of the sampled localities.

Finally, can civilians remain neutral – that is, avoiding both cooperating and non-cooperating with an armed group – in a conflict zone? Neutrality is only an option when the armed group does not make demands or establish any rules – it is impossible to accomplish otherwise, because civilians can only obey, disobey, or migrate.[35] Leaving the territory is the only option for many civilians who do not wish to engage in any form of cooperation *or* non-cooperation with armed groups. To be sure, sometimes civilians are forced to flee, which means that migrating is not always a choice. However, many civilians in conflict zones consider migrating even without being ordered to do so. In the sampled localities, 26 percent of all respondents reported leaving their hometown at some point; among them, 68 percent reported not being forcedly displaced.

It bears emphasis that this is a typology of acts, not a typology of individuals. Civilians do not necessarily opt for only one form of cooperation or non-cooperation with armed actors. They may obey most of the time and engage in spontaneous support occasionally. They may obey some rules and disobey others. They may enlist and then defect. But only by using a subnational lens to identify the defining features of the LOC can we advance our understanding of civilian behavior in conflict zones.

---

[34] The wording of the questions in Spanish is as follows: "Mientras [el grupo armado] estaba haciendo presencia en esta comunidad, en algún momento usted ... Decidió no hacer algo que el grupo le pidió que hiciera? Habló con un combatiente o comandante para pedirle que cambiara su comportamiento? Expresó su desacuerdo con el grupo sobre algo? Desobedeció una regla o una orden del grupo? Le pidió ayuda a un miembro del grupo?"

[35] For this reason, in Arjona (2017) the typology does not include neutrality. The typology was meant to apply to situations of order – that is, where there was a social contract (usually implicit rather than explicit) between the armed actor and the civilian population. Such a contract implies that there are some rules that civilians have to follow, and, therefore, locals can either obey or disobey – there is no room for neutrality. However, in a contested zone or a place where the armed actor has not established regulations, neutrality is indeed possible. This is why it is included here as an option in the typology.

What do we gain by relying on a more nuanced conceptualization and typology of civilian cooperation? To start with, our questions about civilian choice have to somehow incorporate the menu of alternatives available to those interacting with armed organizations. Explaining why civilians support a rebel group necessarily requires a more focused discussion of obedience, voluntary cooperation, and enlistment. Furthermore, insofar as different types of civilian cooperation result from distinct causal paths, identifying those types is a necessary step toward building a theory of civilian choice. Consider, for example, obedience and spontaneous support: These are evidently different choices, and understanding them most likely requires different explanations. Yet, building such explanations would be impossible without first distinguishing between the two alternatives.

A more nuanced conceptualization of civilian choice can also contribute to our understanding of key phenomena. Civilian behavior during wartime is likely to shape several dynamics at the micro, meso, and macro levels. Consider, for example, how civilian cooperation is assumed to be crucial for both rebel and counterinsurgent success. A better conceptualization and theorization of civilian cooperation can illuminate our understanding of rebel behavior and counterinsurgency. Violence, indoctrination, the provision of public goods, and other aspects of rebel behavior could be better understood if we relied on improved models of wartime civilian choice. For example, taking civilian resistance into account is important not only because it can negatively affect rebels' success but also because rebels are likely to incorporate their expectation of such resistance when electing their strategies to conquer, rule, and victimize civilians (Arjona, 2016). In addition, whether or not civilians resist armed actors can also influence subnational patterns of rebel and counterinsurgent success. Furthermore, insofar as civilian choice influences rebel and counterinsurgent success at the local level, a better understanding of its determinants can also shed new light on national-level outcomes such as the duration and termination of war.

Wartime civilian choice is also likely to influence local communities after war has ended. Whether people obeyed, joined, supported, or resisted armed groups may impact the social fabric and accepted institutions of the community, the community's capacity to engage in collective action, its members' interests in politics, and members' overall perception of the state. Internally displaced persons, too, can transform the political, economic, and social realities of the places where they go, even in the post-conflict period (Steele, 2017).

Finally, a better understanding of civilian choice vis-à-vis armed groups in situations of civil war can illuminate our understanding of phenomena in other contexts. For example, despite the differences between rebels and criminals, several organized criminal groups control territory and engage in behaviors similar to those of rebels in their interaction with local communities

(Arjona, 2017). Improvements in our theories of civilian behavior vis-à-vis political armed actors can shed new light on how civilians respond to the presence of drug trafficking organizations, gangs, and other similar groups at the local level.

7.4 CONCLUSION

When studying a phenomenon that results from the choice of an individual, we often identify, either implicitly or explicitly, a unit as the locus of that choice – that is, the place we consider to be the most salient context where the decision-making takes place. In this chapter, I argue that our specification of the locus of a choice, and our corresponding knowledge of it, has critical implications for concept formation because it guides our views of the ontology of the phenomenon, helping to define the elements of that phenomenon and specify the menu of options available to the decision-maker. Devoting effort to selecting and specifying the LOC for the behaviors we study; relying on validated and explicit assumptions about the spatial unit(s) that constitute the LOC; and clearly communicating the assumptions and decisions that underlie our concepts can improve the quality of our theories and contribute to the advancement of knowledge about the phenomena we study.

I illustrated my argument by discussing how the conceptualization of civilian support – a key phenomenon in the study of civil war – improves as scholars adopt SNR and treat the locality as the locus of civilian choice. As our understanding of local realities in conflict zones advances, so too do our conceptualizations and explanations of wartime civilian support and, more generally, civilian behavior. Future research that centers on the locality can further advance our conceptualization of other phenomena related to conflict and violence, such as the behavior of non-state armed groups toward civilians; civilian–combatant interactions; the responses of state actors to non-state armed actors; and the coping strategies that individuals and communities rely on in the aftermath of war as they transition into peace.

Delving deeper into the subnational units that constitute the LOC for human behaviors can catalyze similar improvements in concept formation and theory building in comparative politics more broadly. As research on subnational politics shows, there is great spatial variation at subnational levels in the intensity and quality of state presence (O'Donnell, 1993; Soifer, Chapter 3, and Trejo & Ley, Chapter 6, in this volume), democracy (Gibson, 2005), public goods provision (Otero, 2016; Kale & Mazarehi, Chapter 9, in this volume), and subnationalism (Singh 2015, Singh, Chapter 8, in this volume), among other important factors. Carefully specifying which subnational units form the relevant context for key decisions cannot only improve our conceptualization of key phenomena of interest; it can also help make our explanations more powerful. Just as we have come to recognize the shortcomings of explaining subnational outcomes by relying on theories crafted to explain macro-level phenomena (Introduction, this volume), so too may we find that our concepts need to be refined as we shift our analytic focus across units at different scales.

BIBLIOGRAPHY

Arias, Enrique Desmond. (2006). The dynamics of criminal governance: Networks and social order in Rio de Janeiro. *Journal of Latin American Studies 38*(2), 293–325.
Arias, Enrique Desmond. (2009). *Drugs and democracy in Rio de Janeiro: Trafficking, social networks, and public security.* Chapel Hill: University of North Carolina Press.
Arjona, Ana. (2009). One national war, multiple local orders: An inquiry into the unit of analysis of war and post-war interventions. In Pablo Kalamanovitz & Morten Bergsmo (Eds.), *Law in peace negotiations*, pp. 199–242. Oslo, Norway: Torkel Opsahl Academic EPublisher.
Arjona, Ana. (2014). Wartime institutions: A research agenda. *Journal of Conflict Resolution 58*(8), 1360–1389.
Arjona, Ana. (2016). *Rebelocracy: Social order in the Colombian civil war.* Cambridge, England: Cambridge University Press.
Arjona, Ana. (2017). Civilian cooperation and non-cooperation with non-state armed groups: The centrality of obedience and resistance. *Small Wars & Insurgencies 28* (4–5), 755–778.
Arjona, Ana, & Boucoyannis, Deborah A. (2017, September). *Judicial institutions: The tool for aspiring rulers.* Paper presented at the Annual Meeting of the American Political Science Association, San Francisco, CA.
Arjona, Ana, Kasfir, Nelson, & Mampilly, Zachariah. (2015). *Rebel governance in civil war.* Cambridge, England: Cambridge University Press.
Balcells, Laia. (2010). Rivalry and revenge: Violence against civilians in conventional civil wars. *International Studies Quarterly 54*(2), 291–313.
Balcells, Laia. (2017). *Rivalry and revenge: The politics of violence in civil war.* Cambridge, England: Cambridge University Press.
Barter, Shane Joshua. (2014). *Civilian strategy in civil war.* New York, NY: Palgrave Macmillan US.
Beath, Andrew, Christia, Fotini, & Enikolopov, Ruben. (2011). *Winning hearts and minds through development? Evidence from a field experiment in Afghanistan.* MIT Political Science Department Research Paper No. 2011–14.
Benhabib, Seyla, Shapiro, Ian, & Petranovic, Danilo. (2007). *Identities, affiliations, and allegiances.* Cambridge, England: Cambridge University Press.
Blattman, Christopher, & Miguel, Edward. (2010). Civil war. *Journal of Economic Literature 48*(1), 3–57.
Bowles, Samuel, & Gintis, Herbert. (2002). Social capital and community governance. *The Economic Journal 112*(483), 419–436.
Cederman, Lars-Erik, & Gleditsch, Kristian Skrede. (2009). Introduction to special issue on "disaggregating civil war." *Journal of Conflict Resolution 53*(4), 487–495.
Cockayne, James. (2016). *Hidden power: The strategic logic of organized crime.* Oxford, England: Oxford University Press.

Cohen, Dara Kay. (2013). Explaining rape during civil war: Cross-national evidence (1980–2009). *American Political Science Review 107*(3), 461–477.

Collier, David, & Gerring, John. (2009). Introduction. In David Collier & John Gerring (Eds.), *Concepts and method in social science.*, pp. 1–10. New York, NY: Routledge.

Collier, David, LaPorte, Jody, & Seawright, Jason. (2012). Putting typologies to work: Concept formation, measurement, and analytic rigor. *Political Research Quarterly 65* (1), 217–232.

Davis, Diane E. (2009). Non-state armed actors, new imagined communities, and shifting patterns of sovereignty and insecurity in the modern world. *Contemporary Security Policy 30*(2), 221–245.

Dietrich, Franz, & List, Christian. (2016). Reason-based choice and context-dependence: An explanatory framework. *Economics & Philosophy 32*(2), 175–229.

Drysdale, John. (1996). How are social-scientific concepts formed? A reconstruction of Max Weber's theory of concept formation. *Sociological Theory 14*(1), 71–88.

Dorussen, Han, & Gizelis, Theodora-Ismene. (2013). Into the lion's den: Local responses to UN peacekeeping. *Journal of Peace Research 50*(6), 691–706.

Elster, Jon. (2007). *Explaining social behavior: More nuts and bolts for the social sciences.* Cambridge, England: Cambridge University Press.

Förster, Till. (2015). Dialogue direct: Rebel governance and civil order in Northern Côte D'Ivoire. In Ana Arjona, Nelson Kasfir, & Zachariah Mampilly (Eds.), *Rebel governance in civil war*, pp. 203–225. Cambridge, England: Cambridge University Press.

Galula, David. (1964). *Counterinsurgency warfare: Theory and practice.* New York, NY: Praeger Security International.

Gambetta, Diego. (1993). *The Sicilian mafia.* Boston, MA: Harvard University Press.

Gerring, John. (1999). What makes a concept good? A criterial framework for understanding concept formation in the social sciences. *Polity 31*(3), 357–393.

Gerring, John. (2007). *Case study research: Principles and practices.* Cambridge, England: Cambridge University Press.

Gibson, Edward L. (2005). Boundary control: Subnational authoritarianism in democratic countries. *World Politics 58*(1), 101–132.

Goertz, Gary. (2006). *Social science concepts: A user's guide.* Princeton, NJ: Princeton University Press.

Gregory, Derek, Johnston, Ron, Pratt, Geraldine, Watts, Michael, & Whatmore, Sarah (Eds.). (2009). *The dictionary of human geography.* Hoboken, NJ: John Wiley & Sons.

Griffith, Samuel B., & Mao, Zedong. (1978). *Mao Tse-Tung on guerrilla warfare.* New York, NY: Anchor Books.

Grillo, Ioan. (2012). *El narco: Inside Mexico's criminal insurgency.* New York, NY: Bloomsbury Publishing USA.

Gschwend, Thomas, & Schimmelfennig, Frank. (2007). *Research design in political science: How to practice what they preach.* New York, NY: Palgrave Macmillan.

Harbers, Imke, Jaffe, Rivke, & Cummings, Victor J. N. (2016). A battle for hearts and minds? Citizens' perceptions of formal and irregular governance actors in urban Jamaica. *Política y gobierno 23*(1), 97–123.

Hay, Colin. (2006). Political ontology. In Robert E. Goodin & Charles Tilly (Eds.), *The Oxford handbook of contextual political analysis*, pp. 78–96. Oxford, England: Oxford University Press.

Ibánez, Ana Maria, & Moya, Andrés. (2010). Vulnerability of victims of civil conflicts: Empirical evidence for the displaced population in Colombia. *World Development 38* (4), 647–663.

Johnson, Chalmers A. (1962). *Peasant nationalism and communist power: The emergence of revolutionary China.* Stanford, CA: Stanford University Press.

Kalyvas, Stathis N. (2006). *The logic of violence in civil war.* Cambridge, England: Cambridge University Press.

Kalyvas, Stathis N. (2008a). Ethnic defection in civil war. *Comparative Political Studies 41*(8), 1043–1068.

Kalyvas, Stathis N. (2008b). Promises and pitfalls of an emerging research program: The microdynamics of civil war. In Stathis Kalyvas, Ian Shapiro, & Tarek Masoud (Eds.), *Order, conflict, and violence,* pp. 397–421. Cambridge, England: Cambridge University Press.

Kalyvas, Stathis N., & Balcells, Laia. (2010). International system and technologies of rebellion: How the end of the cold war shaped internal conflict. *American Political Science Review 104*(3), 415–429.

Kaplan, Oliver. (2013). Protecting civilians in civil war: The institution of the ATCC in Colombia. *Journal of Peace Research 50*(3), 351–367.

Kasfir, Nelson. (2004, September 3). The creation of civil administration by guerrillas: The National Resistance Army and the Rwenzururu Kingdom Government in Uganda. Paper presented at the 2004 Annual Meeting of the American Political Science Association, Chicago, IL.

Lilyblad, C. M. (2014). Illicit authority and its competitors: The constitution of governance in territories of limited statehood. *Territory, Politics, Governance 2*(1), 72–93.

Lyall, Jason. (2009). Does indiscriminate violence incite insurgent attacks? Evidence from Chechnya. *Journal of Conflict Resolution 53*(3), 331–362.

Lyall, Jason. (2010). Are coethnics more effective counterinsurgents? Evidence from the Second Chechen War. *American Political Science Review 104*(1), 1–20.

Lyall, Jason, Blair, Graeme, & Imai, Kosuke (2013). Explaining support for combatants during wartime: A survey experiment in Afghanistan. *American Political Science Review 107*(4), 679–705.

Lyall, Jason, & Wilson, Isaiah. (2009). Rage against the machines: Explaining outcomes in counterinsurgency wars. *International Organization 63*(1), 67–106.

Mampilly, Zachariah. (2011). *Rebel rulers: Insurgent governance and civilian life during war.* Ithaca, NY: Cornell University Press.

Masullo, Juan. (2017). Civilian noncooperation in armed conflicts: Refusing to cooperate with armed groups as a self-protection strategy. Working Paper.

McColl, Robert W. (1969). The insurgent state: Territorial bases of revolution. *Annals of the Association of American Geographers 59*(4), 613–631.

Metelits, Claire. (2010). *Inside insurgency: Violence, civilians, and revolutionary group behavior.* New York, NY: New York University Press.

Mouly, Cécile, Idler, Annette, & Garrido, Belén. (2015). Zones of peace in Colombia's borderland. *International Journal of Peace Studies 20*(1), 51–63.

Nagl, John A., Amos, James F., Sewall, Sarah, & Petraeus, David H. (2008). *The US Army/Marine corps counterinsurgency field manual.* Chicago, IL: University of Chicago Press.

North, Douglass C. (1991). Institutions. *The Journal of Economic Perspectives 5*(1), 97–112.

O'Donnell, Guillermo. (1993). On the state, democratization and some conceptual problems: A Latin American view with glances at some postcommunist countries. *World Development 21*(8), 1355–1369.

Otero, Silvia. (2016). *When the state minds the gap: The politics of subnational inequality in Latin America.* (Doctoral dissertation). Political Science, Northwestern University, Evanston, IL.

Packwood, Lane. (2009). Popular support as the COIN objective. *Military Review* (May–June), 67–77.

Petersen, Roger Dale. (2001). *Resistance and rebellion: Lessons from Eastern Europe.* Cambridge, England: Cambridge University Press.

Sartori, Giovanni. (1970). Concept misformation in comparative politics. *American Political Science Review 64*(4), 1033–1053.

Schedler, Andreas. (2011). Concept formation. In B. Badie, D. Berg-Schlosser, & L. Morlino (Eds.), *International encyclopedia of political science*, pp. 371–382. Thousand Oaks, CA: SAGE Publications.

Scott, James C. (1985). *Weapons of the weak: Everyday forms of peasant resistance.* New Haven, CT: Yale University Press.

Scott, James C. (1990). *Domination and the arts of resistance.* New Haven, CT: Yale University Press.

Seawright, Jason. (2016). *Multi-method social science.* Cambridge, England: Cambridge University Press.

Seawright, Jason, & Gerring, John. (2008). Case selection techniques in case study research: A menu of qualitative and quantitative options. *Political Research Quarterly 61*(2), 294–308.

Singh, Prerna. (2015). *How solidarity works for welfare: Subnationalism and social development in India.* Cambridge, England: Cambridge University Press.

Skarbek, David. (2011). Governance and prison gangs. *American Political Science Review 105*(4), 702–716.

Snyder, Richard. (2001). Scaling down: The subnational comparative method. *Studies in Comparative International Development 36*(1), 93–110.

Steele, Abbey. (2017). *Democracy and displacement in Colombia's civil war.* Ithaca, NY: Cornell University Press.

Thompson, Robert Grainger Ker. (1983). *War in peace: An analysis of warfare since 1945.* New London, CT: Orbis.

Trinquier, Roger. (1964). *Modern warfare: A French view of counterinsurgency.* New York, NY: Praeger.

Trinquier, Roger. (2006). *Modern warfare: A French view of counterinsurgency.* Westport, CT: Praeger Security International.

Varese, Federico. (2001). *The Russian mafia: Private protection in a new market economy.* Oxford, England: Oxford University Press.

Weber, Max. (2015). *On the methodology of the social sciences.* Morissville, NC: Lulu Press.

Weinstein, Jeremy M. (2007). *Inside rebellion: The politics of insurgent violence.* Cambridge, England: Cambridge University Press.

Wickham-Crowley, Timothy P. (1987). The rise (and sometimes fall) of guerrilla governments in Latin America. *Sociological Forum 2*(3), 473–499.

Wilkinson, Steven. (2006). *Votes and violence: Electoral competition and ethnic riots in India.* Cambridge, England: Cambridge University Press.

Wolff, Michael J. (2015). Building criminal authority: A comparative analysis of drug gangs in Rio de Janeiro and Recife. *Latin American politics and society 56*(2), 21–40.

Wood, Elisabeth Jean. (2003). *Insurgent collective action and civil war in El Salvador.* New York, NY: Cambridge University Press.

Yee, Eiling, & Thompson-Schill, Sharon L. (2016). Putting concepts into context. *Psychonomic Bulletin & Review 23*(4), 1015–1027.

PART IV

SOCIAL AND ECONOMIC DEVELOPMENT

8

Subnationalism and Social Development

The Subnational Welfare State in India

Prerna Singh

The quality of life that a person leads depends critically on where she leads it. Even taking into account levels of economic development, the chances of an individual surviving through infancy, growing up literate, or living a healthy, long life vary dramatically across regions of the world, in different countries, and even within the same country. What are the causes of such variation in well-being? This is a question of urgent relevance. Even today, millions of children die annually from malnourishment and vaccine-preventable diseases, and over one-fifth of the total world population cannot read or write. Moreover, it is now acknowledged that expanding human capabilities trumps capital accumulation as a driver of economic growth.

This question of variation in social welfare regimes and outcomes has so far been predominantly studied with a national unit of analysis. There are thus prominent national-level theories to explain differences in social welfare policies and outcomes. An influential strand within this body of scholarship emphasizes the significance of political regime type. Until recently, there appeared to be scholarly consensus that democracies instituted a more progressive social policy and were characterized by higher social development outcomes than autocracies (Besley & Kudamatsu, 2006; Boix, 2001; Brown & Hunter, 2004; Brown & Mobarak, 2009; Lake & Baum, 2001). However, important challenges to this view have now emerged (Gerring et al., 2014; Rothstein, 2011; Shandra et al., 2004). Another important set of works has argued for the primacy of state institutions. Huber et al. show that aspects of constitutional structure that disperse political power and offer multiple points of influence on the making and implementation of policy – for example, federalism, presidential government, strong bicameralism, and single-member-district systems – are inimical to robust social policy (1993, pp. 735, 722). In a similar vein, Gerring and Thacker (2008) argue that "centripetal" institutions that centralize authority but are also broadly inclusive, such as unitary sovereignty, a parliamentary executive, and a closed-list PR electoral system, are the optimal constitutional structures for social development.

Immergut (1992) proposes an analogous argument to explain the variation in healthcare systems across Western Europe, in terms of veto points in state institutional structures, that render them vulnerable to interest groups. A distinct line of scholarship emphasizes the significance of the legacy of colonial rule for contemporary social welfare policy and outcomes. Colonization by the British, for instance, has been argued to be associated with better postcolonial developmental outcomes because of the nature of the legal institutions that they implemented (Hayek, 1960; La Porta et al., 1998; North, 2005) as well as the liberal economic model adopted as compared to the Spanish mercantilist model (Lange et al., 2006; Mahoney, 2010). An important work by Acemoglu, Johnson, and Robinson (2001) focuses less on the characteristics of the colonizing power and more on whether or not European colonists could safely settle in a location, the argument being that settler colonies were characterized by less extractive institutions that were more conducive to the enforcement of the rule of law and investment and which have persisted to the present date. Yet another set of scholars, following Weber (1946), have stressed the importance of the state bureaucracy for development (Heclo, 1972).

But what of the often stark variation in social policy and welfare outcomes across provinces and other subnational units within a country governed by the same national political regime; virtually identical legal, financial, and electoral institutions; and a centrally trained and recruited bureaucracy? What explains such subnational variation? This chapter addresses this question through a study of the dramatic variation in social welfare across Indian states.

The chapter begins with a discussion of the benefits offered by a subnational research design for the study of social welfare. It then discusses the rationale for studying subnational welfare in India. Section 8.3 is devoted to a theoretical delineation of the subnational solidarity argument. I then employ a historical case comparison to show how the strength of solidarity at the subnational level, what I call subnationalism, can be a key driver of subnational differences in social policy and welfare outcomes.

8.1 WHY STUDY SUBNATIONAL WELFARE?

A subnational research design, which characterizes some of the classic works of comparative politics and is also an increasingly popular strategy for research today, offers many benefits for the study of the welfare state. Building on the general merits of a subnational research design laid out in the introductory chapter to this volume, I briefly outline here the specific empirical and theoretical advantages for studying the welfare state from a subnational rather than national perspective.

Social welfare outcomes rarely occur uniformly across the territorially defined subnational units of a political system. National averages often conceal significant subnational variation. A country that is classified as "developed" based on national indicators can include within it regions of substantial backwardness. This backwardness could occur across multiple dimensions, for example spatial or racial. In the United States, even within the state of South Dakota, for example, there is a gap in life expectancy of 12 years between a resident of Moody as compared to Bennett County. Further, African Americans in the United States have 2.2 times the infant mortality rate as non-Hispanic whites. A subnational research design better equips us to handle this spatially uneven nature of processes such as social development (Snyder, 2001, p. 94).

Most leading theories of the welfare state have been derived from the study of Western European countries, which tend to be smaller and characterized by a far greater degree of equality in welfare policies and outcomes within their national boundaries as compared to most other parts of the world. The study of social welfare in developing countries, or even other parts of the developed world, such as the United States, on the other hand, appears to require a focus on subnational units. Developing countries such as India, Brazil, South Africa, China, Pakistan, and Indonesia, as well as a developed country such as the United States, are characterized by striking variation in social policies and outcomes within their national boundaries. Differences in the provision of social services and welfare outcomes across cities, provinces, or regions within these countries are sometimes as large as or even larger than differences across national boundaries in Western Europe. A comparison of subnational units allows one to look beyond the commonplace characterization of a developing country such as India as a "socially backward" country or a developed country such as the United States as "socially advanced," to recognize and theorize cases of substantial development and egregious backwardness that underlie such overarching national characterizations.

Moreover, across the world, primary jurisdiction for welfare policy rests with subnational rather than national administrations. Subnational governments, at different levels, are the prime movers, controlling the allocation of expenditures and making key policy decisions. In some federal countries the constitutional division of powers has historically given primary jurisdiction and administrative control over social policies to subnational rather than national governments. In other places, subnational units are gaining increasing control over social policies through processes of decentralization. Under such situations, subnational units are clearly the appropriate unit of analysis for scholars interested in understanding the politics of the formulation of social policy.

Further, in line with multilevel bottom-up theories as outlined in Chapter 1, examining social policy at the subnational level might also provide a useful analytical window onto national welfare outcomes. National welfare outcomes may be driven largely by subnational politics, especially when subnational governments have control over social policy.

In their introduction to this volume, Giraudy, Moncada, and Snyder note the three specific ways in which subnational research can contribute to theory building. Studying the welfare state subnationally offers an example of the third type of theory building, which is the building of multilevel theories that highlight causal relationships across levels of analysis to explain subnational as well as national outcomes of interest. In particular, a subnational study of the welfare state provides an example of a bottom-up multilevel theory that views national and even international phenomena as shaped by subnational factors. Studying the welfare state subnationally provides an opportunity not only to move beyond well-known national-level explanations by uncovering hitherto understudied factors that are more visible and/or work specifically at the subnational level but also, as will be discussed further in the conclusion to this chapter, to provide a fresh analytical lens that illuminates welfare policy and outcomes at the national level. As I have argued elsewhere (Singh, 2017), theories derived from the inductive study of the subnational welfare state can offer a very productive route toward furthering our understanding of problems of welfare provision and underdevelopment across different units of analysis.

8.2   WHY STUDY SUBNATIONAL WELFARE IN INDIA?

The establishment and maintenance of democratic institutions in India in the context of low levels of economic development and high levels of ethnic diversity has been widely studied and lauded (Kohli, 2001; Varshney, 1998). Yet, while India has been relatively successful in guaranteeing civil and political rights, it has failed miserably in ensuring even a minimal range of social rights for its citizens. Social rights figured prominently in the political and intellectual debates of the Indian nationalist movement (Jayal, 2013).[1] However, despite their periodic articulation in political forums and documents and endorsement by political leaders, including Gandhi and Nehru from the 1920s through the 1940s, and intense debates in the Constituent assembly itself, social rights did not make it to the legally enforceable set of fundamental rights in the Constitution of India. These rights were instead relegated to the Directive

---

[1] Niraja Gopal Jayal (2013) discusses how the right to education, for instance, was included in 1925 in the Commonwealth of India Bill – prepared by a committee chaired by Annie Besant, supported by 43 Indian political leaders from different political parties, and submitted to the British House of Commons – and also in the Nehru Report in the 1920s, which prefigured the Constitution of India adopted in 1950 in many important ways. According to the Nehru Report, the right to free primary education was to be made enforceable regardless of caste, class, and ethnic distinctions "as soon as due arrangements shall have been made by competent authority." It also urged the Parliament to draft laws for "the maintenance of health and fitness for work of all citizens." "The Resolution on Fundamental Rights and Economic Changes" presented to the Karachi session of the Congress in 1931 included, in addition to a range of civil rights, a range of social and economic rights, including the right to education. Social rights were also central to a number of the "alternative constitutional imaginings" that were published during the 1940s (Jayal, 2013, pp. 137–143).

Principles of State Policy, which were meant to guide policy but were not justiciable in a court of law. In his famous "Tryst with Destiny" speech on the eve of independence from British rule in 1947, India's first prime minister, Jawaharlal Nehru, had declared the eradication of "ignorance and disease" as one of the most crucial tasks facing the country. Through the Nehruvian period, through the 1950s and 1960s, and in successive decades, India has been characterized by frugal allocations to the social sector, even relative to other developing countries. Today, after six-and-a-half decades of democratic rule and more than two decades of robust economic development, levels of social development in India, measured along virtually any dimension, remain abysmal. Perhaps the starkest indicator of this is that almost *half* of Indian children under five are classified by the World Health Organization (WHO) as suffering from moderate to severe stunting. This is the highest proportion of children in any country in the world. The infant mortality rate in India (42 per 1,000 live births) is more than three to four times those of its BRIC counterparts, Brazil (12.3), Russia (9), and China (11). The infant mortality rate in India is also substantially higher than almost all other countries at its level of economic development. Within its own neighborhood, for instance, countries in South Asia, such as Bangladesh and Nepal, and in Central Asia, Tajikistan and Uzbekistan, which have equivalent or higher incomes to India all have lower infant mortality rates. The maternal mortality rate in India is almost double that of Iraq. In terms of life expectancy, India is ranked at 145 among a total of 197 countries. A woman in India today, on average, lives 20 years less than her counterpart in Hong Kong.

India is also home to the largest number of illiterates in the world. According to the 2011 census, 74 percent of the population is literate, which is equivalent to that of countries such as Guatemala and Uganda. A particularly worrisome portent for the future of Indian education is that the youth female literacy rate (percentage of females aged 15–24) is in the bottom 15 percent of all countries in the world. In the composite rankings of the Human Development Index (HDI), India is ranked 135 out of a total of 187 countries, just below Tajikistan and above Bhutan.

Yet this overall picture of abysmal social development conceals a striking degree of subnational variation in the nature of social policy and, relatedly, in levels of social development. Whereas certain states have been characterized by levels of social development, defined in terms of the education and health of the population, worse than countries in sub-Saharan Africa, other states have witnessed the implementation of a remarkably progressive social policy and development outcomes approaching those enjoyed by middle-income, industrialized countries. In a country the demographic size of India, these divergences translate into dramatic differences in the quality of life for millions. In the 1950s, residents of the state of Bihar, which has a larger population than France, were less than half as likely to be literate as people in Himachal Pradesh. In the 1970s, women in Orissa, which has a larger population than Argentina, were expected to live, on average, over 12 years less than women in Punjab. In the 1990s, children born in Madhya Pradesh, which has a slightly smaller population than Turkey, were five times less likely to survive through infancy than those born in the state of Goa. Even today, women in Maharashtra, with a population equivalent to Mexico's, are four times less likely to die during childbirth than their counterparts in Assam.

As noted earlier, these differences are the product of subnational politics and policies. Under the Indian Constitution, the primary responsibility for developmental policies has rested with states rather than the national government.[2] States play the key role in the formulation and execution of policies regarding both education and health, and they account for nearly 90 percent of total government expenditure on these issues (Mehrotra, 2006, p. 32). In addition to this empirical rationale for focusing subnationally on states in India, it is also notable that a subnational comparison within India, a federal, bicameral, parliamentary democracy with a uniform single-member electoral system, a highly regarded national civil service, and a history of nonsettler British colonialism facilitates the construction of controlled comparisons by holding constant regime type and the state institutions that have been shown to be key determinants of the national welfare state. In this chapter I analyze these dramatic variations across Indian states to develop a more general argument about the causes of differences in subnational social welfare policy and outcomes. This argument is delineated theoretically in the next section.

8.3   THE SOLIDARITY ARGUMENT FOR VARIATIONS IN SUBNATIONAL WELFARE

While recognizing that there can be different sources of solidarity, this chapter focuses on the solidarity that arises out of a sense of identification with or aspiration for a self-governing homeland. The ideology and movement of such a territorially rooted identification incorporate both cultural and political dimensions. Solidarity emerges among people with a belief in a shared past and a common culture, often but not necessarily based on language, who identify with or desire the creation of and control over a political administrative unit that corresponds to a historic homeland.[3] While

---

[2] Article 246 of the Indian constitution divides the various policy areas among three lists – the Union, State, and Concurrent lists. The Union and State lists consist of subjects under the exclusive purview of the central and provincial governments respectively, whereas the Concurrent list is composed of subjects upon which both levels of government have jurisdiction. Health is on the state list. Education was shifted from the state list to the concurrent list by the 42nd Amendment of 1976. A former education minister observed that prior to 1976, "Whether it was primary education or secondary education or university education, the states if they were so inclined, could do what they liked without the Center having any voice in the legislation they passed or in the administration of the system" (quoted in Joshi, 1977, p. 29).

[3] Weber (1946); Deutsch (1966); Anderson (1991); Gellner (1983); Hobsbawm (1992).

the argument is equally applicable to nationalism, it is developed here for subnationalism. Distinguished from nations that necessarily seek sovereign statehood, subnations either explicitly aspire to have or are willing to settle for a political administrative unit within a sovereign state. While the boundaries between nations and subnations are permeable, this distinction is useful for two reasons. First, it is useful empirically because the contemporary international system, with established nations that have entrenched external boundaries, appears to be conducive to the existence of subnationalism.[4] Second, it is useful analytically because recognizing subnationalism as a distinct phenomenon allows for an understanding of the potential differences in the consequences of movements for autonomy versus separatism. Interestingly, the past decade has witnessed a surge of scholarly focus on subnationalism, or substate nationalism as it is also often termed.[5] In line with constructivist theorizing about identity, I find that subnationalism is created by elites, in this case, as an instrumental calculation in the process of competing for political power and that, in doing so, they often recover and reinvent long-standing cultural symbols. Subnationalism percolates to the broader population through the activities of sociopolitical movements and organizations, and it stands strongest when it is entrenched in state and/or popular institutions.

How Solidarity Works for Welfare: Subnationalism Leads to Social Development

Social development outcomes are determined primarily by the nature of and popular access to social services. Across most of the world, the provision of social welfare is primarily a state responsibility.[6] The question, then, is why do some states prioritize the social sector while others don't? For an issue such as social policy to make it onto a state's policy agenda, it must be supported by the political elite.[7] I draw on scholarship across the disciplines of social psychology, political philosophy, comparative politics, and economics to argue that the solidarity that stems from a collective, affective identity such as subnationalism

[4] An analysis of the Minorities at Risk 2009 database shows that there are, empirically, at least as many movements for political-institutional units within a sovereign state as there are groups engaged in a struggle for sovereignty.

[5] Moreno and McEwan (2005); Béland and Lecours (2008); Catt and Murphy (2003); Forrest (2004); Keating (2009).

[6] A recent review of the influential body of scholarship that has, following the seminal work of Olson (1965), approached the distribution of public goods as a collective action problem also shows that "bottom-up" processes of groups acting collectively to promote their interests are in fact less important than "top-down" interventions, notably by the state (Banerjee, Iyer, & Somanathan [2007]). While there is increasing privatization of education and health-care provision across the world, and especially in India, a vast majority of citizens, especially the poor, continue to rely on state provision of essential social services.

[7] Kingdon (1984).

constitutes a powerful cognitive and motivational basis for the political elite to support a progressive social policy.

The microfoundations of my argument rest on laboratory as well as field experiments in social psychology that consistently and robustly demonstrate the powerful effects of a shared identity.[8] The Common In-Group Identity Model (CIIM) has gone a step further to show that "if members of different groups are induced to conceive of themselves more as members of a single, superordinate group, attitudes toward former out-group members will become more positive through processes involving pro-in-group bias."[9] In a series of experiments, Roderick Kramer and Marilynn Brewer find that "[i]nclusion within a common social boundary reduces social distance among group members, making it less likely that individuals will make sharp distinctions between their own and others' welfare. As a result, outcomes for other group members, or for the group as a whole, come to be perceived as one's own."[10] Within such groups, there is a perception of common interests and goals and a prioritization of collective, rather than purely individual or sectional, welfare.[11] These positive behavioral effects for the group-identity manipulation have been found to occur consistently even when the basis for superordinate group identification was "seemingly trivial."[12] In-group favoritism is likely, then, to be even stronger when, as is the case for subnations, the basis for the superordinate group identification is a set of powerful emotional symbols such as a common history, culture, or language.

While the CIIM leaves the nature of the superordinate identity open, studies in political theory in the liberal-nationalist paradigm emphasize how a shared national identity can foster support for collective welfare through an additional channel: ethical obligations. When individuals perceive themselves as members of a nation or subnation, they prioritize and work for the common good because of the "deep and important obligations [that] flow from identity and relatedness."[13] The crux of the argument is the power of what Yael Tamir calls "the magic pronoun."[14] The obligations we have to those we consider "our own" are different from and more wide-ranging than the obligations we have to others. A sense of belonging together triggers prosocial behavior that transcends purely reciprocal compromise, on which interpersonal relationships in general might be said to be loosely based. Individuals who view themselves as compatriots belonging to a national or subnational group meet "not as advocates for this or that sectional group, but as citizens whose main concerns are the pursuit of common ends."[15]

Bringing together and building on this diverse body of scholarship, I argue that attachment to an overarching subnational identity encourages a perception

---

[8] Tajfel and Turner (1985).   [9] Dovidio and Gaertner (1999), p. 103.
[10] Kramer and Brewer (1984), p. 1045.   [11] Tajfel and Turner (1985); Brewer (1979).
[12] Kramer and Brewer (1984), p. 1056.   [13] Tamir (1993), p. 99.   [14] Tamir (1993), p. 95.
[15] Miller (1995), p. 48.

of shared interests and a sense of mutual commitments on the part of individuals from divergent subgroups. I also argue that these individuals are, in turn, more likely to support policies that further the collective good of the subnational community as a whole and have an inherently redistributive element. Education and health policies are examples of these, insofar as government schools and health centers are most likely to be used by the poor and marginalized, especially in developing countries. Elites bound by shared subnationalism are more likely to push to include education and health on the policy agenda. If subnational identification has taken root among the masses, their constituents are also likely to be in favor of public goods, which is likely to serve as an additional, though not necessary, impetus for the political elite to back social policy.

In contrast, in states lacking a superordinate subnational identity, the positive effects of in-group bias extend only to members of the same subgroup, for example coethnics, and not to all members of the subnational community. Individual perceptions continue to be structured in "us" and "them" terms; there is little conception of the more inclusive "we." In such states, political elites are unlikely to push for social welfare for the subnational community. If and when social policies are introduced, they are likely to be targeted toward elites' ethnic groups and not be universal in nature.

This argument that the elite are motivated by a shared subnational solidarity to prioritize social welfare policy might strike some as a far too rosy view of the elite and more generally, of individual motivations and behavior. Yet it is important to point out that we are surrounded by situations where people accept the costs of behaving prosocially. For example, many, even most, people pay their taxes honestly despite the very low probability of detection and small expected penalties for doing otherwise; vote even though the probability of casting the decisive vote is miniscule; contribute generously to a range of charitable causes and/or volunteer often substantial amounts of their time; and mail back lost wallets with the cash intact.[16]

Interestingly, Adam Smith, who is most prominently associated with his advocacy of self-interest in his book *The Wealth of Nations*, did not believe that human beings are driven only by selfish motives. In his first book, *The Theory of Moral Sentiments*, he wrote, "How selfish soever man may be supposed, there are evidently some principles in his nature, which interest him in the fortune of others, and render their happiness necessary to him, though he derives nothing from it, except the pleasure of seeing it."[17] Moreover, the subnationalism argument I propose may be seen as building on and contributing to the growing research in social science as well as neurology on the centrality of affect in decision-making.[18] Insofar as the solidarity generated by subnational identification is an affective process that generates a set of ideas

---

[16] Meier (2006).   [17] Smith (1759), p. 3.
[18] Peters et al. (2006); Gigerenzer (2007); Damasio et al. (1994).

about the importance of the welfare of the subnational community as a whole, my argument is also in line with the so-called ideational turn in political science that argues for ideas as an important, primary source of political behavior.[19]

Moreover, the perception and prioritization of the common good that a sense of subnational identity is hypothesized to generate is by no means irrational when we broaden our conception of rationality. Max Weber, for example, famously proposed a conceptualization of different forms of rationality, in particular the distinction between formal rationality and substantive rationality. While formal rationality refers to a simple means-ends rational calculation – one has a goal and takes rational steps that are based on past experience, observation, logic, or science to attain that goal – the concept of substantive rationality, on the other hand, refers to goal-oriented rational action within the context of ultimate ends or values. In my argument, that would be promotion of the welfare of the subnational community as a whole.[20] In a different but analogous way, one might think of working for the collective welfare in terms of self-interest, but a shared sense of belonging leads to a shift in identity "from the personal level towards the higher, more inclusive group level ('me' becomes 'we'-identity)" and consequently to a "transformation of motivation" whereby self-interest at the personal or subgroup level is redefined at the collective level.[21] Favorable outcomes for other group members are related to favorable outcomes for oneself.[22] The notion that the welfare of the collective enters into an individual's utilitarian calculus is akin to the move away from the long-standing divide between idealist and materialist theories. Instead we move toward a recognition of the interplay between ideas and interests, specifically that the ideas held by individuals affect how they define their interests in the first place.[23]

To summarize, as Figure 8.1 shows, in states with a powerful subnational identity, governments are more likely to prioritize the social sector, which is, in turn, a necessary condition for and primary driver of social development. Societal involvement with public services might also, as Figure 8.1 indicates, augment the developmental efforts of an active government. Studies with very different theoretical leanings have shown that shared identity – in particular, attachment to a superordinate political identity such as a nation – can produce emotional arousal and/or an interest in politics and, consequently, a propensity toward political action.[24] Such popular involvement, however, is supplementary to state action, which is the primary channel through which I hypothesize that subnationalism influences social development.

---

[19] Béland and Cox (2010).   [20] Elwell (2013).   [21] De Cremer and Van Vugt (1999).
[22] Tyler and Smith (1999).   [23] Campbell (2002); Blyth (2002).
[24] Huddy and Khatib (2007); Rahn (2004); Miller (1995), p. 10; Abizadeh (2002); Mason (2000), p. 117.

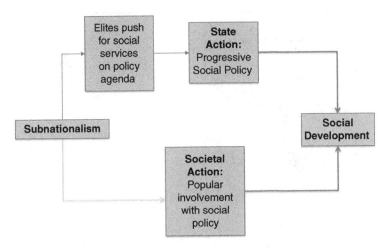

FIGURE 8.1 The Solidarity Argument: How Subnationalism Produces Social Development

8.4 SUBNATIONAL SOLIDARITY AND SOCIAL WELFARE ACROSS INDIAN STATES

The argument I present is developed through a study of social policy and development, operationalized in terms of education and health, across Indian states. I offer a historical case comparison of two Indian provinces from the mid-nineteenth century to the present that were chosen to maximize variation on the primary independent variable, the strength of subnationalism.

Subnationalism and Social Development in Kerala and Uttar Pradesh: A Comparative Historical Analysis

This part of the chapter juxtaposes two Indian states, the southern province of Kerala with the north-central province of Uttar Pradesh (UP) (see Maps 8.1 and 8.2). The two cases are selected to exemplify variation on the explanatory variable, the strength of subnational identification. I seek to delineate the sequences and mechanisms by which subnational solidarity leads to differences in the progressiveness of social policy, which in turn contributes to highly divergent levels of social development. Subnational solidarity began to emerge in the late nineteenth century in Kerala but has remained persistently absent in UP.[25] In modern times, Kerala, demographically the size of Canada, is globally acclaimed as a model of social welfare, whereas UP, demographically the size of Russia, is widely considered a "basket case," characterized by development outcomes that are worse than many countries in sub-Saharan Africa. It is important to note that this was not always the case. I show that in Kerala

[25] Singh (2015b).

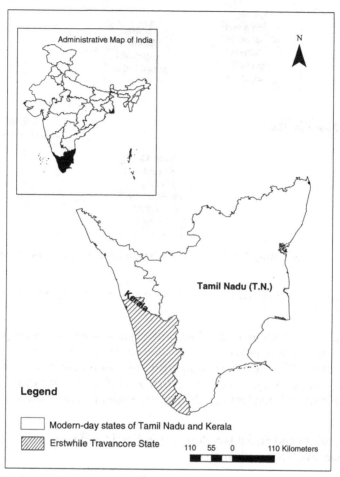

MAP 8.1 Travancore State with the Present-Day Location in India

progressive social policy was introduced and an increase in education and health indicators occurred only after and as a consequence of the emergence of a sense of subnational community.

Equivalent Starting Points: No Subnationalism, Low Social Development (Until the Mid- to Late Nineteenth Century)

In the mid-nineteenth century, neither of the regions that correspond to the present-day states of Kerala or UP had experienced the emergence of a subnational identity.[26] The two regions were characterized by broadly

---

[26] During the colonial period, the present-day state of Kerala was composed of two princely states, Travancore and Cochin, and the northern district of Malabar, part of neighboring Madras

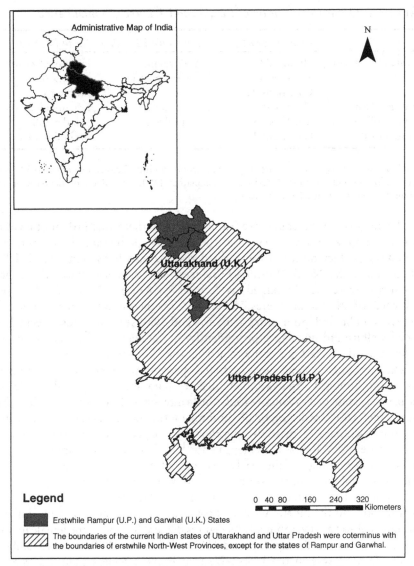

MAP 8.2 North-West Provinces with the Present-Day Location in India

Presidency. Insofar as Travancore constitutes the bulk of Kerala today, most of my analysis of the colonial period refers to Travancore, but developments in Cochin followed a very similar pattern. The region that now constitutes UP was composed of the directly ruled North-Western Provinces and Oudh, which was known after 1902 as the United Provinces of Agra and Oudh, and after 1935, simply as the United Provinces.

TABLE 8.1 *Ethnic Composition of Kerala and UP in the Colonial Period*

	Religion 1881 (%)	Language 1881 (%)	Caste 1931 (%)
Kerala (Travancore)	Hindus 73	Malayalam	Fractionalization
	Muslims 6	speakers 81	index 0.9
	Christians 21		Brahmins 11
Uttar Pradesh	Hindus 86	Hindustani	Fractionalization
(North-Western	Muslims 13	speakers 98	index 0.8
Provinces)	Christians 1		Brahmins 11

Religion and language figures are from the Report on the Census of India, 1881; caste fractionalization index is from Banerjee and Somanathan (2001), calculated on the basic of caste population totals from the 1931 census.

similar linguistic landscapes (see Table 8.1), and there was little mobilization around language in either region at the time. The subnational community in Kerala was, in fact, far more deeply divided along caste lines than it was in UP.[27] At the time, the North-Western Provinces, and their successor, the United Provinces, were widely hailed as "model province[s]," among the "best governed of all Indian states,"[28] while Travancore was characterized by recurrent debt and poor infrastructure and was seen as "misgoverned."[29] Social welfare did not figure prominently on the agenda of either of the two states. Statistical abstracts show that from the 1850s to the 1880s, the North-Western Provinces spent less than 0.1 percent of their total revenue on education. Similarly, analyses of budgetary data show that until the 1870s, the princely state of Travancore took "little interest in the education or health of the people" and "spent practically nothing on the social services."[30] According to some scholars, Christian missionaries played an important role in Travancore's development achievements[31] and undertook important social initiatives beginning in the early decades of the century, but these were contingent on government support[32] and were restricted in scope and, as such, only led to limited gains. In the mid- to late nineteenth century, both Travancore and the North-Western Provinces were characterized by similarly low levels of social development. As Figures 8.2 and 8.3 show, the female literacy rate in Travancore during the mid-1870s and early 1880s was virtually as minuscule as it was in the North-Western Provinces—less than 0.5 percent.

---

[27] By all accounts, the caste system in Kerala was the most orthodox and oppressive of all Indian states, with rigid rules of pollution based not only on touch, like in the rest of India, but also on proximity, as well as strictly enforced injunctions on the use of public facilities by lower castes. During his visit to Kerala in the late nineteenth century, the social reformer Swami Vivekananda famously termed it "a madhouse of caste." Chasin and Franke (1991), p. 75; Desai (2005), p. 463.

[28] Pai (2007), p. xvi; Crooks (1897), p. 3.   [29] Jeffrey (1976), p. 64; Tharakan (1984), p. 1961.

[30] Singh (1944), p. 9.   [31] Gladstone (1984); Mathew (1999).   [32] Kawashima (1998), p. 99.

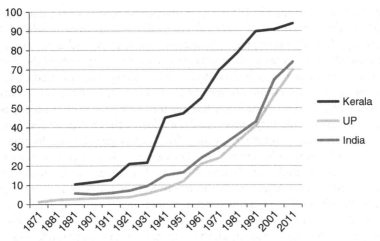

FIGURE 8.2 Total Literacy Rates in Kerala, UP, and India, 1871–2011

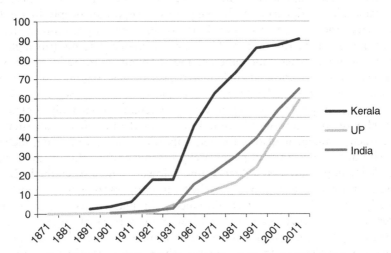

FIGURE 8.3 Female Literacy Rates in Kerala, UP, and India, 1871–2011

In addition, medical reports from Travancore during the 1870s note a very high rate of mortality in the region as compared to other Indian provinces.[33]

Subnationalism Is Produced in Kerala but not in Uttar Pradesh (Mid- to Late Nineteenth Century)

In line with constructivist theorizing that sees identities as socially constructed rather than primordially given, I trace the emergence of subnationalism in Kerala

[33] Singh (1944), p. 342.

and its lack of emergence in UP to the instrumental actions of the elite that were shaped by the exigencies of political competition and were unrelated to the underlying ethnic demographics. Subnationalism was evoked if it was a useful tool for the challenger elite in their attempt to confront the power of the dominant elite; it was a strategic decision unrelated to levels of ethnic fragmentation. Nothing about the underlying ethnic composition of either state made the espousal of a subnational appeal more or less attractive for challenger elites. Instead, as I will detail, a subnational identity was evoked if it allowed the challenger elite to present themselves as a single front clearly distinct from and opposed to the dominant elite.

In the mid-nineteenth century, the socioeconomic and political settings in both Travancore and the North-Western Provinces were dominated by a minority elite – non-Malayali Brahmans in Kerala and Muslims in the North-Western Provinces. At roughly similar points in the mid- to late nineteenth century, these regions witnessed key exogenous changes – a combination of challenges to the caste system, changes in agriculture and trade, and limited opportunities for Western-style education. In Kerala, the Protestant Christian missionaries who had arrived in the region in the early 1800s played an important role in triggering a challenge to the rigid and deeply hierarchical caste system there, both ideologically (through their propagation of the idea that all are equal in the eyes of God) and in material terms (through their support of lower caste movements and campaigns to reduce the state-sanctioned discrimination against lower castes). The region also witnessed important changes in agriculture – the abolition of caste-based rural slavery, the granting of predominantly lower-caste tenants ownership rights over 200,000 acres of state-owned land, and the swift move from subsistence to commercial farming. It also witnessed important changes in trade, including a massive increase in coconut product exports due to rising European demand, which led to unprecedented affluence among lower castes, especially the Izhavas whose traditional caste occupation is the tending and tapping of coconut palms. Similarly, in the North-Western Provinces, the massive expansion of trade triggered by the growth of railways created an increasingly wealthy class of middlemen, predominantly from the Hindu merchant castes. Around this time, the two regions also saw the emergence of the first opportunities for citizens to gain some literacy in English, the official language of administration, through missionary schools in Travancore and select government schools and colleges opened on the initiative of colonial officers in the North-Western Provinces. As a result, an upwardly mobile elite began to surface from nondominant groups – Nairs, Syrian Christians, and Izhavas in Travancore and Hindu merchant castes in the North-Western Provinces – and started to demand political power commensurate with their improved socioeconomic status.[34]

---

[34] It is important to clarify, in light of any potential concerns about endogeneity, that access to English education was very limited – in 1891, less than 0.1 percent of the population of Travancore or UP had any knowledge of English.

Administrative reforms that emphasized merit as a criterion for recruitment to government service, instituted in Travancore in the 1860s and in the North-Western Provinces in the 1870s, presented precisely such an opportunity.

As the challenger elites took advantage of these opportunities, they came into conflict with the dominant elites who sought to maintain their hegemony over political power. At this time, Travancore and the North-Western Provinces were characterized by equivalent levels of linguistic, religious, and caste fractionalization (see Table 8.1). The challenger elites in both states had access to similar sets of symbols and identities rooted in language, religion and class. From these, they selected and emphasized the ones that were most likely to advance their position by allowing them to come together in a united front that was distinguished from and in opposition to the dominant elites. In Travancore – which in the late nineteenth century was, as Table 8.1 shows, less homogenous than the North-Western Provinces in terms of language, religion, and caste – these elites united around a subnational identity; in the North-Western Provinces, by contrast, challenger elites united around religion. In Travancore, a subnational identity allowed the Nair, Syrian Christian, and Izhava challenger elites to come together as native Malayalis in clear opposition to the "foreign" non-Malayali Brahmans.[35] The espousal of a Malayali subnational identity was therefore a purely instrumental calculation on the part of the challenger elites insofar as it allowed them to come together in a minimum coalition of "natives" (Malayali) defined against a common "outsider" contender (the non-Malayali Brahmins).

Once it was evoked, however, a shared Malayali identity which drew on ancient myths of a shared origin, common heroes, and culture took on a powerful emotional valence. Regional newspapers throughout the 1880s bring up the forging of a "glorious" Malayali identity in explicit contradistinction to the "deceitful and treacherous" foreign Brahmans who "devoted all their energies to surpassing and exploiting Malayalis" and were "sucking the life blood of the country."[36] One of the most striking examples of the growing Malayali subnationalism among challenger elites is the "Malayali Memorial" from 1891, a powerful, emotionally worded united protest for greater native representation in public services that had over ten thousand signatories and claimed to embody the grievances of the Malayali community as a whole.[37]

In the North-Western Provinces, on the other hand, the adoption of subnational symbols was not an appealing strategy for the Hindu merchant challenger elites. Rather than distinguish them, such a strategy would have brought them into the same subnational in-group as the dominant Muslim

---

[35] The Nair, Syrian Christian, and Izhava elites did not give up their caste or religious identities; they continued to look at their caste brethren and coreligionists as "natural allies" but they calculated (correctly) that adopting a shared, linguistic identity and mounting a single, united Malayali challenge was likely to be a more effective strategy in their competition with a common, powerful enemy than having each group act on its own. Jeffrey (1976), pp. 147, 168.

[36] Jeffrey (1976), pp. 111, 114.   [37] Koshy (1972), pp. 31–32.

elite whom they were seeking to displace from political power. Religion, not subnationalism, was thus the identity that was more useful to them. It is important to clarify that while the two main religious groups, Hindus and Muslims, are characterized by fundamental differences, they are also connected by a shared symbolic repertoire. Historians have stressed that divisions *within* these communities during this period were often greater than differences between them.[38] The impetus to advance their interests vis-à-vis the dominant Muslim elite, however, pushed the Hindu challenger elite to undermine unifying symbols, notably the common spoken language, Hindustani, and instead deploy Hindi written in the Devanagri script as a means to define and coalesce the inchoate Hindu community. The anxious Muslim elite retaliated by championing Urdu written in the Persian script as the exclusive language of the "Muslim nation" and berating Hindi as nothing but an inferior form of Urdu.[39]

The diffusion of elite identities to the population at large was contingent on their espousal by a sociopolitical movement or association. In Travancore, for example, the Aikya Kerala (United Kerala) movement to consolidate all Malayalam-speaking regions into a single united province, which emerged in the 1920s, proved essential for the transmission of Malayali subnationalism to the masses. Beginning in the late 1930s, cadres of the Communist Party, which was founded on an explicitly subnationalist ideology and took over as the vanguard of the Aikya Kerala movement, further facilitated the spread of popular Malayali subnationalism. In a parallel process in the United Provinces, political-religious organizations such as the Hindu Mahasabha and the Muslim League played a critical role from the 1920s onward in the mass dissemination of the mutually reinforcing and divisive religious-linguistic identities of Hindi-Hindu versus Urdu-Muslim.

Differences in the Strength of Subnationalism Trigger a Divergence in Developmental Trajectories in the Late Nineteenth Century Until the End of the Colonial Period

Malayali subnationalism served as an important trigger for the introduction of a progressive social policy and the beginning of social gains in Kerala. An analysis of important local newspapers, such as the *Malayala Manorama*, which were controlled primarily by upper castes, and the proceedings of the Sri Mulam Popular Assembly, a partially representative but predominantly upper-caste body established in the early 1900s, shows how the growing "Kerala-wide consciousness of a shared community"[40] served as a powerfully effective frame that fostered the emergence of consensus on the part of upper-caste elites regarding the importance of equal social rights for all Malayalis.[41]

---

[38] Robinson (1975), p. 33.   [39] Das Gupta and Fishman (1971), p. 93.

[40] Chiriyankandath (1993), p. 650.

[41] Koshy (1972), p. 45. This is not to deny the considerable sociopolitical conflict in the region during this period. The states of Travancore and Cochin were characterized by continued

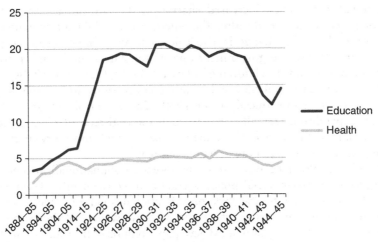

FIGURE 8.4 Government Spending on Education and Health as a Share of Total Government Expenditures, Travancore, 1885–1945

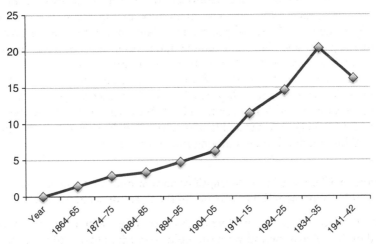

FIGURE 8.5 Number of State Educational Institutions, Travancore, 1864–1942

Figures 8.4 and 8.5 show how the Travancore government's expenditure on education as a proportion of its total expenditure, as well as the number of state

competition between different castes, notably Izhavas and Nairs. Malabar, which was at this time a part of Madras Presidency, witnessed the Moplah rebellion, an uprising by Muslim peasants against British rule and Hindu Nair landlords. During the 1930s and 1940s, Left mobilization and militancy intensified as represented by the Punnapra-Vayalar uprising, a struggle led by the Communist Party against the Travancore government in which over 150 people were killed.

educational institutions, increased sharply in the late nineteenth and early twentieth centuries, shortly after the emergence of Malayali subnationalism among the elite. The change is also evident in the content of social policy. By the early 1900s, the government opened up state schools and introduced vaccination programs to children of all castes. In the 1920s and 1930s, a range of affirmative-action policies, including fee concessions and scholarships for lower castes, were introduced. In the 1940s, 25 percent of Travancore's total medical expenditure was allocated to stem the outbreak of diseases such as cholera and smallpox, one of the main causes of high mortality, particularly among the lower castes, in the previous century.[42]

In the United Province, by contrast, the absence of subnationalism impeded the emergence of a strong social policy agenda and, consequently, developmental gains. Corresponding to the lack of subnational solidarity, there was little conception on the part of the elite of the collective welfare of the people of the state as a whole. An analysis of local newspaper reports of the times shows that in the context of antagonistic religious attachments, demands for the extension for social services were framed almost exclusively in ethnic terms. Hindu and Muslim elite invariably mobilized and petitioned the government for the exclusive advancement of their own religious community and against concessions to the demands of the other.[43] Social policy, as a result, did not occupy a prominent place on the policy agenda.[44] The limited initiatives in education and health that were adopted were a result either of the personal, progressive instincts of a few British administrators[45] or the efforts of Christian missionaries.[46] These differences in state social policy resulted in Travancore gaining a steadily growing developmental lead over the North-Western Provinces. By the 1940s, Travancore and neighboring Cochin had established themselves as forerunners in social and human development among Indian provinces.

Continued Differences in the Strength of Subnationalism Consolidate Divergent Developmental Trajectories in the Postindependence Period

Despite its relative lead, the absolute levels of social development in Travancore at the end of the colonial period were still quite low. More than half the population was illiterate, and on average a man was expected to live less than 30 years.[47] UP's levels of social development, while abysmal in absolute terms, had not yet fallen below those of other Indian provinces as they would in subsequent decades.

---

[42] Singh (1944), p. 434.

[43] At the close of the nineteenth century, for example, the Hind Pratap (Allahabad), opposing the memorial of the Muhammadan Association of Calcutta, wrote, "[I]t would be as unwise to do anything to improve the condition of the Mussalmans as to feed a serpent. If they attain to power, they will only oppress the poor Hindus." British Library (1942).

[44] Robinson (1975), p. 317.

[45] His Majesty's Secretary of State for India in Council (1908), p. 139.   [46] Varma (1994), p. 9.

[47] Ramachandran (1997), p. 225.

The years following India's independence from the British Empire in 1947 mark a critical period in the developmental trajectories of both provinces.

Subnationalism in the regions that would constitute the new state of Kerala reached a crescendo in the 1950s during the time of the linguistic agitations. Movements for the redrawing of provincial boundaries in India go back to the colonial period. The British administration faced frequent demands for the redrawing of state boundaries along linguistic lines in the early years of the twentieth century. The Congress party, which was at the helm of the nationalist movement, supported such demands from 1905 onward and at its annual session in 1920 adopted a new constitution that organized the party along 21 linguistically defined units. After gaining independence, however, the Congress government decided that despite popular demand, because of the "formative state" of the nation it was not "an opportune time" for the creation of linguistic provinces. They feared that such an undertaking might unleash "forces of disruption and disintegration" (Windmiller, 1954). But by the early 1950s, the mobilizations by language groups reached a crescendo and began to take a violent turn. In 1953, the central government was forced to appoint the States Reorganization Commission (SRC), which conceded the principle of the linguistic reorganization of Indian states and also recommended the specific boundaries of the provinces.

An examination of the petitions submitted by the Aikya Kerala campaign to the States Reorganization Commission (SRC), a body appointed by the Indian government to assess the demands for linguistic states, shows that Malayali subnationalism had been inextricably linked to the collective welfare of all Malayalis. In petition after petition submitted to the SRC, the creation of a United Kerala State was presented as an essential condition for "the development of the Malayalis."

Petitions were submitted not just from the princely states of Travancore and Cochin but also from Malabar, which was part of neighboring Madras Presidency, directly controlled by the British government. The petitions submitted by organizations and individuals in Malabar were flush with the idea that the government of the newly constituted state of Kerala, composed of "conationals," would be obligated to look after their welfare, which had been neglected by "foreigners" in the Madras government who had meted out "stepmotherly treatment" to the Malayali District.[48] The campaigners for a united Kerala from Travancore-Cochin, in turn, seemed more than willing to take up the responsibility of Malabar's development and vehemently refuted the argument, which was not empirically unfounded, that the region's relative backwardness would constitute a costly liability for a state already in a relatively precarious socioeconomic position. They argued that "Malabar has immense possibilities for development, [and] this is possible only in an Aikya Kerala."[49]

[48] Nair (1954); Pocker Sahib (1954); Wynad Taluk (1954).
[49] Communist Party of India (1954), p. 3.

Malayali subnationalism remained strong and a key driver of social spending and development through most of the postindependence decades. This is particularly evident in the activities of the Communist Party, which was formed in the 1930s and won its first elections in 1957. The party was defined by its leader, E. M. S. Namboodiripad, as Kerala's "national party."[50] The embodiment of a subnational consciousness has been an important factor, among others, in the success of the Communist Party.[51] Scholars such as Victor Fic emphasize the significance of a subnational identity to the victories of the Communists almost to the negation of Marxist ideology.[52] Similarly, Selig Harrison argues that the party's popular support and electoral victories, especially in the early years, can be explained, "above all, by its ability to manipulate the regional patriotism of all Kerala."[53] The Communists' subnationalism was inextricably intertwined with a focus on Malayali welfare and exemplified by their "development-defined ideal vision of a unified Malayalee people."[54] In the first elections for Travancore-Cochin state in 1951, the party's manifesto pushed voters to choose "A Government That Will Take Care of the Malayalee Nation."[55] The role played by a shared subnational solidarity in the Communist Party leaders' prioritization of social welfare was also strikingly apparent, both as an overall goal and in key social schemes, in the Communist government's evocation of an important subnational hero, the ancient Malayali king Mahabali. As legend has it, Mahabali ruled over a united, solidaristic Kerala with great concern for the well-being of his people. At the time of the creation of Kerala in the mid-1950s, as the leader of the Communist Party and the first chief minister of the united state of Kerala, E. M. S. Namboodiripad had explicitly characterized his vision of the state as "the Mavelinadu (the land of Mahabali) of the future."[56] One of the most significant social initiatives in the state has been the opening of "Maveli (Mahabali) stores," which sell grain and other essential items at controlled prices. Interestingly, social programs, especially those that are more difficult to implement, such as the state's family planning program, have been couched "in terms of the national interest (of Kerala)."[57] In addition, the promotion of Malayali welfare has figured prominently as a justification for the Communist Party's periodic demands for increased autonomy from New Delhi.[58] The link between a vigorous subnationalism and progressive social policy in Kerala appears to be epitomized by the fact that subnationalist occasions are celebrated with the institution of new social policies. In 2006, for example, Chief Minister V. S. Achutanandan announced, "The 50th anniversary of the formation of Kerala is intended for launching the most comprehensive developmental programs in the history of the State."

---

[50] Harrison (1960), p. 195.   [51] Nossiter (1982).   [52] Fic (1970).
[53] Harrison (1960), p. 193.   [54] Devika (2002), p. 53.   [55] Harrison (1960), p. 193.
[56] Devika (2002), p. 57.   [57] Devika (2002), p. 51.   [58] Nossiter (1982), p. 265.

It bears emphasis that in Kerala, the Communist government's commitment to the social sector, which is part of its broad and deep commitment to redistribution – made apparent with the institution of land reforms in the 1960s and 1970s[59] – is far greater than the commitment of Communist Party governments in other Indian states, such as West Bengal, where, incidentally, the left has enjoyed longer and more stable tenures than in Kerala. Moreover, the Indian National Congress – the other major political player in Kerala and one that has retained a distinct subnational identity, functioning, in stark contrast to UP's Congress, more like a regional party than a wing of the central Congress – has also been committed to the social sector, attempting to match and even outdo the Communist governments in providing social services.[60]

Despite Kerala having lower levels of economic development than the national average for most of the postindependence period, state expenditures on education and health have been consistently higher than the average for all other Indian states.[61] The state's commitment to the social sector is apparent in the fact that, despite endemic social unrest during the 1960s and 1970s; political turmoil and instability (the average span of a government from the 1950s through the 1990s was two-and-a-half years);[62] precarious financial situations through the 1980s; and New Delhi's liberalizing market reforms of the 1990s, no government, whether Communist or Congress, has ever reversed a major public service or redistributive program in Kerala.[63] Moreover, social policy has had a distinctly redistributive edge, with an overwhelming emphasis on the provision of primary education and the initiation of schemes for the more deprived sections of Malayali society.

In UP, by contrast, identification with the Indian nation through the 1980s and with religion and caste since the 1990s has impeded the emergence of a subnational developmental agenda. With the founding of Pakistan in 1947 and the associated decrease in activity and relevance of the Muslim League, the Hindu–Muslim cleavage receded but by no means disappeared from postindependence UP politics. The void, however, was not filled with the rise of subnational solidarity. Instead, drawing on the province's historic importance as the birthplace of Hinduism and the nerve center of some of the most influential ancient and medieval empires; its demographic weight, which gave it the single largest number of seats in the newly constituted national

[59] These reforms were not only successful – Kerala is today characterized by one of the more egalitarian patterns of landholding seen in developing countries – but also relatively peaceful (Herring, 1983, 1991).

[60] Venugopal (2006). In the over 70 years since the institution of elections, all but one chief minister of Kerala from the Congress Party have devoted their political careers entirely to state politics.

[61] It is important to acknowledge that foreign remittances in the form of money sent by Malayali workers in the Gulf have provided an important spur for the economy of Kerala. Still, these remittances became substantial in the mid-1980s and only began to assume a significant share of state income in the 1990s.

[62] John (1992). [63] Heller (2005), p. 82.

Source: Shankar's Weekly, Vol VI, Nos. 1-26, 31 May 1953

FIGURE 8.6 Cartoon Depiction of Indian State of Uttar Pradesh

legislature; and its strategic geographic location, the elite in UP successfully portrayed their province, as depicted humorously in Figure 8.6, as the "heartland" of India.[64] UP legislators, for example, proposed to name the province "Aryavrat," a term synonymous with India as a whole, and designate Allahabad, the capital of UP, as the national capital.[65] Political elites in UP tended to see their careers not as being devoted to working in and for the state but instead as a waystation on the road to the national political stage. From the time of prominent UP politician B. D. Pant, who had been at the helm of the state from 1937 but relinquished the chief ministership to take a post in the national cabinet in 1955 (incidentally leaving the state's politics in disarray), chief ministers, the equivalent of governors in other federal systems, in UP have tended to be heavily involved with national politics. Eleven out of 20 chief

---

[64] Kudaisya (2007), p. 10.

[65] This close identification with the national sphere was explicitly, and often positively, contrasted with the absence of subnational identification in UP. Jawaharlal Nehru, for example, wrote that the state has "less provincialism than in any other part of India. For long they have considered themselves, and been looked upon by others, as the heart of India" (cited in Kudaisya [2007], p. 10). B. D. Pant, the first chief minister of UP, declared it to be "unaffected by either linguism or provincialism" (India Parliament, Lok Sabha [1956], p. 1504).

ministers held a position in the national government at some, usually later, points in their career. In short, UP politics were dominated by the national Congress to the extent that it was seen as a "jagirdari" or fief.[66] From the 1950s to the 1980s, and especially under Prime Minister Indira Gandhi, UP chief ministers were selected by the center rather than from within the state. Reflecting this political intertwining, by the 1960s there was a familiar saying: "India, that is Bharat, that is UP."[67] National election-survey data from 1971 show that, like the UP elite, nonelite residents of UP also tended to be far more concerned, especially when compared to people from Kerala, with the actions of the national government (36 percent versus 19 percent, respectively) than with the state government (13 percent versus 41 percent, respectively). In successive elections, the UP electorate tended to vote on national rather than state issues. In 1984, for example, "voters self-consciously rejected local considerations to cast a vote for the party, the Congress, which was perceived as the best party for the good of the country."[68]

This close identification with the nation led to a preoccupation with the national good and effectively blocked the emergence of any sort of subnational developmental agenda in UP.[69] During debates over the state's reorganization, for example, in stark contrast to the elite in Kerala, the UP political elite who did counter the many and powerful proposals for the division of the state and argued for the maintenance of the province's boundaries did so less in terms of how maintaining the status quo would benefit the people of UP and more in terms of how it would benefit the Indian nation.[70] Through the early postindependence decades, the UP elite remained preoccupied with furthering national interests, notably the implementation of Hindi as the national language of India, placing this matter on the top of their policy agenda to the relative neglect of the critical developmental issues facing the state.[71] Election campaigns in UP almost entirely eschewed the issue of the state's development and focused nearly exclusively instead on questions of all-India relevance. During the 1960s, for example, the Jan Sangh ran against the ruling Congress party and succeeded because of its opposition to the ruling Congress's perceived failure to secure just treatment for the Hindu minority in Pakistan.[72] Similarly, elections in UP in the 1980s focused "nearly exclusively

---

[66] Ramesh (1999), p. 2127.   [67] Sharma (1969), p.181. *Bharat* is the Hindi name for India.

[68] Brass (1986), p. 661.   [69] Zerinini-Brotel (1998), p. 79; Kudaisya (2007), p. 24.

[70] The SRC report noted, "One of the commonest arguments advanced before us by leaders in Uttar Pradesh was that the existence of a large, powerful and well-organized state in the Gangetic Valley was a guarantee for India's unity; that such a state would be able to correct the disruptive tendencies of other states, and to ensure the ordered progress of India. The same idea has been put to us in many other forms such as that Uttar Pradesh is the 'back bone of India'" (1955, p. 246).

[71] Kudaisya (2007), p. 378.

[72] Masaldan (1967), p. 282. The Jana Sangh was a right-wing party that existed from 1955 to 1977. It was widely seen to be the political arm of the Hindu nationalist volunteer organization

on the dangers to the country, posed by internal and external enemies and on the need for Indians to close ranks to save the country."[73]

The grave developmental cost to UP of the subservience of its state agenda to national politics is highlighted by an examination of its budget through these decades. The state government prioritized areas emphasized by New Delhi, whether or not they represented its own most urgent needs. For example, social development was clearly needed in UP, yet, as late as the mid-1980s and in line with central policies, the state spent up to 43.5 percent of its total budget on economic services yet just over 3 percent on social services. And even this limited social expenditure was overlaid by central directives. The most egregious example was the funneling of large proportions of health outlays to family planning activities, which took a heavy toll on the provision of essential health services in the state.[74]

Since the early 1990s, the locus of elite and mass identification in UP has shifted from the nation to ethnic groups. The rise of the Hindu nationalist Bharatiya Janata Party (BJP) in the 1990s is associated with the increased salience of and competition around religious identity.[75] The resurgence of religious identity in UP has been accompanied, and arguably overshadowed, by the development of powerful caste allegiances associated with the emergence of lower-caste movements. Among these are, most prominently, the Dalit movement under Kanshi Ram in the 1980s; the Bahujan Samaj Party (BSP) headed by the charismatic Mayawati in the early 1990s; and the rise of the backward castes under Mulayam Singh Yadav, who founded the Samajwadi Party (SP) in 1992. The emergence of caste-based movements and parties has been, on the whole, a divisive process. In its early years, the Dalit movement was directed explicitly against the upper castes, who constitute approximately 20 percent of the population of UP.[76] Moreover, various lower castes also tend to mobilize in antagonism rather than in alliance with each other. The BSP's initial claim to stand for social justice for the *bahujan samaj* (the majority community), defined to include scheduled castes, scheduled tribes, other backward castes, and minorities, quickly narrowed to the claim of standing exclusively for the Dalits.[77] In fact, in the wake of the bitter breakup of the BSP–SP coalition, the interests of the Dalits and backward castes came to be seen not only as separate but also as opposed.

the Rashtriya Swayamsevak Sangh (RSS). In 1977 it came together in a coalition opposed to the Indian National Congress and formed the Janata Party. After the break-up of the Janata Party, it reconstituted itself as the Bharatiya Janata Party (BJP) in 1980, which is presently the ruling party in India.

[73] Brass (1986), p. 663.   [74] Drèze and Sen (1996), p. 55.   [75] Hasan (1996), p. 97.

[76] Campaign slogans of the BSP exemplify the intensity of Dalit animosity against upper castes: "Tilak, Tarazu, Kalam, Talwar; Inko maaro jute chaar [forehead mark, scale, pen, and sword (the occupational symbols of the four upper castes), Thrash them with four shoes]" (Pai, 2007, p. 263.

[77] Pai (2002), p. 121.

The shift of popular identification away from the nation in UP is evidenced by the more than 50 percent decline (from 36 percent in 1971 to 16 percent in 1996) in those reporting greater concern with the actions of the government in New Delhi.[78] The increased salience of caste is evident in the 1996 National Election Study.[79] Forty-six percent of the respondents in UP reported voting the same as other members of their caste or religious group compared to 5 percent of respondents in Kerala and 26 percent of respondents across all India. Moreover, 26 percent of UP respondents said a political party existed that took special care of their caste or religious group's interests, substantially higher than the 16 percent in Kerala and the 17 percent in UP who had expressed the same sentiment in 1971. By the early 2000s, the depth of caste fragmentation in UP was such that even the BJP felt compelled to seek support along caste lines. Badri Narayan Tiwari notes that the general elections of 2004 witnessed a critical change in the BJP's "language of the political discourse." From the use of "one uniform language" across all castes, the party tried to reach out to different castes by focusing on their "caste glory through references to their caste heroes; it sought to consolidate their caste identity by exhorting them to take pride in their caste-based professions."[80]

This polarization along caste lines led to the conceptualization of welfare in narrow, sectional terms. Political elites from different castes have pushed for goods and services for the exclusive benefit of their own group. Such behavior has tilted the social agenda of UP heavily toward targeted policies and away from universal policies designed to benefit all residents of the state.[81] The schemes of the BSP have been the most striking in this regard. In addition to symbolic policies designed to valorize Dalit heroes and inculcate Dalit pride, the party introduced policies aimed exclusively at the socioeconomic development of Dalits. The largest and most prominent of these was the Ambedkar Village Program (AVP), which targeted a number of welfare schemes to villages with Dalit majorities. While it is important not to underestimate their significance in the ideational empowerment of Dalits, these schemes have had only a limited effect on their material welfare and have arguably taken a toll on the social development of the state as a whole.[82] Mayawati, president of the Bahujan Samaj Party (BSP) and chief minister of UP for four different terms, briefly in 1995 and again in 1997, then from 2002 to 2003 and from 2007 to 2012, was well known for her "iconography spree".[83] Mayawati's construction of dozens of large-scale architectural memorials commemorating herself and Dalit social reformers have been estimated as costing millions of rupees and draining UP's already depleted coffers, leaving precious little for

---

[78] Center for the Study of Developing Societies (1971); Center for the Study of Developing Societies (1996).

[79] Center for the Study of Developing Societies (1996).   [80] Tiwari (2007), p. 138.

[81] Drèze and Gazdar (1997), p. 63, write, for example, of "the absence of a well-accepted consensus on the need to universalize primary education in Uttar Pradesh."

[82] Mehrotra (2007).   [83] Zerinini-Brotel (1998), p. 99.

investment in "key sectors such as education, infrastructure and health," which was especially harmful for "the poorest sections of the population, which includes a substantial section of *dalits*."[84] Social schemes such as the AVP involved the siphoning of funds away from and/or suspending developmental schemes meant for the entire state and concentrating them instead in small Dalit enclaves.[85] This has led to the neglect and alienation of other residents of UP, most notably the non-Dalit rural poor who in some areas are more impoverished than Dalits.[86] The social sector in UP has also been marked by "resilient governmental inertia,"[87] reflected not only in some of the lowest budgetary allocations to education and health of all Indian states through the postindependence decades but also in the UP government's massive underutilization of grants from, and the generally lackadaisical implementation of social schemes sponsored by, the national government and international agencies.

Kerala and UP have been distinguished in the postcolonial period not only by starkly contrasting social policies but also by the extent and nature of societal engagement with the services provided by the state. In Kerala, subnational identification has contributed to a significantly higher degree of interest in, consciousness of, and proclivity to participate in the public life of the state than exists in UP (see Table 8.2). Politically aware Malayalis bound by ties of solidarity tend to act collectively on a range of issues, including monitoring how well schools and health centers are functioning.[88] Separate ethnographic studies by Kathleen Gough and Joan Mencher describe local agitations that have erupted over lapses in the delivery of social services.[89] Social and political associations in Kerala frequently submit demands for improved educational and health-care facilities to higher officials,[90] and failure to meet those demands often results in *gheraoes* where protesters surround politicians and do not allow them to leave until a suitable commitment has been made.[91]

In contrast, consistently low levels of political awareness and participation and the "highly divided nature of the rural society" in UP have "seriously

[84] Pai (n.d.), p. 5. It is interesting that in the run-up to the 2016 elections in the state, which she lost, Mayawati herself pledged to commission "no more memorials" and instead focus on "development." https://www.ndtv.com/india-news/mayawati-of-life-size-statues-fame-swears-off-memorials-pledges-vikas-1395417 (last accessed: December 28, 2018).

[85] Pai (2002), pp. 129–130.   [86] Srivastava (2007), pp. 348.

[87] Drèze and Gazdar (1997), pp. 53, 88.

[88] Ramachandran (1997); Cherian (1999); Franke and Chasin (1997).

[89] Gough (1974) recounts an incident in 1962 when angry neighbors dragged a physician from a cinema and forced him to go to the hospital to deliver the baby of a woman who was in great pain (cited in Franke & Chasin, 1989, p. 45). Similarly, based on her fieldwork in Kerala in the 1960s and 1970s, Mencher notes that, "[I]f a PHC [Primary Health Center] was unmanned for a few days, there would be a massive demonstration at the nearest collectorate [regional government office]"; and the death of a child due to perceived physician neglect would prompt "an enormous procession and a big demonstration outside the PHC [and] the next day questions would have been raised in the state assembly" (Mencher, 1980, p. 1782).

[90] Nag (1989), p. 418.   [91] Franke and Chasin (1989), p. 46.

TABLE 8.2 *Political Consciousness in Kerala and UP*

	Year	Kerala	UP	India
Respondents with "Somewhat" or "Great deal of interest" in election campaign (%)	1967	49	21.6	32
	1996	73	47	35
	2004	53.4	34.2	43
Respondents with "Somewhat" or "Great deal of interest" in politics and public affairs (%)	1967	53	22.8	34
	1996	50	47	35
	2004	49	37	43

Source: Center for the Study of Developing Societies, national election studies 1967, 1996, 2004.

constrained" collaborative public action to ensure the effective functioning of social services provided by the state and resulted in a long-standing pattern of popular indifference and inertia toward those services.[92] In my interviews with more than 30 bureaucrats who had served as district collectors – civil servants in charge of the overall administration of the district – in different districts of UP at various points from the 1960s to the 2000s, not one recalled petitions or demonstrations protesting the malfunctioning of social services.[93] Public vigilance has been essential to ensuring the effective functioning of health centers and primary schools in Kerala.[94] In contrast, the failure of village communities to discipline teachers and doctors has contributed to the "chaotic functioning" of social services in UP.[95] An especially egregious example of this is the Palanpur village school, which Jean Drèze and Haris Gazdar found to be "virtually non-functional" due to systematic absenteeism by the local teacher for as long as 10 years between 1983 and 1993. Revealingly, the UP government itself highlights "public apathy" as one of the main causes for the disarray of social services in the state.[96]

Together, these differences in top-down state policies and bottom-up social activism have generated stark variation in the levels of social development between Kerala and UP. Kerala has made remarkable gains in the post-independence years and attained educational and health levels equivalent to the top 30 to 40 percent of countries across the globe, whereas UP has some of the worst human development indicators in the world.[97] This is all the more

[92] Drèze and Sen (2002); Drèze and Gazdar (1997); Sinha (1995).
[93] Interviews by the author conducted from August 2006 to December 2008.
[94] Drèze and Sen (2002), p. 92. By contrast, A UNICEF educational survey conducted in 1999 found that Kerala had one of the lowest rates of teacher absenteeism in the country (Mehrotra [2007], p. 264). A study of health centers in Kerala in the 1980s found that "all the staff were regularly at work" (Franke & Chasin [1989], p. 46).
[95] Drèze and Gazdar (1997), p. 92.   [96] See http://up.gov.in/upecon.aspx.
[97] What is even more striking is that even UP's Dalits, the primary beneficiaries of social schemes in recent years, remain far more socially deprived than their counterparts not only in Kerala but

TABLE 8.3 *Economic Development across Case Study States*

	1960s	1970s	1980s	1990s	2000s
Kerala	688.3	786.2	998.9	1467.1	2123.8
Uttar Pradesh	766.2	817	1022.8	1199	1433.6

Note: Real net state domestic product deflated by consumer price index for agricultural workers (Rs per capita).

striking because for much of the post-independence period when Kerala was making its most important social achievements, from the 1950s to the 1980s, it was also characterized by lower levels of state incomes than UP (see Table 8.3).[98]

8.5 CONCLUSION

Access to basic public goods and services has a profound influence on the quality of life. In a world in which millions of people, especially in developing countries, continue to be dogged by illiteracy and ill health, understanding the conditions that promote or hinder social welfare is of critical importance to scholars, activists, and policymakers alike. This chapter advances a new theoretical argument for, and offers a comparative historical analysis to specify, the ways in which a shared subnational identity has influenced public goods provision and social welfare across Indian states over time. I am not suggesting that social welfare policies and outcomes are a product only and/or entirely of the strength of a province's subnationalism. Indeed, Chapter 9 in this volume by Kale and Mazrahi points to the key role played by a vibrant civil society in promoting the implementation of policies for the welfare of the indigenous inhabitants (Scheduled Tribes) across Indian states. My aim is

virtually in all other Indian states, most of which have instituted far fewer social policies targeted explicitly toward Dalits. The relative extent of UP's underdevelopment is underscored by the fact that Dalit women in Kerala have, for the most part, better social indicators than upper-caste women in UP.

[98] It is important to note, however, that Kerala's income surpasses UP's in the 1990s and 2000s. A very important factor in boosting Kerala's economy is foreign remittances in the form of money sent by migrant workers in the Gulf countries. Since the end of the fixed exchange rate system in the early 1990s, remittances have constituted, on average, over 20 percent of the state's total economic output. Remittances started acquiring significance only by the early to mid-1980s when international labor migration began to acquire momentum. From the 1950s to the early 1980s, when the most significant social improvements in Kerala occurred, the difference between modified state income, taking into account remittances, and state domestic product was minimal, indicating that the latter alone was a reasonable gauge of the state's economic development. The rise in Kerala's income since the 1990s has been linked to the investment in and building of human capital.

instead to put the spotlight on subnationalism, a relatively novel and underexplored variable that, even after taking into account a range of plausible alternative explanations, provides an additional significant and substantial fillip to social expenditures and development. It is important to note that the subnationalism argument is not limited to India. The generalizability of the thesis is highlighted strikingly in recent work by Daniel Béland and André Lecours that shows how both Quebecois and Scottish subnationalism produced strong collective bonds and a solidaristic ethos that the members of these political communities used to demand and justify uniquely progressive social policies.[99]

Subnationalism is clearly an explanation that emerges from the study of the subnational welfare state. Still, as I delineate elsewhere (Singh, 2017), it points to the potential for analyses of subnational welfare states to generate new insights, and reanimate forgotten ones, about the national welfare state. An understanding of how differences in the strength of subnational solidarity produce variation in social welfare policies and development outcomes opens an analytical window for exploring how differences in the strength of national solidarity might influence the emergence and maintenance of national welfare states and development outcomes.

Nationalism has come to be strongly associated with odious tendencies such as intolerance, xenophobia, and chauvinism,[100] with one distinguished political theorist going so far as to call it "the starkest political shame of the twentieth century."[101] This chapter, however, seeks to depart from these pejorative understandings. In emphasizing the constructive potential of nationalism, it seeks to recover an argument whose provenance extends at least as far as back as Friedrich List and John Stuart Mill who, while disagreeing on a number of other issues, shared a sense of national solidarity as an important determinant

---

[99] In both Quebec and Scotland, demands for greater autonomy – including at times, independence – have been framed in terms of the necessity of enacting more generous social benefits than elsewhere in the Canada or the United Kingdom in line with the special sense of shared obligations that Quebeckers and Scots feel toward each other's welfare. Indeed, the Quebec government has been known for seminal social policies such as the $5 per day childcare, the universal prescription drug insurance plan, and the lowest university tuition rates in North America. Just over a decade after devolution, Scotland has become the "happening place" for social policy in the UK (Béland & Lecours, 2008, p. 129) with the Scottish Parliament's decision to abolish up-front tuition fees in higher education and the enactment of a universal personal long-term care program for the elderly. Strikingly, the campaign for Scottish independence, which became prominent in the run-up to the 2014 referendum, was called the "Common Weal" and it proposed a fairer Scotland through a move from a politics of "me first" to "all-of-us first" through a range of social policies including, in an interesting parallel with Quebec, subsidized childcare. See http://www.allofusfirst.org.

[100] Kedourie (1993); Hroch (1995); Snyder (2000); Pavkovic (2000); Saideman and Ayres (2008); Cederman, Weidmann, and Gleditsch (2011); Schrock-Jacobson (2012).

[101] Dunn (1979), p. 55.

of economic prosperity[102] and representative democracy,[103] respectively. Interestingly, Mancur Olson also described patriotism as "the strongest non-economic motive for" allegiance.[104] Most directly, this chapter resonates with and stresses the importance of studies that have shown an empirical association between national identification and social welfare in different parts of the world at various points in time. Scholars have, for example, drawn a link between the "societal cohesion"[105] and "aura and practice of social solidarity"[106] generated by World War II and the establishment of welfare states in Europe. Summarizing such research, Nicola McEwen and Richard Parry write, "During the Second World War, explicit associations were made between the solidarity and national consciousness engendered by the war, and the task of constructing a post-war welfare state."[107] Keith Banting and Will Kymlicka write, "[C]itizens have historically supported the welfare state, and been willing to make sacrifices to support their disadvantaged co-citizens because they viewed these citizens as 'one of us,' bound together by a common identity and common sense of belonging."[108] Analyses of surveys in the United States and Canada cross-nationally show that a sense of national attachment fosters support for public services such as schools and health care[109] and redistributive preferences more generally.[110] Studies such as these support the general causal logic of my overarching argument about the potential welfare-enhancing consequences of strong shared identities.

BIBLIOGRAPHY

Abizadeh, Arash. (2002). Does liberal democracy presuppose a cultural nation? Four arguments. *American Political Science Review* 96(3), 495–510.

---

[102] List outlined a critical role for the national economy, which was the outcome of national ideas, national institutions, and people's desire to belong to a nation, in a country's industrial and economic development. Specifically, according to Levi-Faur (1997), p. 170, for List, national solidarity was a key factor in an individual's long-term investment decisions: "an individual is not simply a producer or a consumer; he is a member of a national community and this fact has crucial significance to his willingness to invest in the future. Individuals who are not members of such communities are more liable to make short-term decisions, since mere 'individuals do not concern themselves for the prosperity of future generations – they deem it foolish "to make certain and present sacrifices in order to endeavor to obtain a benefit which is as yet uncertain and lying in the vast field of the future (if events possess any value at all); they care but little for the continuance of the nation" (List [1885 (1841)], p. 173).

[103] According to Mill, a common national culture was necessary for the working of representative institutions. He wrote, "It is in general a necessary condition of free institutions that the boundaries of government should coincide in the main with those of nationalities ... Among a people without fellow-feeling, especially if they read and speak different languages, the united public opinion, necessary to the working of representative government, cannot exist" (Mill [2004 (1861)], p. 298).

[104] Olson (1965), p. 13.   [105] Wilensky (1975).   [106] Furniss and Tilton (1977).

[107] McEwen and Parry (2005), p. 45.   [108] Banting and Kymlicka (2006), p. 11.

[109] Transue (2007); Johnston et al. (2010).   [110] Shayo (2009).

Acemoglu, Daron, Johnson, Simon, & Robinson, James A. (2001). The colonial origins of comparative development: An empirical investigation. *American Economic Review* 91(5), 1369–1401.

Alesina, Alberto, Baqir, Reza, & Easterly, William. (1997). *Public goods and ethnic divisions*. NBER Working Paper No. 6009. Cambridge, MA: National Bureau of Economic Research.

Alesina, Alberto, Devleeschauwer, Arnaud, Easterly, William, Kurlat, Sergio, & Wacziarg, Romain. (2003). Fractionalization. *Journal of Economic Growth* 8(2), 155–194.

Anderson, Benedict. (1991). *Imagined communities: Reflections on the origin and spread of nationalism*. New York, NY: Verso.

Banerjee, Abhijit, Iyer, Lakshmi, & Somanathan, Rohini. (2005). History, social divisions, and public goods in rural India. *Journal of the European Economic Association* 3(2–3), 639–647.

Banerjee, Abhijit, Iyer, Lakshmi, & Somanathan, Rohini. (2007). Public action for public goods. *Handbook of Development Economics* 4, 3117–3154.

Banerjee, Abhijit, & Somanathan, Rohini. (2001). *Caste, community and collective action: The political economy of public good provision in India*. Mimeograph. Cambridge: Massachusetts Institute of Technology.

Banting, Keith, Johnston, Richard, Kymlicka, Will, & Soroka, Stuart. (2006). Do multiculturalism policies erode the welfare state? an empirical analysis. In Keith Banting & Will Kymlicka (Eds.), *Multiculturalism and the welfare state: Recognition and redistribution in contemporary democracies*, pp. 49–91. New York, NY: Oxford University Press.

Beck, Nathaniel, & Katz, Jonathan N. (1995). What to do (and not to do) with time-series cross-section data. *American Political Science Review* 89(3), 634–647.

Béland, Daniel, & Cox, Robert H. (Eds.). (2010). *Ideas and politics in social science research*. New York, NY: Oxford University Press.

Béland, Daniel, & Lecours, André. (2008). *Nationalism and social policy: The politics of territorial solidarity*. Oxford, England: Oxford University Press.

Besley, Timothy, & Kudamatsu, Masayuki. (2006). Health and democracy. *American Economic Review* 96(2), 313–318.

Blyth, Mark. (2002). *Great transformations: Economic ideas and institutional change in the twentieth century*. New York, NY: Cambridge University Press.

Boix, Carles. (2001). Democracy, development, and the public sector. *American Journal of Political Science* 45(1), 1–17.

Boustan, Leah Platt, Ferreira, Fernando, Winkler, Hernan, & Zolt, Eric. (2010). *Income inequality and local government in the United* States, *1970–2000*. NBER Working Paper No. 16299. Cambridge, MA: National Bureau of Economic Research.

Brass, Paul R. (1986). The 1984 parliamentary elections in Uttar Pradesh. *Asian Survey* 26(6), 653–669.

Brewer, Marilynn B. (1979). In-group bias in the minimal intergroup situation: A cognitive-motivational analysis. *Psychological Bulletin* 86(2), 307–324.

British Library. (c.1868–1942). Indian newspaper reports.

Brown, David S., & Hunter, Wendy. (2004). Democracy and human capital formation education spending in Latin America, 1980 to 1997. *Comparative Political Studies 37* (7), 842–864.

Brown, David S., & Mushfiq Mobarak, Ahmed. (2009). The transforming power of democracy: Regime type and the distribution of electricity. *American Political Science Review 103*(2), 193–213.

Campbell, J. (2002). Ideas, politics, and public policy. *Annual Review of Sociology 28* (1), 21–38.

Catt, Helen, & Murphy, Michael. (2003). *Sub-state nationalism: A comparative analysis of institutional design.* New York, NY: Routledge.

Cederman, Lars-Erik, Weidmann, Nils B., & Skrede Gleditsch, Kristian. (2011). Horizontal inequalities and ethnonationalist civil war: A global comparison. *American Political Science Review 105*(3), 478–495.

Center for the Study of Developing Societies. (1971). *National Election Studies 1971.* Available at: http://www.lokniti.org/media/PDF-upload/1536314741_55699000_download_report.pdfx (last accessed: December 29, 2018).

Center for the Study of Developing Societies. (1996). *National Election Studies 1996.* Available at: http://www.lokniti.org/media/PDF-upload/1536126469_69559400_download_report.pdf (last accessed: December 28, 2018).

Chasin, Barbara H., & Franke, Richard W. (1991, October 24). The Kerala difference. *New York Review of Books 38.*

Charnysh, Volha, Lucas, Christopher, & Singh, Prerna. (2014). The ties that bind: National identity salience and pro-social behavior toward the ethnic other. *Comparative Political Studies 48*(3), 267–300.

Cherian, P. J., & Hemachandran, S. (Eds.). (1999). *Perspectives on Kerala history: The second millennium.* Trivandrum, India: Kerala Gazetteers, Government of Kerala.

Chhibber, Pradeep, & Nooruddin, Irfan. (2004). Do party systems count? The number of parties and government performance in the Indian states. *Comparative Political Studies 37*(2), 152–187.

Chiriyankandath, James. (1993). Communities at the polls: Electoral politics and the mobilization of communal groups in Travancore. *Modern Asian Studies 27*(3), 643–665.

Cleary, Matthew R. (2007). Electoral competition, participation, and government responsiveness in Mexico. *American Journal of Political Science 51*(2), 283–299.

Colley, Linda. (2005). *Britons: Forging the nation, 1707–1837.* New Haven, CT: Yale University Press.

Communist Party of India. (1954). *Memorandum submitted to the States Reorganization Commission National Archives of India.* File no. 25/13/54-SRC. New Delhi, India: National Archives of India.

Connor, Walker. (1993). *Ethnonationalism: The quest for understanding.* Princeton, NJ: Princeton University Press.

Crooks, George R. (1897). *The story of the Christian church.* New York, NY: Eaton & Mains.

Das Gupta, Jyotirindra, & Fishman, Joshua A. (1971). Inter-state Migration and Subsidiary-Language Claiming: An Analysis of Selected Indian Census Data. *International Migration Review 5*(2), 227–249.

Datt, Gaurav, & Ravallion, Martian. *Why have some Indian states done better than others at reducing rural poverty?* World Bank Policy Research Paper number 1594. Available at: https://elibrary.worldbank.org/doi/abs/10.1596/1813-9450-1594 (last accessed: December 28, 2018).

De Cremer, David, & Van Vugt, Mark. (1999). Social identification effects in social dilemmas: A transformation of motives. *European Journal of Social Psychology 29*(7), 871–893.

Desai, Manali. (2005). Indirect British rule, state formation, and welfarism in Kerala, India, 1860–1957. *Social Science History 29*(3), 457–488.

Deutsch, Karl Wolfgang. (1966). *Nationalism and social communication: An inquiry into the foundations of nationality.* Cambridge, MA: MIT Press.

Devika, J. (2002, October). *Domesticating Malayalees: Family planning, the nation and home-centered anxieties in mid-20th century Keralam.* CDS Working Paper, no. 340, presented at a Center for Development Studies seminar, Thiruvananthapuram, India.

Dovidio, John F., & Gaertner, Samuel S. (1999). Reducing prejudice: Combating intergroup biases. *Current Directions in Psychological Science 8*(4), 101–105.

Drèze, Jean, & Gazdar, Haris. (1997). Uttar Pradesh: The burden of inertia. In Jean Drèze & Amartya Sen (Eds.), *Indian development: Selected regional perspectives*, pp. 33–128. Oxford, England: Oxford University Press.

Drèze, Jean, & Sen, Amartya (Eds). (1996). *India: Economic development and social opportunity.* Oxford, England: Oxford University Press.

Drèze, Jean, & Sen, Amartya (Eds). (2002). *India: Development and participation.* Oxford, England: Oxford University Press,

Dunn, John. (1979). *Western political theory in the face of the future.* Cambridge, England: Cambridge University Press.

Esping-Andersen, Gøsta. (1987). Citizenship and socialism: De-commodification and solidarity in the welfare state. In Martin Rein, Gøsta Esping-Andersen, & Lee Rainwater (Eds.), *Stagnation and renewal in social policy: The rise and fall of policy regimes: workshop: papers.* Armonk, NY: M. E. Sharpe.

Esping-Andersen, Gøsta. (1990). *The three worlds of welfare capitalism.* Princeton, NJ: Princeton University Press.

Fantasia, Rick. (1989). *Cultures of solidarity: Consciousness, action, and contemporary American workers.* Berkeley: University of California Press.

Fic, Victor M. (1970). *Kerala: Yenan of India.* Bombay, India: Nachiketa Publications.

Forrest, Joshua. (2004). *Subnationalism in Africa: Ethnicity, alliances, and politics.* Boulder, CO: Lynne Rienner Publishers.

Franke, Richard W., & Chasin, Barbara H. (1997). Power to the Malayalee people. *Economic and Political Weekly 32*(48), 3061–3068.

Franke, Richard W., & Chasin, Barbara H. (1989). Kerala: Radical reform as development in an Indian state. *Food First Development Report*, no. 6. San Francisco, CA: Institute for Food and Development Policy.

Furniss, Norman, & Tilton, Timothy Alan. (1977). *The case for the welfare state: From social security to social equality.* Bloomington: Indiana University Press.

Geertz, Clifford. (1973). *The interpretation of cultures: Selected essays.* New York, NY: Basic Books.

Gellner, Ernest. (1983). *Nations and nationalism.* Oxford, England: Blackwell Publishing Ltd.

Gerring, John, & Thacker, Strom C. (2008). *A centripetal theory of democratic governance.* New York, NY: Cambridge University Press.

Gerring, John, Thacker, Strom C., & Alfaro, Rodrigo. (2012). Democracy and human development. *Journal of Politics 74*(1), 1–17.

Gerring, John, Thacker, Strom C., Lu, Yuan & Huang, Wei. (2014). Does diversity impair human development? A multiple-level test of the diversity debit hypothesis. *World Development 66*, 166–188.

Gibson, James L., & Gouws, Amanda. (2005). *Overcoming intolerance in South Africa: Experiments in democratic persuasion.* New York, NY: Cambridge University Press.

Gladstone, John Wilson. (1984). *Protestant Christianity and people's movements in Kerala: A study of Christian mass movements in relation to neo-Hindu socio-religious movements in Kerala, 1850–1936.* Trivandrum, India: Seminary Publications.

Glennerster, Rachel, Miguel, Edward, & Rothenberg, Alexander D. (2013). Collective action in diverse Sierra Leone communities. *Economic Journal 123*(568), 285–316.

Goertz, Gary. (2005). *Social science concepts: A user's guide.* Princeton, NJ: Princeton University Press.

Gough, Kathleen. (1974). Indian peasant uprisings. *Economic and Political Weekly 9* (32/34), 1391–1412.

Guibernau, Montserrat. (2008). *The identity of nations.* Cambridge, England: Polity.

Habyarimana, James, Humphreys, Macartan, Posner, Daniel N., & Weinstein, Jeremy M. (2007). Why does ethnic diversity undermine public goods provision? *American Political Science Review 101*(4): 709–725.

Harrison, Selig S. (1960). *India: The most dangerous decades.* Princeton, NJ: Princeton University Press.

Hasan, Zoya. (1996). Communal mobilization and changing majority in Uttar Pradesh. In David Ludden (ed.), *Contesting the nation: Religion, community, and the politics of democracy in India*, pp. 81–97. Philadelphia: University of Pennsylvania Press.

Hayek, Friedrich. (1960). The constitution of liberty. South Bend, IN: Gateway Editions Ltd.

Heclo, H. Hugh. (1972). Review article: Policy analysis. *British Journal of Political Science 2*(1), 83–108.

Heller, Patrick. (1996). Social capital as a product of class mobilization and state intervention: Industrial workers in Kerala, India. *World Development 24*(6), 1055–1071.

Heller, Patrick. (2000). Degrees of democracy: Some comparative lessons from India. *World Politics 52*(4), 484–519.

Heller, Patrick. (2005). Reinventing public power in the age of globalization: Decentralization and the transformation of movement politics in Kerala. In Raka Ray & Mary Fainsod Katzenstein (Eds.), *Social movements in India: Poverty, power, and politics.* Lanham, MD: Rowman & Littlefield Publishers.

Herring, Ronald J. (1983). *Land to the tiller: The political economy of agrarian reform in South Asia.* New Haven, CT: Yale University Press.

Herring, Ronald J. (1991). From structural conflict to agrarian stalemate: Agrarian reforms in South India. *Journal of Asian and African Studies 26*(3–4), 169–188.

Hibbs, Douglas A. (1977). Political parties and macroeconomic policy. *American Political Science Review 71*(4), 1467–1487.

His Majesty's Secretary of State for India in Council. (1908). *Imperial Gazetteer of India.* Oxford, England: Clarendon Press.

Hiskey, Jonathan T., & Seligson, Mitchell A. (2003). Pitfalls of power to the people: Decentralization, local government performance, and system support in Bolivia. *Studies in Comparative International Development 37*(4), 64–88.

Hobsbawm, Eric. (1992). *Nations and nationalism since 1780: Programme, myth, reality.* Cambridge, England: Cambridge University Press.

Horowitz, Donald L. (1985). *Ethnic groups in conflict.* Berkeley: University of California Press.

Hroch, Miroslav. (1995). National self-determination from a historical perspective. *Canadian Slavonic Papers/Revue Canadienne des Slavistes 37*(3/4), 283–299.

Huber, Evelyne, Ragin, Charles, & Stephens, John D. (1993). Social democracy, Christian democracy, constitutional structure, and the welfare state. *American Journal of Sociology 99*(3), 711–749.

Huddy, Leonie, & Khatib, Nadia. (2007). American patriotism, national identity, and political involvement. *American Journal of Political Science 51*(1), 63–77.

Huntington, Samuel P. (1996). *The clash of civilizations and the remaking of world order.* Haryana, India: Penguin Books India.

Immergut, Ellen M. (1992). *Health politics: Interests and institutions in Western Europe.* New York, NY: Cambridge University Press.

India Reorganization Commission. (1955). *Report of the States Reorganization Commission, 1955.* New Delhi, India: Government of India Press.

Jayal, Niraja Gopal. (2013). India's minority leaders. In Atul Kohli & Prerna Singh (Eds.), *Routledge handbook of Indian politics*, pp. 62–68. Abingdon, England: Routledge.

Jeffrey, Robin. (1976). *The decline of Nayar dominance: Society and politics in Travancore, 1847–1908.* New York, NY: Holmes & Meier Publishers.

John, Oommen. (1992). Political instability in Kerala: An analysis. *Indian Journal of Political Science 53*(4), 524–535.

Johnston, Richard, Banting, Keith, Kymlicka, Will, & Soroka, Stuart. (2010). National identity and support for the welfare state. *Canadian Journal of Political Science 43*(2), 349–377.

Joshi, Kashinath Laxman. (1977). *Problems of higher education in India: An approach to structural analysis and reorganization.* Bombay, India: Popular Prakashan.

Kawashima, Koji. (1998). *Missionaries and a Hindu state: Travancore, 1858–1936.* New York, NY: Oxford University Press.

Keating, Michael. (2009). Social citizenship, solidarity and welfare in regionalized and plurinational states. *Citizenship Studies 13*(5), 501–513.

Kedourie, Elie. (1993). *Nationalism*, 4th ed. Hoboken, NJ: Wiley-Blackwell.

Key, V. O. (1949). *Southern politics in state and nation.* Knoxville: University of Tennessee Press.

Kincaid, John, Moreno, Louis, & Colino, Cesar (Eds.). (2010). *Diversity and unity in federal countries.* A Global Dialogue on Federalism Series, vol. 7. Montreal, Canada: McGill-Queen's Press.

Kingdon, John W. (1984). *Agendas, alternatives, and public policies.* Boston, MA: Little, Brown.

Kohli, Atul. (1987). *The state and poverty in India: The politics of reform.* New York, NY: Cambridge University Press.

Kohli, Atul. (2001). *The success of India's democracy.* Cambridge, England: Cambridge University Press.

Korpi, Walter. (1983). *The democratic class struggle.* Boston, MA: Routledge & Kegan Paul.

Koshy, M. J. (1972). *Genesis of political consciousness in Kerala.* Trivandrum, India: Kerala Historical Society.

Kramer, Roderick M., & Brewer, Marilynn B. (1984). Effects of group identity on resource use in a simulated commons dilemma. *Journal of Personality and Social Psychology 46*(5), 1044–1057.

Kudaisya, Gyanesh. (2007). Constructing the "heartland": Uttar Pradesh in India's body-politic. In Sudha Pai (Ed.), *Political process in Uttar Pradesh: Identity, economic reforms, and governance*, pp. 1–31. Essex, England: Pearson Longman.

Laitin, David D., Petersen, Roger, & Slocum, John W. (1992). Language and the State: Russia and the Soviet Union in comparative perspective. In Alexander J. Motyl (Ed.), *Thinking theoretically about Soviet nationalities: History and comparison in the study of the USSR*, pp. 129–68. New York, NY: Columbia University Press.

Lake, David A., & Baum, Matthew A. (2001). The invisible hand of democracy: Political control and the provision of public services. *Comparative Political Studies 34*(6), 587–621.

Lange, Matthew, Mahoney, James, & Vom Hau, Matthias. Colonialism and development: A comparative analysis of Spanish and British colonies. *American Journal of Sociology 111*(5), 1412–1462.

La Porta, Rafael, Lopez-de-Silanes, Florencio, Shleifer, Andrei, & Vishny, Robert W. (1998). Law and finance. *Journal of Political Economy 106*(6), 1113–1155.

Levi-Faur, David. (1997). Friedrich List and the political economy of the nation-state. *Review of International Political Economy 4*(1), 154–178.

Lieberman, Evan S. (2005). Nested analysis as a mixed-method strategy for comparative research. *American Political Science Review 99*(3), 435–452.

List, Friedrich. ([1841] 1885). *The national system of political economy*. Trans. Sampson S. Lloyd. London, England: Longmann, Green, and Company.

India Parliament, Lok Sabha. (1956). *Lok Sabha debates on the Report of the States Reorganisation Commission, 14th December to 23rd December, 1955*. New Delhi, India: Lok Sabha Secretariat.

Mahoney, James. (2010). *Colonialism and postcolonial development: Spanish America in comparative perspective*. Cambridge, England: Cambridge University Press.

Masaldan, Prakash Narain. (1967). Politics in Uttar Pradesh since 1947. In Iqbal Narain (Ed.), *State politics in India*, pp. 273–285. Meerut, India: Meenakshi Prakashan.

Mason, Andrew. (2000). *Community, solidarity, and belonging: Levels of community and their normative significance*. New York, NY: Cambridge University Press.

Mathew, E. T. (1999). Growth of literacy in Kerala: State intervention, missionary initiatives and social movements. *Economic and Political Weekly 34*(39), 2811–2820.

McEwen, Nicola, & Parry, Richard. (2005). Devolution and the preservation of the United Kingdom welfare state. In Nicola McEwen & Luis Moreno (Eds.), *The territorial politics of welfare*, pp. 41–61. New York, NY: Routledge.

McQuoid, Alexander. (n.d.). *Does diversity divide? Public goods provision and soviet emigration to Israel*. Manuscript. Department of Economics, Columbia University.

Mehrotra, Santosh. (2007). Intersections between caste, health and education: Why Uttar Pradesh is not like Tamil Nadu. In Sudha Pai (Ed.), *Political process in Uttar Pradesh: Identity, economic reforms, and governance*, pp. 367–403. Essex, England: Pearson Longman.

Mehrotra, Santosh, & Panchamukhi, Parthasarthi R. (2006). Private provision of elementary education in India: Findings of a survey in eight states. *Compare: A Journal of Comparative and International Education 36*(4), 421–442.

Meier, Stephan. (2006). *A survey of economic theories and field evidence on pro-social behaviour*. FRB of Boston Working Paper No. 06–6.

Mencher, Joan P. (1980). The lessons and non-lessons of Kerala: Agricultural labourers and poverty. *Economic and Political Weekly 15*(41/43), 1781–1802.

Miguel, Edward. (2004). Tribe or nation? Nation building and public goods in Kenya versus Tanzania. *World Politics 56*(3), 327–362.

Miguel, Edward, & Gugerty, Mary Kay. (2005). Ethnic diversity, social sanctions, and public goods in Kenya. *Journal of Public Economics 89*(11–12), 2325–2368.

Mill, John Stuart. ([1861] 2004). *Considerations on Representative Government*. Available at: http://www.gutenberg.org/files/5669/5669-h/5669-h.htm (last accessed: December 28, 2018).

Miller, David. (1995). *On nationality*. Oxford, England: Oxford University Press.

Mirza, Rinchan Ali. (n.d.). *Occupation, diversity and public goods: Evidence from Pakistan through partition*. (Unpublished doctoral dissertation). University of Oxford.

Moreno, Luis, & McEwen, Nicola. (2005). Exploring the territorial politics of welfare. In Nicola McEwan & Luis Moreno (Eds.), *The territorial politics of welfare*, pp. 1–40. New York, NY: Routledge.

Nag, Moni. (1989). Political awareness as a factor in accessibility of health services: A case study of rural Kerala and West Bengal. *Economic and Political Weekly 24*(8), 417–426.

Nair, K. V. S. (1954). Memorandum submitted to the States Reorganization Commission. File no. 25/13/54-SRC. New Delhi, India: National Archives of India.

Nossiter, T. J. (1982). *Communism in Kerala: A study in political adaptation*. Berkeley: University of California Press.

North, Douglass C. (2005). The contribution of the new institutional economics to an understanding of the transition problem. In UNU-WIDER (Ed.) *Wider perspectives on global development*, pp. 1–15. London, England: Palgrave Macmillan.

Olson, Mancur, Jr. (1965). *The logic of collective action: Public goods and the theory of groups*. Cambridge, MA: Harvard University Press.

Pai, Sudha. (2002). *Dalit assertion and the unfinished democratic revolution: The Bahujan Samaj party in Uttar Pradesh*. New Delhi, India: Sage Publications.

Pai, Sudha. (2007). *Political process in Uttar Pradesh: Identity, economic reforms, and governance*. New Delhi, India: Dorling Kindersley.

Pai, Sudha. (n.d.). Kanshi Ram: The Man and his Legacy. An Essay. EconPapers. Available at: http://econpapers.repec.org/paper/esswpaper/id_3a639.htm (last accessed: December 28, 2018).

Peters, E., Västfjäll, D., Gärling, T., & Slovic, P. (2006). Affect and decision making: A "hot" topic. *Journal of Behavioral Decision Making 19*(2), 79–85.

Pavkovic, Aleksandar. (2000). *The fragmentation of Yugoslavia: Nationalism and war in the Balkans*. Houndsmill: Macmillan.

Pocker Sahib, B., Uppi Sahib P., et al. (1954.). Memorandum submitted to the States Reorganization Commission. File no. 25/13/54-SRC. New Delhi, India: National Archives of India.

Pol, Louis G., & Thomas, Richard K. (2001). *The demography of health and health care*. Amsterdam: Springer Netherlands.

Rahn, Wendy M. (2004, September). *Feeling, thinking, being doing: Public mood, American national identity, and civic participation*. Paper presented at the annual meeting of the Midwest Political Science Association, Chicago, IL.

Ramachandran, V. K. (1997). On Kerala's development achievements. In Jean Drèze & Amartya Sen (Eds.), *Indian development: Selected regional perspectives*, pp. 205–356. Delhi, India: Oxford University Press.

Ramesh, Jairam. (1999). Future of Uttar Pradesh: Need for a new political mindset. *Economic and Political Weekly 34*(31), 2127–2131.

Renan, Ernest. (1990). What is a nation? Trans. Martin Thom. In Homi K. Bhabha (Ed.), *Nation and Narration*, p. 19. London, England: Routledge.

Robinson, Francis. (1975). *Separatism among Indian Muslims: The politics of the United Provinces' Muslims, 1860–1923.* London, England: Cambridge University Press.

Rothstein, Bo. (2011). *The quality of government: Corruption, social trust, and inequality in international perspective.* Chicago, IL: University of Chicago Press.

Rugh, Jacob S., & Trounstine, Jessica. (2011). The provision of local public goods in diverse communities: Analyzing municipal bond elections. *Journal of Politics 73*(4), 1038–1050.

Sachs, Natan. (2009, September 3–6). *Experimenting with identity: Islam, nationalism and ethnicity.* Paper presented at the annual meeting of the American Political Science Association, Toronto.

Sáez, Lawrence, & Sinha, Aseema. (2010). Political cycles, political institutions and public expenditure in India, 1980–2000. *British Journal of Political Science 40*(1), 91–113.

Saideman, Stephen M., & Ayres, R. William. (2008). *For kin or country: Xenophobia, nationalism, and war.* New York, NY: Columbia University Press.

Secretary of State for India in Council. (1908). *Imperial gazetteer of India*, vol. XXIV. Oxford, England: Clarendon Press.

Schrock-Jacobson, Gretchen. (2012). The violent consequences of the nation: Nationalism and the initiation of interstate war. *Journal of Conflict Resolution 56* (5), 825–852.

Shandra, John M., Nobles, Jenna, London, Bruce, & Williamson, John B. (2004). Dependency, democracy, and infant mortality: A quantitative, cross-national analysis of less developed countries. *Social Science & Medicine 59*(2), 321–333.

Shariff, Abusaleh, & Ghosh, P. K. (2000). Indian education scene and the public gap. *Economic and Political Weekly 35*(16), 1396–1406.

Sharma, Phool Kumar. (1969). *Political aspects of states reorganization in India.* New Delhi, India: Mohuni Publications.

Shayo, Moses. (2009). A model of social identity with an application to political economy: Nation, class, and redistribution. *American Political Science Review 103* (2), 147–174.

Singh, D. Bright. (1944). *Financial developments in Travancore (1800–1940, AD).* (Doctoral dissertation). University of Kerala.

Singh, Prerna. (2011). We-ness and welfare: A longitudinal analysis of social development in Kerala, India. *World Development 39*(2), 282–293.

Singh, Prerna. (2015a). Supplementary material. Available at: https://www.cambridge .org/core/journals/world-politics/article/subnationalism-and-social-development-a-comparative-analysis-of-indian-states/996C8B2099C9E8C5E4679565BEA35D87 #fndtn-supplementary-materials (last accessed December 29, 2018).

Singh, Prerna. (2015b). *How solidarity works for welfare: Subnationalism and social development in India.* New York, NY: Cambridge University Press.

Singh, Prerna. (2017). The theoretical potential of the within-nation comparison: How sub-national analyses can enrich our understandings of the national welfare state. *American Behavioral Scientist 61*(8), 861–886.

Singh, Prerna, & vom Hau, Matthias. (2014). The ethnic diversity and public goods provision hypothesis revisited: Exploring the effects of ethnicity on state capacity. In Badru Bukenya, Sam Hickey, and Kunal Sen (Eds.), *The politics of inclusive development: Interrogating the evidence*. Oxford, England: Oxford University Press.

Sinha, A. (1995). Village Visit Reports. Compendium of selected field reports of the 60th foundational course. Lal Bahadur Shastri National Academy of Administration.

Sinnott, Richard. (2006). An evaluation of the measurement of national, subnational and supranational identity in crossnational surveys. *International Journal of Public Opinion Research 18*(2), 211–223.

Smith, Anthony D. (1991). *National identity*. Reno: University of Nevada Press.

Snyder, Jack L. (2000). *From voting to violence: Democratization and nationalist conflict*. New York, NY: W. W. Norton & Company.

Snyder, Richard. (2001). Scaling down: The subnational comparative method. *Studies in Comparative International Development 36*, 93–110.

Srivastava, R. S. (2007). Economic change among social groups in Uttar Pradesh, 1983–2000. In Sudha Pai (Ed.), *Political process in Uttar Pradesh: Identity, economic reforms, and governance*. Essex, England: Pearson Longman.

States Reorganization Commission. (1955). *Report of States Reorganization Commission*. Delhi, India: Manager of Publications.

Stepan, Alfred, Linz, Juan J., & Yogendra, Yadav. (2011). *Crafting state-nations: India and other multinational democracies*. Baltimore, MD: Johns Hopkins University Press.

Tajfel, Henri, & Turner, John C. (1985). The social identity theory of inter-group behavior. In Stephen Worchel & William G. Austin (Eds.), *Psychology of intergroup relations*, pp. 7-24. Chicago, IL: Nelson Hall.

Tamir, Yael. (1993). *Liberal nationalism*. Princeton, NJ: Princeton University Press.

Taylor-Gooby, Peter. (2008). The new welfare state settlement in Europe. *European Societies 10*(1), 3–24.

Tharakan, P. K. Michael. (1984). Socio-economic factors in educational development: Case of nineteenth century Travancore. *Economic and Political Weekly 19*(46), 1959–1967.

Thompson, Edward Palmer. (1963). *The making of the English working class*. New York, NY: Vintage Books.

Tiwari, Badri Narayan. (2007). BJP's political strategies: Development, caste and electoral discourse. In Sudha Pai (Ed.), *Political process in Uttar Pradesh: Identity, economic reforms, and governance*. Essex, England: Pearson Longman.

Transue, John E. (2007). Identity salience, identity acceptance, and racial policy attitudes: American national identity as a uniting force. *American Journal of Political Science 51*(1), 78–91.

Tyler, Tom R., & Smith, Heather J. (1999). Justice, social identity, and group processes. In Tom R. Tyler, Roderick M. Kramer, & Oliver P. John (Eds.), *The psychology of the social self*, pp. 223–264. Mahwah, NJ: Lawrence Erlbaum Associates, Inc.

Varma, Uma. (1994). *Uttar Pradesh state gazetteer*. Uttar Pradesh, India: Government of Uttar Pradesh Department of District Gazetteers.

Varshney, Ashutosh. (1998). *Democracy, development, and the countryside: Urban–rural struggles in India*. Cambridge, England: Cambridge University Press.

Venugopal, P. (2006, November 3). State up against new challenges. *Hindu.*

von Herder, Johann Gottfried. (2002). *Herder: Philosophical writings.* Trans. Michael N. Forster. Cambridge, England: Cambridge University Press.

Weber, Eugen. (1976). *Peasants into Frenchmen: The modernization of rural France, 1870–1914.* Redwood City, CA: Stanford University Press.

Weber, Max. (1946). *From Max Weber: Essays in sociology.* Trans. H. H. Gerth & Charles Wright Mills. Abingdon, England: Routledge.

Wilensky, Harold L. (1975). *The welfare state and equality: Structural and ideological roots of public expenditures.* Berkeley, CA: University of California Press.

Wilkinson, Steven I. (2008). Which group identities lead to most violence? Evidence from India. In Stathis N. Kalyvas, Ian Shapiro, & Tarek Masoud (Eds.), *Order, conflict, and violence*, pp. 271–300. New York, NY: Cambridge University Press.

Wimmer, Andreas. (2013, October). *State formation, political development and nation building.* Paper presented at a workshop on ethnicity and state capacity. Weatherhead Center for International Affairs and the Harvard Academy for International and Area Studies, Harvard University, Boston, MA.

Windmiller, Marshall. (1954). Linguistic regionalism in India. *Pacific Affairs* 27(4), 291–318.

Wynad Taluk, A. K. C. (1954). Memorandum submitted to the states reorganization commission. File no. 25/13/54-SRC. 2. New Delhi, India: National Archives of India.

Zerinini-Brotel, Jasmine. (1998). The BJP in Uttar Pradesh: From Hindutva to consensual politics? In Thomas Blom Hansen & Christophe Jaffrelot (Eds.), *The BJP and the compulsions of politics in India*, pp. 72–100. Oxford, England: Oxford University Press.

9

Indigenous Welfare, Tribal Homelands, and the Impact of Civil Society Organizations

A Subnational Analysis of Federal India

Sunila S. Kale
Nimah Mazaheri

As the historian Ramachandra Guha wrote on the 60th anniversary of India's independence, India's indigenous communities have "gained least and lost most from six decades of democracy and development " (2007, Abstract). In India, indigenous communities – called *adivasi* (original inhabitants) in Hindi and designated as Scheduled Tribes (STs) by the government – make up 8.6 percent of the total population. Since Indian independence in 1947, the central government has enacted a variety of measures to protect and advance the rights of STs.[1] For instance, the Indian Constitution reserves seats for STs in federal and state elected bodies as well as educational institutions. For many decades, the central government has earmarked various kinds of funds to distribute to state governments specifically for ST welfare and development. More recently, the Forest Rights Act of 2006 was enacted to protect property and customary rights of indigenous communities to forest lands. Still, despite these efforts, it is undeniable that indigenous communities on the whole have been left out of most of India's economic and political advances in the postcolonial era, and progress in terms of welfare has been uneven across India. Why is this so?

To answer this question, it is essential to adopt a subnational perspective. Although India's central government plays an important role in enacting protective legislation and earmarking funds for ST welfare, it is state governments that implement and administer these policies within their territories. Furthermore, since *adivasis* are unevenly distributed across Indian states, only a subnational focus can address how variation in government programs impacts ST welfare. This chapter seeks to describe and explain the variation across Indian states with respect to implementation of policies designed to benefit ST welfare and rights. We examine four mainland Indian states with very high percentages of STs – Chhattisgarh, Jharkhand, Madhya Pradesh, and

---

[1] We use the terms indigenous, *adivasi*, tribal, and Scheduled Tribe or ST interchangeably throughout this chapter. In Indian public and governmental discussion, the terms *adivasi*, tribal, and ST are used more commonly.

Odisha (formerly Orissa) – and focus on developments since the year 2000 (Table 9.1 displays the Scheduled Tribe populations across India's states as of 2011, the year of the last full census).[2] These states share a wide range of demographic, political, and socioeconomic factors that facilitate our ability to make subnational comparisons and isolate causal variables.

Our strategy here can be considered as an example of the "freestanding units" approach in that we treat our cases as causally independent in terms of the welfare outcomes that we seek to measure.[3] Adopting this strategy is facilitated by the fact that a higher-level variable, such as Indian national policymaking, is less relevant during our period of analysis because India entered an era of competitive federalism starting in the early 1990s. Since then, state governments have adopted individually tailored approaches to local development and social welfare, and likewise civil society must react and respond to the programs and policies that state governments implement and administer.

Among the states with a high percentage of STs, two of them – Chhattisgarh and Jharkhand – are especially amenable to a subnational paired comparison because they were created simultaneously by an act of parliament in November 2000 that redrew federal boundaries. In both states, STs make up a very high share of the population (31 percent in Chhattisgarh and 26 percent in Jharkhand), but, of the two, only Jharkhand was intentionally created as a "tribal homeland." From the standpoint of existing theories about social demography and public goods, we would thus expect Jharkhand to be a "most likely case" for improvements in ST rights and welfare. In fact, we find that Jharkhand has performed worse than Chhattisgarh in many areas of ST rights and welfare. Furthermore, Jharkhand fares poorly relative to Odisha and Madhya Pradesh, states with smaller percentages of STs and origins that are not rooted in tribal movements.

Our analysis focuses on two measures of ST rights and welfare as our dependent variable: the allocation of funds and implementation of programs meant to benefit ST populations; and the implementation of the FRA, a law designed to secure property rights for "traditional forest dwellers," the vast majority of whom are indigenous communities. To explain the variation among these four states, we hone in on differences in the vibrancy of civil society organizations (CSOs) as our key independent variable. We argue that the role of CSOs is a better predictor of a state's attention to the needs and rights of tribal communities than other presumably more important factors, such as

---

[2] We focus on mainland India and leave out a discussion of India's northeast, where Scheduled Tribe populations are in some cases substantially larger. Physically linked to India by a narrow strip of land, the political history and sociological profile of India's seven northeastern states is distinct from other parts of India, particularly in how communities have been classified by the government. Differences between the northeast and the rest of India have become more pronounced over time, especially after several decades of insurgency and the active presence of the Indian military. On politics and insurgency in the northeast, see Baruah (2007).

[3] For a full typology of subnational research design, see the introductory chapter to this volume.

TABLE 9.1 *Total Population and Scheduled Tribe Population across India's States as of 2011*

State	Total Pop.	ST Pop.	% ST Pop.
Lakshadweep	64,473	61,120	95%
Mizoram	1,097,206	1,036,115	94%
Nagaland	1,978,502	1,710,973	86%
Meghalaya	2,966,889	2,555,861	86%
Arunachal Pradesh	1,383,727	951,821	69%
Dadra & Nagar Haveli	343,709	178,564	52%
Manipur	2,855,794	1,167,422	41%
Sikkim	610,577	206,360	34%
Tripura	3,673,917	1,166,813	32%
Chhattisgarh	25,545,198	7,822,902	31%
Jharkhand	32,988,134	8,645,042	26%
Odisha	41,974,218	9,590,756	23%
Madhya Pradesh	72,626,809	15,316,784	21%
Gujarat	60,439,692	8,917,174	15%
Rajasthan	68,548,437	9,238,534	13%
Assam	31,205,576	3,884,371	12%
Jammu & Kashmir	12,541,302	1,493,299	12%
Goa	1,458,545	149,275	10%
Maharashtra	112,374,333	10,510,213	9%
Andaman & Nicobar Isl.	380,581	28,530	7%
Andhra Pradesh	84,580,777	5,918,073	7%
Karnataka	61,095,297	4,248,987	7%
Daman & Diu	243,247	15,363	6%
West Bengal	91,276,115	5,296,953	6%
Himachal Pradesh	6,864,602	392,126	6%
Uttarakhand	10,086,292	291,903	3%
Kerala	33,406,061	484,839	1%
Bihar	104,099,452	1,336,573	1%
Tamil Nadu	72,147,030	794,697	1%
Uttar Pradesh	199,812,341	1,134,273	1%
Chandigarh	1,055,450	0	–
Delhi	16,787,941	0	–
Haryana	25,351,462	0	–
Puducherry	1,247,953	0	–
Punjab	27,743,338	0	–
India	1,210,854,977	104,545,716	8.6%

Source: Census of India, 2011.

subnational identity and social homogeneity. We gather evidence from a variety of central and state government reports and databases, media accounts, and reports from nongovernmental organizations. Interviews conducted in Odisha allow us to flesh out the causal mechanisms that link CSOs, the government, and welfare outcomes.

Our chapter is organized as follows: Section 9.1 connects our study to the larger literatures on social heterogeneity, public goods, and support for welfare programs, highlighting the important contribution that the method of subnational comparative analysis can bring to these bodies of work. Section 9.2 outlines our justification for case selection. In Sections 9.3 and 9.4, we discuss our empirical measures of ST welfare and development and tie these to a discussion of how CSOs facilitate better outcomes. The chapter concludes by pointing to future directions of research.

9.1   EMPIRICAL PUZZLE AND THE VALUE OF SUBNATIONAL COMPARISON

A large body of social science research aims to understand why the provision of public goods and services varies so dramatically from one place to the next. One prominent set of arguments focuses on the role played by social heterogeneity in producing variation in public goods provision. For example, based on subnational comparison of US cities and metropolitan areas, Alesina, Baqir, and Easterly (1999) find that greater levels of social heterogeneity are linked to reduced spending on public goods, either because such heterogeneity makes collective action less likely or because there is less likely to be consensus around preferences for public goods. The importance of a common identity for the support for collective goods has also been demonstrated to be relevant in the Indian context (Singh, 2015).[4] A distinct but topically related literature looks at the relationship between welfare provision and social diversity. Here the focus is not on public goods per se but on the willingness of the larger population to support redistributive policies that benefit specific populations. According to one set of arguments, higher levels of social diversity make welfare funding less likely. This argument has been used to explain the gap in welfare provision between the United States, with its high levels of social heterogeneity, and Europe, with its relatively more homogenous populations (Alesina, Glaeser, & Sacerdote, 2001; however, see Habyarimana et al., 2007).

---

[4] Singh (Chapter 8 in this volume) suggests that the causal links between subnational identity formation and welfare provision emerge out of long-range historical developments of cohesive collective identity formation. Given Singh's argument and findings based on Kerala, we might expect to see the effects of Jharkhand's identity as an indigenous homeland coming to bear in the future. It is also the case that Singh's argument about collective identity and our argument about the significance of civil society actors are not mutually exclusive. Rather, the "we-ness" that Singh references may be materialized in the kinds of civil society networks that we show to be significant in implementing welfare policies.

We show that a subnational comparative analysis in India represents a useful terrain in which to examine the argument that social makeup and social identity condition welfare provision. Subnational comparison of India's political units offers several advantages. The first stems from the distinct way that subnational political boundaries are created. Most often, changes to national-level social composition are either the result of long-standing conflict or longer-run historical processes of migration or demographic change. In the former case, during the twentieth and twenty-first centuries, this conflict has taken the form of civil conflicts, anti-colonial agitations, or often a combination of the two that could themselves have an independent impact on the capacity of states to build welfare programs as well as the willingness of populations to support such programs.

Alternately, social composition might change because of longer-run processes of migration, emigration, and demographic change. In recent decades, scholars of European welfare states have focused on the effects of migration on the support and funding for welfare programs, fearing that such migration will fray the social contract upon which these programs were first based (Mau & Burkhardt, 2009). But such migration and emigration are often produced and propelled by other forces, like economic growth or decline, that could have an independent effect on welfare provision.

By addressing this question at the subnational level, we add a third potential way in which jurisdictional boundaries and social demography change. In federal systems, redrawing internal boundaries tends to be employed as a solution to political conflict. Furthermore, it is a solution that happens in an instant rather than playing out over a long time period, as is the case with migration-induced changes to social demography or long-standing civil conflicts that may end in shifts to political boundaries. Situating our research in the Indian context at the subnational level is particularly useful since, although the central government designs most welfare measures, their implementation occurs at the subnational level.

As with changes to national populations, many of the major transformations in demographic composition at the subnational level (that are not associated with conflict) tend to occur over long periods of time. For instance, the movement of migrants in and out of regions over time can transform the social composition of states and thereby shape the government's commitment to redistribution. New identity formation can also affect composition, but this process is often the product of social and political forces that similarly emerge over longer stretches of time.[5] However, because the Indian Constitution makes it relatively easy (compared to other federal polities) to redraw internal

---

[5] The constructivist position on ethnicity (Chandra, 2004) emphasizes that identities are not fixed or primordial but rather are the product of social and political forces that may bring to the fore specific aspects or facets of ethnic identity at specific moments. For the most part, we consider these to be long-run processes. In the short run, ethnic identity can be considered reasonably stable, particularly in the context of the decade-long time period of the present study.

boundaries, India provides a propitious empirical context to study whether and how changing federal boundaries impacts the implementation of welfare programs that benefit certain communities.[6]

A final advantage of structuring our analysis as a subnational comparative one is that it leverages the geographic concentration that is a common demographic characteristic of indigenous communities.[7] Rather than a uniform spread of indigenous communities across national territories, there is pronounced geographic concentration that can overlap with subnational political jurisdictions or cut across them. This is true of indigenous communities in India, who tend disproportionately, although not exclusively, to live near or in forested lands and away from core urban areas and their hinterlands.[8] In India, therefore, a subnational comparative framing is necessary to understand why there is variation in indigenous rights and welfare.

Applied at the subnational level, the findings from the literatures on public goods and welfare states would predict the following: 1) in political jurisdictions that are more socially homogenous, there will be higher support for public goods, and 2) following Singh (2015), states that were formed on the basis of a clearly defined subnational identity will be more robust welfare states. Our analysis of Indian states with large indigenous populations does not support these hypotheses. Instead, we find that civil society organizations are an intervening variable that connects social identity to welfare outcomes. In the absence of a CSO sector that is well organized and has systematic links to the bureaucracy, even a state formed on the basis of a strongly articulated social identity will fail to advance a welfare agenda that benefits its indigenous citizens.

---

[6] Part I of the Indian Constitution empowers the federal government to admit new states, join existing states, and partition existing states to create new units by an act of parliament. While the central government is required to share any such proposal with the concerned state legislatures, there is no requirement for state-level consent. In other federal polities, as in the United States, there is an additional requirement that the concerned states agree to the proposed redrawing of boundaries.

[7] In some parts of the world, indigenous communities that had once been more geographically concentrated are now more diffusely settled after decades of urban migration. Such is the case in Latin America, where close to half of all indigenous people now live in urban areas. See World Bank (2015, pp. 29–43).

[8] Although just over 30 percent of India's total population resides in urban areas, the share of the ST population across urban India is only 10 percent. We do not mean to imply that India's *adivasis* have no relation to non-tribal communities; indeed there are commercial and political ties that have bound India's various sub-communities together over a long history. Furthermore, there is a current of debate among historians and anthropologists regarding whether the term "indigenous" is empirically appropriate in the Indian context, where centuries of migration into, out of, and across the subcontinent make it difficult to discern who authentically belongs to any one place. For a discussion, see Shah (2010, pp. 21–24). Nevertheless, because Scheduled Tribes are a government category – and one that, when compared to other social categories in India, fares poorly on most socioeconomic measures – we believe that understanding what produces spatial variation in government efforts to promote ST welfare and rights is an important undertaking.

In pointing to the role of CSOs to explain subnational variation in indigenous welfare and rights, we draw from and add to another prominent stream of literature on public goods that emphasizes the catalytic role played by non-state actors. For example, Ostrom (1996) compares Brazil and Nigeria to demonstrate that successful provision of public goods and services can be greatly enhanced when states actively encourage and make use of non-state actors, theorized as "co-production." Likewise, Evans (1996) conceptualizes state–society "synergy" as a form of cooperation that can facilitate diverse developmental goals, including the provision of public goods and welfare. Not all state–society interfaces are the same, nor do they have the same effects: Roy (2008) finds that CSOs that cross caste lines and have coherent political linkages are more effective in empowering marginalized groups. Other studies of public–private partnerships, such as Harriss (2006), warn that many of the most effective CSOs in urban India are also those that champion middle-class interests exclusively; in this case, successful coproduction has the potential to further entrench deep-seated caste- and class-based inequalities.

We observe considerable subnational variation in the extent to which state governments form links with CSOs in the context of the politics of indigenous rights in India. This variation has meaningful consequences for indigenous rights and welfare. First, we look at variables that measure the vibrancy of CSOs – how large and active the sector is – to show that there is significant subnational variation.[9] A final section provides a more detailed analysis of the implementation of one of India's most important indigenous rights measures – the Forest Rights Act – to show that what matters is not merely the vibrancy of civil society but also the extent of the linkages between government agencies, the bureaucracy, and CSOs. The most effective CSOs in our analysis are those with a statewide presence that have both nodes in the provincial capital and arms stretching to the local level, as this organizational form allows CSOs to serve as a kind of ligament connecting the sources of power and money in the state capital to intended beneficiaries in the districts. After describing the logic for our case selection in the next section, subsequent sections further develop and provide evidence for our argument.

9.2 CASE SELECTION

Our case selection helps control for several rival explanations for variation in indigenous welfare and public goods provision, the most prominent of which focus on social heterogeneity and the cohesion of subnational identity. In what follows we address this hypothesis, along with other potential explanations that

---

[9] This is in keeping with other scholarship that measures civil society vibrancy to explain political outcomes, such as Putnam (2000). For an example from the literature on ethnic conflict, see Varshney (2003).

hinge on income, state capacity, civil conflict (the armed Maoist movement), and political party ideology.

Our cases are two of the states newly created in 2000 with large percentages of STs – Chhattisgarh and Jharkhand – and two other states with large percentages of tribal communities, Madhya Pradesh and Odisha (see Map 9.1).

We focus on the time period after the creation of the new states in 2000 until 2017. Since little more than a decade and a half has elapsed since the creation of Chhattisgarh and Jharkhand, our time frame is too limited to reveal whether or not the implementation of policies has had a measurable effect on welfare. In our selection of empirical materials we are careful to evaluate evidence of *effective implementation* of welfare and rights policies, even if these have not directly translated into *material improvements* in welfare. The most recent data drawn for the study are from 2017. These four states are geographically contiguous and span the densely forested regions of eastern and central India. As we will show, they have a range of demographic, political, social, and economic features in common, which allows us to employ a "most similar" systems approach in a subnational research design.[10]

However, the states differ in two central ways: the origins and impetus for state formation; and the vibrancy of their civil societies. Our analysis demonstrates that the first factor – contrary to expectations – is not consequential in affecting the degree to which states implement programs to improve ST welfare and rights. Although movements for autonomy of indigenous communities are often predicated on the idea that having their own political jurisdiction will more effectively advance indigenous rights and welfare, the state that was created most explicitly as a tribal homeland – Jharkhand – does not outperform the other states in our analysis. On the contrary, along many measures Jharkhand severely underperforms.

Our selection of cases allows us to control for a number of other factors that might explain variation in the dependent variable. For instance, although many of the funds for welfare programs come from the central government, in some cases state governments are also expected to contribute funds, and in all cases state governments must contribute bureaucratic capacity. We might expect income, therefore, to be a good predictor of support for welfare and tribal rights, as wealthier states have more resources than poorer ones for supporting STs. Income is also directly related to levels of bureaucratic capacity. However, the per capita income for these four states was nearly the same in 1999–2000, and income growth since then has been similar, although Chhattisgarh has led the group.[11] All four states are routinely categorized as having lower levels of

---

[10] Despite the obvious advantages of comparative analysis of states in India, until recently the bulk of research on India has traditionally been a study of individual states (see Jenkins, 2004; Harriss, 1999, p. 3367).

[11] In 1999–2000, income per capita (at factor cost, constant prices) was 11,629 Rs in Chhattisgarh, 11,549 Rs in Jharkhand, 12,384 Rs in Madhya Pradesh, and 10,622 Rs in Odisha.

MAP 9.1 States in India Selected for Analysis

bureaucratic capacity than states with much more robust welfare outcomes, such as Kerala and Tamil Nadu. Similarities in income and bureaucratic capacity precede this period, as well, as these four states were together considered part of India's low-income, low-growth "BIMAROU" region.[12]

By 2016–2017, Chhattisgarh's per capita income grew 512 percent, Jharkhand's grew 369 percent, Madhya Pradesh's grew 319 percent, and Odisha's grew 481 percent. Data retrieved from Reserve Bank of India (http://www.rbi.org.in).

[12] The acronym BIMARU plays on the Hindi word for "sick" and refers to the states Bihar, Madhya Pradesh, Rajasthan, and Uttar Pradesh, with an additional "o" sometimes added to include Odisha.

They are likewise similar in terms of education levels and the extent of urbanization (low relative to other states) during the period of our analysis.[13]

Along with having roughly equal levels of development, the four states share a similar ecological profile. This is relevant because many STs live in forested areas and are dependent on forest resources for their livelihoods. While one might expect that states with more forest cover would devote more resources to maintaining these forests – thereby indirectly benefiting ST communities – we can rule out this factor given that the states are all close with respect to their share of forest cover and have similar proportions of "open," "very dense," and "moderate dense" forests.[14]

The four states have demographic features in common. As noted, they are the mainland Indian states with the highest share of STs in their populations. According to the 2011 Census, Chhattisgarh's population is 31 percent STs, Jharkhand's is 26 percent, Madhya Pradesh's is 21 percent, and Odisha's is 23 percent. The states have similar shares of "Scheduled Castes" (SCs), the people who are commonly referred to as "Dalits." According to the 2011 Census, Chhattisgarh's population is 13 percent SCs, Jharkhand's is 12 percent, Madhya Pradesh's is 16 percent, and Odisha's is 17 percent. They also have a similar percentage of "Other Backward Classes" (OBCs), another category of disadvantaged people in India. According to the National Sample Survey Organization, OBCs make up between 32 and 46 percent of each state's population (as cited in Singh et al., 2008, p. 5).

An important factor that shapes politics in this region is the "Naxalite movement," an ongoing violent conflict between the government and Maoist insurgent groups. Many *adivasis* are drawn to the Naxalite movement in part due to the government's failures to address the needs of indigenous communities. Thus, it may be that funding for STs is tied to a broader strategy from state governments to address Naxalism. However, we can rule out this factor because all four states have large ST populations as well as many "Naxal-affected districts," as defined by the Indian Planning Commission. If state policy decisions about STs are driven mainly by the imperative of dealing with Naxalism, we should not observe such wide variation among these states in the implementation of policies designed to benefit STs.

Finally, in explaining cross-state variation in the implementation of policies benefiting indigenous citizens, we can largely rule out political party affiliation,

[13] Per the 2011 Census, the literacy rate was 71 percent in Chhattisgarh, 68 percent in Jharkhand, 71 percent in Madhya Pradesh, and 73 percent in Odisha. The percentage of the population that resides in rural areas was 77 percent in Chhattisgarh, 73 percent in Jharkhand, 72 percent in Madhya Pradesh, and 83 percent in Odisha.

[14] As of 2011, the percentage of each state's geographic area under forest cover was 41 percent in Chhattisgarh, 29 percent in Jharkhand, 25 percent in Madhya Pradesh, and 31 percent in Odisha. The states have a similar proportion of open/very dense/moderate dense forests, although Chhattisgarh has a higher percentage of moderate dense forest (Government of India-Central Statistical Office, 2012).

which Kohli (1987) finds to be an important determinant of subnational development spending. During most of the time period since November 2000, these four states were ruled by, or had an alliance with, the same political party: the Bharatiya Janata Party (BJP). In Jharkhand, BJP-affiliated chief ministers have governed the state for 72 percent of the time since November 2000. Both Chhattisgarh and Madhya Pradesh have been governed by a BJP-affiliated chief minister for 82 percent of the time since November 2000.[15] Although Odisha's chief minister for the last 17-plus years, Naveen Patnaik, is leader of a different political party (the Biju Janata Dal), he had an alliance with the BJP until March 2009.[16]

Despite their many similarities, the four states differ in two crucial respects: the origins of state formation; and the vibrancy of civil society organizations. With respect to the first factor, the origins of Odisha and Madhya Pradesh lie in the years prior to or shortly following India's independence in 1947. By contrast, Chhattisgarh and Jharkhand were created in 2000. Why did the Indian government decide in 2000 to carve out these new states?[17] Although some suggested that this was in response to the electoral needs of national political parties or a way to satisfy the demands of industry, Tillin (2013) argues persuasively that a more complex combination of political and social factors was at play.

For the purposes of our study, it is critical to highlight that Jharkhand's origins were rooted in a clearly articulated demand for a tribal homeland, whereas Chhattisgarh's were not.[18] In Jharkhand, demands for independence emerged as far back as the 1920s via a tribal-based movement. According to Shah, the movement "initially revolved around the idea that the culturally autonomous indigenous people, or adivasis, were exploited and oppressed by the high-caste Hindu governments that had ruled them" (2010, p. 6). By contrast, no such tribal-based movement was at the heart of Chhattisgarh's independence. According to Tillin, "They [*adivasis*] were not behind the demand ... for [Chhattisgarh's] statehood and they have not been

---

[15] These figures are calculated as of September 20, 2017, and exclude periods of President's rule, a constitutional provision that allows the national parliament to suspend an elected state assembly when that body is deemed to have failed in its mandate to maintain stability and order.

[16] Given that federal–state dynamics affects fiscal transfers in India (Singh & Vasishtha, 2004), it might be argued that this factor explains why some states commit more to ST welfare than others. We argue that this is unlikely to be the case for two reasons. First, the period of analysis (post-2000) comes well after a period of major policy devolution during which states were granted more autonomous decision-making power. Second, many of the centrally sponsored programs for STs are supposed to tie funding levels to the size of a state's ST population, even if this is not always achieved in practice. The utilization and implementation of these funds, however, varies from state to state.

[17] Alongside Chhattisgarh and Jharkhand, another state (Uttarakhand) was made independent in November 2000.

[18] See Tillin (2013) for a comprehensive analysis of how multiple causes unfolded over time to shape the rise of three new states – Chhattisgarh, Jharkhand, and Uttarakhand – in India in 2000.

well represented in the administration of the new state" (2008). The case of Jharkhand is therefore important to our study because it is the only instance where social identity was central to state formation. If the positive relationship between increasingly homogenous and cohesive social identity and welfare predicted by the theories of Alesina, Glaeser, and Sacerdote (2001) and Singh (2015), among others, is true, we should find evidence for it in Jharkhand.

In Madhya Pradesh and Odisha, on the other hand, tribal identity is not central to subnational identity. Despite the reservations that ensure ST representation in the state assemblies, the tribal members of these states' political institutions have been more or less marginalized, consigned to playing junior roles in parties and governments dominated by upper-caste politicians. In Madhya Pradesh, one reason for this involves the overlap between current political constituencies and many of the region's historic princely states, which gives social ties from an older political order a continuing influence over the state's politics (Jaffrelot, 2008). In Odisha, by contrast, it is not princely ties but the upper-caste urban political elite that has maintained its political dominance since independence (Mohanty, 2014).

The four states also differ in terms of the vibrancy of civil society organizations and the extent to which these organizations center on issues that affect ST welfare. One way to measure the vibrancy of CSOs is to examine state-level data on voluntary organizations (VOs) and nongovernmental organizations (NGOs). A source of data on VOs/NGOs is the "NGO Partnership System" of the Government of India's National Institution for Transforming India (or "NITI Aayog," formerly the Indian Planning Commission), which was established to build links between the government and the voluntary sector.[19] According to the most recent data, Odisha has the strongest presence of VOs/NGOs on a per capita basis and Jharkhand has the weakest.[20] If we examine only organizations that indicate

---

[19] Any VO/NGO that is registered as a trust/society/private limited nonprofit company (not an individual) under section-25 of the Indian Companies Act (1956) can sign up with the NGO Partnership System (http://www.ngosindia.com/resources/ngo_registration1.php). Although the vast majority of Indian CSOs began as citizen-led initiatives, the role of the central and state government in sponsoring CSOs is certainly a factor that contributes to how many there are in a state. Since the 1990s, international funding for CSOs in India has gradually been withdrawn, while funding from the government, private corporations, and a variety of other sources has become more important. State governments also have increasingly relied on CSOs in service delivery for state-sponsored schemes and targeted projects. Yet, there are reports that competition among CSOs to manage these projects is fierce and that corruption distorts which CSOs are selected by the state (Goswami & Tandon, 2013). Thus, it appears that the actual number of CSOs in a state is substantially larger than the number of CSOs that directly emerge due to state funding opportunities.

[20] According to data available from NITI Aayog, as of September 20, 2017, the number of VOs/NGOs in each state is the following: 494 in Chhattisgarh, 520 in Jharkhand, 2,090 in Madhya Pradesh, and 1,522 in Odisha. This indicates that Odisha has the most VOs/NGOs per capita while Jharkhand has the least (data retrieved from http://ngodarpan.gov.in).

"Tribal Affairs" as a key issue, Odisha again tops the group and Chhattisgarh is at the bottom. Jharkhand and Madhya Pradesh lie in the middle and have similar levels of VO/NGO presence on tribal affairs.[21]

For our argument, it is not only the presence of CSOs but their active support from and integration with government agencies that is important. One way to measure this is to examine the value of state government grants for VOs/NGOs whose work focuses on improving the welfare of tribal communities. Here as well, Odisha is at the top of the group both in terms of total funds and when measured on the basis of funds granted per tribal individual in the state. From 2010–2011 to 2016–2017, the government in Odisha granted 26.75 crore Rs[22], as against 4.07 crore Rs in Chhattisgarh, 22.97 crore Rs in Jharkhand, and 6.02 crore Rs in Madhya Pradesh.[23]

Next, we describe the variation across two areas of ST welfare and rights: the implementation of programs meant to benefit ST populations and the implementation of the FRA. These two empirical areas serve different purposes for our overall argument. Our discussion of ST welfare challenges the expectation that a state created as a tribal homeland should do a better job administering tribal development and welfare programs. We find no evidence to support this prediction. Our analysis suggests that the relationship between a state's subnational "identity" and the implementation of welfare policy is not as straightforward as the literature implies but is mediated by civil society organizations whose vibrancy varies across states in India. To substantiate this, we focus on implementation of the FRA, which allows us to specify more precisely the mechanisms by which CSOs influence the implementation of welfare and rights initiatives that benefit India's tribal communities. The discussion focuses on the state that has most effectively implemented the FRA – Odisha – and briefly compares it with a state that has a worse record of implementation: Jharkhand.

9.3 THE IMPLEMENTATION OF INDIGENOUS WELFARE AND DEVELOPMENT POLICIES ACROSS INDIAN STATES

The existing literature leads us to expect that states with higher percentages of STs, Chhattisgarh and Jharkhand, are more likely to implement policies designed to benefit ST welfare and rights than the states with lower

[21] As of September 20, 2017, there is one VO/NGO with "Tribal Affairs" as a key issue for every 77,454 tribal individuals in Chhattisgarh, one for every 50,556 tribal individuals in Jharkhand, one for every 45,996 tribal individuals in Madhya Pradesh, and one for every 23,335 tribal individuals in Odisha (data retrieved from http://ngodarpan.gov.in).

[22] One crore is equal to 10 million in the South Asian numbering system. "Rs" is shorthand for Rupees.

[23] Ministry of Tribal Affairs Annual Report, various years; retrieved from https://www.tribal.nic.in/Statistics.aspx.

TABLE 9.2 *Rank of Performance (1=best, 4=worst) on Measures of ST Welfare and Development among Four Indian States*

Category	Chhattisgarh	Jharkhand	Madhya Pradesh	Odisha
SCA-TSP project on forest villages for STs	2	4	1	3
Article 275(1) grants-in-aid for ST welfare	2	3	4	1
Housing for STs (IAY)	1	3	4	2
Loan institutions for ST entrepreneurs (SGSY)	3	2	4	1
Value of Loans for ST entrepreneurs (SGSY)	2	4	3	1
Rural work for STs (MGNREGA)	2	3	4	1
Primary health centers in rural tribal areas	1	4	3	2
Primary health sub-centers in rural tribal areas	1	3	4	2
Community health centers in rural tribal areas	3	2	4	1
Funds for education of STs	2	3	4	1
Funds for improving literacy among female STs	3	4	2	1
Funds for residential schools in tribal areas	3	4	2	1
Number of residential schools sanctioned in tribal areas	3	4	1	2
Average Rank	**2.15**	**3.31**	**3.08**	**1.46**

percentages of STs, Madhya Pradesh and Odisha. Likewise, we would expect a state like Jharkhand, given its origins in a tribal movement, to be particularly centered on expanding ST welfare and rights. However, the evidence (discussed here and summarized in Table 9.2) sharply breaks with these expectations. Despite Jharkhand's origins as a tribal homeland, the state government has had comparatively little success in implementing programs designed to benefit ST welfare. In most areas of social policy targeting indigenous people, Jharkhand performs worse than Chhattisgarh and worse than the two older states, Madhya Pradesh and Odisha. Another consistent pattern is that the older states with lower percentages of STs, Madhya Pradesh and Odisha, tend to perform better than, or just as well as, the newer states with higher percentages of STs. Between the two older states, Odisha is more often the leader.

Since 2001, the share of social service expenditures that states devoted to the welfare of minority and indigenous communities (STs, SCs, and OBCs) has

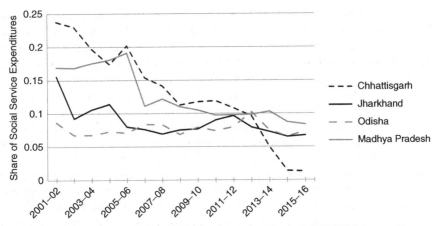

FIGURE 9.1 State Government Expenditure on Welfare of ST/SC/OBC as a Share of Total Expenditures on Social Services

declined in most states (see Figure 9.1).[24] Although Chhattisgarh and Madhya Pradesh devoted the highest average shares during the 2000s, the share of the budget allocated to this category steadily declined over time. Nevertheless, both states set aside higher shares for minority and indigenous communities than Jharkhand (at least until 2012–2013), the one state that was initially established as a tribal homeland. Jharkhand's share of spending for these communities was in fact very similar to Odisha's, a state with a lower percentage of STs and whose origins are not rooted in a tribal movement.

Since we do not know how much of this spending is targeted specifically for STs (and what this spending is used for), it is more informative to compare states in terms of their implementation of tribal-focused programs and initiatives. Many of the programs and initiatives were initially spearheaded by the Indian central government, and the ratio of funding is typically 75 percent central and 25 percent state. One of the first such programs is the "Tribal Sub Plan" (TSP), launched in the mid-1970s. The TSP is designed to support the welfare of STs, boost income generation of ST families, and promote education of STs. As a "sub plan," the TSP is meant to function within states' own five-year and annual economic plans to support STs. But when we examine the data, it is likewise impossible to tell where funds are spent and how much is targeted to ST communities. Furthermore, there are numerous reports of TSP funds being misallocated, diverted, or unspent, such that it is difficult to ascertain the real value of TSP expenditures that benefit ST welfare.[25]

---

[24] Data retrieved from Reserve Bank of India (http://www.rbi.org.in).

[25] Problems in the TSP are frequently reported (see National Campaign on Dalit Human Rights, n.d.). According to Panda, "The main limitations of the sub-plan strategy are absence of proper organisation, faulty process of identification of target groups and above all lack of proper coordination between different departments" (2006, p. 139).

A better estimate of the extent to which states prioritized securing funds from the central government that could be utilized to boost ST welfare is the "Special Central Assistance" to the TSP (or SCA-TSP), designed as an additive to the TSP. Here, funds are released from state governments directly to local tribal development organizations. The SCA-TSP is mostly intended to support income-generation programs in agriculture, horticulture, sericulture, and animal husbandry. From 2006 to 2011, Jharkhand stands out among the group as having received the least and under-utilized the most SCA-TSP funds. Although Jharkhand largely corrected these issues between 2011 and 2016, the state still underperformed in utilization of SCA-TSP funds given the size of its tribal population and especially compared with Odisha.[26] However, both Jharkhand and Odisha received little funding for the SCA-TSP project for the development of "forest villages." Whereas Chhattisgarh and Madhya Pradesh received 159 Rs and 170 Rs, respectively, for each tribal individual in the state, Jharkhand and Odisha received a fraction as much – about 4 Rs and 5 Rs, respectively.[27]

Another important source of funds for ST welfare and the development of tribal regions are grants-in-aid provided by the central government under Article 275(1). Although an upward trend in funding is observed and there is more parity among states in recent years, from 2009–2010 to 2016–2017, Jharkhand secured the second-lowest amount of funds per tribal individual (Madhya Pradesh was the lowest). Odisha secured the most funding among the four states, roughly 24 percent more than Jharkhand.[28]

Beyond these sources, various central government ministries collaborate with state governments to help improve ST welfare. Two prominent programs originating from these collaborations are Indira Awaas Yojana (IAY) and Swarnajayanti Gram Swarozgar Yojana (SGSY). IAY was launched by the Ministry of Rural Development in 1985 and is used to build or upgrade homes for rural people who live below the poverty line. From 2009–2010 to 2014–2015, Chhattisgarh built one house for every 71 tribal individuals, and Odisha and Jharkhand were marginally fewer at one house for every 72 and 74 tribal individuals, respectively. By contrast, Madhya Pradesh built one house for every 133 tribal individuals.[29] SGSY, started in 1999, is intended to boost rural employment by creating "self-help groups" (*swarozgaris*), financial intermediaries that provide micro-loans to entrepreneurs. About 46 percent of

[26] Data retrieved from "State-wise Fund Released and Utilisation under Special Central Assistance (SCA) to Tribal Sub Plan (TSP) in India" (various years) (http://www.indiastat.com).

[27] Data retrieved from "Selected State-wise Funds Released for Development of Forest Villages under Special Central Assistance to Tribal Sub Plan in India" (2005–2009, 2010–2012) (http://www.indiastat.com).

[28] Data retrieved from "Selected State-wise Funds Utilisation under Article 275 (1) of Constitution by Ministry of Tribal Affairs in India" (various years) (http://www.indiastat.com) and Government of India-Ministry of Tribal Affairs (http://www.tribal.nic.in).

[29] Data retrieved from "Number of Houses Constructed to Scheduled Caste/Scheduled Tribe (SC/ST) under Indira Awaas Yojana (IAY)" (various states; various years) (http://www.indiastat.com).

all individuals who benefit from SGSY belong to either an ST or an SC community. Odisha appears to have been the most successful at implementing SGSY for STs. In 2011–2012, after normalizing by a state's ST population, Odisha assisted 38 percent more self-help groups for STs than Jharkhand, 71 percent more than Chhattisgarh, and 139 percent more than Madhya Pradesh. Odisha also led the group in terms of the value of credit and subsidy disbursed under SGSY (over 90 crore Rs in total).[30]

The issue of unemployment among indigenous communities is increasingly a concern for Indian states. One of the most widely discussed employment programs in the world today is the Mahatma Gandhi National Rural Employment Guarantee Act (MGNREGA). Launched in 2005, MGNREGA guarantees at least 100 days of wage employment per year to every household whose adult members volunteer to do unskilled manual labor. From 2013–2014 to 2016–2017, Odisha averaged the highest share of total person-workdays that were worked by a tribal individual in the state. About 41 percent of all person-workdays in Odisha were worked by a tribal individual over this period, whereas this value was 38 percent in Chhattisgarh, 36 percent in Jharkhand, and 33 percent in Madhya Pradesh.[31]

The provision of health services for ST communities varies significantly across states, with Odisha and Chhattisgarh achieving better performance in recent years. One of the basic requirements for ensuring the health of India's rural populations is the establishment of primary health centers (PHC), PHC sub-centers (PHCS),[32] and community health centers (CHC).[33] These are state-owned facilities that provide basic medical care, maternal and child health, vaccinations, etc. As of March 2016, Odisha and Chhattisgarh led the group in terms of the provision of PHCs and PHCSs in rural tribal areas, and Odisha led the group in CHCs (see Figure 9.2).[34]

In terms of education for STs, Odisha again consistently outperforms the other states. From 2007–2008 to 2009–2010, Odisha released the most funds for the education of their tribal population.[35] Between 2003–2004 and

---

[30] Data retrieved from "Number of Scheduled Caste/Scheduled Tribe (SC/ST) Swarozgaris Assisted and Subsidy Disbursed under Swarnajayanti Gram Swarozgar Yojana (SGSY)" (various states) (http://www.indiastat.com) and Government of India-Ministry of Rural Development (http://www.rural.nic.in).

[31] Data retrieved from http://nrega.nic.in.

[32] PHCSs are "the most peripheral and first contact point between the primary health care system and the community" (http://www.mohfw.nic.in).

[33] CHCs are the largest and most encompassing health-care facilities, intended to provide specialist health care to the rural population.

[34] Data retrieved from "State-wise Number of Sub Centres, Primary Health Centres (PHCs) and Community Health Centres (CHCs) in Tribal Areas in India" (various years) (http://www.indiastat.com).

[35] Data retrieved from "Funds Released for Education of Tribal Population" (various states) (http://www.indiastat.com).

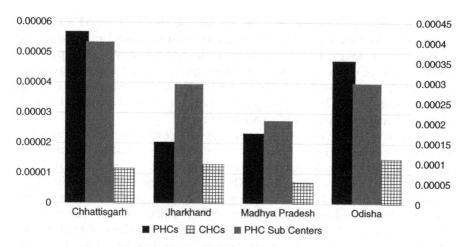

Left axis: PHC SubCenters (in gray) as share of rural tribal population
Right axis: PHCs (in black) and CHCs (in black/white grid) as share of rural tribal population

FIGURE 9.2 Number of Rural Health Services in Tribal Areas (as Share of Rural Tribal Population), as of March 31, 2016

2007–2008, Odisha led the group – with Madhya Pradesh also performing well – in terms of funds released to NGOs and state organizations for improving female literacy in tribal areas (see Figure 9.3).[36]

Jharkhand and Chhattisgarh, however, released few funds toward this effort. Similar patterns are observed in funding for residential schools (*ashrams*) in tribal areas, one component of the TSP. Between 2005–2006 and 2014–2015, significantly more funds were used to establish residential schools in Odisha and Madhya Pradesh than the other states.[37] Over these years, most states made strides in establishing schools in tribal areas. Whereas in Madhya Pradesh, 112 schools were approved (one for every 69,847 tribal individuals), the figure for Chhattisgarh is 77 (one for every 101,596 tribal individuals), and for Odisha, 97 (one for every 98,874 tribal individuals). But contrary to the expectation that Jharkhand would be a leader in increasing access to education in tribal areas, just two additional schools were established in the state (one for every 4,322,521 tribal individuals).

[36] Data retrieved from "Selected State-wise Grants Released under Scheme of Educational Complex in Low Literacy Pockets for Development of Female Literacy in Tribal Area in India" (various years) (http://www.indiastat.com).

[37] Data retrieved from "State-wise Amount Released under Scheme of Establishment of Ashram Schools Tribal Sub-Plan (TSP) Areas in India" (various years) (http://www .indiastat.com).

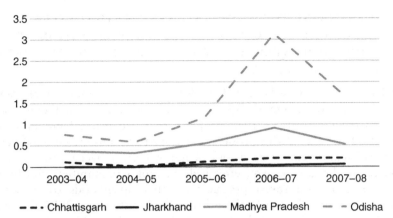

FIGURE 9.3 Funds Released to NGOs and State-Run Organizations for Improving Female Literacy in Tribal Areas (Rs per Tribal Individual)

Taken as a whole, a few patterns emerge from these data. Despite Jharkhand's origins as a tribal homeland, the state government has had surprisingly little success in implementing programs designed to benefit ST welfare. Some of the areas where the state does perform well are with regard to SGSY and the provision of CHCs, although this is the least directly accessible health service for the rural population. Across most other measures, outcomes are worse in Jharkhand than Chhattisgarh, the other new state, and worse than the two older states, Madhya Pradesh and Odisha. The other consistent pattern is that the older states with lower percentages of STs – Madhya Pradesh and Odisha – perform better than, or just as well as, the newer states with higher percentages of STs. Between the two older states, Odisha is much more often the leader.

In order to explain the observed variation, the next section hones in on differences in the vibrancy of civil society organizations and their linkages with the state government and bureaucracy. As noted, Odisha stands out in terms of the sheer number and funding capacity of state-based voluntary and nongovernmental organizations devoted to ST welfare and rights. We demonstrate that this factor is critical for Odisha's ability to implement the FRA, one of the most important pieces of legislation devised to protect the property and customary rights of STs. We briefly contrast Odisha's experiences with the puzzling case of Jharkhand, whose political origins would suggest that the state would be a leader in indigenous welfare and development policies. By focusing on the FRA, we seek to specify the causal mechanisms by which civil society organizations influence the implementation of initiatives intended to benefit ST welfare and rights.

9.4   IDENTIFYING THE CAUSAL MECHANISMS THAT EXPLAIN
      SUBNATIONAL VARIATION IN THE IMPLEMENTATION OF
      INDIGENOUS WELFARE AND DEVELOPMENT POLICIES: INDIA'S
      FOREST RIGHTS ACT, 2006

If India's *adivasis* have benefited the least from postcolonial development, arguably the most troubled aspect of their position within Indian society concerns the insecurity of their property rights to forest lands and forest products. The roots of this problem reach far back into the colonial period, when British authorities vested control and ownership over forests and forest resources in the government, effectively making communities who lived in forests or relied on forest products for their livelihoods trespassers on government land. To rectify these historical injustices, in 2006 the Indian central government passed the Forest Rights Act.[38] The FRA allows forest-dwelling individuals and communities, the majority of whom are indigenous, to file petitions with the state government asking for recognition of their rights to forests and forest products. The law requires claimants to provide proof that their ancestors (up to three generations) used the forests for homes or livelihoods. Although the act attempts to right the historical injustices against those who live in and near India's forests, critics have pointed out a number of shortcomings, including a privileging of individual over community claims (thereby subverting indigenous understandings of property as a community resource) and a dilution of the draft bill's most progressive aspects as it moved from the drafting table to the parliamentary floor (Prasad, 2006–2007). Notwithstanding its shortcomings, the FRA represents one of the most significant potential advances for India's *adivasi* minorities.

The FRA splits authority over its implementation across several political jurisdictions. The Indian Parliament authored the act but also empowered the central government's Ministry of Tribal Affairs to issue additional rules for implementation, which it has done several times. State governments are required to formulate the rules and create the bureaucratic infrastructure for administering the FRA, including forming a State Level Monitoring Committee that compiles statistics and oversees implementation. State governments play another critical role, as they are charged with publicizing and making information about the act accessible to the public. Local bodies at the third tier of government – *panchayat* institutions – are authorized to compile claims and have the authority to adjudicate whether claims filed under the FRA are valid or not. Once these claims have been assembled and examined by the *gram sabha*, or village committee, those deemed valid are forwarded to a subdivisional-level committee and from there to the district-level committee for final decisions. This last level serves as the appellate body for those who

---

[38] The full name of the act is The Scheduled Tribes and Other Traditional Forest Dwellers (Recognition of Forest Rights) Act, 2006.

disagree with the findings of either the *gram sabha* or the subdivisional-level committee.

An analysis of the FRA highlights how non-state actors drive subnational variation in the implementation of policies designed to advance ST welfare and rights. Subnational variation in the vibrancy of civil society helps explain why there are vastly different numbers of claims made under the FRA across Indian states. Table 9.3 displays the state-level variation in the implementation of the FRA.

Overall, FRA implementation has been most successful in Odisha. Although Chhattisgarh has a higher number of claims per tribal individual than Odisha, the percentage of claims rejected in Chhattisgarh is much greater (59.4 percent versus 27.3 percent). What is especially surprising, though consistent with what we show in Section 9.3, is that there are far fewer FRA claims filed in Jharkhand than elsewhere. In Jharkhand, only 1.2 claims have been filed for every 100 tribal individuals in the state, a figure that contrasts with Chhattisgarh, Odisha, and Madhya Pradesh, where the numbers of claims filed are 11, 6.4, and 3.8, respectively. With respect to titles distributed, Chhattisgarh and Odisha have had more success than Jharkhand or Madhya Pradesh. In the case of communal claims, Madhya Pradesh and Odisha rank far above Jharkhand (data for Chhattisgarh are not available). For every 10,000 tribal individuals, 28 communal claims were filed in Madhya Pradesh and 14 were filed in Odisha – compared to 4 in Jharkhand. A similar pattern can be seen in community titles distributed. For every 10,000 tribal individuals, 17.8 titles were distributed in Madhya Pradesh, 5.7 titles were distributed in Odisha, but just 2.1 titles were distributed in Jharkhand.[39]

We argue that Odisha's relative success in FRA implementation stems from the participation of civil society groups in three spheres: publicity and translation; community training and empowerment; and inter-bureaucratic coordination. Compared to the other states, Odisha has more VOs/NGOs per capita, more VOs/NGOs focusing on tribal issues, and more VOs/NGOs that were awarded grants for addressing ST welfare. But it is not just the size and mobilization capacity of the nongovernmental sector that explains the success of FRA implementation: the degree to which this sector coordinates with the government also plays a crucial role.[40] Akin to Ostrom's (1996) insight about

---

[39] Sarap et al. (2013) show that in Odisha there has been greater emphasis on individual over community claims, for which they blame the lack of publicity about the full extent of rights and protections under the act, especially as they pertain to communal property rights.

[40] For scholars of non-state actors, particularly those who focus on development, a vital concern is the risk of cooptation. Whereas cooperation between state and non-state actors can produce larger gains, there is always the risk of CSOs losing their autonomy in the process. While our interviews for this project did not directly address this issue, the line between cooperation and cooptation is something about which the larger canvas of activists in Bhubaneswar, Odisha's capital city, is concerned. For a recent analysis of CSO–state relations in the context of another Indian state, see Harrison (2017).

TABLE 9.3 *Implementation of Forest Rights Act in Chhattisgarh, Jharkhand, Madhya Pradesh, and Odisha, as of November 30, 2016*

A. State	B. No. of claims filed*	C. No. of titles distributed*	D. No. of claims rejected	E. Number of claims filed for every 100 ST individuals	F. Percent of titles distributed to number of claims received	G. Percent of claims rejected (D) to total adjudicated (C + D)
Chhattisgarh	860,364 (NA)	347,789 (NA)	507,907	11	40.42%	59.4%
Jharkhand	103,625 (3,403)	52,573 (1,850)	25,791	1.2	50.85%	32.9%
Madhya Pradesh	574,795 (42,156)	206,960 (42,156)	374,718	3.8	37.96%	64.4%
Odisha	618,384 (13,433)	399,996 (5,513)	150,133	6.4	64.18%	27.3%

Source: Data in columns B, C, D, and F from Ministry of Tribal Affairs, *Annual Report 2016–17* (New Delhi: Government of India, 2017), p. 255. Remaining columns tabulated by authors. The above represents the most recent data available as of writing.

* Figures in parentheses indicate the number of total claims and titles that represent communal as opposed to individual claims. Data on communal claims are unavailable for Chhattisgarh.

the role of non-state actors in the "coproduction" of public goods, civil society has become a key actor in the promotion of ST welfare and rights in Odisha.

Civil society was crucial in lowering barriers to information about citizens' rights under the FRA and the bureaucratic mechanics required for citizens to make appeals. The FRA was passed in 2006, the law was published in the official government gazette in 2007, and the Ministry of Tribal Affairs issued the rules to implement the law in January 2008. From January 2008 onward, CSOs in Odisha played a multifaceted and increasingly active role raising awareness about the FRA. First, the primary civil society organization involved in advancing property rights for STs in Odisha, Vasundhara, used its network of activists throughout the state to begin publicizing the act.[41] Vasundhara was formed in the early 1990s by a group of students from the Indian Institute of Forest Management, who during field visits to forested areas in Odisha became aware that communities who rely on forests for livelihoods, many of whom are STs, had developed sophisticated communal means to protect their forest lands (Singh, 2013).[42] These methods were quite distinct from the scientific management techniques of the Indian Forest Department, particularly in the way that they acknowledged human settlements as part of the forest ecology rather than as a problem that had to be removed.

From the 1990s onward, activists in Vasundhara were single-mindedly focused on legalizing these communal practices by advancing the rights of forest-dwelling and forest-dependent communities. In fact, Vasundhara was one of the key civil society organizations involved in drafting and pushing for the adoption of the FRA in 2006, which itself was the outcome of a national network of CSOs that came together around the specific goal of drafting and garnering political support for the FRA. According to the director of Vasundhara, the alacrity and organizational capacity with which civil society organizations in the state responded to the FRA is one of the key reasons that its implementation has been so much more successful in Odisha.[43] Alongside Vasundhara's activities, the Odisha government's own Scheduled Caste and

---

[41] In addition to Vasundhara, several other CSOs in Odisha focus on land issues and implementation of the FRA, including Orissa Development Action Forum, Foundation for Ecological Security, and Living Farm. These CSOs also play an important role in bringing to the state's attention instances where the FRA is not being implemented correctly at the local level. For example, many CSOs provided this kind of input to the government during a state-level consultation held in 2010 (Report on issue of implementation of the Forest Rights Act in Orissa, 2010).

[42] In her essay on the making of environmental subjectivities in Odisha, Neera Singh describes her early work with Vasundhara and how this was prompted in part by her encounter with communities in Odisha that had developed joint forest management techniques outside the purview or direction of government officials.

[43] Interview with Mr. Y. Giri Rao at Vasundhara's head office in Bhubaneswar, July 24, 2014. Several researchers who have worked for many years on Odisha's political economy and forest rights and management echoed this view of the importance of civil society organizations. This was expressed in conversations we had with several activists and academics during a visit to

Scheduled Tribes Research and Training Institute began translating the act and its rules into various tribal languages and dialects. These translations were a key early effort that facilitated the dissemination of knowledge of the FRA far more widely than would have been possible otherwise.

A second initiative that was convened jointly by the state government and CSOs took place in 2010. Young people from various tribal communities across Odisha were selected to attend a workshop in the state capital, Bhubaneswar, where they were given detailed information about the mechanics of the FRA. Participants were coached through the process of filling out the manifold forms required for the implementation of all rights and welfare programs in India, including the FRA. The young people then returned to their communities and were able to serve as "brand ambassadors" for the program.[44] Scholars who study the anthropology of the postcolonial state in South Asia have noted the barriers to access posed by the bureaucracy's labyrinth of records and forms for precisely those citizens who are the putative beneficiaries of government programs (Gupta, 2012; Hull, 2012). Educating individuals from tribal communities about the bureaucracy's documentary world, then, served as an important way to lower such barriers to access. According to the state government bureaucrat most directly involved in the implementation and oversight of the FRA, this training event was a significant cause of the "quantum jump" that took place in FRA applications after 2010.[45]

A final role played by CSOs involved facilitating coordination across bureaucratic agencies. Historically, several different bureaucracies have laid claim to the management and protection of India's forests. While the state-level forest department is the official owner of the forests, the state-level revenue department controlled land, including forest land. The tribal affairs department, by contrast, served and represented the interests of tribal communities in India, the majority of which were reliant on forests for livelihoods or as homes. The jurisdictional overlap of these agencies resulted in an antagonistic relationship that the FRA had the potential to further deepen. By appointing tribal affairs ministries at the central and state levels as the nodal administrative agency for the FRA, the legislation threatened to undermine the authority of the forest and revenue departments.[46] In Odisha, bureaucrats in the tribal affairs ministry have been alert to these interagency conflicts – which they

Odisha in July 2014. Among those who shared their views on this subject were Dr. B. Nayak and Dr. K. Kumar.

[44] Interview on July 24, 2014, with Dr. A. B. Ota, director-cum-additional secretary of ST & SC Development, Minorities & Backward Classes Welfare Department.

[45] Interview with Dr. A. B. Ota, July 24, 2014.

[46] This is not to imply that officials in these two ministries were predisposed to oppose the FRA; indeed one retired principal secretary of the forest and environment department confessed that he was extremely uncomfortable with the policy that was in place before the FRA, which focused on evicting ostensible squatters from government land: "How do we evict people who have been living in the forests for so long?" Interview with Dr. A. Behera in Bhubaneswar, July 24, 2014.

recognize could jeopardize the operations not only of state-level bureaucracies in the capital city, Bhubaneswar, but also of their various field and district offices – and have tried to mitigate them in various ways.

First, the Tribal Research Institute hosted training sessions for officials of the forest department, functionaries from other state bureaucracies, and CSOs, and when these various disparate groups came together "a lot of hiccups could be cleared up that enabled smoother implementation."[47] Second, and perhaps more importantly, some of the central government funding for Odisha's Tribal Sub Plan (TSP) was apportioned for use by the district collectors' offices for FRA implementation. With these funds, the collectors' offices were instructed to hire retired revenue inspectors and other retired government employees with land and revenue-related expertise to facilitate the implementation of the FRA. This move can be interpreted as an effort to secure the consent of those bureaucratic actors most likely to obstruct the FRA. The various state-level ministries in Bhubaneswar also issued jointly signed letters to field staff. Together, these measures served to "narrow down the gap" that existed among these government agencies.[48] Ultimately, the compliance of these various ministries and their willingness to cooperate was strengthened by the pronounced support for the FRA by the chief minister's office. As one member of a CSO put it, although the three-and-a-half-term chief minister, Naveen Patnaik, is widely considered to be pro-mining, he has also turned out to be "pro-tribal."[49]

Odisha's success in FRA implementation contrasts sharply with Jharkhand's experience. In 2010, a committee jointly convened by the central Ministry of Tribal Affairs and Ministry of Environment and Forests (MoTA/MoEF) investigated the reasons for Jharkhand's poor performance. The notes from the committee's field visit found "limited enthusiasm for the implementation of the Act" (MoEF/MoTA, 2010, p. 9) and a lack of adequate publicity to inform the state's citizenry. In many villages, as of 2010, the bureaucratic machinery required to implement the FRA was still not in place, and, even where it existed, few claims were being submitted. Although some officials blamed the slow progress on the Maoist threat, claiming that it dampened the enthusiasm among civilians for government programs that might put them at risk with Maoist cadres, the committee heard no complaints along these lines from either villagers or formal complaints from officials in the districts or in Jharkhand's capital of Ranchi (MoEF/MoTA, 2010, p. 5).

Jharkhand's slow start publicizing and implementing the FRA has resulted in a number of problems, of both informational and procedural natures. A study by Tapas Kumar Sarangi found that, as late as 2009, claim forms were not systematically distributed to the population. In some instances, claim forms

---

[47] Interview with Dr. Ota, Bhubaneswar, July 24, 2014.
[48] Interview with Dr. Ota, Bhubaneswar, July 24, 2014.
[49] Interview with CSO activist, Bhubaneswar, July 24, 2014.

were printed but officials either did not distribute them or demanded bribes to do so (2013, p. 41). Furthermore, state government agencies tasked with raising awareness about the FRA, such as Jharkhand's Department of Social Welfare, have "failed to do much" according to a report by the Asian Indigenous and Tribal Peoples Network (AITPN) (2012, p. 19). The lack of information about how the FRA works and how to properly file claims has prevented many forest-based communities in Jharkhand from understanding their communal rights as enshrined in the FRA. The activist Dayamani Barla says that most villagers in Jharkhand are neither aware of the community land rights provisions of the FRA nor offered any support for filing communal claims (Prasad, 2013).

From a procedural standpoint, state agencies and local government institutions tasked with assisting in implementation in Jharkhand are often unclear about the roles they are supposed to play. According to the FRA's guidelines, *panchayats* are supposed to elect a Forest Resource Committee (FRC) whose role is to "assist the *gram sabha* in its function to collate, verify and approve claims to rights." Yet, in Dumka district, AITPN's report concluded that "FRC members and even the secretary themselves did not know that they were part of the FRC, nor what it meant. Neither the FRCs nor Gram Sabhas were found to be involved significantly at any stage in the implementation of the FRA" (2012, p. 8). There are also reports that district officials in Jharkhand are adopting their own approaches to implementing the FRA since the state government has not provided proper guidance (Sarangi, 2013, p. 41). It is important to emphasize that these outcomes are due not to a lack of resources but to a failure to prioritize the FRA and educate the Jharkhand public about it.

Whereas in Odisha civil society quickly stepped in to publicize the FRA and coordinate with governmental agencies, this process has been slower in Jharkhand. The MoTA/MoEF committee observed that there was little involvement from CSOs in Jharkhand and even found evidence of antagonism between grassroots activists and state government agencies (MoEF/MoTA, 2010, p. 9). There are some signs that this may be changing as a result of a new agreement underwritten by support from the UK Department for International Development (DFID) to facilitate more cooperation between the state government and CSOs. In May 2014, a formal Memorandum of Understanding (MOU) between the government of Jharkhand and NGOs was signed to "build synergies between the state and civil society for addressing the critical gaps" in the FRA. The agreement's members are Jharkhand State Tribal Cooperative Development Corporation Ltd.; Poorest Areas Civil Society Program (PACS), which is an initiative of DFID; and Jharkhand Van Adhikaar Manch (a forum of 22 local CSOs, the organization of which was facilitated by PACS).

As a response to the MOU, the Jharkhand government expressed gratitude that CSOs would assist with FRA implementation. J. P. Lakra, tribal welfare commissioner for the state government, cheered the MOU, stating, "Collaborative efforts of the administration and civil society would immensely help in ensuring that the provisions of the act are realized on ground as envisaged" (Lens Eye, 2014). Summarizing the significance of the MOU, journalist Amit Gupta (2014) wrote: "The main takeaway ... will be better awareness among forest dwellers of the fact that something like the forest rights Act exists ... If full-scale ignorance and half-baked applications of forest dwellers have played spoilsport, so have bureaucratic lethargy and chaos." The next few years will be critical in determining whether Jharkhand's government and civil society can work together toward better implementation of the FRA.

9.5 CONCLUSION

The role of CSOs is a better predictor of the amount of attention a state government in India gives to the needs and rights of indigenous communities than factors that are conventionally viewed as more important, such as whether the state's origins are rooted in a movement for an indigenous homeland or if indigenous communities represent a high percentage of the population. Our subnational analysis of four Indian states demonstrates this with respect to the implementation of programs designed to improve indigenous welfare and legislation intended to protect the rights of indigenous communities to forests. We found that the one state established in response to an indigenous movement's claims for a homeland, Jharkhand, has largely underperformed compared to other states. Moreover, we found that older states with smaller indigenous populations, such as Odisha, often outperformed newer states with larger indigenous populations. An analysis of the divergent fortunes of the Forest Rights Act in Odisha and Jharkhand illustrated the important role played by civil society organizations in the successful implementation of this legislation.

As this chapter demonstrates, it is essential to adopt a subnational perspective if we are to understand why there is such extreme variation in the implementation of policies and programs designed to assist indigenous communities across India today. Part of the reason why a subnational perspective is essential is because of the rise of competitive federalism in India after 1990. Since the central government devolved more authority to state governments to design and implement their own development policies, researchers seeking to understand the causes of local variation across India must necessarily look to state-level institutions and state-level dynamics for possible clues. Further, it is difficult to envision how one can understand changes pre- and post-2000 for the six Indian states whose political borders were redrawn overnight by the central government (Bihar, Chhattisgarh, Jharkhand, Madhya Pradesh, Uttar Pradesh, and Uttarakhand) unless a subnational perspective is embraced. Indeed, there is good reason to want to study these particular states given that their collective population comprises over 35 percent of India's entire population.

Our findings not only make a scholarly contribution to the writings on public goods and welfare states; they also offer insights to policymakers about the consequences of creating new political units in federal systems. Jharkhand's lackluster performance at implementing programs and legislation designed to protect indigenous citizens shows that states founded on a clearly defined indigenous group identity are not necessarily better at ensuring the welfare and rights of these groups, despite claims to the contrary routinely made by their leaders. This is true even when movements organized around these very identities played a central role in the push for independence. Whether or not new states can provide better protections and benefits to disadvantaged social groups should be treated not as an assumption but as an empirical question to be evaluated. In this respect, the Indian government's decision to create another new state in June 2014, Telangana, will, in due course, offer further evidence for assessing the relationship between the creation of new political units and both policy and political economy outcomes.

Finally, while this chapter did not address the role of electoral politics, it seems reasonable to suppose that states with more political representation from STs are more likely to work toward ensuring their welfare and rights. This notion already has empirical support in India, as scholars have demonstrated that the policy of reservations impacts political outcomes (Chattopadhyay & Duflo, 2004; Pande, 2003). Although ST-reserved seats in state assemblies are apportioned according to population, analysis of detailed election results can reveal the extent to which ST politicians are competitive more generally, across both reserved and non-reserved constituencies. In Chhattisgarh's 2008 and 2013 state assembly elections, an ST candidate either won or was among the top five candidates in terms of vote share for 43 percent and 33 percent of open, non-reserved seats, respectively. Yet, in Jharkhand's 2005, 2009, and 2014 elections, these values were lower, at just 20 percent, 25 percent, and 16 percent, respectively.[50] This suggests that STs may be more directly involved in Chhattisgarh's politics and are, in turn, better able to influence policymaking. Having elected representatives in formal political institutions may very well help VOs and NGOs connect to and coordinate with the state government on the provision of goods and services to benefit STs. While more research needs to be done on the role of electoral politics in the making and implementation of policies designed to benefit India's indigenous citizens (see Basu, 2012), the contrasting fortunes of indigenous candidates seen across Chhattisgarh and Jharkhand seems to offer further reason to be skeptical that increasing social homogeneity by creating ethnic homelands, alone, will translate directly into policies that actually benefit these ethnic groups.

---

[50] These figures exclude votes for "None of the above." Data retrieved from the Election Commission of India (http://eci.nic.in).

BIBLIOGRAPHY

AITPN. (2012). *The state of the Forest Rights Act*. New Delhi, India: Asian Indigenous and Tribal Peoples Network.

Alesina, Alberto, Baqir, Reza, & Easterly, William. (1999). Public goods and ethnic divisions. *The Quarterly Journal of Economics 114*(4), 1243–1284.

Alesina, Alberto, Glaeser, Edward, & Sacerdote, Bruce. (2001). Why doesn't the United States have a European-style welfare state? *Brookings Papers on Economic Activity 2*, 187–254.

Baruah, Sanjib. (2007). *Beyond counter-insurgency: Understanding the politics of northeast India*. New Delhi, India: Oxford University Press.

Basu, Ipshita. (2012). The politics of recognition and redistribution: Development, tribal identity politics and distributive justice in India's Jharkhand. *Development and Change 43*, 1291–1312.

Chandra, Kanchan. (2004). *Why ethnic parties succeed: Patronage and ethnic headcounts in India*. Cambridge, England: Cambridge University Press.

Chattopadhyay, Raghabendra, & Duflo, Esther. (2004). Women as policy makers: Evidence from a randomized policy experiment in India. *Econometrica 72*, 1409–1443.

Evans, Peter. (1996). Government action, social capital and development: Reviewing the evidence on synergy. *World Development 24*(6), 1119–1132.

Goswami, Debika, & Tandon, Rajesh. (2013). Civil society in changing India: Emerging roles, relationships, and strategies. *Development in Practice 23*(5–6), 653–664.

Government of India-Central Statistical Office. (2012). *Compendium of environment statistics India*. New Delhi, India: Ministry of Statistics and Programme Implementation.

Guha, Ramachandra. (2007). Adivasis, Naxalites and Indian democracy. *Economic and Political Weekly 42*(32), 3305–3312.

Gupta, Akhil. (2012). *Red tape: Bureaucracy, structural violence and poverty in India*. Durham, NC: Duke University Press.

Gupta, Amit. (2014, May 30). Triple power ink for forest rights: State part of tripartite agreement to align act with (land) deed. *The Telegraph*.

Habyarimana, James, Humphreys, Macartan, Posner, Daniel, & Weinstein, Jeremy. (2007). Why does ethnic diversity undermine public goods provision? *American Political Science Review 101*(4), 709–725.

Harriss, John. (1999). Comparing political regimes across Indian states: A preliminary essay. *Economic Political Weekly 34*, 3367–3377.

Harriss, John. (2006). Middle class activism and the politics of the informal working class: A perspective on class relations and civil society in Indian cities. *Critical Asian Studies 38*(4), 445–465.

Harrison, Tom. (2017). NGOs and personal politics: The relationship between NGOs and political leaders in West Bengal, India. *World Development 98*, 485–496.

Hull, Matthew. (2012). *Government of paper: The materiality of bureaucracy in urban Pakistan*. Berkeley: University of California Press.

Jaffrelot, Christophe. (2008). The uneven plebeianisation of Madhya Pradesh politics. *Seminar 591*(November), 28–32.

Jenkins, Rob (Ed.). (2004). *Regional reflections: Comparing politics across India's states*. New Delhi, India: Oxford University Press.

Kohli, Atul. (1987). *The state and poverty in India: The politics of reform.* Cambridge, England: Cambridge University Press.

Lens Eye. (2014, May 29). MoU between Tribal Cooperative Development Ltd., Jharkhand Adhikaar Manch & Poorest Areas Civil Society. Available at: http://www .lenseye.co/mou-between-tribal-cooperative-development-ltd-jharkhand-van-adhikaar-manch-poorest-areas-civil-society-for-the-effective-implementation-of-forest-rights-act-2006-in-the-state/ (last accessed January 4, 2019).

Mau, Steffen, & Burkhardt, Christoph. (2009). Migration and welfare state solidarity in Western Europe. *Journal of European Social Policy 19*(3), 213–229.

Ministry of Environment and Forests and Ministry of Tribal Affairs. (2010). Implementation of Forest Rights Act in Jharkhand: Report of field visit, 15–19 July 2010. New Delhi, India.

Ministry of Environment and Forests and Ministry of Tribal Affairs. (2010). Report on issue of implementation of the Forest Rights Act in Orissa. Bhubaneswar, India.

Ministry of Tribal Affairs. (2012). *Annual report, 2011–12.* New Delhi, India: Government of India.

Ministry of Tribal Affairs. (2017). *Annual report, 2016–17.* New Delhi, India: Government of India.

Mohanty, Manoranjan. (2014). Persisting dominance: Crisis of democracy in a resource-rich region. *Economic and Political Weekly 49*(14), 39–47.

National Campaign on Dalit Human Rights. (n.d.). Status of Special Component Plan for SCs and Tribal Sub Plan for STs. New Delhi, India.

Ostrom, Elinor. (1996). Crossing the great divide: Coproduction, synergy, and development. *World Development 24*(6), 1073–1087.

Panda, Nishakar. (2006). *Policies, programmes, and strategies for tribal development: A critical appraisal.* New Delhi, India: Kalpaz.

Pande, Rohini. (2003). Can mandated political representation increase policy influence for disadvantaged minorities? Theory and evidence from India. *American Economic Review 93*, 1132–1152.

Prasad, Archana. (2006–2007, December 30–January 12). Survival at stake. *Frontline 23*(26), 4–10.

Prasad, Rachna Kumari. (2013, November 30). Right to forest land: Who benefits? *Mainstream 51*(50), 28–38.

Putnam, Robert. (2000). *Bowling along: The collapse and revival of American community.* New York, NY: Simon & Schuster.

Roy, Indrajit. (2008). Civil society and good governance: (Re-)conceptualizing the interface. *World Development 36*(4), 677–705.

Sarap, Kailas, Sarangi, Tapas Kumar, & Naik, Jogindra. (2013, September 7). Implementation of Forest Rights Act 2006 in Odisha: Process, constraints and outcome. *Economic and Political Weekly 48*(36), 61–67.

Sarangi, Tapas Kumar. (2013). *Legalising rights through implementation of Forest Rights Act 2006: A critical review on Odisha and Jharkhand.* RULNR Working Paper Number 20, Hyderabad, India.

Shah, Alpa. (2010). *In the shadows of the state: Indigenous politics, environmentalism, and insurgency in Jharkhand, India.* Durham, NC: Duke University Press.

Singh, D. P., Goyal, Jaya, Saritha, C. T., & Srinivasan, K. (2008, September 25–26). *Population estimates of social groups: Reliability of large scale survey of NSS and*

NFHS. Paper presented at National Seminar of NSS 62nd Round Survey Results. New Delhi, India.

Singh, Neera. (2013). The affective labor of growing forests and the becoming of environmental subjects: Rethinking environmentality in Odisha, India. *Geoforum 47*, 189–198.

Singh, Nirvikar, & Vasishtha, Garima. (2004). Patterns in centre-state fiscal transfers: An illustrative analysis. *Economic and Political Weekly 39*(45), 4897–4903.

Singh, Prerna. (2015). *How solidarity works for welfare: Subnationalism and social development in India*. Cambridge, England: Cambridge University Press.

Tillin, Louise. (2008). Politics in a new state: Chhattisgarh. *Seminar 591*, 23–27.

Tillin, Louise. (2013). *Remapping India: New states and their political origins*. Oxford, England: Oxford University Press.

Varshney, Ashutosh. (2003). *Ethnic conflict and civic life: Hindus and Muslims in India*. New Haven, CT: Yale University Press.

World Bank. (2015). *Indigenous Latin America in the twenty-first century: The first decade*. Washington, DC: World Bank.

Local States of Play: Land and Urban Politics in Reform-Era China

Meg Rithmire

Urbanization in China during the past three decades has constituted the largest construction project in the planet's history. The proportion of Chinese citizens living in cities has increased from 18 percent in 1978 to 51 percent in 2011.[1] China has 15 of the world's 100 fastest-growing cities with populations above one million. China also has 89 cities with over a million residents (UN, qtd. in Normille, 2008, pp. 740–743). Urban construction – the building of factories, shopping malls, residential compounds, and so forth – has constituted the primary metaphor for and manifestation of China's economic progress. At the same time, land conflict became China's most politically explosive issue in the past 15 years. The contention surrounding the politics of land control is evident in the extraordinary amount of protest, conflict, and violence associated with land expropriation; distorted and inefficient land use patterns in the countryside; unsustainable urban sprawl; high levels of land-financed local government debt; diminishing arable land; and the apparent inability of central authorities in Beijing to rein in most of these practices (Yu, 2007; Hsing, 2010; Man & Hong, 2011; Wang et al., 2010, 2011).

China's unprecedented efforts at urban construction – and the social and political battles that accompany them – are the product of the country's third twentieth-century land revolution:[2] the commodification of land that began in the late 1980s. According to Article 10 of the Constitution of the People's Republic of China (PRC), all urban land is owned by the state, and all rural

---

[1] National Bureau of Statistics via China Data Online. Chinese citizenship is based on place of household registration, or *hukou*. An estimated 150 million people with rural household status live precariously in Chinese cities; these rural-to-urban labor migrants are frequently called the "floating population." See Fan (2008, p. 71).

[2] The first land revolution comprises the land redistributions (1940s–1953) followed by collectivization (1956–1957) that were the foundations of Chinese Communist Party (CCP) policy during the revolution and after the establishment of the PRC (1940s–1957). The second land revolution is decollectivization and the return to household farming in the 1960s and 1970s.

land is owned by the collective.[3] Prior to 1986, land use rights were allocated to state units or farmers essentially free of charge by urban governments or village governments. In 1986, however, the Land Management Law (revised in 1988 and again in 1998) separated ownership rights from use rights, permitting landowners to lease land use rights for fixed terms in exchange for capital in the form of land use fees (Ho & Lin, 2003, pp. 681–707). Land markets thus became legal in rural and urban China for the first time in PRC history.

Yet land was not the same kind of commodity in all parts of China. As I will show, because the national-level institutions governing property rights over land were vague, local circumstances shaped land markets differently across China. Local land markets did not differ simply in degree, for example, with some markets being larger or more developed than others. Rather, they differed in *kind*, meaning that the very rules governing property rights over land varied from place to place. This subnational variation raises an issue at the very heart of political economy: what drives the emergence and development of property rights over land?

I compare the experiences of three cities in a single Chinese region using a *most similar systems* research design (Przeworski & Teune, 1970).[4] The cities of Changchun, Dalian, and Harbin all began the post-1978 reform era as part of a similar regional political economy – the Northeastern rust belt (东北 *dongbei*), which comprises the provinces of Heilongjiang, Liaoning, and Jilin (see Map 10.1). Yet their fates subsequently diverged because of the distribution of preferential policies from Beijing, which granted some cities early and privileged access to foreign capital and global markets. These seismic transformations in subnational political economies allow me to observe the formation of land markets and changes to urban property rights in cities with similar historical legacies and socioeconomic conditions. Because national-level changes in property rights law, coupled with the territorially uneven implementation of national government policies giving cities access to foreign markets and capital, had contrasting local effects, this analysis exemplifies what this volume's Introduction terms a "top-down" strategy of subnational research, where causes located at higher scales have effects on lower scales. In this case, a major shift in China's national-level property rights law helps explain striking subnational variation in local-level political economies.

---

[3] The "collective" refers generally to the unit of organization for Chinese villages during the Maoist era (1949–1976). Decision-making in rural China is concentrated in village teams, which are generally based on "natural villages" as they existed pre-1949, and in the "administrative village," a group of teams that were united into a production brigade during the Maoist era. In general, the administrative village, typically referred to as the "village," makes decisions about land allocation since the 1990s. See Hsing (2010) and Hui (2003).

[4] Also known as Mill's method of difference. The cases are similar but differ in the outcome or dependent variable.

MAP 10.1 Cities in China Selected for Analysis

10.1 LAND AND PROPERTY RIGHTS IN CHINA: THE VALUE OF A SUBNATIONAL PERSPECTIVE

Dominant explanations in economics and political science of the emergence and effects of property rights institutions typically focus on the national level and over the long term. These analyses invariably set property rights at the center of the institutions required for productive investment and economic growth (Acemoglu & Johnson, 2005, pp. 949–995; North & Weingast, 1989, pp. 803–832; North & Thomas, 1973; North, 1990). The Chinese economic reforms that began under Deng Xiaoping in 1978 introduced markets and market mechanisms yet did not include the adoption of clear, formal, Western-style institutions governing property rights. Scholars have proposed various ways of reconciling this fact with China's extraordinary economic growth, including arguing that decentralization acts as a growth-enhancing de facto property right; that informal institutions offer sufficient guarantees; and that political relationships ensure the security of firms and investments (Clarke, 2003, pp. 89–111; Montinola, Qian, & Weingast, 1995, pp. 50–81; Tsai, 2002, 2008, pp. 116–141). Still others have argued that it is precisely this ambiguity over property rights that permitted adaptive behaviors and innovative, market-oriented activities in China within a Leninist political system (Heilmann & Perry, 2011; Naughton, 1995).

A similar debate occurs in the context of property rights over land. One widely accepted viewpoint stipulates that a lack of clear property rights institutions has led to a number of predatory practices and perverse outcomes in Chinese land markets and land politics. Local governments enjoy the fiscal benefits of land rents as the designated "owner" of urban land as well as rights to requisition land in the "public interest." Coupled with collective ownership over rural land, which prevents individuals and families from liquidating holdings, the lack of clear urban property rights produces a perfect storm of urban sprawl, land grabbing and confiscation, forced evictions, and inadequate recourse for dislocated urban and rural residents (Cai, 2003, pp. 662–680; Guo, 2001, pp. 422–439; Hsing, 2010). Other scholars interpret the conflict surrounding land development and property rights in China as a form of growing pains, arguing that Chinese property rights institutions are evolving and that ambiguities have allowed adaptive flexibility in land arrangements that have served both social and economic interests well (Ho, 2005; Lin, 2009).

Studying land markets and property rights from a national standpoint, however, obscures the vast majority of changes in property rights practices and institutions, which occur at the subnational level. In fact, because local governments are the de facto "owners" of land and therefore the key actors driving land development, theories that privilege the role of national-level actors and institutions can neither explain this local variation nor accurately capture the dynamics of land conflict in China.[5] A subnational approach to the growth of land markets reveals a spectrum of political motives for property rights practices that is far richer than either predation or, alternatively, local adaption. Moreover, these political logics driving property rights vary systematically across contrasting political and economic contexts.

I argue that local institutions and practices of property rights over land emerged as instruments of political expediency for local governments facing different constraints as a result of Beijing's sequencing of economic reforms in China. Instead of looking to national policy, local governments innovatively allocated property rights over land in ways that best served their own most acute interests. Some local governments aggressively promoted land markets, asserting themselves as the monopoly owner of urban land in order to capitalize on its monetary value. Other local governments, by contrast, treated land not as an economic asset to be sold to the highest bidder but as a political asset to be distributed to important constituencies, honoring their claims to property and turning a blind eye to informal and illegal land use on their behalf. In short, the introduction of land markets offered opportunities for local governments to pursue different political goals that reflected preferences shaped by distinct subnational political economies.

---

[5] For an account of how local governments came to be the primary owners of land, see Rithmire (2017).

Attention to the genesis of property rights practices at the local level illuminates a political logic that is difficult or impossible to observe with the conventional focus on institutional change at the national level. National-level analyses tend to emphasize changes in economic structure or national political systems as impetuses for changes in property rights (Demsetz, 1967, pp. 347–359; North & Thomas, 1973; North, 1992). I find instead that decisions about property control are made in a sometimes ad hoc fashion as the product of political bargaining over issues that are not necessarily related to the distributional consequences of property rights arrangements (Libecap, 1989).[6] Put more simply, sometimes property rights are not about property rights at all but rather figure as political resources in larger arenas. In the conclusion (Section 10.6), I return to the broader idea that the subnational vantage point offers great promise for analyzing the multilevel politics of institutional change.

10.2   THE LOCAL POLITICS OF LAND IN CHINA'S RUSTBELT

I compare the process of land commodification from the late 1980s through the 2000s in three cities that entered the reform period as part of a single Chinese region – the Northeastern rustbelt – and, as a result, share quite similar political and economic histories. The provinces of Heilongjiang, Jilin, and Liaoning comprise the Northeast macro-region, referred to in China as the "old industrial base" (老工业基地 *lao gongye jidi*) or what Westerners may call a "rustbelt." The three provinces were the heart of Japanese Manchuria between 1931 and 1945. Despite the atrocities of Japanese imperial occupation, the three northeastern provinces entered the PRC period with substantial inherited infrastructural and industrial capacity: the majority of China's industrial output was generated in Manchuria by the end of World War II (Naughton, 2007, p. 48). This inherited capacity, as well as the region's historic connection to Russia and proximity to the PRC's close ally in the 1950s, the Soviet Union, made the Northeast the heartland of Maoist, state-led industrialization (Zeng & Liang, 1994). Beyond economic growth and state investment, it was in the Northeast where the socialist model of urban organization was most thoroughly developed because of the region's heavy share of state-owned enterprises and formal sector workers.

Despite their shared location in the same region and similar levels of socioeconomic development in 1978, when the central government initiated the suite of market reforms known as "Reform and Opening," the economic fortunes of the three cities have diverged over the past three decades. In 2005, Dalian's GDP per capita was the largest among the three and nearly twice that of Harbin. Urban public revenues in Dalian are double those of Changchun and 20 percent more than Harbin, despite the fact that it is smaller in both size and

---

[6] Libecap also views property rights changes as results of political bargaining, but he sees that bargaining as limited to the distributional consequences of property rights arrangements.

population. Harbin and Changchun continue to funnel nearly half of total capital investment into state-owned enterprises (SOEs), whereas Dalian spends a comparable amount not on SOE investment but on real estate development (see Table 10.1 for basic comparative data).[7] Besides wealth, the most striking difference among these cities lies in their varied levels of global economic integration. Dalian receives considerably more foreign direct investment (FDI) than the other two. Data on employment by foreign firms are instructive in this regard: over half of Dalian's workforce was employed by foreign firms (including those from Hong Kong, Taiwan, and Macao) in the 2000s, compared to just 26 percent in Changchun and 8 percent in Harbin.[8]

While these macroeconomic data offer evidence of the divergent paths taken by the three urban economies, they only partially reveal what these economies look like, how they got there, and the constituencies that exercised voice or, alternatively, lost it in the process. Looking more deeply into the experiences of these cities during the reform era, I find striking differences not only in economic outcomes, such as levels of FDI and wealth, but also in the foundational rules of economic reform, investment, and organization. Following scholars like Richard Locke and Gary Herrigel, who have identified subnational variation in political economic organization in Italy and Germany respectively, we can think of these different sets of foundational rules as comprising distinct urban "economic orders" (Herrigel, 1996; Locke, 1995).[9] Participants in these contrasting urban economic orders – from local officials to private entrepreneurs to publicly owned firms to citizens and workers – held different shared expectations about the rules of economic activity, especially about the extent and nature of the local government's role in the economy.

These shared expectations and understandings that underpin local economic orders were forged during the reform era, as local officials attempted to pursue economic growth and political survival. While inherited economic and social conditions matter tremendously, they do not, especially in the cities I examine, explain the most fundamental differences in local market practices, such as the role of the state in directing investment. Instead, the distribution of preferential policies from Beijing and, therefore, the differential timing and sequencing of economic reform and opening to global capital led local governments to take on different roles in the local economy. Since Deng Xiaoping, the CCP has referred to the post-1978 economic reforms as "economic reform and opening up" (改革开放 *gaige kaifang*). Though these two terms go together, they are quite different policies: "economic reforms"

---

[7] Fixed Asset Investment (*guding zichan touzi*).

[8] Data compiled from Harbin, Dalian, and Changchun statistical yearbooks, various years. These data are from 2008.

[9] Herrigel uses the term "economic order" precisely because it is more encompassing than "industrial structure" or "industrial organization" (pp. 22–23). Both Herrigel and Locke explored variation in a broader array of economic activity than inter-firm relations: for example, the structure of inter-group relations, associational patterns, and links to the national center.

TABLE 10.1 *Harbin, Dalian, and Changchun: Demographic and Socioeconomic Statistics*

	1985 (*1987)	2000	2010
Population (million)			
Harbin	3.8	9.35	9.92
Dalian	4.85	5.51	5.86
Changchun	5.89	6.99	7.59
Urban built-up area (km²)			
Harbin	156	165	359
Dalian	84	234	406
Changchun	105	154	388
GDP* (RMB billion)			
Harbin	6.37	100.27	366.49
Dalian	10.09	111.08	515.82
Changchun	6.31	81.1	332.9
GDP per capita* (RMB)			
Harbin	1,317	10,563	36,951
Dalian	2,022	19,366	77,704
Changchun	1,055	11,550	43,936
FDI* (US$ million)			
Harbin	–	203.14	700.10
Dalian	49.9	1,305.97	10,030.25
Changchun	–	143.83	698.79
Employed persons (million)			
Harbin	2.02	1.72	1.35
Dalian	2.37	.929	.942
Changchun	2.96*	.982	.928

Sources: Population and Urban Size: 1985 data are from *China urban statistical yearbook, 1985* (1985, pp. 26, 44); 2000 and 2010 data are from EPS Net.com, China City Data, accessed September 2013; population figures for Dalian and Harbin are reported slightly differently in local yearbooks (9.41 million for Harbin, 5.45 million for Dalian); see *Harbin statistical yearbook, 2001* (2001) and *Dalian City yearbook, 2001* (2001); Harbin 2010 city size data are from the National Bureau of Statistics via CEIC, China Premium Database, accessed September 2013.

GDP: 1987 data are from the city yearbooks, various years; Dalian GDP per capita, author's calculation; 2000 GDP and per capita and 2010 GDP data are from China Data Online (China Data Center, University of Michigan), accessed September 2013, except for the 2000 Harbin GDP per capita data, which are from *Harbin statistical yearbook, 2001* (2001, p. 460). 2010 GDP per capita data are from EPS Net.com, China City Data, accessed September 2013.

FDI: Dalian FDI data for 1987 are from *Dalian City gazetteer* (2004, p. 268). 2000 and 2010 data are from EPSnet.com, accessed September 2013.

Employment: 1985 data are from *Fifty years of Chinese cities, 1949–1998* (1999); 2000 and 2010 data are from China Data Online, accessed September 2013; Changchun 1987 data are from *Changchun yearbook, 1988* (1988).

typically involve changes to the public sector, such as privatizing or restructuring state-owned enterprises (SOEs), layoffs, and the retreat of the state from provision of social welfare and services. "Opening up," on the other hand, involves gaining access to global capital and global markets. The sequencing of these two major economic changes has a major impact on the role of the local government in the economy.[10] Cities that opened to global capital before dismantling state socialism were able to accumulate capital (through FDI) and establish a constituency for reforms (foreign-invested and export-oriented firms) before undertaking politically painful corporate restructuring and social welfare retrenchment. In such cities, local governments were able to use their role in distributing FDI to induce compliance with corporate restructuring and social welfare reform. In contrast, cities that undertook "reform" before opening adopted painful reforms in a climate of capital scarcity and without established constituencies for reform. In these cities, local officials faced resource constraints and were more dependent on local power bases, including SOEs and the newly emergent capitalist class. Unable to distribute access to global capital as a resource, these governments were more creative in distributing political resources in exchange for compliance with reforms. As we shall see, land was one such resource.

Dalian was designated a "coastal open city" in 1984, allowing the city to court international investors with preferential tax and labor policies; this was nearly a decade before the central government extended this access to Harbin and Changchun. Ironically, in the city that opened early and widely to global capital and markets, local governments ended up with the most concentrated control of the economy. By contrast, in Harbin and Changchun – cities that only later gained access to global markets and investments – local government ended up as a far less dominant actor, sharing economic and political power with various stakeholders.

For the purposes of this study, the distribution of preferential policies from Beijing can be understood as exogenous – that is, determined by factors unrelated to local property rights institutions or pre-reform urban political economies. An extensive body of literature explores the origins and consequences of the Chinese Communist Party's (CCP) decision to open coastal areas to market reforms and global capital first before implementing these economic reforms inland (Fan, 1995, pp. 421–49, 1997, pp. 620–639; Wang & Hu, 1999). That Dalian is a coastal city certainly privileged it over its regional neighbors in being allowed to open to global capital. There is plenty of evidence, some of it presented in this chapter, that inland cities – Harbin and Changchun in particular – were also eager to open up to foreign investment, but Beijing's preference for experimentation and gradualness in introducing market reforms meant that, to paraphrase Deng Xiaoping, some would get rich before

---

[10] For an argument about how the national sequencing of these policies affected the power of the CCP nationally, see Gallagher (2002).

others. As I show, the timing of those policies was fundamental to the establishment of contrasting local economic orders.

Conceptualizing Local Economic Orders across Urban China

Local economic orders – in which state and societal actors share expectations about the rules of economic activity and, especially, the role of the local government in the economy – differ along two main dimensions: intra-governmental relations; and state–firm relations. Intra-governmental relations include the degree of administrative or bureaucratic coherence within the local government. For example, to what extent are the highest levels of local government authority, that is, mayors and party secretaries, able to discipline and direct officials below them? To what extent are economic objectives coordinated across municipal government departments? These relations can be described along a continuum from coherent to fragmented.[11] Local economic orders also differ in state–firm relations, because local governments vary in the kind and degree of authority they exercise over firms. Across Chinese cities, some local governments have maintained a planning role throughout the reform era, directing local investment, "picking winners" among local firms, and fostering environments that nurture successes among specific types of firms or those engaged in particular industries. By contrast, other local governments play a less commanding role, following developments in local markets and firms rather than engineering them. State–firm relations may thus be conceptualized along a continuum between directive and reactive (Segal & Thun, 2001, 557–588; Rithmire, 2014). Table 10.2 organizes these dimensions into a typology of local economic orders.

Dalian exemplifies a **statist** economic order, where the local government itself serves as the key coordinator and steward of economic development.[12] Dalian's municipal bureaucracy can be described as coherent, under the consolidated authority of the highest level of municipal officials, and the local government's relationship with firms was directive, because the government set economic policy objectives that guided firm activities. Dalian, like many cities that benefited from early access to foreign capital as a result of preferential policies from Beijing, designated a development zone outside the urban core to rebalance the concentration of economic power in favor of pro-reform coalitions while leaving the downtown, pre-reform power base undisturbed during the early stages of reform and opening. By later introducing dual pressures for downtown enterprises to restructure (i.e., undergo privatization and/or layoffs) and physically relocate, the city government established itself as both the sole claimant to urban land and the critical link between foreign investors and local firms. This empowered role for the local government allowed Dalian to be among

---

[11] For an example of this analysis applied to Chinese cities and beyond, see Zhang (2013).
[12] For this perspective on statism, see Hall (1986) and Levy (2006).

TABLE 10.2 *A Typology of Local Economic Orders*

		Intra-governmental relations	
		Fragmented	Coherent
State–firm relations	Directive	Decentralized Statist* (no cases)	Statist (Dalian)
	Reactive	Distributive (Harbin)	Regulatory (Changchun)

* Though there are no city cases that exemplify this type in this chapter, fragmented inter-governmental relations and a directive state best describes China's national economic order. Other scholars have used terms like "fragmented authoritarianism" or "decentralized authoritarianism" to describe the CCP regime overall, in which the role of the state in the economy is quite large but manifests at various levels of the administrative hierarchy. See Lieberthal and Oksenberg (1988); Yang (2004).

the first cities in China to initiate land markets in order to generate capital and prestige for the local government.

Harbin – which, as a result of national policies, did not have access to global capital until the mid-1990s – instead pursued decentralization of authority over policies such as housing, enterprise reform, and the expansion of private entrepreneurship, distributing control of urban land to assuage losers of economic reforms and spur growth. This strategy of decentralization and bottom-up growth typifies what I call a distributive economic order, where the local government focuses primarily on dispensing resources to groups, such as firms or workers, with each distributive decision improvised and isolated rather than connected to any overarching economic strategy (Lowi, 1964, pp. 667–715).[13] Intra-governmental relations in Harbin, both vertically through the hierarchy of municipal power and horizontally across policy arenas, can best be described as fragmented, and the government acted reactively in its dealings with firms, allowing them to drive economic policy. In Harbin, land became a resource for distribution and informal property rights were used as a political strategy. Over time, as multiple claimants to urban land became increasingly entrenched, both socially and physically, *de facto* land claims became powerful constraints on the government's ability to regulate land and execute urban planning projects.

[13] This conception of a distributive state borrows heavily from Theodore Lowi's characterization of *distributive* policies, as opposed to *regulatory* and *redistributive* ones. Lowi (1964, p. 690) says, "Distributive policies are characterized by the ease with which they can be disaggregated and dispensed unit by small unit, each unit more or less in isolation from other units and from any general rule … These are policies that are virtually not policies at all but are highly individualized decisions that only by accumulation can be called a policy." Clearly, the Harbin local government did not only make distributive policies, but Lowi's description of distributive policies aptly captures the general character of the relationship between state and society in Harbin.

Changchun, like Harbin, opened late to global capital and only after undertaking market reforms of the state sector. Still, Changchun's municipal leaders were neither as bureaucratically fragmented as Harbin's nor as aggressive as Dalian's. Instead, they were eager to assert control over the city's large automobile sector that was under the direct control of Beijing. Local officials in Changchun saw land commodification as an opportunity to both expand their administrative power and achieve prosperity for the community at large. Changchun thus exemplifies what I call a regulatory economic order, where the local government reacts to economic trends by setting guiding goals in various policy arenas and is capable of disciplining its bureaucracy to pursue these goals.[14] Changchun's government established policies that regularized relationships among firms, workers, and state agencies in a more systematic way than in Harbin, yet it did not pursue intervention and stewardship on the scale seen in Dalian.

Local property practices are but one arena where we see the consequences of these different economic orders. The next sections provide narratives of the development of land markets and property rights practices in the three cities. I focus on how the sequencing of economic reforms and opening to global markets – and, by extension, each city's relationship with the central government in Beijing – produce local economic orders. Still, other variables, including leadership, regional normative or cultural practices, and specific institutional legacies also have effects on local economic orders. My aim is not to provide a comprehensive theory of the origins of local economic orders. Instead, I highlight how a top-down subnational analysis offers a stronger understanding of contrasting economic orders within a single country and, in turn, how this variation produces different property rights outcomes.

10.3   A STATIST ECONOMIC ORDER IN DALIAN

With its coastal location at the tip of the Liaodong peninsula, Dalian was well positioned in the 1980s to benefit from opening to international trade and investment through the central government's coastal development policy (Fan, 1995, p. 623). Dalian's authorities, united under the power of a strong party secretary, Bo Xilai, sought to segregate the activities of the new globally oriented economy from those of the old, creating competition both between private and public firms and among state-owned enterprises.[15] Through

---

[14] I borrow this concept from Lowi (1964, p. 690) as well. He says, "Regulatory policies are also specific and individual in their impact, but they are not capable of the almost infinite amount of disaggregation typical of distributive policies ... because individual decisions must be made by application of a general rule."

[15] Bo, the son of a major CCP patriarch, Bo Yibo, would go on to become governor of Liaoning Province, minister of commerce, and then party secretary of the southwestern provincial municipality of Chongqing, where he gained popular fame – and notoriety – for his campaign against organized crime and revival of Maoist-era mobilization strategies (e.g., singing red songs). In

development zoning first and then by reforming the state sector through forced enterprise relocation, the government of Dalian recalibrated the spatial distribution of power in the city and managed urban interests in a way that established it as the arbiter rather than the target of political conflict.[16] Coherent intra-governmental relationships and a directive role over local firms allowed the city government to monopolize property rights over city land.

Development Zoning

In May of 1984 Dalian was designated as one of 14 coastal open cities, a designation that handed decision-making power over foreign capital to the municipal authorities, allowing them to attract and approve FDI at the local level. The city's authorities looked outside the downtown urban core for the physical space to anchor new forms of economic activity. Even before Beijing conferred special status on Dalian, the city's 1980 master plan included the preliminary designation of a development zone (开发区 *kaifaqu*) in the Maqiaozi village in suburban Jinzhou County, a full 35 kilometers from the city center.[17]

Though the strategy of designating a specific space for internationally oriented development may strike any present observer of urban China as unexciting, in 1984 directing new investment an hour's driving distance from a traditional urban center was novel (see Map 10.2 for a map of Dalian City). The Dalian Economic Development and Technology Zone (or Dalian Development Area, DDA) was the very first such space in China.[18] The DDA offered a number of formal benefits to foreign firms to entice them either to invest in local enterprises or to relocate to the DDA, including a lower tax rate and no real estate taxes for the first three years of the investment period (Chung, 1999).[19] The strategy of development zoning gained greater momentum in the early 1990s after political elites in Beijing signaled that economic reforms would continue following the uncertainty of the Tiananmen protests and crackdown in 1989.[20] In October 1992, the Dalian Tax Free Zone was established adjacent to the DDA in Jinzhou County, becoming China's "first domestically located,

---

2012, Bo fell from power in a political scandal involving his wife and the murder of a British businessman. He was sentenced to life in prison for abuse of power and corruption in 2013.

[16] This section draws heavily from Rithmire (2013).

[17] On the 1980 city plan, see Liu (2001), p. 112.

[18] Dalian's Economic and Technology Development Zone was the first open zone within the jurisdiction of a city. The Special Economic Zones (SEZs) – Shenzhen, Zhuhai, Shantou, and Xiamen – were designated as entirely open cities in 1979.

[19] See also *Dalian City Foreign Trade and Opening Gazetteer* (2004), pp. 518–539.

[20] For the few years following the use of the military to crack down on, and massacre, advocates for democratic change in Beijing, many in China were unsure whether market-oriented economic reforms would continue or if the political crackdown signaled a return to a command economy. See Baum (1992).

MAP 10.2 Dalian City

foreign-run" economic area.[21] Space was also designated for high-technology parks around the DDA and to the southwest of the city center. Seventeen smaller "development zones" were established between 1992 and 1999 (15 in 1992 alone) throughout the city; but only one of the special zones is located within the four core urban districts.

In Dalian, these special designations allowed the city government to direct the spatial distribution of growth and investment and provided a space in which to experiment with reforms. One of the most important experimental policies was the creation of land markets as a novel means of local government financing. Converting what was essentially farmland into a strategic industrial and commercial base required a great deal of capital, an estimated 38 billion Renminbi (RMB) (over 5 billion US dollars) in the DDA's first 10 years. Much of this sum came from funds raised by leasing land in the development zone as the municipal government aggressively asserted its role as landowner, interpreting the 1986 (revised 1988) land law as having granted land leasing and market creation powers exclusively to local governments.[22] The typical

---

[21] *Dalian City Construction Gazetteer* (2004), p. 548. The benefits of the tax-free zone included exemption from domestic taxes (as long as partial assembly was done in the zone) and access to warehousing and transport provided by the city itself.

[22] *Dalian City Construction Gazetteer* (2004), p. 478.

model for a development project in the DDA's embryonic period (1985–1992) involved the construction of infrastructure by local entities (local government, development companies run by city agencies, and state-owned productive enterprises), after which land was leased to foreign investors and domestic commercial developers with lease fees accruing directly to the local government itself.[23] By the early 1990s, having seen the economic benefits of land commodification for local government finances through experimenting outside the city, Dalian authorities began applying the same model of development in the congested downtown area. At this time, Bo Xilai explicitly advanced the idea of "managing the city as an important state asset." This idea, which appears again and again in discussions of Dalian's 1990s transformation, straightforwardly means generating revenue by using land as "a key state-owned resource."[24]

Sequencing of Reforms

The politically and economically difficult enterprise reforms were undertaken in Dalian later in the 1990s, as enterprises were forced to relocate from downtown into new development zones and specially designated industrial zones as part of the city's massive enterprise relocation (般企 *banqi*) campaign. The year 1992 became the turning point after which the "old" city area became a target for redevelopment rather than a place to be avoided in favor of the periphery. The campaign was carried out jointly by the Municipal Bureau of Industry and Commerce (MBIC), Urban Planning and Land Resource Management Bureaus, and the Dalian Municipal Housing Authority, who held authority over approximately 83 percent of residential housing in the downtown core.[25] Between 1994 and 2001, these institutions relocated 115 enterprises from Zhongshan and Xigang Districts alone, freeing over 3 million square meters of land that fell directly under the city government's management.[26]

The relocation campaign targeted enterprises desperate for capital: municipal authorities would guarantee capital infusions for the enterprises in exchange for turning over downtown land. The typical process involved the city

---

[23] For example, the case of the West Pacific Petro-Chemical Factory (*xitaiping yang shiyou huagong youxian gongsi*), established in 1990 (October) jointly between Sinopec, the Dalian Urban Construction company (the corporate wing of the Dalian City Construction Bureau), Daqing city foreign trade conglomerate, China Chemical Engineering Corporation, Zhonghua Oil International (Hong Kong), and Daodaer (France). These parties invested a total of 1.03 billion yuan, 20 percent of which was foreign contributed. See *Dalian City Construction Gazetteer* (2004), p. 478

[24] See "Taking on the Opening Mission and Responsibility" (2001). See also Bo (2003).

[25] Former MBIC official (served 1991–1997), interview, January 2008, Dalian; Housing data from 1985–1986 National Housing Survey; see *Dalian 1986 Yearbook* (1986), p. 62.

[26] Exhibit in Dalian Modern Museum (Dalian Xiandai Bowuguan), visited February 2008. Note that, citywide, there were only 282 large and medium enterprises (SOEs) in 1993. *Dalian 1994 Yearbook* (1994).

government leasing development zone land at a very low cost to an enterprise (an MBIC official in an interview insisted that land was essentially "given away") and then leasing out the enterprise's former downtown location with a promise that some of the capital acquired would be given to the relocated enterprise for facility upgrading and technological investments.[27] Critically, the city would also assist with finding foreign joint-venture partners for enterprises that agreed to move, enabling the city simultaneously to reclaim downtown land from enterprises and guide the restructuring of a firm's management and ownership. For example, the Bohai Beer Factory, which occupied 30,000 square meters downtown, was designated for relocation in 1995. The MBIC negotiated its acquisition by a Hong Kong investment firm, turning over half of the land-lease fee to the factory's domestic owners when the Land Management Bureau secured the former area for a Korean commercial venture (a large mall).[28] And when Sanyo, a major Japanese electronics company, located its production facilities in the DDA in 1996, the DDA assisted with the creation of a large conglomerate firm in which Sanyo was partnered with 16 SOEs relocated from the downtown core. These SOEs were competing with each other to suffer the least number of layoffs.[29] Municipal authorities, in this instance, concurrently reclaimed factory-occupied land and implemented enterprise restructuring.

For the city officials, securing the acquiescence of factory managers who faced underperforming enterprises and painful downsizing in any case was not especially challenging. The thorny parts of the relocation campaign – and the ones rarely discussed in public celebrations of the remaking of the city – concern the movement of the housing compounds that had dominated downtown neighborhoods and relocating the workers who occupied them.[30] In interviews, city officials and urban planners referenced opposition to the relocations of the 1990s. One urban planner recalled many petitions and attempts at protest in 1994 and 1995 but said that because the local party organizations, residential committees, and work units themselves did not support the residents, their efforts at collective organization failed.[31] Another official clearly stated the dilemma facing residents: they stood to lose both their homes and their jobs should they choose to resist relocation. Enterprises often laid off a substantial portion of their work force when they moved and underwent restructuring; therefore, residents and workers within the same

---

[27] Former MBIC official, interview, 2007.   [28] Example cited in Liu (1999), p. 16.

[29] DDA management committee members, group interview, March 2008, Dalian.

[30] Credible estimates of the numbers of residents relocated in the 1990s are scarce. The December 1995 "Dalian City Residential Neighborhood Work Law" set an agenda of creating 95 small residential districts (formally part of the "Hong Kong of the North" campaign) and 175 more in 1996, relocating over 280,000 people in less than a year, which suggests some idea of scale. See *Dalian Patriotic Cleanliness Campaign* (2001).

[31] Urban Designer at Dalian Urban Planning Bureau, group interview, October 2007, Dalian. On the importance of these networks, see Cai and Shi (2006).

firm were actually competing with each other to accept the compensation and relocation arrangements.[32]

The relocation campaign began in conjunction with Bo Xilai's assumption of the city's leadership in 1993 and campaigns to "beautify the city" and transform Dalian into a "commerce and trade, finance, tourism, and informational city."[33] The combination of linking employment prospects with acquiescence to relocation, the offer of substantial compensation packages for residents by leasing out the land on which they had formerly resided, and ideological campaigns to pressure compliance foreclosed any viable attempts at collectively resisting eviction and relocation.

Land markets emerged in Dalian as the linchpin of a strategy of capital accumulation on behalf of the municipal government itself. From the outset of land commodification in the late 1980s, Dalian's authorities asserted themselves as the sole claimants to urban property rights and envisioned land as an asset directly under their control. Land leasing began in the relatively safe experimental zones, allowing the municipal government simultaneously to enlarge its coffers and develop a new economic base outside the old city as well as cultivate new pro-reform constituencies. By developing first outside the city and then asserting control over downtown land, the municipal government was able to position itself at the center of land, labor, and foreign capital markets, strengthening its capacity to direct and control the local economy.

10.4   A DISTRIBUTIVE ECONOMIC ORDER IN HARBIN

Harbin's urban landscape is more a pastiche of power bases than a canvass onto which the local government projects political power and generates wealth. These power bases consist of firms and residential occupants who perceive themselves as de facto – if not de jure – claimants to property rights over land the city has sought to appropriate or reallocate. Unlike Dalian, Harbin had nearly no access to foreign capital early in the reform period, and therefore reforms to the public sector were introduced in a climate of resource scarcity. As officials in Harbin weathered the economic reforms of the 1980s and 1990s under this set of political and economic conditions, the municipal government pursued a strategy of steadily relinquishing control over urban land in its dealings with public sector enterprises, laid-off workers, and an emerging private sector.

Public Sector Firms

Whereas Dalian's officials during the 1980s circumvented potentially messy programs of reform and contests over urban property with centrally located

---

[32] Former MBIC official, interview, 2007.
[33] See "Taking on the Opening Mission and Responsibility" (2001), p. 16.

SOEs by looking outside the city center and to global firms, Harbin's city officials – lacking the power to engage global markets that the central government had granted Dalian – steadily reinvested, politically and economically, in large state-owned enterprises. Scholars have documented Heilongjiang province's "anti-reform conservativism," tracing its continued struggle with market reforms and global opening to the difficulties overhauling the state socialist economy in the early reform period (Christoffersen, 2002; Sullivan, 1988, pp. 198–222). Yet Harbin officials, rather than taking an "anti-reform" posture opposed to politically difficult layoffs and privatization plans, actually did introduce reforms to the state sector. However, the reforms in Harbin aimed to revitalize threatened enterprises by diversifying their economic activities and further decentralizing authority over their operations. This approach to reform produced a concomitant strategy of distributing and decentralizing control over urban land.

Harbin's 1985 master plan sought to limit industrial "sprawl" and rationalize the layout of the city by concentrating infrastructure investments in existing compounds, mostly located in clusters for heavy enterprises created early in the PRC period within the city's six core urban districts. Harbin's four largest industrial compounds and its three central districts were slated to receive investment to "rehabilitate" facilities and housing.[34] The plan expressly avoided the acquisition of new urban land and confined new industrial construction to existing compounds. In the 1980s, Harbin officially acquired only four plots of new land for urban construction, all of which surrounded major industrial compounds within Daoli and Nangang districts.[35] As early as 1986, as they sought to plan infrastructural improvements, the city's highest officials were wrestling with urban industrial firms over land rights. A 1986 project to build a new transport tunnel through Nangang and Xiangfang Districts interfered with the land operated by a local factory, whose manager asked for over 8 million RMB in compensation. The factory's compliance with the construction of the transport tunnel required the intervention of the mayor himself, who went to the factory manager with the requested money and personally counted out each bill to reach a "mutual understanding" with the manager.[36] This strategy of devolving economic and territorial power to enterprises empowered a variety of urban interests vis-à-vis Harbin's municipal authorities. Whereas in Dalian enterprises were becoming dependent on city officials for funding and survival, in Harbin city officials were becoming dependent on the acquiescence of enterprise managers in order to carry out basic urban planning.

---

[34] Harbin City Management Department (1984), p. 6–7. The industrial clusters in Pingfang, Sankeshu, Haxi, and Dongli were each among the 156 national "key point" projects for industrial construction in the first Five Year Plan. See *Harbin City Construction Gazetteer* (1998).

[35] Harbin City Management Department (1984), p. 8; Yu (2002), p. 11.   [36] Gu (1987).

Laid-Off Workers: Housing and Redistribution

Layoffs and factory closures, especially in the late 1980s through the mid-1990s, created potentially destabilizing sets of "losers" to market reforms, and the redistribution of urban land and control of territory served as a key way to assuage these groups (Hurst, 2009, pp. 43–44). Harbin in the 1980s became nationally famous for rehabilitating dilapidated housing compounds that were part of major industrial clusters and doing so without relocating residents. Deng Xiaoping held a Housing Work Conference in Beijing in 1978 and set the national target for living space per person at five square meters by 1985.[37] Realizing that state investment alone would be insufficient to ameliorate urban China's housing shortage, the central government began to encourage investment in new housing with contributions from the central state, local governments, investors, enterprises, and individuals.

In Harbin, new funds for housing were disbursed directly to enterprises.[38] In conjunction with the Municipal Construction Bureau, the enterprises used the money to renovate work-unit housing and build new housing within compounds. The flagship projects were the renovation of Harbin's two most famous slums, the "36" and "18 corner" slums, both of which in the 1950s were turned into work-unit housing compounds attached to machinery plants under the Harbin MBIC. These plants were some of Harbin's first to undergo privatization and layoffs in the 1990s.[39] One Harbin urban planner in charge of such a project in Nangang District in the late 1980s viewed renovating housing as a form of "insurance" for soon-to-be laid-off workers, since they would get ownership over an apartment that they could either choose to rent out at a higher price or keep for themselves, in which case the security afforded by home ownership would make them more willing to take entrepreneurial risks.[40] Investing in housing compounds of threatened enterprises was thus a strategy for compensating the potentially contentious losers of reforms.

Harbin's approach to urban land control was one of decentralization, permitting local neighborhoods and enterprises to draw up and implement their own detailed local plans, albeit with the approval of the municipal planning agency. An essay by Yu Binyang, a prominent urban planner in Harbin, offers a telling description of the process of planning in the 1980s:

Harbin has had a difficult time incorporating widely accepted and national standards of good living environments. For example, average living space per person is much lower than in the rest of the country, but neighborhoods and surroundings are much more convenient. Harbiners do not want to demolish large parts of the old city to build green

---

[37] *Contemporary China's Construction* (1990), pp. 108–110.
[38] Xinhua News Agency (1980); *Harbin Party History Materials*, Part 3 (n.d.). The Municipal Party Committee actually devolved control over housing assignments to worker congresses (*gonghui*) after unrest over unfair housing assignments.
[39] Interview with vice director of Harbin Society of Urban Planners, October 2007.
[40] Interview with senior urban planners, retired, November 2007.

space, and new space for commerce and the tertiary industry has developed somewhat organically in the downtown area without a great deal of demolition and reconstruction.[41]

Yu concludes that local discretion over the built environment is a condition particular to Harbin and one that has contributed to the distinctive quality of Harbin's urban form. In short, while the government of Dalian was centralizing intra-governmental relations, buoyed by the authority to attract foreign investment granted to the city by the national government, Harbin's government was decentralizing them, giving local officials latitude to distribute control of land in exchange for cooperation with reforms to the state-run economic sector.

Emergent Private Industry: Informal Property Rights and the Informal Sector

As formal sector workers experienced layoffs and wage cuts or anticipated their inevitability, many turned to petty commerce and street-level services as a means of livelihood. In Harbin, these activities emerged in areas that boasted a rich tradition of private and commercial activity prior to nationalization in 1956 – Daoli and Daowai Districts. Daoli District, home to Harbin's celebrated Central Street and the center of the Russian émigré bourgeoisie in the 1920s, became the epicenter of commercial and service enterprise development during the reform period. Daowai houses the Muslim quarter surrounding the city's largest mosque and was settled very densely by Chinese laborers in the early twentieth century. Both districts have a long tradition of vibrant private enterprise, and the commercial impulse was quick to return under conditions of economic liberalization.[42]

To be sure, the growth (or return) of commercial streets and bourgeois clusters was far from spontaneous. The Harbin MBIC was instrumental in fostering an advantageous environment, institutionally and spatially, for these small commercial endeavors. As early as 1980, the MBIC encouraged experimentation with private business and issued instructions to ease the registration process for urban private enterprises. By 1981, the city had registered over 12,000 private enterprises, 21 times the number registered at the end of 1978.[43] Critically, the onus of encouraging, registering, and approving private enterprise rested with lower levels of government, such as district governments (区 *qu*) or street offices (街道办事处 *jiedao banshichu*).

---

[41] Yu (2002), p. 76. This essay was selected by the municipal government as the third most outstanding essay on Harbin published in 2002 – a sign that Yu's views were reflecting those of the authorities.

[42] Daowai before 1949 was home to 4,950 self-owned stores and businesses – 63 percent of such businesses citywide. *Daowai District Social and Economic Development Comprehensive Statistical Yearbook, 1978–1987* (1988), p. 3.

[43] *Heilongjiang Province Private Enterprise Economic Yearbook* (2004), p. 102.

The blossoming of commercial activity – shoe repair, craftsmanship, barber shops, food stalls, teahouses, bakeries – emerged under the purview of street offices that were extensively integrated with local communities. The central municipal branch of the MBIC and its local arms acted as advocates for urban private enterprise, designating spaces for operations and turning a blind eye to entrepreneurial activities when they contradicted other local governmental policies.[44]

By the late 1990s, land control had become one of the most politically salient issues in Harbin, taking a close second place to labor issues even during the most intense strike wave of the decade in 1997.[45] Harbin's economic policies generated land strategies that emboldened existing occupants and encouraged new claimants to downtown land in the form of a new class of urban entrepreneurs. In addition to struggles with firms and residents, various arms of the municipal administration dealt differently with their constituencies in struggles over land control, precluding the municipal government from exercising the kind of unified government control over land seen in Dalian.

10.5 A REGULATORY ECONOMIC ORDER IN CHANGCHUN

Changchun's municipal officials were eager to embark on reforms and open to the global economy, and they demonstrated a resigned awareness that Changchun faced constraints because it lacked the preferential central government policies required to attract much-needed foreign investment into the city's enterprises. The greatest challenge faced by local officials was the overwhelming reliance of the city's economy on the automobile sector. Changchun's emergence as a motor city began with the construction of the First Auto Works (FAW) in 1956, an enormous automobile manufacturing SOE whose "Liberation"-brand trucks and "Red Flag" limousines were once the pride of the city and the country.[46]

FAW has always been a centrally owned and operated SOE, meaning that the rights of control over the enterprise, the firm's land, and access to profits all belong to the central government in Beijing instead of the local government.

---

[44] Interview with members of Daowai District Commerce Association, March 2008. Business owners throughout Jingyu market credited the MBIC, chiefly its Daowai District organ, for their survival during the hard times of the 1990s.

[45] For 1997, issues of insurance, pension, and wages for laid-off or retired workers accounted for 25 percent of collective visits or letters (that is, group visits and petitions to register grievances with local governments), and city construction, relocation, and planning accounted for another 20 percent. *Harbin Yearbook, 1998* (1998), p. 83.

[46] Changchun was selected as the site of China's first auto manufacturing plant because of its well-developed rail networks and strategic location close to the Soviet Union but far from the eastern coast; with the onset of the Korean War in 1950, central planners began to consider ways to protect industry from the more militarily vulnerable coastline. *Changchun Coach Company Gazetteer, 1954–1990* (1993), pp. 14–15.

FAW is an albatross to the city because its fortunes are linked to a large enterprise over which it has little control. Politically, the president of FAW, appointed by the Central Party Organization Department in Beijing, holds a higher rank in the CCP than the mayor of Changchun (Thun, 2006, 181). Still, when central SOEs downsize, experience wage arrears, or seek to reduce their social welfare burdens by contributing less toward social insurance, housing, and pensions, the resulting displaced workers become the local government's problem. These massive enterprises also occupy large tracts of urban land, generating conflict between SOEs who stand to gain from liquidating land holdings and local governments who seek these same financial gains and are also charged with urban development projects.

In the 1980s, like many cities in China, Changchun faced dire capital shortages as well as pressing needs for investment in urban infrastructure and technological upgrading of enterprises. Throughout the decade, Changchun's municipal officials eagerly embraced the reform atmosphere by encouraging the growth of an embryonic private and commercial sector. At the beginning of the 1980s, housing renovation was concentrated in the city's poorest and most overcrowded areas and in neighborhoods likely to absorb returnees from the countryside. Toward the end of the decade, municipal officials focused their development efforts on work units undergoing reforms or experiencing wage arrears. The critical difference between Changchun and Harbin, however, was the high level of coherence and autonomy from societal interests among municipal bureaucratic units in Changchun, as opposed to the fragmented nature of the Harbin bureaucracy.

Housing and Redistribution

As Changchun began implementing piecemeal reforms of public enterprises in the middle of the 1980s, housing investment and ownership reforms were undertaken in ways that both targeted potential losers of reform and reasserted the municipal government's control over urban land. In some instances, the devolution of authority over wages and bonuses to enterprises resulted in enterprise managers paying workers greater amounts, which, in turn, exacerbated overall losses (Steinfeld, 1998, pp. 86, 112), and many Changchun enterprises were in such dire straits that they accumulated wage arrears.[47]

---

[47] This was apparently the case especially at some larger SOEs, such as the tractor, bicycle, and washing machine factories, some of the first factories to be completely bankrupted in the early 1990s. Reports of unrest at these enterprises because of wage nonpayment in *Changchun Yearbook, 1989* (1989), p. 51; *Changchun Daily* (1988a, 1988b). Changchun's workers were also active in the spring of 1989. At least 16 "ringleaders" were arrested at FAW for initiating strikes and protests across Changchun. They organized at least one year prior to the onset of the Tiananmen protests. Mayor Shang Zhanling also cited groups of workers bombarding factory floors to recruit workers and stage strikes as well as block street intersections. See BBC News (1989a, 1989b).

Reactions to these reforms, especially in the midst of nationwide macroeconomic instability and inflation in 1988 and 1989, generated significant unrest. First Party Secretary Ma Ximing noted in 1990 that "instability at factories and work units has been the primary obstacle to implementing reforms," and reports from the research office of the Changchun Party Committee state that many of the city's enterprises saw a 50 percent drop in production levels or even stopped production altogether.[48]

In this climate, the Real Estate Bureau undertook large-scale housing commodification – a process that did not occur in most of China until 1998 – as a way to liquidate some enterprise assets and also placate workers through asset redistribution.[49] In 1988, city officials noted that enterprises lacked capital for the maintenance of housing compounds and their ancillary facilities: "Nurseries have insufficient rooms inside or play space outside. Public green areas are trampled and constructed upon; some have become office space, some residential areas, and some have become spontaneous markets."[50] The city's Party Committee called for strengthening urban planning by enhancing the status of the Urban Planning Office. The Urban Planning Office was established in 1989 to facilitate the rehabilitation of the urban landscape by "having one office in charge of urban planning and urban management."[51] In the same year, the Land Management Bureau (LMB) initiated sweeping citywide campaigns to conduct building censuses and register occupancy claims with the municipal government. In September of 1989, the city also established the Real Estate Market Management Office, which was essentially charged with regulating property rights over land.

The establishment of the independent Urban Planning Bureau, with orders to work closely with the land and real estate officials, set the stage for coherent regulatory policy over land; in the parlance of the city's own annals, the administrative changes signaled a "new stage for the management of land assets in Changchun."[52] The division of labor among the agencies was relatively clear: the LMB was the accountant and owner-manager of urban land, the real estate authorities were charged with leasing out land to generate revenue, and the UPB were the strategic planners and enforcers of the city's plans for the urban landscape. The personnel staffing these agencies in Changchun frequently moved back and forth among them, and flexibility in urban plans allowed them to adapt practices to maximize economic growth, control over land, and political stability. According to interviewees who worked in the UPB in the early 1990s, there were few conflicts between agencies, and the

---

[48] Ximing (1990); *Changchun Yearbook, 1991* (1991), pp. 3, 41. In 1988, 1,088 of the 6,474 "letters and visits" (*xinfang*) of complaints to government offices in Changchun concerned wage non-payment. *Changchun Yearbook, 1989* (1989), p. 144.

[49] State Council of the People's Republic of China (1998).

[50] *Changchun Yearbook, 1989* (1989), p. 56.   [51] Changchun City (1988).

[52] *Changchun Yearbook, 1989* (1989), pp. 302–303.

key motivation for empowering urban planners was the perceived crisis in city revenues in the late 1980s and the readily visible dilapidation of the urban environment. One former official remarked, "All of the offices in charge of land understood that in order for problems [in the city's economy] to be solved, we had to solve the problems of the city's layout, and the only way to have money to do that would be to utilize the land."[53] In 1989, when the three agencies were founded, 82 percent of urban land was under the control of work units (according to their own estimation and records). By 1995, this ratio had changed substantially, with 20 percent of urban land for construction under the control of central SOEs, 40 percent under the control of collectives and local SOEs, and 40 percent under private control – that is, leased out with revenues accruing to the municipal government.[54]

Urban Expansion in Changchun under Globalization

Changchun opened to the global economy in 1992 when Beijing approved the city's first development zone, established southeast of the city center.[55] Initial investment in infrastructure made the zone ready for the establishment of foreign-invested firms, after which city authorities depended on capital from land-leasing to fund further local development. For the few first years of the zone, the leasing of land was critical to finance further infrastructure construction. In keeping with established patterns regarding land control inside the city's core, the development zone authorities set up a branch of the LMB with an office to coordinate with the UPB; all land transactions and usage rights would go through the LMB, which worked under the direction of the development zone management committee.[56] The zone's LMB branch began to work with municipal industry and commerce officials to initiate a "dual track" reform process for enterprises experiencing losses in the city center: "On the one hand we constructed a modern industrial open zone, and on the other reformed

---

[53] Former vice director of the UPB, present professor of urban planning and architecture, interview, Jilin University, July, 2009.

[54] Calculations are my own based on yearbook data. These estimates are conservative since the yearbook in 1996 only displays data on urban land for construction throughout the city's jurisdiction, rather than just in the five core districts referenced in the 1989 data. Therefore, much of the 40 percent of urban construction land for collectives reported for 1995 was rural land controlled by town and village enterprises (TVEs), which means that the actual proportion of land leased out was likely much higher than 40 percent. *Changchun Yearbook*, 1996 (1996), p. 143.

[55] *Changchun Economic and Technology Development Zone (ETDZ) Gazetteer, 1992–2004* (2008), pp. 33–34. As in Dalian, the area was primarily farmland prior to the designation of the ETDZ. The acquisition process, according to official reports, involved payouts of 8,000 RMB to occupants between 18 and 35 years of age and 16,000 RMB to those over 35 in addition to the national standard for peasants losing land for agricultural production (3 times annual income plus predetermined prices per meter for various crops).

[56] *Changchun EDTZ Gazetteer* (2008), p. 33.

SOEs by allowing them to move to the development zone, vacating valuable land [in the city center] for development. They took the capital they raised through the real estate transactions to build new and better facilities in the development zone," after which the development zone authorities would help "graft on" foreign capital, "generating good results for all parties."[57] Forty SOEs underwent such a process in the 1990s.[58]

Although the process of creating the development zone in Changchun was similar to that in Dalian during the "enterprise relocation" campaign in the 1990s, differences in the development zones themselves had contrasting consequences for the level of integration between the development zones and their host cities. Unlike Dalian's zone, the development zone in Changchun is only 5 kilometers from the city's symbolic center at the People's Square, a distance that residents can walk in less than one hour, and at least six bus routes traffic the route. The decision to locate the new zone as close as possible to the city was driven by several strategic reasons.[59] Whereas the Dalian Development Area's labor base consisted mostly of rural-to-urban migrants, city officials in Changchun were concerned about unemployment and social order in the city center, and they thought that establishing a zone with preferential policies nearby would allow enterprise relocation and employee transfers to occur (as opposed to the labor displacement experienced in Dalian). The city thus invested funds in transportation infrastructure (roads and buses) instead of workers' dormitories, and even as of 2012 a relatively small portion of land use in the development zone was devoted to housing.[60] The combination of the zone's proximity to the city center, investment in transportation links, and the fact that that housing reform and commodification of land preceded the moves of many SOEs to the development zone helps explain why Changchun has experienced remarkably little suburbanization compared to other large Chinese cities.[61]

The Changchun municipal government, through bureaucratic coordination among relevant agencies, established itself as the sole allocator of the rights to use, generate income from, and transfer urban property. In a climate of capital scarcity as a result of the sequencing of reform and opening, the city government was pressured to redistribute to residents and upgrade urban infrastructure at the same time as it was implementing politically contentious reforms, such as social welfare retrenchment and corporate restructuring, to the city's economy. Changchun's intra-governmental coherence, I have suggested, stems from the

---

[57] Yu (2001). Yu served as the director of the ETDZ management committee for 13 years.

[58] Yu (2001).   [59] Yu (2001).

[60] In the 1996 plan, 12.8 percent was devoted to housing. In the overall land use composition citywide (for urban construction land), the proportion for housing stayed between 27.43 percent and 29.72 percent throughout the 1990s. Zhang (2000); Lu, Qi, & Li (2010), p. 46.

[61] Geographers rank Changchun's level of suburbanization as extremely low for the 40 largest Chinese cities according to population. The built area of the city has remained essentially within a 10 square kilometer area since the onset of reforms. See Wang, Li, & Ding (2001).

city's simultaneous dependence on and alienation from its largest economic constituent, FAW and its affiliates, whose social and political burden the city bears without enjoying most of its economic fruits. Changchun's leaders were eager to find ways to finance necessary upgrades and construction, and they turned to the control of land as a way to generate income both for the city and for capital-starved enterprises. Yet, compared to Dalian, the role in the economy played by city government in Changchun was much more reactive, allowing both public (e.g., FAW) and private sector actors to pursue their own economic objectives while simultaneously carving out an independent space for local government authority. As a result, the municipal government in Changchun regulated but, in contrast to the outcome in Dalian, did not dominate property rights.

10.6 CONCLUSION: LOCAL AND NATIONAL NARRATIVES OF LAND

In the opening to this chapter, I presented a series of undesirable outcomes related to land policy in China – disputes between urban residents and governments and between rural residents and governments, inefficient patterns of land use, dramatic reduction of arable land, urban sprawl, and real estate bubbles. The conventional wisdom, drawing on the neo-institutionalist tradition, views these negative outcomes as the inevitable results of a lack of institutional clarity over property rights in reform-era China (Guo, 2001, pp. 422–439; Ho, 2005; North & Thomas, 1973). In this view, most of the problems stem from local government predation and expropriation, behaviors that can only be prevented with institutionalized property rights supported by an independent court system.

Although the lack of clear property rights is a national phenomenon, we do not observe predation and expropriation in every city. In the period under study here (1988 through to the late 1990s), when property rights were least clear, we surprisingly observe not large-scale predation and expropriation but rather the harnessing of property rights over land by local officials in ways that helped them manage the different political challenges they faced. Of course, as seen in Dalian, some city government officials actively introduced and promoted land markets for their own enrichment. In Changchun and Harbin, however, city officials relied on the regulation and distribution of urban land not for personal enrichment but as a potent political tool for forging accommodations among key local stakeholders with conflicting interests. These agreements, in turn, made it possible for urban development to proceed.

The findings presented here also challenge a second expectation: that Chinese land markets would steadily liberalize together with an evolution of property rights institutions toward greater clarity. From this standpoint, the beneficiaries of secure land-lease rights – especially the private sector and foreign investors – are expected to push for greater security of land rights by seeking formal restrictions on the state's taking powers and also stronger judicial enforcement of property rights (Ho & Lin, 2003, pp. 681–707). This line of reasoning leads to the prediction that China's coastal areas, which enjoy higher levels of foreign investment and where market forces have been active for longer, will see stronger demands both for property protections and more transparent land markets.

Yet the evidence and analysis presented in this chapter do not support the hypothesis that greater market liberalization and opening to global capital produce stronger claims for land rights. In fact, the city that opened earliest and implemented liberalizing economic reforms first, Dalian, subsequently ended up with the most, not the least, local state intervention in land markets and control of urban property. Conversely, Changchun, a city that was not authorized by the central government to open its economy to global markets until far later, developed transparent policies over land markets. Moreover, these policies were not a "demand-driven" response to pressure from private or foreign interests but resulted from an initiative led by city government officials. And in Harbin, another latecomer to globalization, municipal authorities succumbed to claims to land rights staked by both private (capitalist) and public sector (socialist) actors. The municipal governments across all three cities adopted strategies for establishing land markets that reflected their own political and economic needs, which, in turn, stemmed largely from differences in the timing of economic liberalization and the opening of urban economies to foreign trade and investment.

Sharp variation in the local political economies of Chinese land markets strengthens the case for a subnational approach to the politics of property rights. Dominant approaches to property rights institutions, with few exceptions, focus exclusively on national-level institutions (Haber, Maurer, & Razo, 2003; North, 1990; North, Wallis, & Weingast, 2009; Larsson, 2012; exceptions include Libecap, 1989; Verdery, 2003). This national-level focus directs attention toward formal institutions and large, structural explanations for changes in property rights. Indeed, scholars have taken the establishment of formal national institutions – land laws and judicial enforcement institutions – as the paramount indicator for how property rights are practiced and whether they are secure. By contrast, local-level analysis lays bare the political bargains and accommodations that produce informal property rights and, sometimes, underlie formal institutions that are later adopted. By combining attention to local-level variables and the sequencing of national policies into a multilevel theory, as I have done here, we can better understand why similar cities adopted such different property rights practices.

In the Chinese case, local property rights practices emerged as local officials responded to both national-level policies and local political conditions. National policies from Beijing determined when and, crucially, in what order cities would open to global capital and implement economic reforms to dismantle elements of state socialism. This "top-down" process sorted cities into different local economic orders because it either afforded or, alternatively, denied them access to global capital before they took on politically difficult economic reforms such as privatizations and layoffs. Given these different realities, local officials responded to local political concerns, such as desires to promote urban growth or assuage political losers, as they crafted property rights practices in their cities.

In this volume's introduction, the editors discuss several multilevel analytical strategies, including the top-down approach I adopt here, a bottom-up approach in which subnational choices affect national outcomes, and a reciprocal vertical approach where subnational behavior both causes and is caused by political choices at higher levels. Scholarship on property rights in diverse geographic and institutional environments has increasingly adopted multilevel strategies, paying attention especially to reciprocal causality, in explaining the origins of property rights institutions and their effects on other important political phenomena. Combining a top-down and bottom-up approach, Alisha Holland explains local tolerance of squatting, street vendors, and other informal and illegal property rights practices in Latin America by looking to the electoral strategies of local officials. She argues that inadequate national social policy leaves the urban poor reliant on informal and illegal survival strategies, and local governments vary in their tolerance of illegal activities, a phenomenon she calls "forbearance," depending on local electoral institutions. Holland further argues that widespread forbearance by local governments as a strategy for redistribution mitigates demand for more inclusive national welfare policy, demonstrating how subnational causes have national-level effects (Holland, 2017). Scholars of property rights in the former socialist world have effectively employed a bottom-up strategy to explain why national-level property rights institutions are "hollow" – that is, they assign rights by law that few citizens actually enjoy in practice. In her study of post-soviet Ukraine, Jessica Allina-Pisano blames this disjuncture on what she calls "sub rosa resistance," by which local state actors produce a façade of compliance with central policy while subverting those policies they deem less advantageous for themselves and, sometimes, the communities they serve, in favor of the status quo (Allina-Pisano, 2004, pp. 555–556). Catherine Boone's study of rural land-tenure regimes examines both national and subnational variation in the rules governing access to and authority over land in Africa, arguing that different land tenure regimes produce distinct electoral dynamics, patterns of political violence, redistributive politics, and ethnic competition. Although Boone focuses on explaining the effects of land-tenure regimes, she also views property rights regimes themselves as products of contingent choices made by local and national elites in response to political pressure (Boone, 2014).

For decades, social science research has puzzled over which kinds of property rights institutions best facilitate economic growth and social well-being; indeed, property rights institutions are one arena where the ideas of social scientists have manifested in the policies and institutions countries have adopted, and with mixed outcomes (Mitchell, 2005, pp. 297–320). Recent research on the making of property rights institutions and the realities of property rights practice at different scales, however, suggests that the focus on institutional design may have been somewhat misplaced. Even in a case like China, with a centralized authoritarian regime and a strong state, we observe striking variation in property rights practice at different scales across subnational units. Whether scholars are interested in property rights as independent or dependent variables, they will likely produce much richer political insights by employing a subnational lens to study how politics across multiple levels of government shape a phenomenon that is foundational to a range of broader outcomes.

BIBLIOGRAPHY

Acemoglu, Daron, & Johnson, Simon. (2005). Unbundling institutions. *Journal of Political Economy 113*(5), 949–995.
Allina-Pisano, Jessica. (2004). Sub rosa resistance and the politics of economic reform: Land redistribution in post-soviet Ukraine. *World Politics 56*(4), 555–556.
BBC News. (1989a, June 8). Mayor of Changchun urges protesters to act "reasonably."
BBC News. (1989b, July 13). Counter-revolutionary clique arrested in Changchun.
Boone, Catherine. (2014). *Property and political order in Africa: Land rights and the structure of politics.* New York, NY: Cambridge University Press.
Baum, Richard. (1992). Political stability in post-Deng China: Problems and prospects. *Asian Survey 32*(6), 491–505.
Cai, Yongshun. (2003). Collective ownership or cadres' ownership? The non-agricultural use of farmland in China. *The China Quarterly 175*, 662–680.
Cai, Yongshun, & Shi, Fayong. (2006). Disaggregating the state: Networks and collective action in Shanghai. *The China Quarterly 186*, 314–332.
Christoffersen, Gaye. (2002). The political implications of Heilongjiang's industrial structure. In John Fitzgerald (Ed.), *Rethinking China's provinces*, pp. 221–246, New York, NY: Routledge.
Chung, Jae Ho (Ed.). (1999). *Cities in China: Recipes for economic development in the reform era.* New York, NY: Routledge.
Clarke, Donald C. (2003). Economic Development and the Rights Hypothesis: The China Problem. *The American Journal of Comparative Law 51*(1), 89–111.
Demsetz, Harold. (1967). Toward a theory of property rights. *The American Economic Review 57*(2), 347–359.
Fan, C. Cindy. (1995). Of belts and ladders: State policy and uneven regional development in post-Mao China. *Annals of the Association of American Geographers 85*(3), 421–449.
Fan, C. Cindy. (1997). Uneven development and beyond: Regional development theory in post-Mao China. *International Journal of Urban and Regional Research 21*(4), 620–639.
Fan, C. Cindy. (2008). Migration, Hukou, and the city. In Yusuf Shahid & Tony Saich (Eds.) *China urbanizes: Consequences, strategies, and policies*, pp. 65–89. Washington, DC: World Bank.

Gallagher, Mary E. (2002). Reform and openness: Why china's economic reforms have delayed democracy. *World Politics 54*(3), 338–372.

Guo, Xiaolin. (2001). Land expropriation and rural conflicts in China. *The China Quarterly 166*, 422–439.

Haber, Stephen H., Maurer, Noel, & Razo, Armando. (2003). *The politics of property rights: Political instability, credible commitments, and economic growth in Mexico, 1876–1929*. Cambridge, England: Cambridge University Press.

Hall, Peter A. (1986). *Governing the economy: The politics of state intervention in Britain and France*. New York, NY: Oxford University Press.

Heilmann, Sebastian, & Perry, Elizabeth J. (2011). *Mao's invisible hand: The political foundations of adaptive governance in China*. Cambridge, MA: Harvard University Asia Center: Distributed by Harvard University Press.

Herrigel, Gary. (1996). *Industrial constructions: The sources of German industrial power*. Cambridge, England: Cambridge University Press.

Ho, Peter. (2005). *Institutions in transition: Land ownership, property rights, and social conflict in China*. Oxford, England: Oxford University Press.

Ho, Samuel P. S., & Lin, George C. S. (2003). Emerging land markets in rural and urban China: Policies and practices. *The China Quarterly 175*, 681–707.

Holland, Alisha. (2017). *Forbearance as redistribution: The politics of informal welfare in Latin America*. Cambridge, England: Cambridge University Press.

Hsing, You-tien. (2010). *The great urban transformation: Politics of land and property in China*. Oxford, England: Oxford University Press.

Hurst, William. (2009). *The Chinese worker after socialism*. New York, NY: Cambridge University Press.

Larsson, Tomas. (2012). *Land and loyalty: Security and the development of property rights in Thailand*. Ithaca, NY: Cornell University Press.

Levy, Jonah D. (2006). *The state after statism: New state activities in the age of liberalization*. Cambridge, MA: Harvard University Press.

Libecap, Gary D. (1989). *Contracting for property rights*. Cambridge, England: Cambridge University Press.

Lieberthal, Kenneth, & Oksenberg, Michel. (1988). *Policy making in China: Leaders, structures, and processes*. Princeton, NJ: Princeton University Press.

Lin, George C. S. ([1995] 2009). *Developing China: Land, politics and social conditions*. London, England: Routledge.

Locke, Richard M. (1995). *Remaking the Italian economy*. Ithaca, NY: Cornell University Press.

Lowi, Theodore J. (1964). American business, public policy, case-studies, and political theory. *World Politics 16*(4), 677–715.

Man, Joyce Y., & Hong, Yu-hung. (2011). *China's local public finance in transition*. Cambridge, MA: Lincoln Institute of Land Policy.

Mitchell, Timothy. (2005). The work of economics: How a discipline makes its world. *European Journal of Sociology 46*(2), 297–320.

Montinola, Gabriella, Qian, Yingyi, & Weingast, Barry R. (1995). Federalism, Chinese style: The political basis for economic success in China. *World Politics 48*(1), 50–81.

Naughton, Barry. (1995). *Growing out of the plan: Chinese economic reform, 1978–1993*. New York, NY: Cambridge University Press.

Naughton, Barry. (2007). *The Chinese economy: Transitions and growth*. Cambridge, MA: MIT Press.

Normille, Dennis. (2008). China's living laboratory in urbanization. *Science 319*, 740–743.

North, Douglass C., & Thomas, Robert Paul. (1973). *The rise of the Western world: A new economic history*. Cambridge, England: Cambridge University Press.

North, Douglass C., & Weingast, Barry R. (1989). Constitutions and commitment: The evolution of institutional governing public choice in seventeenth-century England. *The Journal of Economic History 49*(4), 803–832.

North, Douglass C. (1990). *Institutions, institutional change, and economic performance*. Cambridge, England: Cambridge University Press.

North, Douglass C. (1992). *Transaction costs, institutions, and economic performance*. San Francisco, CA: ICS Press.

North, Douglass C., Wallis, John Joseph, & Weingast, Barry R. (2009). *Violence and social orders: A conceptual framework for interpreting recorded human history*. Cambridge, England: Cambridge University Press.

Przeworski, Adam, & Teune, Henry. (1970). *The logic of comparative social inquiry*. New York, NY: Wiley-Interscience.

Rithmire, Meg. (2013). Land politics and local state capacities: The political economy of urban change in China. *The China Quarterly 216*, 872–895.

Rithmire, Meg. (2014). China's "new regionalism": Subnational analysis in Chinese political economy. *World Politics 66*(1), 165–194.

Rithmire, Meg. (2017). Land institutions and Chinese political economy: Institutional complementarities and macroeconomic management. *Politics & Society 45*(1), 123–153.

Segal, Adam, & Thun, Eric. (2001). Thinking globally, acting locally: Local governments, industrial sectors, and development in China. *Politics & Society 29* (4), 557–588.

Steinfeld, Edward. (1998). *Forging reform in China: The fate of state-owned industry*. New York, NY: Cambridge University Press.

Sullivan, Lawrence. (1988). Assault on the reforms: Conservative criticism of political and economic liberalization in China, 1985–1986. *The China Quarterly 114*, 198–222.

Thun, Eric. (2006). *Changing lanes in China: Foreign direct investment, local governments, and auto sector development*. New York, NY: Cambridge University Press.

Tsai, Kellee S. (2002). *Back-alley banking: Private entrepreneurs in China*. Ithaca, NY: Cornell University Press.

Tsai, Kellee S. (2006). Adaptive informal institutions and endogenous institutional change in China. *World Politics 59*(1), 116–141.

Verdery, Katherine. (2003). *The vanishing hectare: Property and value in postsocialist Transylvania*. Ithaca, NY: Cornell University Press.

Wang, Hui, Tao, Ran, Wang, Lanlan, & Su, Fubing. (2010). Farmland preservation and land development rights trading in Zhejiang, China. *Habitat International 34*(4), 454–463.

Wang, Hui, Wang, Lanlan, Su, Fubing, & Tao, Ran. (2011). Rural residential properties in China: Land use patterns, efficiency and prospects for reform. *Habitat International 36*(2), 201–209.

Wang, Shaoguang, & Hu, Angang. (1999). *The political economy of uneven development: The case of China*. Armonk, NY: M. E. Sharpe.

Yang, Dali L. (2004). *Remaking the Chinese leviathan: Market transition and the politics of governance in China.* Stanford, CA: Stanford University Press.

Zhang, Yue. (2013). *The fragmented politics of urban preservation: Beijing, Chicago, and Paris.* Minneapolis: University of Minnesota Press.

CHINESE BIBLIOGRAPHY

Bo, Xilai. (2003). How to operate a city as state asset [*Ruhe jingying chengshi zhefen guoyou zichan*]. In Liu Changde (Ed.), *Symphony of a city: The idea and practice of Dalian City* [*Chengshi jiaoxiang: Dalian shi linian yu shixian*], pp. 8–13. Beijing, China: Qinghua University Press.

Changchun City. (1988). Document 45.

Changchun coach company gazetteer, 1954–1990 [*Changchun keche chang zhi, 1954–1990*]. (1993). Changchun, China: Jilin People's Press.

Changchun Daily [*Changchun Ribao*]. (1988a, May 3).

Changchun Daily [*Changchun Ribao*]. (1988b, May 5).

Changchun economic and technology development zone (ETDZ) gazetteer, 1992–2004 [*Changchun jingjing jishu kaifaqu zhi, 1992–2004*]. (2008). Changchun, China: Jilin People's Press.

Changchun yearbook, 1988 [*Changchun nianjian, 1988*]. (1988). Changchun, China: Jilin renmin chubanshe.

Changchun yearbook, 1989 [*Changchun nianjian, 1989*]. (1989). Changchun, China: Jilin renmin chubanshe.

Changchun yearbook, 1991 [*Changchun nianjian, 1991*]. (1991). Changchun, China: Jilin renmin chubanshe.

Changchun yearbook, 1996 [*Changchun nianjian, 1996*. (1996). Changchun, China: Jilin renmin chubanshe.

China urban statistical yearbook, 1985 [*Zhongguo chengshi tongji nianjian, 1985*]. (1985). Beijing, China: Xin shijie chubanshe.

Contemporary China's Construction [Xiandai Zhongguo de jianshe]. (1990). Beijing, China: Academy of Social Sciences Press.

Dalian City construction gazetteer [*Dalian shi zhi: Chengshi jianshi zhi*]. (2004). Dalian, China: Dalian Publishing Company.

Dalian City foreign trade and opening gazetteer Dalian City foreign trade and opening gazetteer [*Dalian shi zhi: waijing waimao zhi*]. (2004). Dalian, China: Dalian Publishing Company.

Dalian City gazetteer: Foreign economy and foreign trade [*Dalian shi zhi: waijing waimao zhi*]. (2004). Beijing, China: Fangzhi chubanshe.

Dalian City yearbook, 2001 [*Dalian shi nianjian, 2001*]. (2001). Beijing, China: Zhongguo tongji nianjian.

Dalian patriotic cleanliness campaign, 1988–1998 [*Dalian shi aiguo weisheng yundongzhi, 1988–1998*]. (2001). Dalian, China: Dalian Patriotic Cleanliness Campaign Committee.

Daowai District social and economic development comprehensive statistical yearbook, 1978–1987 [*Haerbin shi Daowai qu shehui jingji fazhan tongji zonghe nianjian, 1978–1987*]. (1988). Harbin, China.

Fifty years of Chinese cities, 1949-1998 [*Xin Zhongguo chengshi wushinian, 1949–1998*]. (1999). Beijing, China: Xinhua chubanshe.

Gu, Wanming. (1987). Treating urban illness: Harbin city's renovation strategy [*Yizhi chengshi bing: Haerbin chengshi gaizao lueji*]. *Liaowang Magazine 44*(3), 21–22.

Harbin City construction gazetteer [*Harbin Shi: Chengshi guihua, tudi, shizheng gongyong jianshe zhi*]. (1998). Harbin, China: Heilongjiang Renmin Chubanshe.

Harbin City Management Department. (1984). *Harbin City 1985 master plan.* Archives of the Urban Planning Society of Municipal Harbin.

Harbin party history materials, Part 3 [*Ha'erbin dangshi ziliao*]. (n.d.). Harbin Municipal Archives, D235.351/01–3.

Harbin statistical yearbook, 2001 [*Ha'erbin tongji nianjian, 2001*]. (2001). Harbin, China: Ha'erbin nianjianshe.

Harbin yearbook, 1998 [*Haerbin nianjian, 1998*]. (1998).

Heilongjiang Province private enterprise economic yearbook [*Heilongjiang sheng minying qiye jingji nianjian*]. (2004). Harbin, China: Heilongjiang Renmin Chubanshe.

Hui, Qin. (2003). *Nong min zhongguo: Li shi fan si yu xian shi xuan ze.* Zhengzhou, China: Henan ren min chu ban she.

Liu, Changde (Ed.). (1999). *Symphony of a city: The idea and practice of Dalian City* [*Chengshi jiaoxiang: Dalian shi linian yu shixian*]. Beijing, China: Qinghua University Press

Liu, Changde (Ed.). (2001) *Dalian City planning 100 years, 1899–1999* [*Dalian chengshi gui hua yi bai nian*]. Dalian, China: Dalian Naval Affairs University Publishing House.

Lu, Shichao, Qi, Yong, & Li, Bingxin. (2010). Study on evolution and driving force of urban construction land structure of Changchun City [*Changchun shi chengshi jianshe yongdi jiegou yanbian jiqu dongle fenxi*]. *Journal of Jilin Institute of Architecture and Civil Engineering* [*Jilin jianzhu gongcheng xueyuan xuebao*] *27* (5), 46.

State Council of the People's Republic of China. (1998, July). Notice on further deepening reform in the urban housing system and accelerating housing construction [*Guowuyuan guanyu jinyibu shenhua chengzhen zhufang zhidu gaige jiakuai zhufang jianshe de tongzhi*]. State Council, No. 23.

Taking on the Opening Mission and Responsibility: An Interview with Dalian Urban Planning and Land Resource Management Bureau chief Wang Zhenggang [*Jianfu kaituo de shiming yu zeren: fang Dalian shi guihua he guotuziyuanju Wang Zhenggang juzhang*]. (2001). In Liu Changde (Ed.), *Dalian city planning 100* years, 1899–1999 [Dalian chengshi gui hua yi bai nian], pp. 15–16. Dalian, China: Naval Affairs University Publishing House.

Wang, Qichun, Li, Chenggu, & Ding, Wanjun. (2001). Study on urban area structure of Changchun City [*Changchun Shi chengshi dihou jiegou tixi yanjiu*]. *Scientia Geographica Sinica* [*Dili Kexue*] *21*(1), 81–88.

Ximing, Ma. (1990, December 23). Speech to the 7th plenum 6th plenary session of Changchun CCP.

Xinhua New Agency. (1980, November 28). Foreign Broadcast Information Service (FBIS) *Daily Report.* Naples, FL: Readex.

Yu, Binyang. (2002). Create the concept of modern urban planning and act as the 'dragon head' of city management. In Yu Binyang (Ed.), *21st century Harbin City planning measures research* [*21 shiji Ha'erbin chengshi guihua duice yanjiu*], pp. 73–80. Harbin, China: Harbin Chubanshe.

Yu, Binyang (Ed.) (2002). *21st century Harbin City planning measures research* [21 *shiji Ha'erbin chengshi guihua duice yanjiu*]. Harbin, China: Harbin Chubanshe.

Yu, Deman. (2001). Boosting construction of development zones as a way of running cities [*Jiakuai kaifaqu jianshe, tansuo chengshi jingying jingyan*]. *Urban Studies* [*Chengshi Xuexi*] 8, 23–26

Yu, Jianrong. (2007). *Organized peasant resistance in contemporary China: An investigation of Hengyang County of Hunan Province* [*Dang Dai Zhongguo Nong Min De Wei Quan Kang Zheng: Hunan Hengyang Kao Cha*]. Xianggang, China: Zhongguo wen hua chu ban she.

Zeng, Juxin, & Liang, Bin. (1994). Comparative research on regional economic growth in China [*Zhongguo quhou jingji zengzhang bijiao yanjiu*]. *Economic Geography* [*Jingji Dili*] 14(1), 16–20.

Zhang, Hongbo. (2000). Research on industrial layout in Changchun Economic and Technology Development Zone [*Changchun Jingji Jishu Kaifaqu gongye buju yanjiu*]. *Journal of Changchun Teachers' College* [*Changchun shifan daxue xuebao*] 19(2), 70–77.

CONCLUSION

II

Empirical and Theoretical Frontiers of Subnational Research in Comparative Politics

Agustina Giraudy
Eduardo Moncada
Richard Snyder

Subnational research (SNR) plays a growing and increasingly prominent role in comparative politics. It advances knowledge about fundamental themes that define the field, including regimes, states, and development. The contributions to this volume show how looking inside countries provides a powerful way to discover new and humanly important phenomena hidden from view by the dominant national lens. Moreover, SNR spurs theoretical innovation, especially multilevel theory building; offers new strategies for comparative research; and can be combined fruitfully with vanguard methodologies.[1] These achievements of SNR point to key areas where more work needs to be done. In this concluding chapter, we discuss empirical and theoretical challenges for future research.

II.I EMPIRICAL FRONTIERS: COLLECTING, STANDARDIZING, AND AGGREGATING SUBNATIONAL DATA

A major empirical challenge of SNR concerns the availability of subnational data. The "whole-nation bias" (Rokkan, 1970, p. 49) in comparative politics historically led to a focus that emphasized country-level data.[2] As a result, a gap exists in the availability of comprehensive, systematic, and readily accessible subnational data. Although subnational researchers have slowly but

An initial draft of this chapter was presented at the Workshop on Subnational Politics organized by the Department of Political Science at the Catholic University of Chile (PUC), November 30–December 1, 2017, in Santiago, Chile. We thank the participants in the Workshop, especially Rodrigo Mardones, for helpful comments on the draft. We also thank Carla Alberti and Juan Pablo Luna for organizing the Workshop and inviting us to present this material there.

[1] For further examples of the substantive, theoretical, and methodological contributions of recent subnational research, see Sybblis and Centeno (2017).

[2] Wimmer and Glick Schiller (2002, p. 307) discuss a related problem, "methodological nationalism," which they argue "reduces the analytical focus to the boundaries of the nation-state."

steadily started to fill this data gap by carrying out the vital and often painstaking work of collecting and organizing qualitative and quantitative subnational data,[3] important hurdles remain. These obstacles include a scarcity of cross-sectional subnational data, which constrains case selection, descriptive analysis, and hypothesis testing, as well as a lack of historical subnational datasets, which hampers longitudinal research.

The production and collection of subnational data is especially difficult in the Global South, where limited state capacity and resources, informality, and armed conflict, among other factors, can hinder the ability of both national and subnational government agencies to consistently gather systematic data on which social scientists can draw (see Auerbach, LeBas, Post, & Weitz-Shapiro, 2018).[4] This problem is especially acute in the many policy areas that are now administered by local governments as a result of the wave of decentralization in the late twentieth century. Local government agencies across much of the Global South simply lack the institutional infrastructure, technical expertise, and resources to develop and systematically implement measures for evaluating trends and outcomes across policy areas.

Subnational researchers have tackled the problem of data scarcity by turning to new tools for spatial analysis. Geographic Information Systems (GIS) has enabled the construction of new datasets both for discrete spatial objects, such as borders of countries, regions, cities, and villages, and for continuous variables over space, such as population density, violence, economic productivity, and topographical elevation (Gleditsch & Weidmann, 2012, p. 465). High-resolution satellite imagery and other remote sensing tools offer further exciting possibilities for generating new subnational data (Auerbach, LeBas, Post, & Weitz-Shapiro, 2018). For example, satellite imagery makes it possible to collect data about inaccessible places, such as conflict zones that pose high safety risks to researchers.[5] Satellite imagery can be combined with other kinds of geocoded information to provide rich new subnational data, as seen in Nemeth et al. (2014), which uses multiple forms of geocoded data to gain fresh insights into the causes of domestic terrorism. Likewise, recent studies of civil war have successfully harnessed GIS and spatial data to produce fine-

---

[3] See, for example, Baldwin (2014); Cammett and Issar (2010); Charron and Lapuente (2013); Díaz-Rioseco (2016); Durán-Martínez (2018); Giraudy (2015); Ingram (2016); Hollenbach et al. (2016); Niedzwiecki (2018); Touchton and Wampler (2014); Trejo and Ley (2018); Freidenberg and Suárez-Cao (2014); Resnick (2014); Rodrigues-Silveira (2012); Steele (2011); Yasuda (2017); Zukerman-Daly (2012).

[4] See Lecours and Hallen (2016) for a vivid example of how the lack of data collection by Latin American national and subnational governments on the number of tobacco-related deaths hinders the adoption of potentially life-saving public health policies. See also Nori-Sarma et al. (2017) on the challenges researchers face in obtaining and deciphering municipal-level mortality registry data.

[5] As King (2009) notes, satellite imagery can also help researchers overcome barriers posed by the absence of reliable official government statistics.

grained subnational data and measures of key variables.[6] The proliferation of satellite and geocoded data as a way to address the problem of subnational data scarcity, however, raises another problem: the use of different measures and scales across studies. This underscores the importance of recent efforts to standardize subnational data on armed conflict and political violence along these and other dimensions.[7] Still, as Imke Harbers and Matthew C. Ingram remind us in Chapter 2, the spatial perspective arrived later in political science than in other social science disciplines, and the spatially attuned studies seen in recent research on armed conflict and violence are still the exception and not the rule.

Another important task facing future subnational research concerns the lack of historical datasets on key political processes and policy areas. Recent research on subnational democracy provides an illustrative example. Because of the lack of historical datasets about subnational regimes (McMann, 2018), the vast majority of these studies focuses on the Third Wave democratization period (1974–2010), when subnational data became more readily available.[8] This temporal data limitation imposes an important constraint on our understanding of subnational political regime dynamics. Many of the outcomes we seek to explain result not from swift shocks but from gradual changes in institutions that unfold over long periods of time (Pierson, 2003; Mahoney & Thelen, 2010, p. 3). Subnational democratization can be both a result and cause of slow-moving processes, and good longitudinal data is thus required to understand its origins and consequences.

An important effort to supply systematic subnational data on political regimes that span longer periods of time can be seen in the Varieties of Democracy dataset (V-Dem), which bills itself as "the largest database on democracy in history." V-Dem has recently added 22 indicators of subnational democratic institutions and practices for all countries, except microstates, from 1900 to 2012. This will help equip researchers to assess the evolution of subnational regimes, develop more sophisticated descriptive analysis, and test hypotheses across time periods both within countries and across subnational units in multiple countries.

---

[6] See, for example, Buhaug and Rød (2006); Hegre et al. (2009); Lyall (2009); Østby et al. (2009); Schutte and Weidmann (2011). See also Hollenbach et al. (2016) for a study that combines satellite imagery and other kinds of geocoded data to analyze state-building and resource allocation across territory in post-conflict settings.

[7] An innovative example is the xSub initiative, based at the University of Michigan, which aggregates and harmonizes subnational data on violence around the world. See http://www.cross-sub.org; and Zhukov et al. (2017) on the initiative's rationale and objectives. Available at: https://sites.lsa.umich .edu/zhukov/wp-content/uploads/sites/140/2017/08/xSub_Aug2017pdf (last accessed January 1, 2018).

[8] See, for example, Solt (2003); Benton (2012); Borges (2007); Gervasoni (2010); Giraudy (2010, 2013, 2015); Lankina and Getachew (2006, 2012); Rebolledo (2011); and Reisinger and Moraski (2010).

The work on state capacity by Mariano Sánchez-Talanquer (n.d.) offers another good example of a recent effort to widen the temporal scope of subnational data. Focusing on Colombia and Mexico, Sánchez-Talanquer aims to explain striking variation in the ability of modern states in the Global South to provide security, collect taxes, acquire knowledge about their societies, and improve the welfare of citizens. Combining newly uncovered archival documents and other unexamined primary sources with historical census data and contemporary measures of state activity, he offers fine-grained subnational data at the municipal and submunicipal levels on taxation, construction of mass education systems, extension of state systems of civil registration, provision of local security, and other core state activities. The new georeferenced historical datasets are analyzed with a variety of causal identification strategies, including spatial statistics and other quantitative techniques that exploit discontinuities between neighboring municipalities. Together with qualitative analysis of primary evidence, these quantitative tests show that domestic struggles and cleavages, not interstate warfare and external threats, determined the types of state capacity that developed as well as their geographical distribution within countries.

In addition to the collection and standardization of subnational data, another task for future SNR concerns aggregation – that is, assessing how subnational variation affects national-level concepts and measures of regimes, states, and development. For example, as discussed in Chapter 1 and also Chapter 5 by Caroline Beer, Chapter 9 by Sunila Kale and Nimah Mazaheri, and Chapter 8 by Prerna Singh, SNR shows that wide variation exists inside countries in the extension of political and social rights.[9] Yet existing national measures of democracy, authoritarianism, state capacity, and welfare states fail to consider the extent to which these phenomena are uniformly present across the national territory. As Agustina Giraudy and Jennifer Pribble (2018) argue, the lack of a territorial component in national-level concepts and measures severely hampers our understanding of key political phenomena.

Consider research on democracy and universal welfare states.[10] Conceptually, full democracy and welfare state universalism both rest on the idea that all citizens, regardless of where they reside in a country, will have an equal opportunity to exercise their political and social rights. In other words, a full democracy and a universal welfare state can be said to exist only if all citizens across all the national territory can vote, engage in civic activities, express their thoughts freely, and have access to health care and education as well as other forms of social protection. Although a territorially even distribution of political and social rights is implicitly a core attribute of democracy and welfare universalism, it has not been incorporated explicitly into national-level

---

[9] See also Luna and Medel (2017).
[10] This and the next paragraph draw on Giraudy and Pribble (2018).

measures of these concepts.[11] Empirically, because existing national-level measures of democracy and welfare state universalism do not account for the uneven territorial extension of rights, they provide limited, and potentially misleading, information for assessing whether countries are fully democratic and universalistic in the provision of welfare benefits.

Giraudy and Pribble (2018) thus propose Territorial Gini Indexes, which they use to adjust existing national-level measures of democracy and welfare state universalism. In turn, Giraudy and Pribble use the resulting Adjusted Measures of Democracy/Welfare State Universalism to show that certain Latin American countries that are celebrated for advances toward full democracy and welfare universalism appear less impressive when territorial variation in the extension of political and social rights is considered. For example, the performance of Chile, widely viewed as a regional leader in achieving welfare state universalism, looks far less impressive when the national measure of universalism is adjusted for territorial inequality.[12] With regard to democracy, Argentina and Mexico perform less well with the new national Adjusted Measure of Democracy than with unadjusted national measures, and, contrary to conventional wisdom, Mexico surprisingly performs better than Argentina in the 1990s. Including within-country territorial variation in national-level measures of welfare states and democracy thus offers an alternative and more accurate assessment.

In sum, by drawing on innovative techniques such as these for collecting, standardizing, and aggregating subnational data, researchers can make further progress in overcoming the empirical challenges to SNR posed by the scarcity of subnational datasets.

11.2 THEORETICAL FRONTIERS: CHALLENGES OF SUBNATIONAL UNIT SELECTION AND OPPORTUNITIES FOR THEORY-BUILDING

The welcome efforts to increase the supply and variety of subnational data raise theoretical challenges.[13] As Robert A. Dahl cautioned about the worldwide explosion in the amount of social science data over the past 50 years, "The problem now is an excess of information ... Theoretical frameworks are crucial for dealing with all this information, because information that can't be tied to a theoretical framework just becomes a book of facts, or random

---

[11] This mismatch between the definitions of these concepts and their operationalization results in a lack of what Goertz (2006) calls "concept-measure consistency."

[12] See Otero-Bahamon (in press) for a related study of "social subnational inequality" in contemporary Latin America.

[13] See Branch (2016) on the theoretical and conceptual challenges that the GIS revolution poses for scholars of international relations.

knowledge" (Munck & Snyder, 2007, p. 145). Several key theoretical issues arising from the proliferation of new subnational data merit emphasis.

As discussed in Chapter 1, a subnational focus offers researchers the exciting possibility of working with a far larger and more diverse set of territorial units of analysis. While this opens opportunities for innovative research designs, it also poses challenges of selecting the appropriate unit. Hillel Soifer's Chapter 3 addresses this problem of unit selection, noting that subnational research faces a conundrum, long recognized by geographers yet seldom addressed by political scientists: the modifiable areal unit problem, or MAUP. The MAUP stems from the fact that, according to the geographer Stan Openshaw (1984, p. 3), the spatial units in many studies are "arbitrary, modifiable, and subject to the whims and fancies of whoever is doing, or did, the aggregating." Moreover, the relationships among variables can be extremely sensitive to changes in both the size and shape of the areal unit used to measure the data. Openshaw (1984, p. 22ff) highlights the potentially devastating consequences of the MAUP for statistical inference: aggregating the same data into different spatial units can produce correlation coefficients for a single pair of variables ranging from -0.93 to $+0.99$ (Soifer & Alvarez, 2017, p. 3). The implications of the MAUP for social science research are quite significant. For example, Cho and Baer (2011, pp. 416–418) show that research on racial attitudes in the United States employs a wide variety of different units of analysis, including census block groups, census tracts, cities, metropolitan areas, counties, states, parishes, public housing projects, and even prison cells. In turn, findings and conclusions about the determinants of racial attitudes vary across studies using different units. Soifer succinctly summarizes the consequences of the MAUP: "as the unit of analysis varies, so too will our results."

To manage the problems posed by this sensitivity of results to changes in units, Soifer recommends that the choice of units "should begin with theory" – that is, with the causal claim the researcher wants to evaluate. He proposes dividing theories into three categories: those that are *unit-independent* and can apply to any unit of analysis; those that are *unit-specific* and apply only to particular units of analysis; and those that are *unit-limiting* because they can be evaluated with some units of analysis yet not others.[14] Ana Arjona's Chapter 7 in this volume offers a good example of unit selection driven by theory that is "unit-limiting." She argues that localities, which include a variety of small units such as neighborhoods, hamlets, and villages, are the appropriate units for making causal claims about civilian cooperation with rebels during civil wars. This is because these small units comprise the spatial context, or what she calls the "locus of choice," where civilians make decisions about whether to cooperate with or, alternatively, resist efforts by rebel organizations to

---

[14] Singh (2017) distinguishes between theories developed at the subnational level that are scalable to the national level and those that are not scalable, that is, "unit specific" in Soifer's terms. In his Chapter 3, Soifer notes that unit-independent theories are rare in political science, because most causal claims are only applicable in certain contexts.

establish their rule. Moreover, a focus on subnational units facilitates more precise conceptualization of the different forms that civilian cooperation and noncooperation alike can take. Arjona harnesses a subnational perspective to develop a more nuanced typology of civilian behavior in conflict zones. Making this conceptual advance requires shifting from a focus on national-level determinants of civilian behavior in wartime settings to a subnational approach centered on the specific locality where these consequential choices occur.[15] Arjona's theory-driven selection of local units of analysis thus provides a foundation for a stronger understanding of civilian cooperation in civil wars.

Theoretical considerations can also lead scholars to combine different kinds of subnational units in a single study. Although these units may differ in important respects, they can be analytically equivalent from the standpoint of the theory the researcher is building or testing. This principle of cross-system equivalence, which is routinely invoked as a guide for developing valid indicators in comparative research (Przeworski & Teune, 1970), can also help scholars address the challenge of unit selection. For example, the level at which collective bargaining between workers and employers takes place varies across countries and also across sectors within countries, ranging from the company to industry to national levels.[16] Achieving cross-system equivalence in a comparative study of labor politics may thus require a focus on different kinds of units depending on the locus of collective bargaining.[17] Likewise, similar political duties and powers may be located at quite different levels of government across countries, rendering municipalities in one country and states in another analytically equivalent units. An illustrative study that combines national and subnational units is Patrick Heller's (2001) comparative analysis of democratic decentralization in the Brazilian city of Porto Alegre, the Indian state of Kerala, and the country of South Africa. Despite the fact that these three cases are very different kinds of units – that is, a city, a state, and a country – Heller justifies the comparison because they share a key political attribute: All were governed by grassroots, left-of-center political parties. Still, the three cases vary in the degree to which marginalized societal groups were incorporated into decision-making about the allocation of public resources. To explain the contrasting roles of marginalized groups, Heller focuses on a pair of critical relations, state–civil society and political party–social movements, at the city, state, or national level depending on the case.[18]

---

[15] In her Chapter 7, Arjona discusses three seminal works that paved the way for the shift to the local level in the study of civilian behavior during civil wars: Peterson (2001); Wood (2003); and Kalyvas (2006).

[16] See Hsueh (2011) for a comparative study of subnational variation in government–business relations across economic sectors in China.

[17] See Locke and Thelen (1995) on ways to achieve equivalence in comparative research through what they call "contextualized comparisons" that focus on different, yet analytically equivalent, factors across cases.

[18] Gallagher's (2016) study of the judicial fate of cases of homicides and disappearances in domestic courts in Mexico and Colombia offers another good example of combining

In addition to cross-system equivalence, another rationale for juxtaposing different kinds of units concerns "matched comparisons" that can help control for variables across cases. Consider a subnational comparative study of Argentina and India where the size of the population is an explanatory or control variable. The population of 10 of India's 29 states is greater than the entire population of Argentina (41.22 million in 2010), with India's largest state, Uttar Pradesh, alone having a population (199.58 million in 2011) nearly five times the size of Argentina's.[19] Matching subnational units on the basis of population may thus require studying different kinds of units in each country, for example cities in India and provinces in Argentina. By bringing into focus a wide variety of different units inside countries, a subnational perspective gives researchers greater flexibility to select units of analysis in ways that bolster cross-system equivalence and strengthen comparative research design. Taking advantage of this increased maneuverability, however, requires researchers to make effective use of theory to guide the choice of units.

But formal administrative units – e.g., a city, county, or a state – do not necessarily map neatly onto the *subjective* understandings individuals hold of the spatial contexts that inform their political perceptions and behavior. This potential disjuncture between objective and subjective understandings of context has important theoretical implications. For example, in their study of how context shapes racial prejudice, Wong et al. (2012) add a map-drawing exercise to a survey questionnaire as a way to probe whether the administratively defined territorial boundaries of the area where respondents' houses are located overlap with their perceptions of the spatial boundaries of their "local communities." Gauging the overlap between objective and subjective boundaries is important because existing theory predicts that individuals' perceptions about demographics in the places they live – conventionally measured by using objective administrative units – have a strong effect on whether they see racial outsiders as threats. Wong et al. (2012) find striking discrepancies between the formal and subjective units of analysis: Respondents tend to define their communities subjectively as small locales inside the objective, formal administrative units that researchers normally rely on. Moreover, the accuracy of respondents' perceptions of the racial composition of units decreases as the scale increases beyond their subjectively defined understandings of their communities. One strategy to mitigate this discrepancy between objective and subjective units of analysis and, more broadly, the MAUP, is for researchers to

subnational and national units. She analyzes subnational data from three Mexican states (Chihuahua, Guerrero, Nuevo Leon) alongside national-level data from Colombia.

[19] The 10 Indian states with populations larger than Argentina's in 2016 were Uttar Pradesh, Maharashtra, Bihar, West Bengal, Madhya Pradesh, Tamil Nadu, Rajasthan, Karnataka, Gujarat, and Andhra Pradesh. Data on the population of India's states are from India Ministry of Home Affairs, Office of the Registrar General and Census Commissioner (2011, Map 5). Data on Argentina's population are from the United Nations, Department of Economic and Social Affairs: https://esa.un.org/unpd/wpp/DataQuery/ (last accessed: July 14, 2018).

test whether their findings hold at multiple scales (Wong et al., 2012, p. 1157; Soifer, Chapter 3 in this volume). A subnational approach can help implement this recommendation for assessing the robustness of findings by offering researchers a diverse set of units of analysis at different scales.

Another theoretical challenge facing future SNR concerns the distinction between jurisdictional, or formal, and non-jurisdictional, or informal, units that we introduced in Chapter 1. Again, it is helpful to refer to Soifer's Chapter 3, which notes that jurisdictional units often have an advantage regarding data availability, because many measures of phenomena of interest to social scientists are produced by government agencies. Consequently, electoral, economic, and demographic data are often aggregated at the scale of jurisdictional units, such as districts, municipalities, states, provinces, and departments. However, many important phenomena of interest are non-jurisdictional, because they are not contained by formal jurisdictional units, such as criminal groups and other violent non-state actors, vector-borne infectious diseases and other public health threats, environmental degradation, pollution, and natural disasters. The "shapes" of phenomena such as these do not fit neatly, if at all, into the formal grids defined by jurisdictional units. Not only do they cut across jurisdictional boundaries, including international borders, but their spatial distribution and, hence, density can also vary widely both within and across formal jurisdictions.[20] How should researchers handle these "unbound" phenomena that do not fit into jurisdictional units?

One approach to unbound phenomena involves using raster, or grid squares, comprised of standardized rectangles to divide up the area of a country, thereby dispensing with formal jurisdictional units altogether.[21] This approach offers an advantage, especially to those who prefer experimental methods, because it reduces the risk that unit boundaries are endogenous to the outcomes of interest: Raster boundaries are far less likely than political and administrative boundaries to be related causally and systematically to variables of interest to researchers. Still, a raster approach will likely face daunting data challenges, because official and other kinds of data are very unlikely to be collected at the raster level. Moreover, the challenges posed by the incongruence, or lack of "fit," between unbound phenomena and subnational jurisdictional units will not necessarily be surmounted by substituting raster for jurisdictional units.

Regarding the limits of raster as a technique for managing unbound phenomena, it is appropriate to consider James C. Scott's (1998) concept of "high modernism" – that is, the simplifying and standardizing schemes that states devise to render legible, administer, and govern societies. Scott shows the unintended, sometimes tragic, consequences stemming from the failure of these

---

[20] The GIS technique of "hot spot" mapping is premised on spatial variation in the density of phenomena, such as crime.

[21] See, for example, Gleditsch & Weidmann (2012), and Tollefsen et al. (2012), as discussed in Soifer's Chapter 3.

simplifying schemes to consider the complexity and unpredictability of the social and natural worlds. Jurisdictional units can be interpreted as instances of high modernism, potentially vulnerable to the pernicious consequences that Scott argues result from simplifying state schemes. From this standpoint, using a raster grid of standardized rectangles to try to get beyond the limitations of subnational jurisdictional units for studying unbound phenomena would seem to be an exercise in an even higher modernism that may, like state simplifications, prove woefully inadequate for comprehending the phenomena of interest.

An alternative approach to unbound phenomena, rather than dispensing with jurisdictional units by turning to raster, takes the incongruence, or lack of "fit," between unbound phenomena and formal jurisdictions as an opportunity for theory-building. For example, Richard Snyder and Angélica Durán-Martínez (2009a, 2009b) focus on a major change in the boundaries of law enforcement districts in Mexico in the late 1990s, showing how this resulted in a new map of territorially fragmented districts for the administration of justice. Moreover, whereas the geographical distribution of drug-trafficking organizations, the so-called Tijuana, Sinaloa, Gulf and Juárez "cartels," was aligned with the old jurisdictional map, which had divided the country into three large and contiguous administrative districts in the North, Center, and South, the new jurisdictional map undid this spatial alignment.[22] The resulting lack of fit between the redrawn law enforcement map and the geographic distribution of criminal organizations, in turn, fostered both a breakdown of the long-standing state-sponsored protection racket and a massive increase in violence.

The factors that shape the internal dynamics and durability of informal and non-jurisdictional units, such as squatter settlements, regional economies, and criminal fiefdoms, offer further opportunities for theory building. For example, Eduardo Moncada (in press) explores why business firms targeted for illicit taxation by criminal organizations pursue strikingly different forms of resistance, ranging from armed rebellion to peaceful and discreet everyday negotiations. These varied forms of resistance, in turn, have contrasting consequences for the scope and maintenance of criminal fiefdoms that extend across both formal (e.g., an entire municipality) and informal (e.g., a handful of city street blocks) jurisdictions. Moncada proposes and tests a new theory that explains the strategies of resistance to criminal extortion pursued by firms as the result of their economic and political resources, especially how much access they have to financial capital and the state's coercive apparatus.

A further theoretical frontier of SNR concerns subnational units of analysis that are *non-territorial*, such as ethnic and other societal groups, especially ones that are not geographically concentrated. Examples of non-territorial

---

[22] The undoing of the old spatial alignment between jurisdictional districts of law enforcement, on the one hand, and the geographical distribution of drug-trafficking organizations, on the other, was no accident. It was part of a package of anti-corruption reforms introduced by Mexico's federal government in the mid-1990s (Snyder & Durán-Martínez, 2009a, pp. 264–265).

subnational units include ethnic minorities in interwar Europe that were geographically dispersed inside countries, such as the Russians in Latvia, the Jews in Lithuania, and the Protestants in Ireland (Coakley, 1994). Non-territorial units are, by definition, unbound – that is, they cut across and are contained neither by formal or informal territorial subnational units. This incongruence between non-territorial and territorial subnational units produces a dilemma in the case of geographically dispersed ethnic minorities, because the lack of territories where minorities are dominant precludes the possibility of their exercising autonomy or self-government on a territorial basis through federalism or other mechanisms for devolving power to subnational units.[23] Still, just as research on the lack of fit between unbound phenomena and jurisdictional subnational units has spurred analytic and theoretical innovation, the incongruence between non-territorial and territorial subnational units, both formal and informal, may also offer fruitful opportunities for theory building.

11.3   CONCLUSION: ADVANCING KNOWLEDGE ACROSS SCALES

SNR offers a venerable, powerful, and exciting way to do comparative politics. As seen in the contributions to this volume, SNR has made important substantive, theoretical, and methodological contributions to political science. Still, as noted in Chapter 1, we do not claim that all comparative research should be subnational. The nation-state continues to stand as the constitutive unit of global politics, with citizenship and political identities routinely defined in terms of countries. The demand for social science research with a national focus is strong, and it will surely remain so. Just as we do not seek to displace national-level research, we also do not aim to carve out a segregated separate sphere for subnational work. Instead, we hope to foster greater engagement among scholars who study the same or similar problems at different scales. The potential for such cross-scale engagement to advance knowledge can be seen in the recent efforts already discussed to improve national measures of democracy and social welfare by including subnational data on spatial variation. The promise of cross-scale dialogue is further illustrated by the examples this book offers of multilevel theory-building that combines national and subnational perspectives to achieve more powerful explanations of phenomena ranging from women's rights (Beer's Chapter 5) to economic development (Rithmire's Chapter 10) and human security (Trejo and Ley's Chapter 6). We hope this book will inspire others to address empirical and theoretical challenges like these as they seek to understand the many humanly important problems both across and inside countries.

---

[23] On "non-territorial autonomy" as a plausible alternative for such groups, see Coakley (1994).

BIBLIOGRAPHY

Auerbach, A. M., LeBas, A., Post, A. E., & Weitz-Shapiro, R. (2018). State, society, and informality in cities of the Global South. *Studies in Comparative International Development* 53(3), 261–280.

Bahaug, Halvard, & Rod, Jan Ketil. (2006). Local determinants of African civil wars. *Political Geography* 25(3), 315–335.

Baldwin, Kate. (2014). When politicians cede control of resources: Land, chiefs, and coalition-building in Africa. *Comparative Politics* 46(3), 253–271.

Benton, Allison. (2012). Bottom-up challenges to national democracy: Mexico's (legal) subnational authoritarian enclaves. *Comparative Politics* 44(3), 253–271.

Borges, André. (2007). Rethinking state politics: The withering of state dominant machines in Brazil. *Brazilian Political Science Review* 1(2), 108–136.

Branch, Jordan. (2016). Geographic information systems (GIS) in international relations. *International Organization* 70(4), 1–25.

Buhaug, Halvard, & Rød, Jan Ketil. (2006). Local determinants of African civil wars, 1970–2001. *Political Geography* 25(3), 315–335.

Cammett, Melani, & Issar, Sukriti. (2010). Bricks and mortar clientelism: Sectarianism and the logics of welfare allocation in Lebanon. *World Politics* 62(3), 381–421.

Charron, Nicholas, & Lapuente, Victor. (2013). Why do some regions in Europe have a higher quality of government? *Journal of Politics* 75(3), 567–582.

Cho, Wendy K. Tam, & Baer, Neil. (2011). Environmental determinants of racial attitudes redux: The critical decisions related to operationalizing context. *American Politics Research* 39(2), 414–436.

Coakley, John. (1994). Approaches to the resolution of ethnic conflict: The strategy of non-territorial autonomy. *International Political Science Review* 15(3), 297–314.

Díaz-Rioseco, Diego. (2016). Blessing and curse: Oil and subnational politics in the Argentine provinces. *Comparative Political Studies* 49(14), 1930–1964.

Durán-Martínez, Angélica. (2018). *The politics of drug violence: Criminals, cops, and politicians in Colombia and Mexico.* New York, NY: Oxford University Press.

Freidenberg, Flavia, & Suárez-Cao, Julieta (Eds.). (2015). *Territorio y poder: Nuevos actores y competencia política en los sistemas de partidos multinivel en América Latina.* Salamanca, Spain: Ediciones Universidad de Salamanca.

Gallagher, Janice. (2016). The last mile problem: Activists, advocates, and the struggle for justice in domestic courts. *Comparative Political Studies* 50(12), 1666–1698.

Gervasoni, Carlos. (2010). A rentier theory of subnational regimes: Fiscal federalism, democracy, and authoritarianism in the Argentine provinces. *World Politics* 62(2), 302–340.

Giraudy, Agustina. (2010). The politics of subnational undemocratic regime reproduction in Argentina and Mexico. *Journal of Politics in Latin America* 2(2), 53–84.

Giraudy, Agustina. (2013). Varieties of subnational undemocratic regimes: Evidence from Argentina and Mexico. *Studies in Comparative International Development* 48(1), 51–80.

Giraudy, Agustina. (2015). *Democrats and autocrats: Pathways of subnational undemocratic regime continuity within democratic countries.* New York, NY: Oxford University Press.

Giraudy, Agustina, & Pribble, Jennifer. (2018). Rethinking measures of democracy and welfare state universalism: Lessons from subnational research. *Regional and Federal*

Studies. Available at: https://doi.org/10.1080/13597566.2018.1473250 (last accessed January 4, 2018).

Gleditsch, Kristian Skrede, & Weidmann, Nils B. (2012). Richardson in the information age: Geographic information systems and spatial data in international studies. *Annual Review of Political Science 15*, 461–481.

Goertz, Gary. (2006). *Social science concepts: A user's guide*. Princeton, NJ: Princeton University Press.

Hegre, Håvard, Østby, Gudrun, & Raleigh, Clionadh. (2009). Poverty and civil war events a disaggregated study of Liberia. *Journal of Conflict Resolution 53*(4), 598–623.

Heller, Patrick. (2001). Moving the state: The politics of democratic decentralization in Kerala, South Africa, and Porto Alegre. *Politics and Society 29*(1), 131–163.

Hsueh, Roselyn. (2011). *China's regulatory state: A new strategy for globalization*. Ithaca, NY: Cornell University Press.

Hollenbach, Florian M., Wibbels, Erik, & Ward, Michael D. (2016). *State building and the geography of governance: Evidence from satellites*. Working Paper. Texas A&M University.

India Ministry of Home Affairs, Office of the Registrar General and Census Commissioner. (2011). Census 2011: Provisional population totals.

Ingram, Matthew. (2016). *Crafting courts in new democracies: The politics of subnational judicial reform in Brazil and Mexico*. New York, NY: Cambridge University Press.

Kalyvas, Stathis N. (2006). *The logic of violence in civil war*. Cambridge, England: Cambridge University Press.

King, Gary. (2009). The changing evidence base of political science research. In Gary King, Kay Lehman Schlozman, & Norman H. Nie (Eds.), *The future of political science: 100 perspectives*, pp. 91–93. New York, NY: Routledge.

Lankina, Tomila, & Getachew, Lullit. (2006). A geographic incremental theory of democratization: Territory, aid, and democracy in postcommunist regions. *World Politics 58*(4), 536–582.

Lankina, Tomila, & Getachew, Lullit. (2012). Mission or empire, word or sword? The human capital legacy in postcolonial democratic development. *American Journal of Political Science 56*(2), 465–483.

Lecours, Natacha, & Hallen, Greg. (2016). Addressing the evidence gap to stimulate tobacco control in Latin America and the Caribbean. *Pan American Journal of Public Health 40*(4), 202–203.

Locke, Richard M., & Thelen, Kathleen. (1995). Apples and oranges revisited: Contextualized comparisons and the study of comparative labor politics. *Politics & Society 23*(3), 337–367.

Luna, Juan Pablo, & Medel, Rodrigo. (2017). *Local citizenship regimes in contemporary Latin America: Inequality, state capacity, and segmented access to civil, political, and social rights*. Paper presented at the Annual Meeting of the American Political Science Association (APSA), San Francisco, CA.

Lyall, Jason. (2009). Does indiscriminate violence incite insurgent attacks? Evidence from Chechnya. *Journal of Conflict Resolution 53*(3), 331–362.

Mahoney, James, & Thelen, Kathleen. (2010). *Explaining institutional change: Ambiguity, agency, and power*. New York, NY: Cambridge University Press.

McMann, Kelly M. (2018). Measuring subnational democracy: Toward improved regime typologies and theories of regime change. *Democratization 25*(1), 19–37.

Moncada, Eduardo. (in press). Resisting protection: Rackets, resistance, and state building. *Comparative Politics*.

Munck, Gerardo L., & Snyder, Richard. (2007). *Passion, craft and method in comparative politics*. Baltimore, MD: Johns Hopkins University Press.

Nemeth, Stephen C., Mauslein, Jacob A., & Stapley, Craig. (2014).The primacy of the local: Identifying terrorist hot spots using geographic information systems. *The Journal of Politics 76*(2), 304–317.

Niedzwiecki, Sara. (2018). *Uneven social policies: The politics of subnational variation in Latin America*. Cambridge, England: Cambridge University Press.

Nori-Sarma, Amruta, Gurung, Anobha, Azhar, Gulrez Shah, Rajiva, Ajit, Mavalankar, Dileep, Sheffield, Perry, & Bell, Michelle L. (2017). Opportunities and challenges in public health data collection in southern Asia: Examples from Western India and Kathmandu Valley, Nepal. *Sustainability 9*(7), 1106.

Openshaw, Stan. (1984). *The modifiable areal unit problem*. Working paper series on Concepts and Techniques in Modern Geography, Institute of British Geographers, No. 38.

Østby, Gudrun, Nordås, Ragnhild, & Rød, Jan Ketil. (2009). Regional inequalities and civil conflict in sub-saharan Africa. *International Studies Quarterly 53*(2), 301–324.

Otero-Bahamon, Silvia. (in press). Subnational inequality in Latin America: Empirical and theoretical implications of moving beyond interpersonal inequality. *Studies in Comparative International Development*.

Petersen, Roger Dale. (2001). *Resistance and rebellion: Lessons from Eastern Europe*. Cambridge, England: Cambridge University Press.

Pierson, Paul. (2003). Big, slow-moving, and . . . invisible: Macrosocial processes in the study of comparative politics. In James Mahoney & Dietrich Rueschemeyer (Eds.), *Comparative historical analysis in the social sciences*, pp. 177–207. New York, NY: Cambridge University Press.

Rebolledo, Juan. (2011). *Voting with the enemy: Democratic support for subnational authoritarians*. (Doctoral dissertation). Yale University.

Reisinger, William M., & Moraski, Bryon J. (2012). Regional changes and changing regional relations with the centre. In Vladimir Gelman & Cameron Ross (Eds.), *The politics of sub-national authoritarianism in Russia*, pp. 67–84. Aldershot, England: Ashgate.

Resnick, Danielle. (2014). *Urban poverty and party populism in African democracies*. Cambridge, England: Cambridge University Press.

Rodrigues-Silveira, Rodrigo. (2012). *Gobierno local y estado de bienestar: Regímenes y resultados de la política social en Brasil* [Local government and the welfare state: Regimes and outcomes of social policy in Brazil]. Zaragoza, Spain: Manuel Giménez Abad Foundation.

Rokkan, Stein. (1970). *Citizens, elections, parties: Approaches to the comparative study of the processes of development*. New York, NY: David McKay Company.

Sánchez-Talanquer, Mariano. (n.d.). *The geography of state power: Domestic conflicts and uneven state-building in Mexico and Colombia*. Unpublished manuscript.

Schutte, Sebastian, & Weidmann, Nils. (2011). Diffusion patterns of violence in civil wars. *Political Geography 30*(3), 143–152.

Scott, James C. (1998). *Seeing like a state: How certain schemes to improve the human condition have failed*. New Haven, CT: Yale University Press.

Singh, Prerna. (2017). The theoretical potential of the within-nation comparison: How sub-national analyses can enrich our understandings of the national welfare state. *American Behavioral Scientist 61*(8), 861–886.

Snyder, Richard, & Durán-Martínez, Angélica. (2009a). Does illegality breed violence? Drug trafficking and state-sponsored protection rackets. *Crime, Law and Social Change 52*(3), 253–273.

Snyder, Richard, & Durán-Martínez, Angélica. (2009b). Drugs, violence, and state-sponsored protection rackets in Mexico and Colombia. *Colombia Internacional 70*, 61–91.

Soifer, Hillel David, & Alvarez, Amanda M. (2017). *Choosing units of analysis in subnational research: The modifiable areal unit problem and the study of local violence during civil war*. Paper presented at the Annual Meeting of the American Political Science Association (APSA), San Francisco, CA.

Solt, Frederick. (2003). *Explaining the quality of new democracies: Actors, institutions, and socioeconomic structure in Mexico's states*. (Doctoral dissertation). University of North Carolina at Chapel Hill.

Steele, Abbey. (2011). Electing displacement: Political cleansing in Apartadó, Colombia. *Journal of Conflict Resolution 55*(3), 423–445.

Sybblis, Martin, & Centeno, Miguel Angel (Eds.). (2017). The "sub-national turn": The growing importance and utility of "scaling down" [special issue]. *American Behavioral Scientist 61*(8), 799–959.

Teune, Henry, & Przeworski, Adam. (1970). *The logic of comparative social inquiry*. New York, NY: Wiley-Interscience.

Tollefsen, Andreas Forø, Strand, Håvard, & Buhaug, Halvard. (2012). PRIO-GRID: A unified spatial data structure. *Journal of Peace Research 49*(2), 363–374.

Touchton, Michael, & Wampler, Brian. (2014). Improving social well-being through new democratic institutions. *Comparative Political Studies 47*(10), 1442–1469.

Trejo, Guillermo, & Ley, Sandra. (2018). Why did drug cartels go to war in Mexico? Subnational party alternation, the breakdown of criminal protection, and the onset of large-scale violence. *Comparative Political Studies 51*(7), 900–937.

Wood, Elisabeth Jean. (2003). *Insurgent collective action and civil war in El Salvador*. New York, NY: Cambridge University Press.

Wimmer, Andreas, & Glick Schiller, Nina. (2002). Methodological nationalism and beyond: Nation-state building, migration and the social sciences. *Global Networks 2*, 301–334.

Wong, Cara, Bowers, Jake, Williams, Tarah, & Simmons, Katherine Drake. (2012). Bringing the person back in: Boundaries, perceptions, and the measurement of racial context. *Journal of Politics 74*(4), 1153–1170.

Yasuda, John K. (2017). *On feeding the masses: An anatomy of regulatory failure in China*. New York, NY: Cambridge University Press.

Zhukov, Yuri, Davenport, Christian, & Kostyuk, Nadiya. (2017). Introducing xSub: A new portal for cross-national data on sub-national violence. Available at: https://sites.lsa.umich.edu/zhukov/wp-content/uploads/sites/140/2017/08/xSub_Aug2017.pdf (last accessed January 3, 2019).

Zukerman-Daly, Sarah. (2012). Organizational legacies of violence: Conditions favoring insurgency onset in Colombia, 1964–1984. *Journal of Peace Research 49* (3), 473–491.

Index